*A Constitutional History of Georgia*

# A Constitutional History of Georgia

## 1732–1945

*By*

ALBERT BERRY SAYE

ASSOCIATE PROFESSOR OF POLITICAL SCIENCE
THE UNIVERSITY OF GEORGIA

*Athens*

THE UNIVERSITY OF GEORGIA PRESS

Paperback edition, 2010
© 1948 by the University of Georgia Press
Athens, Georgia 30602
www.ugapress.org
All rights reserved
Printed digitally in the United States of America

The Library of Congress has cataloged the hardcover
edition of this book as follows:
Library of Congress Cataloging-in-Publication Data
LCCN Permalink: http://lccn.loc.gov/77016831

Saye, Albert Berry.
    A constitutional history of Georgia, 1732–1968.
  Edition Information: [Rev. ed.]
    xi, 503 p. 23 cm.
  Bibliography: p. 466-477.
    1. Constitutional history—Georgia. I. Title.
JK4316 .S3      1970
342'.75877-16831

Paperback ISBN-13: 978-0-8203-3554-4
ISBN-10: 0-8203-3554-1

*To the Memory of*

**LEWIS H. BECK**

# FOREWORD

IN THE FIRST PARAGRAPH of the Constitution of Georgia of 1861, written by the able hand of Thomas R. R. Cobb, it is said that "The principles of free government cannot be too well understood, nor too often recurred to." In no way can the principles of free government be better understood than by a study of constitutional government as it exists in America, from its beginning in English polity through its development in the American colonies into written constitutions when the colonies became sovereign and independent states, and its subsequent evolution in the constitutions of the several states. The constitutional history of no state is more interesting, nor its study more instructive, than that of the State of Georgia.

In preparing the present work, Professor Saye has performed a distinct and important public service. His work is thorough, scholarly and timely. The adoption of written constitutions by the American people was undoubtedly the greatest political accomplishment of modern times, or perhaps, of any time. Mr. Jefferson said, "Virginia was the first of the nations of the earth to form a fundamental constitution and to commit it to writing and to place it among their archives, where every one should be free to appeal to its text." All the other states soon followed the example of Virginia, and among these no state has made a more notable contribution to American constitutional history than Georgia. Under these state constitutions and the Constitution of the United States,

*Foreword*

formed substantially on the same model, a greater degree of equality of political right and a larger degree of personal freedom have been enjoyed by the American people and the political and property rights of the people have been more stable than in any other country.

The timeliness of a work like the present, which will tend to promote a recurrence to the principles of free government, is obvious, when constitutional government in America, as it has been historically known, both state and federal, is now gravely threatened by an alien philosophy of government which is insidiously seeking to undermine its foundations. Besides the threat of the subversion by alien concepts, thoughtful men are gravely aware that in America itself, there is a growing tendency to shift the boundaries separating the powers of government by encroachment of the executive upon the legislative power; by judicial construction difficult to reconcile with the meaning of the words used when the provisions under construction were adopted; and by frequent amendments, unfairly submitted, and often made to serve temporary expediencies, particular localities and special interests.

The present work cannot fail to increase the pride of Georgians in the rich heritage which their state has in her constitutional history and make them more careful to preserve it.

WALTER MCELREATH
author of
*A Treatise on the Constitution of Georgia*

# PREFACE

THIS VOLUME presents an account of the constitutional history of Georgia from the Charter of 1732 to the revision of the Constitution in 1945. In writing the book I have received assistance from several sources. The Lewis H. Beck Foundation paid the expenses of my study in England while writing the introductory chapters (abridged here from *New Viewpoints in Georgia History* with much of the documentation omitted). The M. G. Michael Research Award at the University of Georgia materially aided the progress of the study. The Faculty Advisory Committee of the University Center in Georgia and Dr. G. H. Boyd, Dean of the Graduate School of the University of Georgia, supported the publication. Too many friends have given encouragement to this study to be listed individually. I only hope that they will not be disappointed in the finished product.

A. B. S.

# CONTENTS

| CHAPTER | PAGE |
|---|---|
| I. The Genesis of Georgia | 3 |
| II. The Execution of a Trust | 12 |
| III. A Model Royal Colony | 47 |
| IV. The Revolution | 71 |
| V. Early State Government | 90 |
| VI. The Federal Union | 117 |
| VII. Constitutional Revision and Land Frauds | 135 |
| VIII. The Constitution of 1798 | 155 |
| IX. Empire State Politics | 196 |
| X. The Civil War | 219 |
| XI. Reconstruction | 250 |
| XII. The Constitution of 1877 | 279 |
| XIII. Late Nineteenth Century | 310 |
| XIV. Early Twentieth Century | 333 |
| XV. Amendments and More Amendments | 365 |
| XVI. The Constitution of 1945 | 393 |
| Bibliography | 416 |
| Governors of Georgia | 428 |
| Appendix | 433 |

*A Constitutional History of Georgia*

CHAPTER I

## The Genesis of Georgia

THERE were half a dozen attempts at setting up new English colonies in America during the two decades prior to 1732. The political and industrial leaders of England envisioned a self-sufficing empire in which the colonies would furnish raw materials and the mother country, manufactures; and colonization of the region south of the Savannah River fitted well into this mercantile ideology. Notable in the promotion literature fostering settlement in the southern region was *A Discourse Concerning the design'd Establishment of a New Colony to the South of Carolina in the Most delightful Country of the Universe,* published in 1717 by Sir Robert Montgomery, a Scottish baronet, with the view of gaining financial assistance for such a project. Sir Robert had secured from the Proprietors of Carolina a tract of land between the Savannah and Altamaha Rivers to which he gave the grandiloquent name, "Margravate of Azilia."

No less imaginative was Jean Pierre Purry, of Neuchâtel, who began his enthusiastic and persistent effort to win fame as a colonizer while an employee of the Dutch East-India Company. He stressed particularly the possibility for silk culture, predicting that within thirty years England might not only meet her own needs, but supply all Europe as well. His persevering endeavors never met with the triumph which he visualized; but he did succeed in giving his name to a small town, Purysburg, on the Carolina bank of the Savannah, where with the aid of British capital he settled about a hundred and twenty Swiss immigrants in December, 1732. Within a few years additional Swiss immigrants came to Purysburg, and this neighboring town was an asset to Savannah during the latter's early years.[1]

The description of Georgia as an Eden, presented with greatest gusto by the speculators Montgomery and Purry, was re-emphasized in *The Trade and Navigation of Great Britain Considered,* published in 1729 by Joshua Gee, a noted writer on commerce.[2]

While speculation upon the economic advantages offered by this region was easy, its occupation would be difficult, for it was inhabited by Indians and claimed by both France and Spain. Nevertheless, the British government was determined upon seizing the disputed prize. South Carolina was already carrying on a profitable fur trade with Indians in the region, and had gone so far as to construct Fort King George near the mouth of the Altamaha River in 1721, but had abandoned it after a few years because of the excessive expense involved in its maintenance. The home government received frequent reports of attacks on South Carolina by hostile frontier tribes urged to action by intriguers of the rival colonial powers. The possible strategic value of a buffer colony south of the Savannah was the primary consideration of the British Government in supporting Oglethorpe's

---
[1] Cecil Headlam and Arthur Percival Newton, editors, *Calendar of State Papers, Colonial Series: America and West Indies, 1732* (London, 1930), xxvii–xxviii.

[2] Subsequent editions of this work appeared in 1730, 1731, 1738, 1750, 1760, and 1767. See also *The Historical Register,* XVI (1732), 181–188.

## The Genesis of Georgia

colonizing project which resulted in the founding of the Colony of Georgia.

James Edward Oglethorpe, called "Father" by the first settlers of Georgia, was born in London on December 22, 1696. His father, Colonel Theophilus Oglethorpe, was of a noble family of Yorkshire which traced its history to a period before the Norman Conquest. A military career was decided upon for Oglethorpe while he was quite young, and although little definite information is now available relative to his early life, it is known that he held certain commissions during the last year of the War of the Spanish Succession. Following family tradition, he was sent to Eton College (date undetermined), and to Oxford University, entering Corpus Christi College, July 3, 1714; little is known of his academic training at either. In 1717 he served in the forces of Prince Eugene of Savoy against the Turks. Two years later he returned to England where he succeeded his brother Theophilus, a voluntary exile because of Jacobite connections, as incumbent of the family estate at Westbrook, Godalming. In 1722 he was chosen a member of Parliament for Haslemere, a position which he held during the succeeding thirty-two years.[3]

The occasion awakening Oglethorpe's determination to relieve the miserable condition of England's imprisoned debtors was, according to a contemporary account, a visit to Fleet Prison while Robert Castell, an acquaintance of his, was confined there. Castell, an architect, seems to have been guilty of no greater crime than the inability to meet an unfortunate debt. He died in prison, and Oglethorpe was "fully convinc'd that the hardships and barbarities put upon him by the warden were the immediate cause of his

---

[3] Amos Aschbach Ettinger, *James Edward Oglethorpe: Imperial Idealist* (Oxford, 1936).

*A Constitutional History of Georgia*

death." From this moment, Oglethorpe resolved "to use his utmost endeavours to get this national grievance redress'd."

On February 25, 1728, the House of Commons, upon a motion by Oglethorpe, appointed a Committee to inquire into the "State of the Gaols." This Committee was revived on February 17, 1729, again upon the motion of Oglethorpe and under his chairmanship.[4] The Committee found conditions of unbelievable horror, and as a result of the Parliamentary investigation the worst offenders among the jail officials were prosecuted, and an act passed which Oglethorpe estimated in 1730 to have set free ten thousand insolvent debtors.[5]

Oglethorpe became a national hero. He was sought out by the most prominent philanthropist of the day, the Reverend Thomas Bray, D.D., himself an active sponsor of prison reform. Bray's life is "a striking instance of what a man may effect without any extraordinary genius, and without special influence."[6] The two oldest societies of the Church of England, the Society for Promoting Christian Knowledge, founded in 1699, and the Society for the Propagation of the Gospel in Foreign Parts, founded in 1701, stand in large measure as monuments to his organizing genius. Although he was connected with a wide variety of other philanthropic activities, Bray's chief interests were the founding of libraries, both in England and her American Colonies, and the conversion and instruction of Negroes.

Oglethorpe made use of his knowledge of the charitable work carried on by Dr. Bray, in particular of a charity trust devolving upon four associates after the benevolent Doctor's death, for setting in motion his scheme

---
[4] *Commons' Journal*, XXI, 237, 444.
[5] R. A. Roberts, ed., *Diary of John Percival, First Earl of Egmont* (Hist. MSS. Reports, 3 vol., London, 1920–23), I, 90.
[6] *Dictionary of National Biography*, VI, 240.

## The Genesis of Georgia

which culminated in establishing the Colony of Georgia. His first move involved two charity legacies.

A certain haberdasher named King left the sum of £15,000 as a charity fund "to be disposed of as his executors should please." One of the three trustees into whose hands this sum passed was the heir of the testator and refused to concur with the two others in any method for disposing of the money, "in hopes, as they were seventy years old each of them, they would die soon, and he should remain only surviving trustee, and then might apply it all to his own use."[7] A lawsuit arose out of a proposal to lodge the money in the Master of Chancery's hands until new trustees should be appointed. Oglethorpe represented and won the case for the two elderly trustees, who then desired that the King fund be annexed to some trusteeship already in being. For this Oglethorpe suggested the D'Allone charity legacy in the hands of four associates of Dr. Bray.

Dr. Bray had encountered and gained the esteem of Abel Tassin D'Allone during a visit made to Holland for soliciting King William's assistance in certain philanthropic undertakings. Upon his death D'Allone bequeathed a portion of his English estate to Dr. Bray and his associates "toward erecting a capital fund or stock for converting Negroes in the British plantations. . . ."[8] Among the four associates chosen by Bray upon whom this fund devolved upon his death was Viscount Percival, later the first Earl of Egmont. Lord Percival was a prominent member in the House of Commons, an influential personage at the Royal Court, and a friend of Oglethorpe, the two having been closely associated since their joint

---
[7] Egmont's *Diary*, I, 44, 90.
[8] Samuel Smith (?), *Publick Spirit Illustrated in the Life and Designs of the Reverend Thomas Bray*, 41. This work, published anonymously at London in 1746, was taken as the official biography by the Associates of Dr. Bray and constitutes the chief source for his life.

7

work on the Committee for investigating conditions in the English prisons. Oglethorpe saw that if he could combine the legacy of King with that of D'Allone he might enlist the weighty support of Lord Percival, as well as others interested in the work of Dr. Bray, for his scheme of establishing a new colony in America. The association of the project with the name of Dr. Bray would certainly be a recommendation for it in the eyes of the public. It is clear too that from the very first Oglethorpe planned to rely heavily upon the contacts which he had established as Chairman of the Parliamentary Committee on Jails.

The first recorded mention of Oglethorpe's plan is found in the *Diary* of Lord Percival for February 13, 1730. At this time the plan involved sending to America "a hundred miserable wretches who being let out of gaol by the last year's act, are now starving about the town for want of employment," as Percival expressed it.[9] By July, 1730, Oglethorpe had formed a "Georgia Society," composed largely of his associates in the House of Commons, to promote his scheme. Already he had "resolved not . . . to confine this charity to prisoners, but to extend it as far as . . . funds would allow to all poor families as would be desirous of it."[10] Two years were to pass before the granting of the Charter of Georgia, and during this interval the objectives of Oglethorpe and the other Trustees were to expand to include also aid to persecuted Protestants abroad. Approximately half of the 2,122 colonists actually sent over on charity during the life of the Georgia Corporation were foreign Protestants. No committee was ever appointed by the Trustees to visit the prisons and select worthy debtors to be sent to Georgia, and in neither diaries nor letters, official records nor

---

[9] Egmont's *Diary*, I, 45.

[10] Benjamin Rand, ed., *Berkeley and Percival: The Correspondence of George Berkeley, afterwards Bishop of Cloyne, and Sir John Percival, afterwards Earl of Egmont* (Cambridge, England, 1914), 277.

## The Genesis of Georgia

press, sermons or any other contemporary source is there any evidence to support the legend that Georgia was originally established as a refuge for released debtors. The evidence is persuasive that fewer than a dozen released debtors ever came to Georgia, and that not a single colonist was selected on the basis of having been imprisoned for debt.[11] The early settlers of Georgia were in the main persecuted Protestants from Germany, and English of the "middle poor," to use Lord Percival's description. Philanthropy which was in the beginning a salient feature of the Georgia enterprise remained so, and this probably accounts in part for the error prevalent in many accounts of the genesis of Georgia.

The British Government, which furnished four-fifths of the money expended by the Trustees of Georgia, was opposed to the migration of her own subjects in the eighteenth century because of the small population of Great Britain in comparison with her rival, France. Immigration from foreign states to the British colonies was welcomed. The arguments used to advantage in securing Parliamentary support for Georgia were, first, the military strength that the new Colony would add to the Empire, and, second, the economic benefit that would arise from the culture of wine, silk, and other needed products. With the passing of years, the latter lost most of its force, and the only convincing argument for support of the Colony left to the Trustees was that Georgia constituted "the Southern Frontier of his Majesty's Dominions in North America."[12]

The prevailing policy of the British Government in the eighteenth century was to concentrate colonial administration in the hands of the Crown; hence the difficulty

---

[11] Albert B. Saye, *New Viewpoints in Georgia History* (Athens, 1943), 9–43.

[12] C.O. 5/671, 222. See Vol. III, 428, for an index to the Parliamentary debates recorded in Egmont's *Diary*.

and long delay that the Trustees of Georgia experienced in securing their charter. A petition for the charter was presented to the Privy Council on September 17, 1730. The record of the steps intervening between the presentation of this petition and the granting of the Charter in its final form is a tedious one of conferences and consultations between the petitioners and boards, commissions, and law officers of the British Government. There were hearings and re-hearings before the Board of Trade, meetings of the petitioners with the Committee of the Privy Council, meetings of small groups of those concerned at the House of Commons, or at Bedford Arms Tavern, and many a hint passed to the governmental officials concerned. No one official or body can be blamed for the long delay in securing approval of the Charter. The fault lay in the loosely organized and, from the point of view of colonial affairs, inefficient administrative system of the day. More than once there were threats of "flinging up" the affair on the part of disgusted petitioners. As in the early stages, Oglethorpe continued to be the guiding spirit of the group and Lord Percival used his personal influence to advantage on several occasions. But despite the diligent efforts and skillful maneuvers of Oglethorpe and his co-workers, it took nearly two years to secure the approval of a Charter acceptable to all parties concerned.

Even after the Charter was approved by the Privy Council in January, 1732, there was still insistence from some quarter upon making Georgia more dependent upon South Carolina. This caused a delay of four more months. Some blamed this delay upon the Duke of Newcastle, Secretary of State for Colonial Affairs; others declared that it was Walpole who was holding up the Charter: both denied the charge. Finally, on April 12, 1732, the King did sign the Charter, and on June 9th it was wit-

## The Genesis of Georgia

nessed at Westminster "by Writ of Privy Seal" and countersigned by Cocks.[13] Although June 9th was taken as the official date of issue, the Charter did not actually pass all necessary offices of the Government until the latter part of June. Even then some errors made in transcribing had to be amended and the document passed under the Seal again sometime during the first week in July.[14]

---

[13] *America and West Indies, 1732*, 146.
[14] Egmont's *Diary*, I, 282–283. An erasure in the official Charter in the Patent Roll leads me to suspect that the date June 9th was not the original date inscribed there.

## CHAPTER II

# The Execution of a Truſt

THE Charter of Georgia, the last of England's thirteen Colonies along the Atlantic Coast of North America, bore much in common with the charters of the earlier Colonies, particularly those of 1609 and 1612 for Virginia and that of 1629 for Massachusetts Bay. But though a composite picture shows certain dominant features to stand out in fairly sharp relief as common to the governments of all the Colonies, no two of them were governed exactly alike. On the basis of the forms of their charters, it has become customary to classify those colonies as "royal," or "crown," which were directly under the control of the King; "charter," or "corporate," in which a charter was granted directly to the colony; and "proprietary," in which the grant was to a landlord or proprietor. If Georgia must be pressed under any one heading of this three-fold classification, the last is the most appropriate; but so long as the term "proprietary" suggests ownership as property rather than the execution of a trust, no more inappropriate label could be chosen for Georgia, as an examination of the Charter will make clear.

## *Provisions of the Charter of 1732*

REGARDED objectively, the Charter is a document about twenty pages in length, written in a cumbersome, legalistic style. There are no divisions into articles or sections nor even into paragraphs, and the sentences are exceedingly long.[1]

The preamble stated in clear terms the threefold objective for establishing the Colony. In the first place, philanthropy combined with relief from domestic unemployment and support of the poor:

> We are Credibly Informed that many of Our Poor Subjects are through misfortunes and want of Employment, reduced to great necessity . . . and if they had means to defray the Charges of Passage, and other Expences incident to new Settlements, they would be Glad to be Settled in any of our Provinces in America whereby Cultivating the lands at present wast and desolate they might . . . gain a Comfortable Subsistence for themselves and families. . . .

In the second place, economic gain, for these unfortunate people might not only gain a comfortable subsistence for themselves and families, "but also strengthen Our Colonies and encrease the Trade, Navigation and Wealth of these Our realms." Finally, the factor of imperial defense in the sanction of the new Colony as a buffer for South Carolina:

> our Provinces in North America have been frequently Ravaged by Indian Enemies, more Especially that of South Carolina, which in the late war by the neighboring Savages was laid waste with Fire and Sword and great numbers of English Inhabitants miserably Massacred And Our Loving Subjects who now Inhabit these by reason of the Smallness of their numbers, will in case of any new war be Exposed to like Calamities in as much as their whole Southern Frontier continueth unsettled and lieth open to the said Savages.

---

[1] The original Charter has been lost. For a photostatic reproduction of the copy in the Patent Roll, see *Georgia's Charter of 1732*, edited by Albert B. Saye (Athens, 1942).

## A Constitutional History of Georgia

The Charter incorporated the petitioners who desired to accomplish these worthy ends as a body politic and corporate, styled, "The Trustees for establishing the Colony of Georgia in America." To this Corporation was granted the territory "in that part off South Carolina in America which lies from the most Northern Stream of a River there commonly called the Savannah all along the Sea Coast to the Southward unto the most Southern Stream of a certain other greater water or River called the Alatamaha [sic] and Westward from the heads of the said Rivers respectively in Direct Lines to the South Seas," together with the islands within twenty leagues of the eastern coast of the said lands. The territory for an empire! But "what cared King George that the grant cut a wide swath through Florida, Louisiana, and Texas? Or that, incidentally, it included Albuquerque, Socorro, and other New Mexico settlements?"[2] The Crown could grant but a seven-eighths interest in this land, however, for George Carteret, one of the eight lord proprietors to whom Charles II had granted Carolina, with the thirty-first degree of north latitude as its southern boundary (thus including this new Georgia grant), had not surrendered his rights as the other seven proprietors had in 1729. But Lord Carteret had promised the Georgia petitioners as early as March, 1731, that he "would do what the King should do," and by an indenture bearing date of February 28, 1732, his interest was legally conferred. This land was "to be holden of us our heirs and Successors as of our honour of Hampton Court in our County of Middlesex, in free and Comon Soccage and not in Capite," meaning simply that the Trustees should take an oath of allegiance to the King and pay an annual quit

---

[2] H. E. Bolton and M. Ross, *The Debatable Land* (Berkeley, California, 1925), 71. With all the subsequent changes in boundary, Georgia remains the largest State east of the Mississippi River.

## The Execution of a Trust

rent fixed at four shillings for every hundred acres of land which the Corporation should grant, but this payment was not to begin until after such land had been occupied for a period of ten years. The "trust" for granting this land was vested in the Trustees and their successors forever.

The twenty-one Petitioners were named in the Charter as Trustees, but following the precedent of corporations under the Virginia Charters and the Company of Massachusetts Bay rather than that of the Council for New England, membership of the Georgia Corporation could be increased indefinitely. New members should be chosen by a two-thirds vote of the Trustees present at a yearly meeting to be held on the third Thursday in March. To insure the charitable aims of the Corporation, Trustees were prohibited from receiving any salary; and should any Trustee accept an office of profit, he would lose his membership in the Corporation. In addition, a Trustee could not hold land in Georgia, nor could land be granted to anyone in trust for his benefit. As Professor Osgood has expressed it, this removal of the possibility of gain from the Trustees was sufficient to make "a radical difference between Georgia and all other proprietary provinces." Whatever service any Trustee rendered the Colony was to be without personal profit, "a condition precisely the opposite of that which lay at the base of all other proprietorships." [3]

It was laid down that the Trustees should prepare such laws as were necessary for the governance of the Colony, provided such laws be not repugnant to the statutes of England, and that they be approved by the King in Council. There were no provisions like those in the Charters of Maryland, Carolina, and Pennsylvania requiring the

---
[3] Herbert L. Osgood, *The American Colonies in the Eighteenth Century* (New York, 1924), III, 36–37.

## A Constitutional History of Georgia

consent of the colonists to the laws. The only liberty specifically guaranteed to the settlers was freedom of religion, "except Papists," although a blanket guaranty of the rights of Englishmen might be drawn from the provision that "all and every the said persons which shall happen to be born within the said Province and every of their Children and Posterity shall have and Enjoy all Liberties Franchises and Immunities of Free Denizens and natural born Subjects within any of our Dominions to all intents and purposes as if they had been abiding and born within this our Kingdom of Great Britain or any other of our Dominions."

In that it would "be too great a burthen upon all the Members of the said Corporation to be Convened so often as . . . [might] be requisite to hold meetings for the settling supporting Ordering and maintaining Such Colony," a smaller body of fifteen members was named in the Charter as a Common Council. After an increase in the membership of the Trustees, the number of Common Councilmen should be increased to twenty-four. Membership was to be during good behavior, with power vested in the Common Council to fill vacancies by election from among the Trustees. It was evidently intended that this smaller body should manage the routine business of the Corporation; yet it was vested with "full power and authority" in numerous matters: it was to apply all monies and effects belonging to the Corporation in such manner as seemed best; enter any covenant or contract deemed advisable; appoint and remove such officers, both for the Corporation and for the government in the Colony, as were thought necessary, and fix their salaries; and, lastly, to grant land to settlers, provided that no more than five hundred acres be allotted to any one person. In view of the importance of these functions, the precaution was set up that no action could be taken at a

## The Execution of a Trust

meeting of less than eight Common Councilmen. This quorum proved difficult to obtain; so it was fortunate that the Charter left to the Board of Trustees, with no stated quorum, many general functions, including the passing of by-laws for the Corporation, approving persons to take subscriptions, setting up courts in the Colony, and making laws for its governance.

Although the Charter represented a marked departure from the prevailing policy of concentrating colonial administration in the Crown, seven provisions more rigid than had accompanied any former proprietary grant insured imperial control: *First,* and most important from this point of view, the authority granted to the Trustees for governing the Colony was for a period of twenty-one years only, after which time control would pass into the hands of the Crown; *second,* no law, as noted above, would have force until approved by the King in Council; *third,* the Governor of the Colony should be approved by the King, and should give security for observing the acts of Parliament relating to trade and navigation, and for obeying all instructions sent to him by the King in pursuance of these acts; *fourth,* the Corporation was required to file an annual report of all receipts and expenditures with any two of several designated Crown officers; *fifth,* reports on the progress of the Colony should be given, "from time to time," to one of the principal Secretaries of State, and to the Board of Trade; *sixth,* all land grants should be carefully registered, and the Crown should receive annual reports upon these grants and reserve the right to make special surveys if deemed necessary to ascertain the quit rents due; and, *seventh,* the chief command of the militia was placed in the royal Governor of South Carolina. Taken as a whole, these clauses provided ample authority for the Crown to see that the Georgia experiment did not pass beyond its control; in any case the departure from the favored colonial policy would be only temporary.

## Oglethorpe Accompanies First Settlers

SUCH then were the provisions of the written document. How did the system work in practice? Many of the provisions of the Charter had an application far different from that anticipated: *e.g.*, the Crown never approved a Governor, for none was ever appointed; only three laws were ever passed, for the Colony was governed through "ordinances" or "regulations" rather than laws; so few of the Trustees participated actively in the work of the Corporation that the quorum of eight for the Common Council proved difficult to obtain, and meetings of four or five members were held more often as a Board of Trustees instead. In fact, the government of Georgia under the Trustees is the most extraordinary in the annals of American history, and one may hope to understand it only by viewing the history of its evolution.

Lord Percival, named first President of the Corporation in the Charter, took his oath of office before the Lord Chief Baron on July 9, 1732, and he in turn swore in the other Trustees when groups of them could be assembled during the following month. In order to secure publicity and raise funds, the promoters of Georgia then began a propaganda campaign which was carried to an extent never dreamed of in the case of any former colony.

Oglethorpe was overcome with enthusiasm. He would go himself and set up the Colony provided a small group should be sent at once. This decision was announced in October (1732), when the funds of the Corporation amounted to but little more than £2,000, a sum far less than that which had been considered a necessary mini-

## The Execution of a Trust

mum for inaugurating the venture, and before the Trustees had formulated any plan of government for the Colony. Raising funds had been the only objective set for the first year.[4] No settlers would have been sent for a considerable time had it not been for Oglethorpe's eagerness and the Trustees' recognition of the difficulty of finding another person so eminently fitted for getting the venture under way. As it was, on November 17, 1732, the 200-ton frigate *Ann* sailed bearing Oglethorpe and a few more than a hundred settlers, carefully selected from among the poor and unemployed of England.[5] The relation which Oglethorpe bore to the Colony is the key to understanding the loose system of government provided.

On learning of Oglethorpe's proposal to go to the Colony, Percival declared that although in his opinion the project had not yet developed sufficiently for sending colonists, he rejoiced that Oglethorpe would go, for "it would be difficult to find a proper Governor, which post he has accepted of."[6] Despite this reference to Oglethorpe as "Governor" by Lord Percival, technically speaking, he never held that title. It was understood at this early stage that Oglethorpe should take such action as was necessary in setting up the Colony without having specific authority conferred upon him by the Trustees; but the failure to grant him general executive authority officially was to prove of great importance in later years. The manner in which he directed affairs in the early days was reported by a visitor from Charleston in March, 1733:

> Mr. Oglethorpe . . . is extremely well beloved by all his People: The general Title they give him, is Father: If any

[4] Egmont's *Diary*, I, 260.
[5] Only a few essential connecting links of general history are given here. For details of the sailing, welcome by South Carolina, choice of the site for Savannah, *etc.*, the reader is referred to the list of excellent general histories of Georgia cited in the bibliography.
[6] *Diary*, I, 293.

## A Constitutional History of Georgia

> of them is sick, he immediately visits them, and takes a great deal of Care of them: If any Difference arises he is the Person that decides it: Two happen'd while I was there, and in my Presence, and all the Parties went away to outward Appearance, satisfied and contented with his Determination; He keeps a strict Discipline; I never saw one of his People drunk, or heard one swear, all the Time I was there: . . . There is no idler there; even the Boys and Girls do their Part. There are four Houses already up, but none finished. . . .[7]

The strong, energetic executive hand needed by the infant frontier Colony was supplied for the moment, but, unfortunately, Oglethorpe did not reside at Savannah for any considerable time once that town had been established. When he returned to England in the spring of 1734, the Colony was left for a year and a half without an executive. He returned to Georgia for most of the year 1736, and after September, 1738, remained in the Colony for a period of almost five years, but his preoccupation with military defense left little time for civil affairs. A more detailed study of his relation to the government of the Colony upon his second and third visits will be given later; yet it is well to bear constantly in mind that the Trustees never appointed a Governor and that it took a decade for any semblance of a united executive authority to evolve in Georgia.

## The Colonial Judiciary

OGLETHORPE continued the complete personal rule described above until July 7, 1733, when he swore in the officials of the "Town Court of Savannah and the Pre-

---

[7] "Account of a Voyage to Georgia," dated March 22, 1733, in *Political State of Great Britain*, XLV (June, 1733), 543–544.

## The Execution of a Trust

cincts thereof." [8] The ordinance of the Trustees creating this Court, the principal element of local government ever provided, was adopted on November 2, 1732, shortly before the first sailing. It provided for three judges, called bailiffs, and a recorder, who were "to preserve the Peace and Administer Justice Without fear or affection, to the Terror of the Evil Doers and to the Comfort of those who do well." For performing these high functions, their jurisdiction was made the broadest possible. They had full authority to ascertain the truth and fact of all crimes, offenses and injuries whatsoever, "by the oath of good and lawful Men . . . & by all other Ways Manners and Means which they shall know of and have in their Power," and to determine the same "according to the Law & Custom of the Realm of England." Furthermore, they might determine all civil cases "between any persons whatsoever." [9]

At the time of the appointment of the bailiffs and recorder, the Trustees also appointed two constables, two tything-men, and eight conservators of the peace. The constables and tything-men were to serve the Court in such matters as summoning juries and executing warrants. From their commissions, there was no distinction between the duties of a constable and a tything-man, as both took an oath "to obey the Warrants Orders and Judgements of the Baliffs & Recorder," but in practice the constables were far more important. They not only served the processes of the Court, but sometimes acted as prosecuting attorneys, and were officers of the militia as well.

---

[8] This day was long celebrated as the anniversary of "Court Day." *Ga. Col. Rec.* IV, 167; VI, 12. See *The* (London) *Weekly Miscellany*, Dec. 1, 1733, p. 3, for a description of the first court day when a public dinner was held and lots assigned.

[9] C.O.5/670, 14–21. A copy of this commission is given in the *Annual Report of the Georgia Bar Association, 1913*, 90–93, as an appendix to a vivid address by Mr. Justice Joseph R. Lamar on "The Bench and Bar of Georgia during the Eighteenth Century."

## A Constitutional History of Georgia

The number of tything-men was later increased, and in addition to serving processes of the Court, they rendered guard service over the "tythings," the name given to the twenty-four districts of ten houses each into which the six wards of Savannah were laid out. The conservators of the peace, like the justices of the peace today, dealt with petty offenses and suits for small sums.

All offices were held at the pleasure of the Trustees. The government set up was municipal in form, but the population of Georgia soon became as scattered as it was cosmopolitan. Before the end of a year Oglethorpe's letters mentioned little settlements like Highgate, Hamstead, Thorpe, Abercorn, Ogeechee, Skidaway, Hutchinson's Island, Tybee, Cape Bluff, Westbrook, and Thunderbolt. The next three years witnessed the rise of dozens of other settlements, among them several important towns: Augusta, begun as a post for Indian trade at the fall line of the Savannah; Ebenezer, on a small tributary of the same river not far distant from the City of Savannah, where the Germans from Salzburg were located; Darien, on the Altamaha River, where husky Scotch Highlanders were set down to meet the brunt of any Spanish attack from Florida; and Frederica, a military post on St. Simons Island. The Trustees were completely befuddled as to the location, population, or anything else relating to most of these communities for which they had the responsibility of providing a government. Oglethorpe complained of their negligence, but they failed ever to provide local officers for other than a few of these outlying settlements.

When in 1735 provision was made for the new outpost of Frederica, the same municipal plan of government as used for Savannah was again followed, with no connection between the two seats of local government.[10] Under

---
[10] C.O.5/670, 243-251.

## The Execution of a Trust

the reorganized government of 1741 on a two-county plan (presently to be explained), the jurisdiction of the court at Frederica was extended over all the southern region, while that at Savannah comprised the northern district.[11] The President and Assistants appointed in 1741 were given appellate jurisdiction over the town courts, but this was of little practical importance at Savannah inasmuch as three of the four assistants there were also bailiffs of the town court. The county government at Frederica was never organized; so in 1743 the President and Assistants at Savannah were given appellate jurisdiction throughout the Colony. Finding that there was but one bailiff at Frederica in 1745, the Trustees suspended even the town court there, so that from that date onward there was no judicial authority outside Savannah other than conservators of the peace who were placed in the larger towns during the last few years of the Trustee period. Finally, in 1745, as though to revert completely to the original judicial system, the Trustees suspended the appellate jurisdiction of the President and Assistants over the Town Court of Savannah, and it was never put into force again.[12] At the time of the surrender of the Charter, other than the conservators of the peace, the judiciary consisted, as in the beginning, of only the court at Savannah, composed of three bailiffs and a recorder. It was then assisted by two constables and nine tything-men for Savannah, and by one constable each for Ebenezer, Augusta, Frederica, the "district of Darien and Medway

---

[11] The jurisdiction of the "Town Courts" had never been strictly limited to the municipalities, for both the ordinances creating them and the commissions to the officers contained the broadening phrase, "and the precincts thereof."

[12] James Ross McCain, *Georgia as a Proprietary Province* (Boston, 1917), 204. Dr. McCain gives a much more detailed account of the evolution of the judicial structure than is attempted here. In an effort at simplification, I have made no distinction between action taken by the Trustees and by the Common Council of the Trustees.

River" and the district of Great Ogeechee. In brief, changes in structure of the judiciary amounted to but a transforming of the Town Court of Savannah into a provincial rather than a municipal court.

But not so much to structure as to personnel and actual operation must one look to discover the true character of the judiciary. To have instituted an elaborate system of courts for a handful of people would have been little short of ridiculous; the crying fault with those established lay in the incompetence of the judges. The Trustees chose the bailiffs and all other officers from among those sent over on charity. It was not likely that those who had made a failure in private matters would make a glowing success in affairs of state. Not one of the bailiffs was fitted for his position, nor ever displayed anything above mediocre ability. It is not to be wondered that the people had little respect for magistrates who possessed neither training nor talent, nor yet social distinction, and who themselves engaged in petty squabbles on the bench. Thomas Causton, a passionate, vindictive, overbearing scoundrel, who in addition to being a bailiff was storekeeper for issuing provisions to the charity settlers, and thus possessed the power, if not the authority, to starve people into submission, lorded it over most affairs when Oglethorpe was away. The people hated Causton and denounced him in violent terms; the ill-advised Trustees trusted him implicitly until 1738 when they found that he had used his authority to draw bills on them to the extent of several thousand pounds for which his records were in a hopeless muddle. He was then suspended from office until his accounts could be cleared, but he died before this was accomplished. Most important among the bailiffs after Causton was Henry Parker, formerly an habitual drunkard, but then somewhat reformed. Some of the bailiffs could neither read nor write.

## The Execution of a Trust

There was frequent debate in open court in which the bailiffs, if not pitted against each other, vied with jurors or the accused about English usage, which the Court was supposed to follow. No lawyers were allowed, one of the inducements offered for migration to Georgia being that it was "a happy, flourishing Colony . . . free from the pest and scourge of mankind called lawyers." But, says Mr. Justice Lamar, "these early settlers did not seem to need the advice of an attorney to make points in order to escape being whipped on the bare back or hung by the neck until they were dead."[13] Open defiance of the Court was not uncommon. Sometimes only the "collaring" of a contemptuous offender by robust tything-men permitted the bailiffs to carry on. In an attempt to lend some dignity to the bench, the Trustees sent over purple robes trimmed with fur for the bailiffs, and also provided them with a copper-gilt mace and a seal, which together probably cost five times as much as the log house in which the Court was held, but all to no avail. The Court had plenty of business, for the people got drunk and caroused, quarreled and fought, stole hogs, committed adultery, murder, and all manner of crimes; and, even though in Georgia, large numbers got into debt and were thrown into jail on that account. The punishments dealt out by the bailiffs were severe: standing in the pillory, sitting in stocks, and whipping on the bare back were common; and many a poor devil was hanged, never having had the advice of an attorney.[14]

It was generally understood from the first that appeal might be made from the local court to the Trustees, and

---

[13] *Georgia Bar Association Report, 1913*, 57.

[14] *Ga. Col. Rec.*, IV, 94, 171, 269, 293, among the many examples. William B. Stevens was usually present at meetings of the Court, and his *Journal*, Vol. IV, and its supplement, in *Georgia's Colonial Records*, is strewn with details of actual cases. This *Journal* is the primary source on the matters discussed here.

in 1741 this was expressly stated as a right in cases involving £100 or more. The Trustees sought to support the bailiffs, and usually sustained their decisions. In a single case, that of Joseph Watson whom the infamous Judge Causton held prisoner on a charge of lunacy, a successful appeal was made to the Privy Council when the Trustees failed to interpose.

## Impractical Legislation

THE Trustees had not only the responsibility of providing an executive and judiciary for the Colony; full legislative power, subject to the approval of the Crown, was vested in them as well. The Charter gave the Georgia Colonists no share whatever in the formation of their laws, although this privilege had been gained before 1732 in all other British Colonies in America. Oglethorpe carried out the first embarcation so hurriedly that no laws were provided by the Trustees. As Egmont expressed it, "We were not particular in establishing the constitution, because till we come to that the laws of England take place."[15] Strange to say, only three laws, all initiated in January, 1734, and ratified by the King in Council in April, 1735, were ever passed during the twenty years of government by the Trustees.[16]

One of these acts prohibited Negro slavery by providing that any slave found in the Colony should be disposed of for the benefit of the Trust, unless the slave had escaped from a neighboring Colony, in which case he should be returned upon claim and payment of costs. Slavery was inconsistent with the whole design of the Trustees. The chief products of the *de luxe* Colony of Georgia were to be silk and wine, whose culture would

---
[15] Vol. I, 286, 295.
[16] *Ga. Col. Rec.*, I, 31–52 for the texts of these laws.

## The Execution of a Trust

require skilled labor rather than brute strength. White servants who could be absorbed into the population after the expiration of an indenture of a few years were better adapted to the circumstances. In the Georgia garden where the air was "healthy . . . serene, pleasant and temperate, never subject to excessive Heat or Cold, nor sudden Changes," and where crops produced an amazing increase, "an hundred fold the common estimate, for a husbandry of little more than scratching the earth and covering the seeds," what could be the result of introducing slaves other than to produce idleness, or to create a gulf between the charity settlers and the adventurers, and thus retard the day when both should occupy the same high plane? [17]

Another law gave Georgia an early lesson in prohibition. In October, 1733, Oglethorpe wrote of a disturbance at Savannah which had caused several deaths while he was away at Charleston, and attributed it to the excessive use of rum. The Trustees immediately ordered "that the drinking of rum in Georgia be absolutely prohibited," and that any rum brought there be staved. Thereafter the Trustees ascribed most of the ills which beset the Colony to the drinking of rum. The law of 1735 was but a confirmation of the "ordinance" of 1733. It prohibited the importation or sale of rum, brandy, "or any other kind of Spirits or Strong Waters by whatsoever Name they are or may be distinguished." This strong wording was nevertheless not intended to outlaw wine, ale, or beer, for the prohibition act itself restricted the sale of these drinks to licensed public houses, and the Trustees sent over strong beer by the tun for supplying their store.

---

[17] E. Merton Coulter, *A Short History of Georgia* (Chapel Hill, 1933), 55; Ga. Col. Rec., I, 49. The quotations are from *A New and Accurate Account of Georgia and South Carolina* by Benjamin Martyn (London, 1732).

## A Constitutional History of Georgia

The third law, "An Act for maintaining Peace with the Indians," restricted trade with the Indians to persons holding a license and set up a number of rigid regulations for their conduct. It required an annual appearance of the trader in person before an Indian Commission at Savannah for a renewal of his license, the payment of an annual fee of not less than £5, and a bond of £100 to insure compliance with the established regulations.

Although commendable in themselves, as was most of the idealistic policy of the Trustees, these acts were, as Professor Osgood concludes, "so far in advance of conditions at the time and place as to be unpractical and to serve mainly as subjects of controversy."[18] The most significant of the three was the exclusion of Negro slaves. The Colonists were soon disillusioned about Georgia being a Garden of Eden: the sun was hot, and there was malaria in the swamps; they had no success in producing either silk or wine. How could they compete with South Carolina where slaves were allowed in the production of rice and lumber? Up rose a mighty protest that dinned the ears of the Trustees. In 1741 the malcontents sent Thomas Stephens, the wayward son of President William Stephens, as colonial agent, with an appeal directed to the King and Parliament. He clamored so loudly against the policy of the Trustees that they had the House of Commons carry out an investigation which found Stephens' charges "false, scandalous and malicious."[19] The ill-advised Trustees, convinced of the wisdom of their policy and thinking the malcontents but a group of idlers, persisted in maintaining the prohibition against slaves; but in 1750, only two years before the surrender of their control, they finally acceded to the continuous demand

---
[18] Osgood, *The American Colonies in the Eighteenth Century*, III, 50.
[19] Egmont's *Diary*, III, 265.

and drew up an act repealing the prohibitory law.[20] The repealing act was never approved by the Crown, but it was immediately effective. Two years earlier the local authorities had reported that numerous Negroes had been introduced into the Province, that attempts to drive them out had been ineffective, and that any further attempt to execute the act against slaves would depopulate the Colony.[21]

The prohibition against rum, like the "noble experiment" of the twentieth century, proved impossible to enforce and was given up much earlier than the ban on slavery. In recognition of the complete failure of the law, the Trustees drew up an act of repeal in 1742, but finding that the Board of Trade objected to certain of its terms, they instructed the local officials to continue to wink at open violation of the prohibition measure.

The system of land tenure is another conspicuous instance of failure by the Trustees, despite heroic efforts and idealistic motives, to adopt measures suited to actual conditions in the Colony. In consideration of the necessity for military defense, the nature of the colonists, and the possibility of profiteering, the Trustees early decided that only fifty acres should be granted to each charity settler. The Charter itself limited grants to five hundred acres for any one person. The fifty-acre grants were more like military fiefs than true possessions as they involved military service in time of war and guard duty in time of peace. The land granted, either to charity settlers or to adventurers who should pay their own expenses and bring over servants, could be neither sold nor mortgaged,

---

[20] C.O.5/681.
[21] *Ga. Col. Rec.*, II, 530.
In a petition to Parliament for support on March 4, 1751, the Trustees stated that there were "349 working Negroes in the Province, besides children too young for Labour." C.O.5/671, 178.

and could be inherited only by a male heir. There were no less than nine distinct grounds for forfeiture, including failure to occupy the land and to plant a specified number of mulberry trees for each acre cleared. Inasmuch as the grants were gifts and could be made on such conditions as the Trustees pleased, no man, it was felt, had a right to complain. "The Board will always do what is right," declared Egmont, "and the people should have confidence in us." [22] The Trustees were indeed lenient in the enforcement of their rules, making special concessions in individual cases where hardships were involved; yet the severe letter of the law drove away many would-be settlers and caused constant complaint in the Colony. The regulations for land tenure, adopted from time to time and frequently revised, were never incorporated into any formal law, with the result that great uncertainty always troubled the colonists lest they lose their tenure. One of them is said to have remarked that the whole laws consist of "tails" and "males," and that all the lawyers in London could not make them plain to a common man.

As noted in the explanation of the terms of the Charter, the Crown reserved a quit rent of 4s. for every hundred acres of land granted, such payment to begin when the land had been occupied for ten years. In practice, however, it proved impossible to collect any quit rent in Georgia either under the Trustees or after the Crown assumed control.

Rather than adopting general laws, in the main the Trustees preferred to deal separately with individual cases. The greater number of their ordinances were specific in nature applying to a particular case; *e.g.*, an ordinance that a certain individual be granted a license for staying in England six months longer before embarca-

---
[22] *Diary*, II, 184.

## The Execution of a Trust

tion, that an inspection be made of the cow pens at Ebenezer, that a guardian be appointed for an infant whose parents had died in the Colony, or that a certain person be allowed to sell his land. Yet there were ordinances broad in nature and general in application, e.g., that of 1741 reorganizing the government of the Colony, or another of the same year to the effect that "The wilful Murder of an Indian in Amity with Great Britain shall be declared Death." The ordinances, usually sent as instructions to the various officials in the Colony in the form of a letter, were given binding effect, and those of general application were laws to all intent and purpose. As already noted, the prohibition against rum was first adopted as an "ordinance" in 1733, and then as a "law" in 1735. Wherein could any distinction possibly be made? The Charter itself gave no definition of laws; nevertheless it laid down that the "laws, statutes, and ordinances" made by the Trustees should meet the double standard of conformity to the laws and statutes of England and approval by the King in Council. Herein was ample ground for the Crown to have intervened had it been so inclined. Despite the Trustees' jealousy and the feeling sometimes expressed that their rights were being encroached upon, in viewing the matter today, the only conclusion is that the British Government voluntarily left the Trustees a free hand in the management of their experiment.

## The Trustees

WHO then were the Trustees, and how did they carry on their work? In view of the high character of its objectives, selection to membership in the Georgia Society was itself a tribute to the patriotic and Christian spirit

## A Constitutional History of Georgia

of each one of the seventy Trustees. Yet the great majority of these men never gave any considerable time to the project. In Egmont's own fitting words, "It is a melancholy thing to see how zeal for a good thing abates when the novelty is over, and when there is no pecuniary reward attending the service." [23] Dr. McCain estimates that a small group of seven "had more to do with the constructive polity of the Trustees than all the other sixty-four members of the Trust combined." [24] The ten most active Trustees whose devotion and courage in supporting the Georgia enterprise deserve especial admiration are Oglethorpe, Egmont, James Vernon, Henry L'Apostre, Samuel Smith, Thomas Tower, John Laroche, Stephen Hales, Edward Digby, and the Earl of Shaftesbury.

The quorum of eight required for the Common Council of Trustees was difficult to obtain from the beginning, and become increasingly more so with the passing of years and interest. The result was that meetings of the Common Council were larger than meetings of the Board of Trustees (for which no quorum was stated in the Charter). Meetings called for the Common Council were carried on as a Board of Trustees when, as was commonly the case, only four or five members appeared. The special functions assigned to the Common Council made membership in it more important, but the more active Trustees were Common Councilmen. The official records are carefully preserved separately as the *Journal of the Trustees* and the *Minutes of the Common Council of Trustees*,[25] but Egmont's *Diary* reveals that in practice the distinction between the two bodies was far less im-

---

[23] *Diary*, III, 124.
[24] *Op. cit.*, 39.
[25] Volumes I and II, respectively, in the *Colonial Records of Georgia*.

*The Execution of a Trust*

portant than the official records indicate. A small group meeting as a Board of Trustees could make decisions and have them ratified when a quorum could be assembled for a Common Council. Sometimes the same meeting was held in part as a Common Council, and in part as a Board of Trustees, usually with a different member presiding. Much work was done through committees, some consisting of two members only, of which the Committee of Correspondence was the most important. Many an important decision was made when a small group dined together at the Cyder House or the Horn, or met by chance at the House of Commons.

## *Lack of Executive Coördination*

THE Trustees spent far more time in securing financial aid from Parliament and in raising subscriptions than in providing a government for the Colony. They knew little about local conditions; so relying upon Oglethorpe to supply a general guidance, they left the Colony for a decade without any legally constituted executive, and with a totally disjointed administration. As specific need arose, a number of administrative officers were appointed, all of whom were placed under the immediate control of the Common Council and directed to send their reports directly to it rather than to any higher executive in the Colony. Among the officers appointed were a storekeeper, schoolmaster, ecclesiastical officer, naval officer, collector, recorder, botanist, a surveyor, several bailiffs, constables, tything-men, and conservators, a register of land grants, secretary of Indian affairs, receiver of fees from the Indian trade, an agent to the Cherokee Indians, another to distribute presents to the Indians, a collector of benefactions for an orphan's home, an overseer of Trust servants for the northern district, another for the southern district, a commissioner for examining and stating the public debt, several missionaries, and a prohibition agent.[26]

The confusion, friction, and general disorder inherent in this loose administrative system were not long in displaying themselves. The officers in Georgia were no doubt unaccustomed to correspondence; certainly the Trustees were unable to learn from them what was going on in the Colony. Oglethorpe himself was negligent in writing to the Trustees. Finally despairing of ever getting satisfactory reports from him, the Trustees determined to send William Stephens as "Secretary for the Affairs of the Trust within the Province of Georgia."

Stephens, a graduate of King's College, Cambridge, had studied law at the Middle Temple, London, and served as a member of Parliament from 1697 to 1727. Having lost both his fortune and his seat in Parliament, in 1736, at the age of sixty-seven, he came to South Carolina to survey a barony of land for Colonel Horsey. Upon this trip he met Oglethorpe. Stephens' interest in Georgia was aroused, leading to his appointment as Secretary of the Colony. His commission, issued on April 18, 1737, bound the other officials in Georgia to "pay due Regard to all and every the Instructions" that he should at any time produce; nevertheless, the elaborate instructions accompanying this commission made him at this time only an agent for gathering information and reporting on conditions in the Colony to the Trustees. Among other things, he was directed to take a census, give an account of the number of forts and their strength, report upon the people's behavior toward the magistrates, send an

---

[26] All of the commissions granted by the Trustees are recorded in C.O.5/670.

## The Execution of a Trust

account of the cultivation of various crops, tell whether the people attended divine worship, and to urge the other officials to send their reports to the Trustees.[27]

Under the circumstances, it was natural that Stephens should have exercised power notably beyond that of simply gathering information. He attended the sessions of Court where the bailiffs often asked his advice upon English usage and consulted him in making their decisions; other officials visited him and sought his advice. He acted with devotion to the welfare of the Colony and unwavering fidelity to instructions from the Trustees, but due to advanced age, he lacked magnetism for arousing enthusiasm among the people. The Trustees, always eager and at times pathetic in their appeals for information, derived more satisfaction from Stephens' diary (or *Journal* as it is called)[28] than from any other source. He knew the views of the Trustees on land tenure, Negroes, and rum, and was anxious to present the state of the Colony in the best light possible; hence he directed his reports toward justifying the policy of the Trustees rather than giving an impartial account of the actual situation.[29]

## Paper Provisions for a Dual Government

LATE in 1741 James Vernon suggested reorganization of the colonial government on a dual county basis, with a President and Council at the head of each. This peculiar form of government was advocated as a means of avoiding friction with the Board of Trade which would have to approve any Governor selected. The other Trustees readily adopted Vernon's idea, and under his

---

[27] C.O.5/670, 323–326; *Ga. Col. Rec.*, II, 90.
[28] Vol. IV and its supplement in *Georgia Colonial Records*.
[29] Egmont's *Diary*, III, 209, 222–223.

leadership details for the new organization were worked out and formally ratified by the Common Council on April 5, 1741.[80] The resolution provided that the Colony should be divided into two counties, called the County of Savannah and the County of Frederica. The former was to be composed of the settlements upon the Savannah and Ogeechee Rivers and as much farther southward as should be determined after a survey and map had been made; the latter county would include the rest of the Colony. The administration of each county was to be under a President and four Assistants, all of whom were to hold office during the pleasure of the Common Council and exercise such authority as it should extend to them. The "instructions" issued on April 20th, in connection with commissions for the officers at Savannah, defined the powers of these officers and are important in that they were not materially altered during the remainder of the Trustee period.[31]

The most notable feature of the plural executive thus established was the meagerness of its powers. In the "private instructions" sent to William Stephens (named President at Savannah), he was told how to inaugurate the new government, asked to continue the journal which he had been sending to the Trustees (for which his salary as Secretary was to be continued), and urged to send over a census, map, and other information. Rather than general executive authority, numerous specific duties were assigned to the President. For example, he was "to take care that God Almighty be devoutly and duly honoured and served . . . according to the Rites of the Church of England," although all Protestant dissenters were to be tolerated. His chief concern should be

---
[80] *Ga. Col. Rec.,* II, 367.
[31] C.O.5/671, 6–19 for these instructions.

## The Execution of a Trust

to see that proper records were kept by the various officers and transmitted to the Trustees. The most definite authority given him was control over the boats and servants of the Trust. The original instructions admonished Stephens to keep "a strict eye" to the observance of the prohibitions against slaves and rum; later in the year he was commissioned to distribute presents to the Indians, and made a joint commissioner with Oglethorpe for licensing and regulating trade with the Indians. For incidental expenses, the President might employ a sum not to exceed £300 per year. His power of removal and appointment was absolute in the case of the clerk to the President and Assistants, conditional upon the advice and consent of the Assistants in the case of constables and tything-men, and limited to suspension and temporary appointment until the pleasure of the Trustees could be ascertained in the case of Assistants. If any minister or schoolmaster set a bad example by his life or doctrines, the President should admonish him "and immediately acquaint the Trustees thereof, that in the Case of his remaining incorrigible, he [might] . . . be recalled."

The Assistants served as a Council, and the President together with any two of them constituted a quorum to act, the President having a deciding voice in case of an even division. The First Assistant presided in the President's absence, but no action was valid until approved by the President, except action upon an appeal from the Town Court, which constituted one of the functions of the Council. In addition to its advisory and judicial function, the Council had the power of issuing public money in payment of colonial expenses in accordance with the directions of the Trustees, but no money was to be issued except by warrant signed by the President upon the advice and consent of a majority of the Assistants. The Council

## A Constitutional History of Georgia

was expressly empowered to license public houses for the sale of liquor, and ordered to revoke such licenses in cases of abuse.[32]

The inhabitants of Savannah wanted to choose their own magistrates and thought little of this executive reorganization. Since the bailiffs of the Town Court became the Assistants, the right of appeal under the new system could mean little. The recorder of the Court was appointed clerk to the President and Assistants, and William Stephens had actually already exercised many of the functions of the new President while bearing only the title of Secretary.

The new county system was never put into operation at Frederica. Oglethorpe, absorbed with the Spanish war, never complied with the Trustees' request that he recommend a suitable person for President in the southern county. Many people fled from this district during the war, so in April, 1743, the Common Council ordered that the bailiffs at Frederica, who had been made Assistants pending the appointment of a President, should be only local magistrates subject to the authority of the President and Assistants of Savannah. For the first time there was now some semblance of a united executive authority throughout the Colony.

Additional Assistants were later added, and as noted previously, the appellate jurisdiction of the President and Assistants was abolished in 1745; but on the whole the executive remained in substantially the same form as established in 1743 until the surrender of the Charter. Georgia was now united under a governmental system resembling in general that of the other British Colonies, but still with an executive notably weaker. With the Trustees' dwindling interest in Georgia, the exigency of the situation led to a gradual assumption of broader

---
[32] *Ibid.*

*The Execution of a Trust*

power by the local executive, so that at the close of the Trusteeship the Colony had a fairly influential *de facto* government.

## *Oglethorpe Absorbed in Military Affairs*

EXECUTIVE power in Georgia had in reality always been *de facto* rather than *de jure,* if the latter be taken to designate an executive power having its foundation in law. Oglethorpe, it will be recalled, never received any formal commission as Governor, but accompanied the first settlers voluntarily and at his own expense as an unofficial guiding hand. In the early days he "exercised paternal power over the settlers, acting as judge, lawgiver, and defender."[33] Throughout the first decade of the Colony's life, he was in residence as an "overseer," to employ the term used by Oglethorpe himself,[34] except when his presence in England was essential to the interest of the Colony. Oglethorpe had no scruples about the extent of his authority in Georgia. President Stephens and all the other officers felt themselves subject to his orders when the General directed his attention to civil matters, but unfortunately, most of his time was occupied with strengthening the Colony's fortifications. The Trustees thought that Oglethorpe went too far with his construction of forts, and relations between them became strained.

The long-smoldering imperial struggle between England and Spain flared into open flame by a formal declaration of war by England on October 23, 1739, beginning the War of Jenkins' Ear. France entered the contest on the side of her Latin sister the following year, and by

---

[33] Edward Channing, *A History of the United States* (New York, 1904), II, 363.
[34] *Berkeley and Percival: The Correspondence of* . . . , 277.

1744 it had spread into a general conflict, known in European history as the War of the Austrian Succession and in American history as King George's War. No detailed account need be given here of the sallying back and forth of the English and Spanish soldiers between Savannah and St. Augustine, nor even of Oglethorpe's saving Georgia from capture by a mighty feat at Bloody Marsh; sufficient has been said to make it evident that Oglethorpe had little time for directing civil affairs in the Colony. With the spreading of the war into a general conflict, the scene of battle shifted to other fields, and on July 23, 1743, Oglethorpe left Georgia, never to return. He continued his membership in the Georgia Corporation until it was dissolved, but in disapproval of the policy pursued, he attended only about one-third of the meetings and was no longer the guiding hand as in earlier years.

One might compile volumes consisting of eulogies of Oglethorpe by visitors to the Colony, by officials and common people there, and by his contemporaries in England; on the other hand, strong condemnation from malcontents in the Province is not lacking. In the light of all the evidence, one cannot but admire his character. Yet the loose system of local government, due to Oglethorpe's occupation with military affairs and the absence of a Governor, was the most fundamental weakness in Georgia's government under the Trustees. From this standpoint one may conclude, that "it would have been better for the province if Oglethorpe had never gone to Georgia, or at least if he had gone there only as commander of the regiment and without any civil authority at all." [35] Yet the verdict of success or failure of Oglethorpe's work is dependent upon the point of view taken of his mission. If the Georgia enterprise be considered as

---
[35] McCain, *op. cit.*, 96.

*The Execution of a Trust*

an experiment in philanthropy with the aim of setting up a Utopia, Oglethorpe failed; if the establishment of a buffer colony as a defense for the British southern frontier in America be placed first in the objectives, as it appears it should, then Oglethorpe was eminently successful.

## *The First Colonial Assembly*

BEFORE closing the discussion of the Trustee period, a significant governmental development near its end should be noted, namely, the rise of a representative assembly. From the earliest days the inhabitants of Savannah had frequently been called together, notably for special "courts" when important communications were received from the Trustees. The Charter, as we have seen, made no provision whatever for local autonomy; nevertheless, there had been instances of cooperative action for the settlement of common problems, as for instance the voluntary convention in 1739 whereby the freeholders who had property in cattle agreed upon regulations for the cattle industry, the formulation of petitions against the laws prohibiting rum and slaves, the choice of a colonial agent by the malcontents in 1741, and the mass meeting on slavery in 1748.

The Trustees did not extend to the settlers so much as the right of even expressing an opinion upon the laws by which they were governed until two years before the surrender of their Charter. Their action in establishing a representative assembly at this late date was partly because the presence of an assembly would strengthen Georgia's chances of being maintained as a province separate from South Carolina, and partly because a representative assembly would aid in giving them an informative account of the condition of the many settlements and their needs.[36]

A resolution of the Common Council of Trustees, dated March 19, 1750, authorized the holding of an assembly in Savannah at a time to be named by the President and Assistants. Representation was to be based upon population: Every town, village, or district having ten families should have one deputy; settlements having thirty families, two deputies; the town of Savannah, four deputies; and Ebenezer and Augusta, two each. Although mentioned along with the three other chief towns in the special allotment, Frederica was to have two delegates only in case her population justified it under the general rule.

The Trustees fixed no specific qualifications for the delegates to the first assembly, but for those of the future most extraordinary qualifications were adopted. Neither age, sex, education, wealth, nor any other of the traditional qualifications was mentioned. The production of silk was the chief consideration. After June 4, 1751, no one should be chosen a deputy who did not have one hundred mulberry trees planted and properly fenced upon every fifty acres of land that he possessed. After June 4, 1753, the qualifications should become more strenuous, for then no one could be a deputy "who had not at least one Female in his Family instructed in the Art of reeling silk," who did not produce fifteen pounds of silk upon every fifty acres which he owned, and who did not strictly conform to the limitation on the number of Negro slaves in proportion to his white servants.[37] These regulations show how tenaciously the Trustees clung to their original objective of producing silk in Georgia. It is doubtful whether any inhabitant could have met them had they

---
[36] *Ga. Col. Rec.* II, 498.
[37] *Ga. Col. Rec.* II, 499.

## The Execution of a Trust

ever become effective; fortunately the Trustees, desirous of some immediate good, did not insist upon them for the first assembly.

The records do not disclose any qualifications set for the electorate, nor do we know anything of the method used in the selection of representatives other than that on December 15, 1750, the President and Assistants issued writs for holding elections in the several districts. As the inhabitants were unaccustomed to elections and unacquainted with the procedure to follow, the President and Assistants, says William Stephens, thought it their duty to hold frequent consultations and provide the needed information.

January 15, 1751, was fixed for the first meeting of the assembly. On that date sixteen leading men of the Province, selected from eleven districts, convened at Savannah. The deliberations opened with an address from President Stephens, and the speaker elected was a Savannah delegate, Francis Harris, senior member of Georgia's one significant commercial firm, Habersham and Harris.

This assembly possessed no power of legislation. There was no need for an upper chamber for a moderating force as in the other Colonies, for the resolution of the Common Council of Trustees establishing it provided that "The Assembly can only propose, debate, and represent to the Trustees What shall appear to them to be for the benefit, not only of each particular Settlement, but of the Province in general." The assembly was to serve primarily as a source of information for the perplexed Trustees. The deputies were enjoined to deliver to the assembly for transmission to the Trustees a written account of the state of the district from which they came, containing a census showing the number of inhabitants, their age, sex, and race, a statement of the quantity of land cultivated by each inhabitant, the manner of cultivation, the number of mulberry trees properly fenced on each plantation, and a report of the progress made by each man or family in the culture of wine, silk, indigo, and cotton. These instructions, like those sent to the various officers at earlier periods, particularly to William Stephens as Secretary, bear testimony that the Trustees never had more than a hazy notion of conditions existing in the Colony which they sought to govern.

The first experiment with a representative assembly proved highly successful. After fifteen days of deliberation, the representatives formulated a list of eleven grievances held to be within the power of the President and Assistants to redress. They voiced a need for standard weights and measures, repair of the court house, regulation of the militia, and improvement of facilities for shipping.[38] Most of these grievances were promptly corrected by the local authorities. The last nine of the twenty-four days in the session were spent in preparing representations to the Trustees. Now that the Trustees had revoked the objectional regulations for land tenure and removed the prohibitions against slavery and rum, the colonists were enthusiastic for a renewal of the Charter. They feared annexation of Georgia by South Carolina, in which case "they might expect to be treated as persons *only fit* to guard her frontier. . . ." The delegates expressed a desire that at future sessions the Assembly should have the power to make bylaws for the Colony which should be in force until disapproved by the Trustees. Other petitions urged the Trustees to apply for a reduction of the quit rent, provide a pilot boat, establish a court of equity, and provide additional regulations for the Indian trade (in particular to prevent Thomas Bo-

---

[38] William B. Stevens, *A History of Georgia* (New York, 1847), I, 248–249. The "Proceedings of the President and Assistants" from Dec. 15, 1750 to May 1, 1752 are now lost. *Ga. Col. Rec.* VI, 369. Stevens was a careful scholar, and his quotations from that source are reliable.

## The Execution of a Trust

somworth from acquiring land reserved for the Indians near Savannah, and to break up a monopoly that a group of seven persons had secured over the Indian trade at Augusta).

The Trustees were pleased with the results of the Assembly and approved most of the representations; yet they thought that colonists who were not yet able to support their government were unqualified to exercise the power of legislation. Nevertheless they promised to take prompt action upon any recommendation which the Assembly should make, and provided that the Assembly should meet annually. Although the benevolent intentions of the Trustees cannot be questioned, the mere fact that they legislated at a distance of three thousand miles for a land which they had never seen, but commonly regarded as a Garden of Eden, made it inevitable that their action should not be consonant with reason. Laws enacted under this system could not represent social thought on the part of the community affected concerning justice. This unwise legislative structure was another fundamental weakness of the government of the Colony.

### Surrender of the Charter

THE Trustees were in negotiation with the Crown for surrender of their Charter before receiving the representation from the colonial Assembly. The warm words of appreciation and praise from the Assembly, in a striking contrast to the many past addresses of condemnation from malcontents, did not alter the Trustees' decision to relinquish control even before the expiration of the Charter. Parliament refused their petition of 1751 for further support, and the Trustees were totally devoid of funds for maintaining the Colony. On April 25th the

Common Council appointed a committee to adjust with the administration the proper means for supporting and setting the Colony for the future.[39] On May 6th, a memorial was presented to the Privy Council praying that sufficient funds be appropriated to enable the Trustees to discharge the obligations already contracted, and stating that for the future proper means should be provided "for putting the Government of the Colony on a more sure Foundation than it is at present thro' the uncertainty of the Trustees being enabled to support it." This memorial was referred to the Committee of the Privy Council, thence to the Board of Trade, which requested reports from the Admiralty, opinions from the Attorney-General, advice from the Lords Justices, and other views extending negotiations over more than a year.[40]

Acting upon the advice of two law officers of the Crown, Ryder and Murray, the Trustees executed under their common seal a deed of surrender of all their interest in Georgia. They gave up not only their authority to govern the Colony, which by the Charter's terms would have expired on June 9, 1753, but also their trusteeship for granting the land which had been placed in the Georgia Corporation forever. The one-eighth interest in the land which the Trustees had secured from Lord Carteret was included. Having closed out their business, on June 23, 1752, the last entry was made in the Trustees' records and their seal defaced. June 25th was taken as the official date for the surrender of the Charter.[41]

---

[39] *Ga. Col. Rec.* II, 506.

[40] The fullest account of these transactions is given in the *Journal of the Board of Trade, 1750–53*, 197 ff.

[41] W. L. Grant and James Munro, eds., *Acts of the Privy Council, Colonial Series* (London, 1910), IV, 128; *Journal of the Board of Trade, 1750–53*, 400.

CHAPTER III

# A Model Royal Colony

DURING the half century between the creation of the Board of Trade in 1696 and the surrender of the Charter of Georgia in 1752, the British Government adopted a well-defined colonial policy now familiarly known as "the old colonial system." The demands of trade and the necessity of adequate military defense against France explain why British statesmen determined to centralize control of the Colonies in the hands of the Crown, and to maintain the greatest uniformity possible in colonial policy.[1] The Trustees' authority over Georgia had been designed as temporary in the first place; Georgia would now become a royal colony conforming to the established colonial pattern. Yet it would have been far too much to expect the inept British colonial administration of that day to provide for the new Colony in advance of the actual transfer of control to the Crown. In any case, the Charter had been surrendered a year before the date of its expiration.

Lest confusion arise in the Colony during the transitional period, the Trustees suggested that the existing officers remain in authority until the establishment of a

---

[1] Charles M. Andrews, *The Colonial Background of the American Revolution* (New Haven, 1924), 17.

## A Constitutional History of Georgia

new administration under the Crown. Accordingly on June 25, 1752, a proclamation was issued by the Lords Justices directing that all persons vested in any offices or places of authority, ecclesiastical, civil or military, in the Colony of Georgia should continue therein until his Majesty's pleasure should further be made known. This action was fortunate, for under the slowly moving colonial administration not until October 29, 1754, did a royal governor arrive in Georgia to set up the new government.[2]

During this interregnum, and in fact for years to come, Benjamin Martyn, former Secretary of the Trustees, was responsible for such attention as Georgia received from the Mother Country. On December 19, 1752, the Board of Trade appointed Martyn as its agent for the affairs of Georgia. He kept the Board informed upon developments in the Colony, supervised the expenditure of Parliamentary grants, and in general acted as the Board of Trade's manager for Georgia affairs.

The government in the Colony remained for the time being under the direction of the President and Assistants. Despite his infirmity, the venerable William Stephens continued as President until September, 1750. Henry Parker, one of the four Assistants, then served as President until the arrival of a packet from the Trustees late in October containing his appointment as Vice-President and Commissioner for Licensing Traders for the Indian Nations. By the same communication James Habersham was named Secretary for the Trustees' Affairs within the Colony, Patrick Graham was made Agent to Distribute His Majesty's Presents to the Indians, and Noble Jones an Assistant.[3] Parker subsequently received the title of President, but he was succeeded in 1752 by Patrick Gra-

---
[2] *Acts of the Privy Council*, IV, 128.
[3] *Ga. Col. Rec.*, VI, 353.

## A Model Royal Colony

ham. When Governor Reynolds arrived in 1754 the local "Board" consisted of Patrick Graham as President, and James Habersham, Noble Jones, Pickering Robinson, and Francis Harris as Assistants. The government of the Colony was then thoroughly reorganized; yet it would be a mistake to consider that a complete break separated the new royal government from the old. Continuity in personnel, regardless of titles, tends toward continuity in policy. The former President and Assistants became members of Governor Reynolds' Council, and he soon complained that the Council sought to reduce his station from that of chief executive to a mere presiding officer of the Council. But though of necessity the nature of any government is to some extent conditioned by historical factors, the changes in the governmental structure and policy in Georgia resulting from the transfer of control from the Trustees to the Crown were of the broadest and most sweeping nature, far surpassing the changes of any other date, the Revolution not excepted.

The Privy Council left the responsibility of devising a plan of government for the new Colony to the Board of Trade. On March 5, 1754, the Board reported "that of the different Constitutions now subsisting in His Majesty's Dominions in America, that Form of Government established by the Crown in such of the Colonys as are more immediately subject to its direction and Government, appears to Us, the most proper Form of Government for the Province of Georgia." In working out this plan, Georgia was made a model royal colony.[4]

At this period the royal province was the normal type of British colony in America. In view of the Revolution of 1689, which definitely marked its supremacy in the

---
[4] *Acts of Privy Council*, IV, 178–79; *Journal of the Board of Trade, 1754–58*, pp. 59, 119. For examples of the use of Georgia as a model colony, see Leonard Woods Labaree, *Royal Instructions to the British Colonial Governors, 1670–1776* (New York, 1935) I, 295, 327.

49

age-old conflict with the King, Parliament might conceivably have taken an active part in the management of colonial affairs. There were certain advances in that direction in the two decades immediately following the Revolution; for instance an attempt was made in the session of 1695–1696 to organize a board with members appointed by Parliament to replace the old Committee of Trade and Plantations which dated from the reign of Charles II. Yet all such attempts failed. Parliament took much interest in trade and in reports upon conditions in the Colonies; yet it left their actual administration in the hands of the Crown which continued to handle it through the established agencies for the regular government of the realm, despite the growing importance of the Colonies in the Empire. The Secretary of State, Treasury, Admiralty, War Office, and other executive boards had a part in the administration of the Colonies. But by far the most important of these agencies dealing with colonial affairs was the Board of Commissioners for Trade and Plantations, or, more briefly, the Board of Trade. This Board, organized by King William in May, 1696, functioned with considerable success for the next eighty-six years.

The government of the Colonies was based upon the principle of government "by royal grace and favor," not government "by the consent of the governed." The system was essentially one of government by instructions. The King sent a royal governor to a colony as his direct agent, charged with the exercise and protection of the royal prerogative. To this executive he issued a royal commission in the form of letters patent under the Great Seal of the Realm, which constituted the legal basis of political authority within the colony. Supplemented by more specific royal instructions, it formed the basis of the provincial constitution so far as written documents went. The commissions to royal governors, highly formal documents phrased in general terms, showed little variation from colony to colony, and the commissions to the royal governors of Georgia were in the usual form. The detailed instructions contained such variations as were necessary to make them applicable to local circumstances. These instructions were drawn up in the office of the Board of Trade, but they were in fact a composite draft, showing the handiwork of nearly all who had a voice in affairs of the Colonies.[5]

The instructions to the first royal Governor of Georgia reflected in many instances experience gained from the administration of earlier Colonies. A dozen or more of the hundred and nine divisions of the General Instructions of August 6, 1754, to Captain John Reynolds explained certain undesirable practices that had arisen in other Colonies and gave the new Governor specific directions for avoiding their recurrence in Georgia. Reading these fifty pages of instructions today, one is impressed with the desire of the Home Government to establish an equitable system of government for the Colony, albeit the economic interests of the Mother Country were not to be compromised. Some of the long provisions were of no real significance, and one at least, number seventy-one, relating to whale fishing, had no place in a list of instructions for a Governor of Georgia.

There were only minor variations between the general instructions given to Georgia's three royal Governors, nor were there many substantial changes made through the "Additional Instructions" sent upon half-a-dozen occasions. The only additional instructions of much significance related to land grants, and these alterations in the original instructions simply reflected the British offi-

---

[5] Leonard Woods Labaree, *Royal Government in America* (New Haven, 1930), 1–36, *passim.*

cials' ignorance of the local conditions. The British policy of colonial government set forth in the commission and instructions to Governor Reynolds in 1754 was well established and underwent little change before the Revolution.[6]

## Powers of the Royal Governor

UNDER the royal government Georgia had a Governor for the first time. Her chief executive bore the impressive title "Captain-General and Governor-in-Chief in and over His Majesty's Colony of Georgia in America," and he was Vice-Admiral of the same. The Governor played a double role: He was, on the one hand, agent of the English Crown, the means of communication between Crown and Colony, a viceroy charged with the responsibility of preserving the royal prerogative; on the other hand he was chief executive, the mainspring of the Colony's government, responsible for the execution of laws passed by the Assembly. His legislative power included the right to initiate laws, call, prorogue, and dissolve the Assembly at will, and to pass a final and absolute veto upon all measures. His commission gave him the power, with the advice and consent of his Council, to establish such courts of justice as he should deem fit, and to appoint the judges. His instructions provided that he and his Council should act as a court of appeals. Furthermore, the Governor in his own right was empowered by his commission to pardon all crimes except treason and willful murder, and in these cases execution might be suspended until the King's pleasure should be known. His commission also stated

---

[6] Albert B. Saye, ed., "The Commission and Instructions of Governor John Reynolds," *The Georgia Historical Quarterly*, XXX (June, 1946), 125-162.

that he could remit fines and forfeitures, a power held by the governors of the other British royal colonies, but this provision was at variance with the seventy-second article of his general instructions which specifically forbade him to remit any fine above the sum of ten pounds until such remission should be approved by the Privy Council.[7] His executive powers were numerous and extensive.

As Captain-General the Governor was empowered to "levy, arm, muster, command, and employ" all persons whatsoever within the Province, and to transport them to any place within the British Colonies in America to resist enemies. With the advice and consent of his Council, he could erect such forts as were deemed necessary, and provide them with ordnance and other equipment. He was empowered to exercise martial law "in time of invasion, war, or other times, when by law it may be executed; and to do and execute all and every other thing and things, which, to our Captain General and Governor in Chief, doth or ought of right to belong." His powers over the colonial troops were thus made of the broadest nature. Yet it was not expedient to extend his authority to British regulars who might be stationed in the Colony, as had been done in the case of the governors in the West Indies. Despite his title, the Governor of Georgia was subordinate in military affairs to the commander-in-chief of the British forces in America.

In addition to his military powers, the Governor was given a number of naval powers as well. He received a special commission as Vice-Admiral which empowered him to try maritime cases. The royal commission authorized him to appoint captains and masters of such ships as he might commission, and to confer upon them the power of enforcing martial law. His general instruc-

---

[7] Contrast the provisions, found in *Ga. Col. Rec.*, XXXIV, 9, 64.

tions allowed him to grant commissions to privateers, under limited conditions, and to try offenses committed by seamen while on the shores of Georgia. He did not have jurisdiction over vessels of the Royal Navy within Provincial waters, nor authority to try offenses committed on board any ship commissioned by the British Admiralty.[8]

To provide for local administration, the Governor's commission gave him a broad power of appointment. In addition to judges and justices of the peace, he was to appoint all other officers necessary for the efficient execution of laws and the administration of justice. His instructions expressly empowered him to remove any subordinate officer, the only restriction being that he give a full account of his action to the Board of Trade. Yet in practice the Governor's control over inferior officers was not as extensive as the terms of his commission would indicate. The home officials found themselves irresistibly tempted to have a share in the colonial patronage. As a result the more important posts in Georgia, as in the other Colonies, were filled by nomination of the Secretary of State or the Board of Trade. The officials thus appointed were subject only to suspension by the Governor, pending a report from the Privy Council. In some instances the principal office-holder drew his salary while residing in England and exercised the office through a deputy in the Colony. Anthony Stokes, Chief Justice of Georgia, took particular note of this "fatal practice" which deprived the Governor of a patronage which could have been used as a means of strengthening the Royal Government.[9]

---

[8] *Ga. Col. Rec.*, XXXIV, 10–13.
[9] *A View of the Constitutions of the British Colonies* (London, 1783), 138.

## A Model Royal Colony

By the terms of the royal commission, no money raised by an act of the provincial assembly should be issued for support of the government except upon a warrant by the Governor, to which the advice and consent of the Council were necessary. By his instructions the Governor was required to keep a careful record of all receipts and expenditures, and to transmit a semiannual audit to the Board of Trade. No act for the issuance of bills of credit should be approved by the Governor until first confirmed by the Privy Council.

Among his many other powers was custody of the Great Seal of the Province. Inasmuch as all public documents and many private ones had to be validated by passing under this seal, for which substantial fees were collected, the charge of this symbol of authority was a desirable privilege as well as an important duty.

The greatest property value in the Colony was its vast expanse of land, which the Governor's commission gave him authority to grant to any person upon such conditions as he and his Council should deem expedient. This authority was conferred upon the Governor in the broadest terms by the wording of his commission, but it was narrowly restricted by detailed provisions for his guidance in the royal instructions. In general, an attempt was made to limit land grants to the size that the holder could cultivate or develop.

Four pages of the royal instructions related to the religious organization within the Province. The Governor was to take care that God be devoutly served throughout the Colony, that the Book of Common Prayer be read, and that the sacrament be administered according to the rites of the Chuch of England. The jurisdiction of the Bishop of London was recognized. The Governor was not to "prefer" any minister without a certificate from the Bishop, nor was any teacher to come from England and set up a school in the Colony without the Bishop's license.

Other lesser powers were set forth in the royal commission and instructions, but it was not intended that the Governor's authority should be limited to enumerated powers. Near the close of his general instructions it was provided that, "If any thing shall happen that may be of advantage and Security to our said Colony, which is not herein or by Our Commission Provided for, We do hereby allow unto you, with the advice and consent of Our Council, to take order for the present therein," pending further instructions from the Home Government.[10] All of these powers were held at the pleasure of the King, and in no case was the Governor to leave the Colony and go to Europe without having obtained leave from the Privy Council.

## The Governor's Council

CLOSE to the Governor in the management of the colonial government stood his Council. The usual number of Councilors in a royal colony was twelve, but the first instructions prepared for the royal Governor of Georgia named only ten. The Board of Trade did not at the moment know of twelve persons in the Colony properly qualified to serve as Councilors; but the number was soon increased to twelve. In addition, the Surveyor-General of the Customs of the Southern District and the Surveyor-General of the local district were to be admitted to sit and vote as Councilors Extraordinary during their residence in the Colony. Members of the Council were appointed by the Crown, but the Governor was empowered

---
[10] *Ga. Col. Rec.*, XXXIV, 79.

## A Model Royal Colony

to make recommendations. He could suspend members of the Council, and in case the number fell below seven, appoint new members up to that number, to serve until the Crown made new appointments. Three was designed as a quorum.

The functions of the Council were threefold: executive, legislative, and judicial. In an executive capacity it served as an advisory board or cabinet, and many of the powers granted to the Governor could be executed only with its advice and consent. The more important of these were the powers of summoning the Assembly, appointing inferior officers, issuing money from the provincial treasury, creating courts of justice, and establishing martial law in time of war. In other matters the Governor was not bound to follow the advice of his Council, although in practice he was not able to disregard the views of this distinguished group. Judging from the official *Proceedings and Minutes of the Governor and Council*, one would conclude that most of the Council's time was occupied with investigating applications and approving land grants.[11] Besides these executive functions, the Council served both as the court of appeals and as the upper house of the General Assembly.

## The Assembly

THE settlers in Georgia had had little legislative experience, but a system of local legislation was a definite part of the government of all British royal colonies. The Governor's commission indicated that he was to have the chief voice in the passage of laws. "You, the said John Reynolds," ran the commission of Georgia's first Governor, and the subsequent commission of Governors

---
[11] *Ga. Col. Rec.*, Vol. VII–XII, *passim*.

## A Constitutional History of Georgia

Ellis and Wright read likewise, "with the consent of Our said Council and Assembly, or the major part of them respectively, shall have full power and authority to make, constitute, and ordain Laws, Statutes, and Ordinances. . . ." A difference in the British and American view of the proper function and power of the local assembly had already arisen in several of the Colonies. It was natural that the British Government, looking upon the colonial government as one by royal grace and favor, should assign the leading role in legislation to the Governor as chief agent of the royal prerogative. Legislation should be tripartite, enacted by the Governor, the Council, and an elective Assembly. The Governors of Georgia were cautioned in their instructions "to observe in the passage of all Laws that the Style of enacting the same be by the Governor, Council and Assembly and no other." [12]

The one legislative assembly held during the Trustee Period, that of January, 1751, had been composed of sixteen members, supposedly apportioned among the various settlements on a basis of population. Governor Reynolds' royal instructions provided for a General Assembly of nineteen representatives to be apportioned among the settlements as follows: four from the City of Savannah and nearby villages, three from Ebenezer, two from Augusta, two from Great and Little Ogeechee, and one each from Vernonburgh, Acton, Abercorn and Goshen, Halifax, Midway River, Darien, Frederica, and the Islands Skidaway, Wilmington, Tybee and Green. An Act of 1758 divided the Colony into eight parishes,[13] and after that date representatives were more commonly referred to as representatives of a certain parish than as representatives of a district. The parish also became the common political subdivision for such purposes as taxation.

---

[12] *Ga. Col. Rec.*, XXXIV, 32.
[13] *Ga. Col. Rec.*, XVIII, 259–260.

## A Model Royal Colony

The general instructions of all three royal Governors provided that the Colony should be divided into counties "as soon as conveniently may be," but this was not carried out before the Revolution. Two years after the extension of the Colony's southern boundary to the Saint Marys River following the Peace of Paris in 1763, four new parishes, St. David, St. Patrick, St. Thomas, and St. Mary, were added. The original parishes were Christ Church (Savannah), St. Matthew (Ebenezer), St. George (Halifax), St. Paul (Augusta), St. Philip (Hardwick), St. John (Sunbury), St. Andrew (Darien) and St. James (Frederica).[14] The Governor never received any royal instruction to increase the number of representatives above the original nineteen, but in the years just before the Revolution, twenty-odd representatives sometimes actually attended the Commons House.

The only positive qualification for an elector stated in the royal instructions was the ownership of fifty acres of land. A representative was required to own five hundred acres within the district from which he was chosen. A negative provision disqualified anyone from either voting or serving as a representative who was a Popish recusant, or who was not twenty-one years of age.[15] In 1761 the King approved an Act of the Georgia legislature for regulating the method of election whereby six months' residence in the Colony and the ownership of fifty acres of land within the district of election were added as qualifications of the electorate.[16] This Act disqualified the Provost Marshal or anyone authorized by him to manage an election as a representative. The method of voting established was anything but secret. The returning officer was to come to the designated voting place at an appointed

---

[14] *Ga. Col. Rec.*, XVIII, 689-90.
[15] *Ga. Col. Rec.*, XXXIV, 31.
[16] *Ga. Col. Rec.*, XIII, 465-466.

time and enter in a book or roll the name of anyone desiring to run. Underneath each candidate's name would be a blank column wherein the name of those voting for him should be inscribed. The Act provided that two days should be set apart for elections. The hours of the polls were fixed from nine to six, but if the candidates present agreed, the closing hour could be made earlier if two hours had elapsed and no additional votes had been cast. Voters should be free from arrest while going to and returning from the polls, and any officer seeking to influence a voter was subject to fine.[17]

There were definite checks upon the local legislative power. In addition to the absolute veto of the Governor, all laws were subject to disallowance by the British Privy Council. Some British colonies had circumvented the Royal disallowance by passing temporary laws. To guard against this practice, the Governor of Georgia was instructed not to give his assent to any law proposed for a less time than two years, except in certain specified instances. Nor was he to consent to the reënactment of any law once disallowed by the Privy Council without the express consent of that body. Moreover, revenue acts, acts affecting the trade of Great Britain, private acts, or acts of an unusual nature were to be suspended until the royal pleasure should be known.[18] Thus, along with their first grant of legislative power, the Georgia Colonists were presented with the concept of a higher standard of legality than legislative will. The check took the form of a veto, but the experience of the Colonists with this royal veto was a step in the direction of law-limited government later to be established under a written constitution with judicial review.

[17] *Ga. Col. Rec.*, XIII, 466. Labaree, *Royal Instructions*, I, 95–96.
[18] *Ga. Col. Rec.*, XXXIV, 33–36.
Not all of the Acts recorded in Volume XIII of the *Colonial Records of Georgia* became laws, for some of them were vetoed by the Crown.

## A Model Royal Colony

Meetings of the General Assembly were called by the Governor, usually convening in October and continuing until the following spring. The term of a member was indefinite, lasting until the Assembly was dissolved by the Governor. As the representatives received no remuneration, they considered long terms of service as a hardship, and sought vigorously, but unsuccessfully, to have the English Government provide for elections at stated intervals. The Commons House elected its own Speaker, subject to the Governor's approval, and sought to follow the usages of the British House of Commons. Most of the familiar legislative procedure used by the House of Representatives in Georgia today, such as the previous question, the Committee of the Whole, the Committee on Ways and Means, and the three readings of bills, were practiced in the first meetings of the Commons House of Assembly.

Serving in the Assembly must have been a liberal education for some of the members. It was but natural that many irregularities should occur at the outset. When the first Commons House assembled in January, 1755, there were disputed elections in three of the eleven districts, and no members were seated from two of them. Before one month was out, four other members were expelled for excessive absences and seditious letters, a fifth was expelled in February, and a sixth in March. At the second session of the Assembly, in 1756, it was claimed that an erasure had been made in the returns from the District of Halifax, so the representative from that district was not seated. The clerk, appointed by the Governor, refused to read the minutes " 'till members returned duly elected and . . . in Town, were admitted; the Governor having declared that he will not look upon any thing done as valid 'till they are admitted." [19] The House proceeded to

---

[19] *Ga. Col. Rec.*, XIII, 95.

choose its own clerk, whereupon it was prorogued by the Governor for a week. Upon reassembling it persisted in refusing to seat the representatives in question, so the Governor dissolved the House. Future sessions of the Assembly were less stormy.

Acting as the Upper House of Assembly, the Governor's Council exercised a concurring and equal voice in the passage of all measures other than money bills, which were required to originate in the Commons House and could not be amended. Joint committees, resembling the modern conference committee, were frequently appointed to resolve differences between the two houses. In the last half of the royal period the Upper House more readily supported the policy of the Home Government as upheld by the royal Governor, and strong friction sometimes arose between the houses. An early instance of this was in 1765 when the Upper House refused to concur in the appointment of Charles Garth as colonial agent. The Commons House did not feel that Benjamin Martyn, agent of the Board of Trade for Georgia Affairs, properly represented the interests of the Colony, and in 1762 (by a joint act of the General Assembly, as it appears in the records) William Knox was named "Agent Assistant to Benjamin Martyn." [20] He was dismissed in 1765 for upholding the position of Parliament in the Stamp Act controversy, and it was over the appointment of his successor that the controversy between the Upper House and the Commons House ensued. An agreement was reached in 1768 when Benjamin Franklin, already stationed in London to guard the interests of Pennsylvania, agreed to serve as Georgia's colonial agent also.[21] The General Assembly did a great deal of quarreling, but it also did much con-

---

[20] *Ga. Col. Rec.*, XVIII, 482.
[21] *Ga. Col. Rec.*, XIX, 199; Coulter, *op. cit.*, 103.

## A Model Royal Colony

structive work. It levied taxes, appropriated money, authorized the issuance of paper currency, established religious worship, limited the interest on loans, suppressed lotteries, regulated the Indian trade, relieved imprisoned debtors, regulated the assize of bread, built roads, light houses, and ferries, organized the militia, prohibited gambling and horse racing, regulated the sale of beef, pork, pitch, tar, turpentine, and firewood, forbade the export of corn, and, without too much regard for individual rights or doctrines of *laissez-faire*, legislated for the general welfare of the Colony.[22]

## The Judiciary

THE chief organ of the judiciary in the royal government was the General Court at Savannah. In legal terminology there were two courts: The General Court, and The Court of Session of Oyer and Terminer and General Gaol Delivery. However, as the same judges presided at both courts and the chief distinction between them was that the former handled civil cases and the latter criminal cases, it is clearer to describe the two courts as simply the General Court.[23] The Governor, with the advice and consent of his Council, appointed the judges. The number varied, but there were usually three.[24] The low caliber of

---

[22] *Ga. Col. Rec.*, XVIII–XIX, *passim.*

[23] In reëstablishing the royal government after the British overran Georgia during the Revolution, the Court of Oyer and Terminer, described as "superfluous" by Chief Justice Anthony Stokes, was abolished. Stokes, *A View of the Constitution of the British Colonies*, 132. See *ibid.*, pp. 259–260, for a copy of the proclamation creating the original General Court.

[24] *Ga. Col. Rec.*, VII, 47, 504; Percy Scott Flippin, "The Royal Government in Georgia," in the *Georgia Historical Quarterly*, X (December, 1926), 261.

the judges had been the fatal flaw in the administration of justice under the Trustees, and this same weakness persisted in the first period of royal control. Soon after his arrival in Georgia, Governor Ellis wrote to the Board of Trade that "Nothing could be more irregular and unprecedented than the proceedings of our Courts owing to the ignorance and partiality of those who have hitherto presided. . . . We find here a Councillor prosecuting a man for *Scandalum Magnatum*. . . ." [25] He urged that a chief justice be sent from England, and this request was granted. During the royal period three chief justices came over, the best known among them being Anthony Stokes, who arrived in 1769 and soon became next to the Governor the most important person in the Colony. His salary of £500 from the Home Government, supplemented by numerous fees, enabled him "to appear in the character of a gentleman." The associate justices who received no salary or fees were, said Stokes, "almost always unacquainted with the law." [26]

In addition to the chief and associate justices, the personnel of the judiciary included an attorney-general, a provost marshal, justices of the peace, and constables. The attorney-general, as the name suggests, served as legal advisor to the Governor and Council and as prosecuting attorney for the Colony. The provost marshal corresponded to the English sheriff, with such duties as summoning juries, issuing summons for elections to the Assembly, serving various writs, and keeping custody of prisoners. In practice the principal provost marshal resided in England and rented out the office to a deputy who was styled "acting provost marshal." The position of the constables was similar to that of bailiffs in Georgia

---

[25] Letter of March 11, 1757. *Ga. Col. Rec.*, XXVIII, Part I-A, p. 7
[26] *A View of the Constitution of the British Colonies*, p. 132.

## A Model Royal Colony

today. They served the justices of the peace as the provost marshal served the General Court.

There was a right of appeal to the Governor and Council in civil cases where the amount exceeded £300, and in criminal cases where the fine was £200 or more. Important criminal cases and civil cases involving an amount above £500 could ultimately be appealed to the Privy Council. Suits involving smaller amounts might also be appealed to the Privy Council if they related to fees, duties, annual rents, or similar matters likely to be recurrent.[27]

The Governor, as noted above, had the power to grant pardons and to suspend the payment of fines, pending a decision on the latter from the Home Government. As Ordinary he had the sole power of probating wills and administering intestate estates; as Vice-Admiral he had jurisdiction of maritime cases.

The General Court, The Court of Sessions of Oyer and Terminer and General Gaol Delivery, The Court of Appeals, The Court of Admiralty, and The Court of Ordinary all functioned during the royal period; yet it was not in any of these, but rather in the Inferior Courts, or Courts of Conscience, held by justices of the peace, that the bulk of litigation was carried on. Every settlement had several justices of the peace, the total number commissioned by the Governor for the Province ranging at different dates between fifty and eighty. They may be compared to justices of the peace today in that their jurisdiction was over petty crimes and minor civil cases in which the amount involved did not exceed £8; nevertheless, the frontier life of the period made justices of the peace far more important in Colonial Georgia than they are today.[28]

---

[27] *Ga. Col. Rec.,* XXXIV, 49–50.
[28] *Ga. Col. Rec.,* VII, 55–61; IX, 543; X, 428; XVIII, 372–388.

*A Constitutional History of Georgia*

## The Established Church

THE British Government encouraged the development of the Anglican Church in Georgia by supplementing the salaries of its ministers; yet with the exception of "Papists," diverse religious groups, notably Presbyterians, Congregationalists, Lutherans, Baptists, and Jews, continued to worship God according to the dictates of their conscience. The act of the General Assembly of 1758 dividing the Province into parishes established the state religion of England. Vestrymen of the several parishes were empowered to assess rates within fixed limits for the repair of churches, relief of the poor, and other parochial services. The vestrymen of Christ Church Parish constituted a principal element in the local government. In addition to their religious functions and care of the poor, they were charged, among other things, with protecting Savannah against fire, preventing the dumping of refuse in the streets, appointing a beadle, and enlarging and enclosing the cemetery. All freemen could vote for vestrymen, and not all of the vestrymen chosen were members of the Church of England. But despite the encouragement given it by the British government and by the Society for the Propagation of the Gospel in Foreign Parts, the Church of England never became so strongly entrenched in Georgia as in some of her sister Colonies. There were rarely more than two Anglican ministers in the Colony at one time. Itinerant ministers of the Presbyterian and Baptist faiths who preached with greater emotional fervor had a stronger appeal to the frontier settlers.[29]

[29] Reba Carolyn Strickland, *Religion and the State in Georgia in the Eighteenth Century* (New York, 1939), 103–110.

A Model Royal Colony

## The Three Royal Governors

As FIRST Governor for the Colony the King sent John Reynolds, a captain in the Royal Navy. Reynolds had been to the port of Savannah a number of times, and was perhaps thought to know something of the local conditions. He arrived at Savannah as Governor on October 29, 1754, and was received with great ovation, including bonfires that night. The people expected a new era to begin with the new government, but their hopes were soon dampened. Reynolds had little judgment in the exercise of civil functions and soon quarreled with almost everyone, not excepting his Council and the Assembly. He was charged with interfering in the administration of justice, dealing with the Assembly in a highhanded manner, waste and graft in the distribution of Indian presents, and the appointment of menial servants to responsible positions. In particular he entrusted to William Little, a former surgeon in the Navy, then the Governor's private secretary, many public duties which were shamefully abused.[30] In response to complaints from all quarters, on July 29, 1756, less than two years after his arrival in Georgia, the Privy Council ordered Reynolds' return to England to give an account of his administration.

Henry Ellis, a young gentleman thirty-six years of age whose distinction as an explorer in search of the Northwest Passage had made him a Fellow in the Royal Society, was selected as the successor of Governor Reynolds. He arrived in Georgia on January 27, 1757, and set about his task of bringing harmony out of discord. On March 11th he wrote to the Board of Trade confirming the reports of the turbulent state of the Colony: "I found

[30] Ga. Col. Rec., XXVII, 273 ff.; XXIV, 171-195, passim.

*A Constitutional History of Georgia*

the people here exceedingly dissatisfied with each other . . . ," he explained. "Few approached me that were not inflamed with resentment and liberal in invectives, urgent that I should take some immediate and violent steps such as a total change of public Officers and a dissolution of the Assembly."[31] Indians flocked into Savannah every week expecting presents in consequence of the change of government. The young Governor must have been discouraged, but proceeded tactfully in his duties and was eminently successful in restoring order and bringing confidence in their government to the colonists of Georgia for the first time. Under his wise leadership the Colony made rapid strides. Unfortunately, he remained in Georgia for only three years because, he said, the warm climate was ill-suited for his health. He retained his interest in the welfare of the Colony, however, and was able to render it some service even after his return to England.[32]

The third and last Royal Governor was Sir James Wright who was probably born in England, but spent his boyhood in South Carolina and later became Chief Justice of that Colony. He was educated for the law, entering Gray's Inn in 1741, served many years as Attorney General of South Carolina, and was employed as her colonial agent in London at the time of his appointment in 1760 as Governor of Georgia.

## The Colony Prospers

WRIGHT made an excellent Governor. He was well liked by most of the people, and respected by all of them. His administration was efficient, his execution of the royal

---
[31] *Ga. Col. Rec.*, XXVIII, Part I, p. 4.
[32] *Ga. Col. Rec.*, XXXIV, 508.

## A Model Royal Colony

instructions faithful. Making Georgia his true and permanent home, he took a sincere personal interest in her advancement. His own success in amassing a personal fortune was conspicuous. By 1771 he owned 523 slaves distributed over eleven plantations. Under him the Colony experienced an unprecedented material prosperity, accompanied by rapid growth in both population and territory. Whereas in the petition of 1751 for the surrender of their Charter the Trustees estimated the population as 1,700 whites and 400 Negroes, by 1760 there were 6,000 whites and 3,000 Negroes. In 1766 the whites numbered 10,000 and the Negroes 8,000, and by 1773 there were 18,000 whites and 15,000 Negroes.[33] Governor Wright spoke enthusiastically of the flourishing state of the Colony, its ever increasing prosperity, and promising future. Formerly, of the three objectives in establishing the Colony, only the military aim had succeeded; now Georgia was to prove an economic asset to Great Britain as well. No longer hoping to become rich from silk and wine, the Colonists busied themselves in planting rice, indigo, corn, peas, tobacco, wheat, and rye; in making pitch, tar, turpentine, shingles, and staves; in sawing lumber from the abundant forests; in raising cattle, mules, horses, and hogs; and in securing deer and beaver skins through trade with the Indians. Immigrants from Virginia began to cultivate tobacco with "most astonish-

---

[33] Wright to Darmouth, Sept. 20, 1773, in *Collections of Georgia Historical Society*, III, 167. The Bureau of the Census in *A Century of Population Growth from the First Census of the United States to the Twentieth, 1790–1900* (Washington, 1909), 7, gives the following summary estimate of Georgia's population in the Eighteenth Century:

| Year | Total | White | Negro |
|---|---|---|---|
| 1752 | 5,000 | | |
| 1760 | 9,000 | 6,000 | 3,000 |
| 1766 | 18,000 | 10,000 | 8,000 |
| 1773 | 33,000 | 18,000 | 15,000 |
| 1776 | 50,000 | | |
| 1790 | 82,548 | 52,886 | 29,662 |

ing success."[34] From these many products, the principal articles of export were rice, indigo and skins to Europe, and lumber, horses and provisions to the West Indies. From fifty-two ship-loads of products valued at £15,744 in 1755, the exports increased to one hundred eighty-six ship-loads valued at £99,383 in 1770, and to two hundred twenty-five loads valued at £121,677 in 1773.[35]

By the Treaty of Paris at the close of the French and Indian War, Florida became a part of the British Empire. In the following year Georgia's southern boundary, long a disputed question, was finally determined upon as the St. Marys River, thus doubling Georgia's territory. The Mississippi River now became the western boundary. Removal of the danger of attack from France or Spain opened the way for an even brighter chapter in Georgia's history. As admirably expressed by one of the two greatest historians of eighteenth century Georgia, "The effect was most salutary: inhabitants flocked in, lands were taken up and cleared, new settlements projected, trade was enlarged, wealth increased, and a day bright with many promises of future aggrandizement dawned upon the long harassed and afflicted colony."[36]

---

[34] "Observations Upon the Effect of Certain Late Political Suggestions" by George Walton, William Few, and Richard Howley, reprinted in George White's *Historical Collections of Georgia* (New York, 1855), 107.

[35] Flippin, "Royal Government in Georgia," *Georgia Historical Quarterly*, IX (Sept., 1925), 187–245.

[36] William B. Stevens, *History of Georgia* (Philadelphia, 1859), II, 26.

CHAPTER IV

# The Revolution

In *A View of the Constitution of the British Colonies* published in 1783, Anthony Stokes, Chief Justice of Georgia under the royal government, explained:

> Georgia continued under the King's Government to be one of the most free and happy countries in the world—justice was regularly and impartially administered—oppression was unknown—the taxes levied on the subjects were trifling—and every man that had industry became opulent—the people there were more particularly indebted to the Crown than those of any other Colony—immense sums were expended by Government in settling and protecting that country—troops of rangers were kept up by the Crown for several years—Civil Government was annually provided for by vote of the House of Commons in Great Britain, and most of the inhabitants owed every acre of land they had to the King's free gift; in short, there was scarce a man in the Province that did not lie under particular obligations to the Crown.[1]

In view of the fact that the Colony fitted perfectly into the British mercantile system and was in a most prosperous state, it is not to be wondered that the revolutionary spirit developed more slowly in Georgia than in her sister Colonies to the north. Indeed, the surprise is

---
[1] Page 139.

rather to be found in the fact that Georgians joined in the Revolution at all, even though constantly "spirited on by . . . northern neighbors who never let them rest or gave them time to cool off." Philanthropy had played a conspicuous role in the establishment of the Colony, and in its infancy Georgia had been the pet of English charity. The British Government had furnished four-fifths of the finance for the Colony during its first twenty years, and after the surrender of control by the Trustees in 1752, Parliament continued to make annual appropriations of around £4,000 for maintaining the civil government of the Colony. The total amount spent by Parliament in support of the Colony was approximately £215,000 sterling, or well over a million dollars in modern currency.[2] No such favorable treatment had been lavished upon any other Colony, and Georgia might well have felt grateful.

Governor Wright, still loved and respected by the people, was well grounded in point of fact when he declared to the Assembly in January, 1775, that "We are in a very different situation and a very different footing from the other colonies."[3] Georgia was not seriously hampered by the British government's abandonment of a long standing "salutary neglect" in favor of a new policy of strengthening and enforcing the regulations of trade at the close of the Seven Years' War. Georgia, wrote Governor Wright in 1766, had "no manufactures of the least consequence: a trifling quantity of coarse homespun cloth, woollen and cotton mixed; amongst the poorer sort of people, for their own use, a few cotton and yarn stockings; shoes for our negroes; and some occasional blacksmith's work. But all our supplies of silk, linens, woollens, shoes, stockings, nails, locks, hinges, and tools

---
[2] Flippin, *Georgia Historical Quarterly*, IX, 189.
[3] *Ga. Rev. Rec.*, I, 36.

of every sort . . . are all imported from and through Great Britain."[4] Furthermore, less than a dozen ships were owned by Georgians, so they "could not be expected to get greatly excited when smuggling New England merchants and traders should be caught and tried for their crimes."[5] The eighteen thousand white inhabitants of Georgia at the outbreak of the Revolution were scattered over a vast area and needed protection from the ten thousand neighboring Indians.[6]

## Philosophy of the Revolution

IN VIEW of her favorable position in the British Empire, why did Georgia revolt, fight a bloody war, and set herself up as an independent state? The American Revolution is best interpreted in terms of a British colonial problem rather than merely an American problem. The colonial system, like all the British Constitution, evolved without any preconceived pattern, and the eighteenth century witnessed the rapid development of two opposing principles within this system: the Colonies, self-absorbed and preoccupied with domestic problems, grew toward intensive self government; the Mother Country, faced with the difficult problem of administering and financing the defense of the Colonies, grew toward imperialism rather than a simple mercantilism. Subordination of the Colonies to the Home Government was accepted by all English statesmen. The concept of a "commonwealth of nations" had not yet arisen. The readjustment of the laws of trade, reform of the administration, and imposition of taxes on the Colonies after the Peace of Paris was as

---

[4] *Ga. Col. Rec.*, XXVIII, Part II-A, pp. 404–405.

[5] Coulter, *op. cit.*, 100.

[6] Estimate by Governor Wright, *Collections of Georgia Historical Society*, III, 167.

natural a development as the former colonial autonomy had been. In the conflict between these two divergent tendencies is found the explanation for the Revolution offered by historians today.[7]

Those who believe like Hegel that ideas are predominant in the movement of history, or even believe that ideas such as those involved in great religious systems—Judaism, Confucianism, Mohammedanism, Buddhism, Christianity—exert an independent influence upon the course of history, will find another explanation for the Revolution in the intellectual developments of the Seventeenth and Eighteenth Centuries. "Conflicting political ideas, and not tea or taxes," declares Professor Van Tyne, "caused the American secession from the British empire. . . ."[8] It often happens that the idea involved is fully developed long before a practice is instituted. There is truth in the exaggerated assertion that once the ideas of the enlightened philosophers had been accepted in France, the French Revolution had occurred before it actually began. Likewise the Intellectual Revolution furnished the general atmosphere of the American Revolution.

The *Georgia Gazette* carried occasional advertisements of treatises on government such as those by Hume, Montesquieu, Voltaire, Locke and Rousseau for sale at the office of the publisher in Savannah. As leaders in the revolutionary movement in Georgia were eclectics, they borrowed freely from these and other sources. Their political philosophy was by no means original, but it nonetheless partook of the noblest thought that mankind has yet produced. If any one writer is to be singled out as the most influential upon the leaders of the American Revo-

---

[7] See Andrews, *The Colonial Background* and George L. Beer, *British Colonial Policy, 1754–1765* (New York, 1907).

[8] *American Historical Review*, XIX (October, 1913), 64.

## The Revolution

lution, then that place should be given to John Locke. Critics of Jefferson later charged that the Declaration of Independence "contained no new ideas"; that it was "a commonplace compilation, its sentiments hackneyed in Congress for two years before," and that Jefferson had "copied from Locke's treatise on Government." Jefferson did not deny these charges other than to say, "I know only that I turned to neither book nor pamphlet while writing it." [9]

The gist of Locke's elaborate inquiry into the origin and character of government is this: Reason is the only sure guide which God has given to men; hence reason is the only foundation of just government. Reason dictates that government should be responsible to the people of the community which it governs; that its power should be limited both by natural law and by the constitutional traditions and conventions inherent in the history of the realm. As government is indispensable, its right of existence is indefeasible; yet it is also derivative in the sense that it exists for the well-being of the nation. Whereas Locke has been empirical in his *Essay Concerning Human Understanding,* in much of this political philosophy he was rationalistic. Yet for those who believe in morals apart from force, and who have faith in human reason to determine the direction of these absolutes, these conclusions of Locke, like the self evident truths of Jefferson a century later, still have an appeal.

This philosophy of natural law, individual rights, and limited government found its most brilliant exposition in the Declaration of Independence:

> We hold these truths to be self-evident, That all men are created equal, that they are endowed by their Creator with certain unalienable Rights; that among these are Life, Liberty and the pursuit of Happiness—That to se-

---
[9] Carl Becker, *The Declaration of Independence* (New York, 1922), 25.

cure these rights, Governments are instituted among Men, deriving their just powers from the consent of the governed,—that whenever any Form of Government becomes destructive of these ends, it is the Right of the People to alter or to abolish it, and to institute new Government, laying its foundation on such principles and organizing its powers in such form, as to them shall seem most likely to effect their Safety and Happiness.

The language of this declaration holding all men to be created equal has given rise to much fruitless discussion. There is little to be gained from taking as an absolute a phrase which can only have meaning when qualified. The natural nobility of mankind furnished an exalted standard for Americans of the Revolutionary Era; it remains so for those who have faith in the worthiness of the lives and purposes of common men and women, for those who with Jefferson believe in "equal rights to all, special privileges to none." The Fathers, says Lincoln, "did not intend to declare all men equal in all respects. They did not mean to say that all were equal in color, size, intellect, moral development, or social capacity. They defined with tolerable distinctness in what respects they did consider all men created equal—equal in certain inalienable rights, among which are life, liberty, and the pursuit of happiness. This they said and this they meant. They did not mean to assert the obvious untruth, that all men were then actually enjoying that equality, nor yet that they were about to confer it upon them. In fact, they had no power to confer such a boon. They meant simply to declare the right, so that the enforcement of it might follow as fast as circumstances should permit. They meant to set up a standard maxim for free society which should be familiar to all and revered by all—constantly looked to, constantly labored for, and even, though never perfectly attained, constantly approximated; and thereby

## The Revolution

constantly spreading and deepening its influence and augmenting the happiness and value of life to all people, of all colors, everywhere." [10]

The Declaration of Independence was penned by a son of Virginia, but it represented a philosophy common to all America. Declarations by revolutionary groups in Georgia gave expression to all the philosophy of natural law, limited government, and inalienable rights sketched above. While not original, these declarations are nonetheless important. There is no more significant fact in Georgia's history than the acceptance of this philosophy. Notable among the earlier philosophical statements was that adopted on August 10, 1774, at a general meeting in Savannah of the inhabitants of the Province. Therein it was stated that "protection and allegiance are reciprocal, and under the British Constitution correlative terms; . . . the Constitution admits of no taxation without representation; they are coeval and inseparable; . . . it is contrary to natural justice and the established law of the land to transport any person to Great Britain or elsewhere to be tried under indictment for a crime committed in the colonies, as the party prosecuted would be deprived of the privilege of trial by his peers from the vicinage. . . ." [11]

A careful study of the many Revolutionary documents reveals that there were few specific grievances on the part of Georgia herself which could be listed as causes for revolt. Revolutionary groups in Georgia voiced opposition to taxation without representation, to the maintenance of ten thousand British troops in America in time of peace, to the Quartering Act, to various measures for trade and navigation, and to most of the other ill-chosen

---

[10] Speech at Springfield, June 26, 1857, quoted in Arthur N. Holcombe, *State Government in the United States* (New York, 1916), 23–24.
[11] *Ga. Rev. Rec.*, I, 15.

colonial measures of George III; yet more excitement could be aroused by proclaiming the danger to the Colonists' liberties in general than by demonstrating any severe grievance suffered by Georgia. But Georgia felt a close kinship for her sister Colonies. She recognized that a union with them was best calculated to afford the protection which she sorely needed against the Indians, and she sympathized with them in the unjust treatment which they were receiving under the harsh British administration of the day. If these sister Colonies could be so oppressively dealt with through "alarming and arbitrary" acts, what guarantee would remain for the preservation of the time-honored liberties which the Georgia Colonists claimed under the British Constitution?[12]

## Revolutionary Spirit Develops Slowly

A CONTEMPORARY brochure entitled *The Particular Case of the Georgia Loyalists* rightly explained "That the principal part of the Inhabitants, at the commencement of these troubles . . . were well affected to his Majesty's person and government, and attached to Great Britain. That it was owing to their loyal disposition that the House of Assembly, though repeatedly solicited by letters and emissaries from the Legislatures of some of the other Colonies, declined to concur with them, in resolves calculated to support their opposition to the British Government. . . ."[13] But while not nearly so violent in the early stages as in the other Colonies, serious opposition did arise in Georgia to the new British colonial policy.

---

[12] *Ga. Rev. Rec.*, I, 8–10, 37–39, 250. *The Georgia Gazette*, July 11, 1774.
[13] *The Particular Case of the Georgia Loyalists: In Addition to the General Case and Claim of the American Loyalists which was lately Published by order of their Agent* (London (?), 1783). Copy in De Renne Collection.

*The Revolution*

Whether or not Parliament had a legal right to tax the Colonies continues to be debated after much scholarly research on the question; the opposition of the Colonies to taxation without representation becomes far easier to support if shifted from the legal to an ethical basis. James Johnston discontinued his *Georgia Gazette*, the Colony's only newspaper, when the Stamp Tax of 1765 became effective;[14] James Habersham held it an insult to common reason to argue that the Colonies were represented in Parliament; and only the influence of Governor Wright prevented the Commons House of Assembly, convened at Savannah on September 2, 1765, from sending delegates to the Stamp Act Congress. The resolutions of the Stamp Act Congress were approved, apparently unanimously, by the Commons House of Assembly on December 14, 1765. Tumultuous gatherings at Savannah led Governor Wright to remove the stamps from the store where the Indian presents were deposited and place them in the guard house. Other than those used in clearing vessels, no stamps were sold in Georgia. Yet when the Commons House was convened on July 15, 1766, to hear the welcome news of the repeal of the obnoxious tax, Governor Wright was able to congratulate the Assembly on having "no votes or Resolutions injurious to his Majesty's Government or tending to destroy the Legal and Constitutional Dependency of the Colonies on the Imperial Crown and Parliament of Great Britain to reconsider."[15]

The British Government was convinced of the justice and necessity of raising taxes from the Colonies to pay a portion of the enormous public debt incurred by the

---

[14] See the issue of May 21, 1766, the first after the resumption of publication, for a lengthy article giving sound reasons against taxation without representation.

[15] *Ga. Col. Rec.*, XIV, 369-371.

French and Indian War, waged partly at least in defense of the Colonies. It also felt that the Colonies should share in the support of the army and navy still maintained for their protection. The repeal of the Stamp Tax was followed by new revenue measures, the Townshend Acts, which imposed duties on glass, lead, paper, and tea imported into the Colonies. Colonial resistance produced the non-importation movement. In Georgia this movement followed much the same line of development as in the other plantation provinces where the planters rather than the merchants, as in the north, took the lead. Spurred to action by a letter from the General Committee of South Carolina, a radical group known as the Amicable Society meeting at Liberty Hall in Savannah issued a call for a public meeting of all inhabitants on Tuesday, September 12 (1769), to consider methods of obtaining relief from the Townshend Acts. At this meeting, attended by "Merchants, Planters, Tradesmen, and others," a committee was appointed to submit a form of agreement to the inhabitants a week later.[16] Perhaps in an effort to prevent the adoption of too sweeping an agreement, the merchants of Savannah held a meeting of their own at the home of Alexander Creighton on September 16th. This meeting of merchants three days before the general meeting denounced the Townshend Acts as "unconstitutional," expressed full sympathy with the non-importation movement, and resolved "That any person . . . importing any of the articles subject to such duties, after having it in their power to prevent it, ought not only to be treated with contempt but deemed enemies to their country. . . ."[17] These efforts of the mer-

---

[16] Arthur Meier Schlesinger, *The Colonial Merchants and the American Revolution* (New York, 1918), 147. See also the *Georgia Gazette*, Sept. 6 and 13, 1769.

[17] Charles C. Jones, *The History of Georgia* (Boston, 1883), II, 113.

## The Revolution

chants proved unavailing. The mass meeting of September 19th adopted a comprehensive agreement patterned after that of South Carolina of July 20th and 22nd. The terms of the agreement were to expire with the repeal of the Townshend duties. The subscribers agreed to import no European or East Indian goods other than an enumerated list of necessities and goods for which orders had already been placed that could not be countermanded. They pledged themselves to sell goods at the customary prices, to promote provincial manufactures, to discard mourning, to import no Negroes from Africa after June 1, 1770, and to import no wine after March 1st of the same year. All trade should be severed with inhabitants of the Province and with transient traders who neglected to sign the agreement within five weeks, and every violator should be deemed "no Friend to his Country." Jonathan Bryan, a member of the Governor's Council, presided at this meeting of September 19th, and for his boldness he was soon dismissed.[18]

The adoption of a non-importation agreement was one thing; the enforcement of the agreement was another matter. In all the plantation provinces, non-importation and the problems of its enforcement was much less a part of the fabric of everyday life than in the commercial provinces. The agreements were not the making of the merchants, and in the general absence of trading centers it was difficult for the planters to instill a fear of discipline in the hearts of the merchants. As a result the non-importation movement was always a failure in the plantation provinces. Whereas in the commercial provinces the imports from England declined by two-thirds in the year 1769 as compared with the year 1768, and fell below the level of 1768 even in the year 1770 when the agreements collapsed, in the plantation provinces imports

---
[18] White, *Historical Collections*, 42–44.

actually increased somewhat in the years 1769 and 1770. In Georgia where the general non-importation association had been reluctantly adopted by the merchants, it was speedily disregarded. On June 27, 1770, a public meeting in Charleston solemnly voted, without a dissenting vote, that Georgians ought "to be amputated from the rest of their brethren, as a rotten part that might spread a dangerous infection." [19]

The year of the adoption of non-importation also witnessed a tactful enunciation of the principle of no taxation without representation by the Commons House of Georgia when it urged the extension of representation to the four parishes recently carved out of the territory lying between the Altamaha and St. Marys River lest the Assembly itself be guilty of violating the principle for which it contended.[20] Two years later serious friction arose between the Commons House and the Governor when Wright refused to sanction the choice of Noble Wymberley Jones, one of the foremost radicals of the Colony, as Speaker. The House resolved "That the rejection by the Governor of a Speaker, unanimously elected, was a high breach of the privileges and liberties of the people, and their representatives," whereupon the Governor dissolved the Assembly. In 1772 while Wright was visiting England, James Habersham, the Secretary of the Colony who had been made Acting-Governor, called the Assembly together. Jones was again elected Speaker, only to be rejected by Habersham. The House proceeded to elect Jones a third time, but he refused to accept the position. Archibald Bulloch was then elected and approved. Acting-Governor Habersham had not known of the third election of Jones, but later upon inspecting the

---

[19] *South Carolina Gazette*, May 17, 1770, quoted in Schlesinger, *op. cit.*, 209.
[20] *Ga. Col. Rec.*, XII, 123-24.

*The Revolution*

minutes he was exasperated and demanded that the section recording the election of Jones be expunged from the records. The House refused and was again dissolved.[21] These instances evidence the rise of discontent, but Georgia had not yet come anywhere near an upheaval such as the Boston Massacre.

## *Emergence of Revolutionary Government*

AT THE close of the year 1773 when Georgia was relatively tranquil, having as her chief concern the establishment of amiable relations with the Indians, Boston defied the attempt of the British Government to force her to pay a tax on tea by holding a "tea party" which started a train of rapidly moving events destined to cause a severance of all political ties with the Mother Country within the brief space of two and a half years. Parliament responded to the colonial defiance of its tax measures with a series of coercive acts, known in the Colonies as Intolerable Acts, directed particularly at reducing Boston to submission. Instead of isolating Massachusetts, these measures caused a storm of protest to sweep over America and rallied twelve other Colonies to her support.

The royal legislatures were to a certain point effective instruments for championing the rights of the Colonists: They had a popular basis, were well organized, were experienced in struggles with the Crown, and possessed a tight grip on the treasury. Their limitations were a lack of dispatch, the hamper of oaths, the possibility of control by a clique subservient to the Crown, and the royal governor's prerogative of dissolution or prorogation. As the revolutionary spirit progressed, these half-fettered legislative bodies were pushed out of the way by pro-

---

[21] *Ga. Col. Rec.*, XVII, 768.

vincial congresses, unhampered by legal restraints. As royal government broke down, provisional governments were established. The process was a gradual one, the transition spanning roughly the years 1774–1776.[22]

In Georgia, news of the Intolerable Acts aroused indignation and created a deep sympathy for Massachusetts. The young and radical element would not stand idly by. Noble Wymberley Jones, Archibald Bulloch, John Houstoun, and George Walton, four of the most prominent citizens, issued a notice in the *Georgia Gazette* on July 14, 1774, decrying the "alarming and arbitrary" imposition of the recent acts and summoned all patriots to assemble at Peter Tondee's Tavern in Savannah on July 27th. Due to the poor facilities for communication, those attending this meeting were all from Savannah and the surrounding territory; so after reading letters from committees of correspondence in Massachusetts, Pennsylvania, Maryland, Virginia, North and South Carolina, and appointing a committee of thirty-one headed by John Glen to draw up a statement of the position of the people of Georgia on the momentous problems of the day, the meeting was adjourned to reconvene on August 10th.[23] At this second meeting bold resolutions were adopted in denunciation of the British Government, but after much debate it was determined that no delegates should be sent to the Continental Congress scheduled to meet in Philadelphia the following September. Nevertheless, some organization to the thus far sporadic opposition was effected through the appointment of "a general committee to act," any eleven of whom were given "full power to correspond with the Committees of the several provinces upon the Continent." [24]

---

[22] Allan Nevins, *The American States During and After the Revolution* (New York, 1924), 26.

[23] *Ga. Rev. Rec.*, I, 11–12.

[24] *Ga. Rev. Rec.*, I, 15–19; Hugh M'Call, *History of Georgia* (Savannah, 1816), II, 273.

## The Revolution

Governor Wright, always vigilant to preserve the royal interest, took active measures to destroy the effect of the meeting of August 10th. A protest meeting, attended by about a third of the inhabitants in and about Savannah, including the Governor's Council and numerous other officers, both civil and military, drew up a "Dissent to the Resolutions of August 10th" which denounced the meeting of that date as one "held by a few persons in a tavern with doors shut," in no sense representative of the people. Agents were sent throughout the Colony to secure signatures to similar statements of dissent, and these, together with other propaganda in the King's behalf, were published in the *Georgia Gazette*. The year 1774 closed without impressive gains by the radicals.[25]

News of the action taken by the First Continental Congress produced a divided opinion in Georgia. In order to bring about some determination relative to the Association and other recommendations of the Continental Congress, "a few well-affected persons in Savannah" published a call for a meeting of delegates from all the parishes to convene at Savannah in a provincial congress on January 18th, the same date upon which the royal legislature had been called to assemble. While every parish sent representatives to the Commons House of Assembly, only five sent delegates to the Provincial Congress. Clearly this extra-legal body could not pretend to represent the Colony. To avoid embarrassment, it adopted the expedient of proceeding to transact the desired business and then submit it in the form of resolutions to the House of Assembly which, it was hoped, might hastily adopt the resolutions before the Governor could interfere.[26] Accordingly, the Provincial Congress drew up a modified form of the "non-importation, non-consumption, non-exportation" agreement which the

---
[25] *Ga. Rev. Rec.*, I, 18-39, *passim*.
[26] White, *Historical Collections*, 61-63.

*A Constitutional History of Georgia*

Continental Congress had adopted the preceding October,[27] named delegates to the Continental Congress, and notified the Commons House of its action. Despite this sly procedure, the scheme of using the Provincial Congress as a caucus for the Assembly failed. Governor Wright, always alert, learned of the transactions going on and prorogued the Assembly until May 9th (1775), by which time he hoped to know "the Final Determination of Parliament relative to American Affairs." [28]

Noble Wymberley Jones, Archibald Bulloch, and John Houstoun, chosen by the Provincial Congress as delegates to the Second Continental Congress, called to meet at Philadelphia on May 10th, declined to serve because they felt unable to pledge themselves for the execution of any measures whatever. In a letter to the President of the Continental Congress, dated April 6, 1775, they declared that there was not enough strength in Georgia to enforce the non-importation measures recently adopted by the Provincial Congress. They found the inhabitants of Savannah "not likely soon to give matters a favorable turn," for the importers were "mostly against any interruption (of the trade) and the customers very much divided. There were some of the latter virtuously for the measures, others strenuously against them, but more who called themselves neutrals than either." [29]

The only parish showing a marked determination to join the other Colonies in their resistance to England was

---

[27] For text of the Association of the Continental Congress, see William Macdonald, *Documentary Source Book of American History, 1606–1898* (New York, 1902), 166–172; for the proposed Georgia 'Association' see *Georgia Revolutionary Records*, I, 43–48.

[28] Wright to Dartmouth, July 18, 1775, in *Collections of Georgia Historical Society*, III, 198. This was the last session of the Assembly, for no quorum could be secured in May and by November 9, 1775, the date next set for reassembling, royal authority in Georgia had been swept away. *Ga. Rev. Rec.*, XII, 419.

[29] White, *Historical Collections*, 62.

## The Revolution

St. Johns, inhabited by Puritans who had migrated from England in 1630 to Dorchester, Massachusetts, where they had remained for fifty years before moving to South Carolina, and thence to St. Johns Parish in Georgia. Through a group meeting in December, 1774, this Parish fully ratified the measures adopted by the Continental Congress. Dissatisfied with the action of the First Provincial Congress in Georgia, these Puritans took steps toward seceding from Georgia and entering an alliance with South Carolina. The movement failed, but South Carolina did recommend these Puritans to the Continental Congress, and Lyman Hall whom they elected in March as their delegate took a part in the deliberation of the Congress although he had no vote.[30]

News of the opening of war in New England produced a burst of excitement in Georgia which swelled the ranks of the patriots from those who had thus far been neutral. Spurred to action by the news of Concord and Lexington, on May 11th the radicals stormed the powder magazine at Savannah and seized the ammunition stored there. The customary celebration of the King's birthday on June 4th was turned into a wild demonstration by the radicals in which a liberty pole was erected. Within the brief space of one month the radicals completely defied royal authority and set up their own government. In response to a call issued in the *Georgia Gazette,* a large number of inhabitants of Savannah and the surrounding country assembled at Savannah on June 22nd and chose a group of fifteen, headed by William Ewen as President, as a Council of Safety whose duty for the moment was to act as a center of liaison.[31] A call was broadcast for the election of new members to a Second Provincial Congress to convene on July 4th.

---
[30] *Ga. Rev. Rec.,* I, 54–62.
[31] *Ga. Rev. Rec.,* I, 66–67.

## A Constitutional History of Georgia

Georgia was now thoroughly aroused. At the appointed date more than a hundred delegates representing every parish and district assembled at Tondee's Tavern. The work of this Provincial Congress in providing a government for the Colony resembled that of similar bodies elsewhere. At the July session, the Association of the First Continental Congress was adopted, and John Houstoun, Archibald Bulloch, the Reverend John Joachim Zubly (later to prove a Tory and resign), Noble Wymberley Jones, and Lyman Hall were sent as delegates to the Second Continental Congress, any three of them to constitute a quorum.

The fragmentary records now available do not permit a complete history of the steps taken in setting up the new government for the Colony, nor a detailed description of its organization and operation, but the general outline is clear. The Provincial Congress itself exercised executive, legislative, and judicial functions, either as a body or through committees. While it was not in session, the Council of Safety, created on June 22nd and recognized by the Provincial Congress on July 17th, exercised full governmental authority. These two central bodies, acting through committees in the several districts, raised troops, commissioned officers, issued paper money, enforced the Association, and took all other action which the exigencies of the time demanded.[32] In August the Council of Safety provided for calling out the militia and expelling all officers who would not subscribe to the Association. All opposition to the Provincial Congress would be silenced, if need be by subjecting the offender to tarring and feathering. Even the rector of Christ Church was removed and a layman appointed in his

---

[32] Portions of the 'Proceedings of the Council of Safety' found in the *Collections of the Georgia Historical Society*, V, 15–127, and in White's *Historical Collections*, 86–92, furnished useful supplements to the scattered proceedings in Vol. I of the *Georgia Revolutionary Records*.

## The Revolution

stead. Soon the royal courts were forcefully closed. "In short my lord," wrote Wright to Dartmouth on September 16, 1775, "the whole Executive Power is Assumed by them, and the King's Governor remains little Else than Nominally so." [33]

The repercussion of Lexington had already sent half the royal Governors scurrying for safety. In those States where the conservatives were strongest, the royal and proprietary Governors remained in their seats even after Bunker Hill, but as impotent spectators of the rapidly strengthening revolutionary governments. In order to prevent Governor Wright from communicating with two British war vessels and a transport which arrived off Tybee early in January, 1776, the Council of Safety, by a resolution of January 18th, ordered the arrest of both Wright and his Council. Still respected, the venerable Governor was paroled and allowed to remain in his home upon giving his pledge not to communicate with the ships; but on February 11th he broke his pledge, escaped, and found refuge on one of the ships at Tybee. The Georgians were glad to see him go. The royal government under which Georgia had made remarkable progress was at an end.

---

[33] *Collections of the Georgia Historical Society,* III, 209.

CHAPTER V

# Early State Government

THE powers of the National Government are today so expanded as to cause the American mind to turn instinctively to the national Constitution when considering the constitutional law of the land. The exalted place given to the document drawn up by the Federal Convention causes us to forget that "the most eventful constitution-making epoch in our history was not the year 1787, but an antecedent period extending from 1776 to 1780."[1] Lord Bryce was careful to point out to his British readers that the American Federal Constitution was largely formed upon the earlier State Constitutions, which were in turn an outgrowth of colonial experience.[2]

Time and time again the Colonists had appealed to their charters and to the great documents of English constitutional history against an invasion of their rights, and in many cases their appeals had been successful. It was precisely because the three leading New England Colonies had been founded upon the charter principle and had retained their charters that New England was more secure in her freedom than other sections. The transfer

---

[1] William C. Morey, "The First State Constitutions," *Annals of the American Academy of Political and Social Science*, IV (September, 1893), 201.

[2] *The American Commonwealth* (New York, 1888), 19 ff.

## Early State Government

of sovereignty from the King to the "King in Parliament," and then by the Revolution of 1776 to the American people, did not abrogate the need for a constitution.

The basic theory upon which the Americans were proceeding in the Revolution was that the people were the source of governmental authority, and that government should of right rest upon the consent of the governed. Now that they had the opportunity to set up their own governments, how nearly would their conduct accord with their doctrine? What method would be used in drawing up constitutions as fundamental laws? The characteristic practice relative to the adoption of written constitutions which developed later involved three main principles: *first,* a distinction between constitutional and statutory law; *second,* a distinction between the constitutional convention and the ordinary legislative body of the state; and *third,* submission of the proposed constitution to a direct vote of the people.[3] There can be no doubt that a distinction was made between constitutional law and ordinary statutes in the Revolutionary Period; but in the adoption of the first State constitution, Massachusetts alone followed the convention method in its perfected form.

Early revolutionary meetings in Georgia, patterned for convenience rather than after any careful plan of representative government, were nothing more than mass meetings, dominated by the radicals of Savannah. The first Provincial Congresses were supposedly modeled after the Commons House of Assembly, but whereas in some of the Colonies, notably Massachusetts and Virginia, these two bodies were practically identical, the First Provincial Congress in Georgia was far smaller and the Second four times larger than the former lower house

---
[3] Arthur N. Holcombe, *State Government in the United States* (New York, 1916), 42.

## A Constitutional History of Georgia

of the royal Assembly. There is no definite information relative to the method used in electing the delegates to these first congresses, but it is probable that they were chosen through mass meetings held on different dates in the several districts, with all present exercising a vote. "For the American people to live under the rule of agencies which had an indefinite tenure, a vague authority, and an irregular mode of functioning was impossible, while to carry on a war through such agencies was preposterous." [4]

Georgia participated in the process of regularization of political authority carried on throughout the continent during the year 1775. Her Second Provincial Congress sought to give future congresses a representative basis by fixing the number of delegates at ninety-six, to be distributed among eighteen districts according to their population. As the radical element then held full sway, a resolution of July 14, 1775, extended the franchise to "every man contributing toward the general tax." These measures constituted a notable improvement, but always a laggard in the revolutionary movement, Georgia was not to give a foundation at all substantial to her revolutionary government until April of the following year.[5]

## Rules and Regulations of 1776

THE Third Provincial Congress, in session at Augusta because of the commencement of hostilities at Savannah, went far toward providing Georgia with a written constitution. But for their brevity, incompleteness, and avowedly temporary character, the "Rules and Regula-

---

[4] Nevins, *The American States During and After the Revolution*, 88
[5] *Collections of Georgia Historical Society*, V, 20; *Ga. Col. Rec.*, I, 254–256.

tions" adopted on April 15, 1776, might be termed the Constitution of 1776. A lengthy preamble reviewed the "unwise and iniquitous system of administration obstinately persisted in by the British Parliament and Ministry" which had resulted in the state of confusion then existing in Georgia. With all officers uncertain of their authority, and "all judicial powers . . . totally suspended to the great danger of persons and property," the members of the Provincial Congress, "as the representatives of the people, with whom all power originates, and for whose benefit all government is intended," felt it their duty to provide rules and regulations as a "temporary expedient" until the advice and direction of the Continental Congress could be secured.[6]

As English speaking people always build their new political institutions upon the old, in the main these Rules and Regulations of 1776 only gave legislative sanction to the revolutionary government that had grown up during the past ten months. Supreme control of the Colony was still to remain in the hands of the Provincial Congress. In addition to the exercise of all legislative power, the Congress was given control over the personnel of both the executive and the judiciary. A chief justice, an attorney general, a provost marshal, and a clerk of the Court of Sessions were to be chosen by the Congress, to serve during its pleasure. The President and Commander-in-Chief was likewise made subservient to the Congress through the provision that he be elected by it for a term of only six months. The chief executive was in fact made little more than the president of a plural executive, for he was bound not only to consult but to follow the advice of his Council in all cases whatsoever. This Council was largely a continuation of the Council of Safety, but was

---

[6] For a copy of these Rules and Regulations, see *Ga. Col. Rec.*, I, 276–277.

in the future to consist of thirteen members plus the five delegates to the Continental Congress, all of whom were to be elected in like manner and for the same period as the President. The provisions relative to the judiciary were inexplicit, but evidently there was to be little change from the judicial structure under the Crown. The Congress itself was to appoint the judges for the General Court, and the President and Council should appoint magistrates (justices of the peace?) for the several parishes. The former rules of proceedings in the courts should be followed as nearly as possible, and all the former laws, both common and statutory, should continue in force if not inconsistent with action taken by the Continental or Provincial Congresses. Salaries were set for the principal officers, and anyone holding a place of profit, civil or military, was made ineligible for membership in either the Congress or the Council of Safety. Archibald Bulloch, President of the two previous Congresses, was elected first President, and under his guidance the Committee of Safety, or Council, continued its vigorous efforts toward establishing order and strengthening the militia of the Province.[7]

## News of the Declaration of Independence

THE promulgation of the Rules and Regulations of April 15, 1776, with their enunciation of popular sovereignty was the nearest approach to a declaration of independence by Georgia; it rested with the Continental Congress to take this decisive step for her.

Lincoln once declared that "The Union is older than the States, and in fact created them as States."[8] The ques-

---
[7] Stevens, *op. cit.*, II, 294; *Collections of Georgia Historical Society*, V, 45–127, *passim*.
[8] Special message to Congress, July 4, 1861, quoted in Nevins, *The American States*, 118.

## Early State Government

tion of whether there was an American state in the Revolutionary period played no mean role in the long and bitter historical controversy over state sovereignty, nullification, and secession. In the case of Georgia, the bulk of historical evidence supports the nationalist point of view. Governor Wright, viewing the scene from Georgia in September, 1775, conceived the position of the Continental Congress in the revolutionary organization to be a "Supreme Legislative and Governing Power over the whole Continent." [9] Despite her tardiness in sending delegates, Georgia was the third Colony to bind herself to abide by the resolutions of the Congress. The Provincial Congresses in Georgia always looked to the Continental Congress for guidance. The preamble to the Rules and Regulations of 1776 stated that before any general system of government could be adopted it was necessary "that application be made to the Continental Congress for their advice and direction," and that the regulations then adopted should be of force only "until the further order of the Continental Congress." [10] When in February of 1776 the Third Provincial Congress selected Button Gwinnett, Lyman Hall, and George Walton, the three delegates who signed the Declaration of Independence for Georgia,[11] rather than closely binding instructions, these delegates were given full discretion to take such action as should appear best calculated for the common good.

Before July 4th most of the Colonies had passed resolutions in favor of independence and had instructed their delegates in the Continental Congress to vote accordingly, but Georgia never took any such action. No, Georgia did

---

[9] Wright to Dartmouth, September 16, 1775, in *Collections of the Georgia Historical Society*, III, 209.

[10] *Ga. Rev. Rec.*, I, 277.

[11] John Houstoun and Archibald Bulloch were also elected at this time, but were not present in Congress at the date of the signing.

*A Constitutional History of Georgia*

not declare her independence. Only on August 8th did a letter from John Hancock reach Georgia telling her that the Continental Congress had declared it for her.[12] Two days later the people were assembled at Savannah where the Declaration was proclaimed and greeted with a dramatic demonstration, including the firing of cannon and the burning of King George III in effigy. The legislature of Georgia never reenacted the Declaration of Independence, as was the case in the other States. By an "Act to extend and enforce the authority of the several laws heretofore passed in the then province, but now State of Georgia," adopted on September 16, 1777, the local laws were expressly subordinated to "the resolves and regulations of the honourable the Continental Congress."[13]

Prior to the Declaration of Independence, four of the original States (New Hampshire, South Carolina, Virginia, and New Jersey) had already adopted written constitutions. The next six months was to see a marked burst of activity in this direction. The fact that it took only a few months to establish such documents in all of the States shows that the colonial experience had paved the way for them.

## Georgia's First Constitutional Convention

A FEW days after receipt of news of the Declaration of Independence, Archibald Bulloch, President of the Coun-

---

[12] *Collections of the Georgia Historical Society*, V, 89. *Ga. Rev. Rec.*, I, 280. No adequate study has been made of the loyalists in Georgia. Considering the fact that until the year before Georgia had been a laggard in the revolutionary movement, taunted and scolded by her neighbors, and further that a great portion of the bloodshed in Georgia during the War was from strife between patriots and loyalists, it is improbable that on July 4, 1776, a popular referendum in Georgia would have given a majority vote for independence.

[13] Robert and George Watkins, *Digest of the Laws of the State of Georgia* (Philadelphia, 1801), 212–213. Compare the preamble of the Act of Attainder passed on March 1, 1778. *Ibid.*, 208.

## Early State Government

cil of Safety, issued a proclamation for the election of delegates to a convention where "business of the highest consequence to the government and welfare of the state, . . . (would) be opened for their consideration." The proclamation stated that the Continental Congress had recommended to the assemblies and conventions of the united colonies, where no government sufficient to the exigencies of their affairs had been established, that they adopt such government as should, in the opinion of the representatives of the people, best conduce to the happiness and safety of their constituents in particular and America in general. It further explained that the terms of the members of the Georgia legislature would expire on the last day of that month (August, 1776). Hence President Bulloch, with the consent of his Council, had thought it fit to order the several parishes and districts to proceed to elect delegates, between the first and tenth days of the next month, to convene in convention in Savannah on the first Tuesday in October.[14]

Both in the election of delegates and on the floors of their constitutional conventions, lively opposition developed between the democratic and conservative elements in all of the States except Pennsylvania and Georgia. The relatively sudden seizure of control by the radicals in these two States presents a contrast to the steady march toward independence in other Colonies where a large Whig element was in control from an early period. In the historical analysis given at some length in the previous chapter it was shown that in Georgia conservative loyalists were in a sufficient majority to retain control of the Colony without marked resistance until July, 1775, and that then within a very short while the radicals gained complete domination. This was to have a marked effect

---

[14] Hugh M'Call, *History of Georgia* (Savannah, 1816), II, 321–322; *Ga. Rev. Rec.*, I, 280–281.

## A Constitutional History of Georgia

upon the personnel of the first constitutional convention.

In most of the States the elections for the early constitutional conventions are said to have been "full and free," but just how appropriate this description would be for Georgia, the fragmentary records of today do not permit one to say with definiteness. The franchise had been extended to "all persons paying toward the general tax" by the Provincial Congress on July 14, 1775. This qualification was reënacted by the Council of Safety on December 8, 1775, at which time it was further provided that elections should be by ballot and that only freeholders in the Province should be qualified to serve as delegates in the Provincial Congress.[15] There had been no change in these qualifications before the elections in September, 1775, for the Constitutional Convention.

At the time of calling this Convention, President Bulloch sent a letter to the several parishes and districts of the State in which he sought to impress upon the people the necessity of choosing "upright and good men" to represent them. "America must stand or fall," admonished Bulloch, "by the virtue of her inhabitants; consequently, the utmost caution must necessarily be used by the people of this State, in choosing men of unsuspected characters, men whose actions had proved their friendship to the cause of freedom, and men whose depth of political judgment qualified them to frame a constitution for the future government of the country." [16]

Definite information about this Convention is now meager. At the time of the compilation of the *Revolutionary Records of Georgia* in 1908 no list of the members could be found. A fragment of the minutes has since been discovered accompanying early printed copies of the Constitution of 1777. From this source we learn that

---
[15] *Collections of the Ga. Hist. Soc.*, V, 19–20.
[16] Quoted from M'Call's *History of Georgia*, II, 322.

*Early State Government*

Button Gwinnett, William Belcher, Joseph Wood, Josiah Lewis, John Adams Treutlen, Henry Jones, and George Wells composed a committee "to reconsider and revise" the Constitution, and that Edward Langworthy served as secretary. In addition to these members, William Few is known to have served in the Convention.[17] An enthusiastic biographer holds that "to Button Gwinnett belongs the distinction of having done the major portion of the work of drafting the Constitution, and that the document reflects his political philosophy, as well as the tenets of the dominant liberal wing of the Whig party of the state of which, at that time, he was the undoubted leader." [18] Some additional light is thrown upon the dim scene of this Convention by the *Proceedings of the Council of Safety*. This source indicates that the Georgia Convention was no exception to those in other States at the time in that its work consisted in legislating and providing for the exigencies of the moment in addition to formulating a constitution. The Convention lasted from October, 1776, to February 5, 1777, but it was not actually in session half of this time.[19] The technique of ratifying the constitutions by popular vote was not yet perfected, so the Georgia Convention itself declared the Constitution which it had framed to be adopted.

## *The Constitution of 1777*

Georgia's Constitution of 1777, framed by the ultrademocratic element within the State without restraint from the conservatives, is certain to awaken a lively interest on the part of a student of government reading it for the first time. This early document clearly foreshadowed

---

[17] White, *Historical Collections*, 410.
[18] Charles Francis Jenkins, *Button Gwinnett* (New York, 1926), 108.
[19] *Ga. Rev. Rec.*, I, 282; *Collections of the Georgia Historical Society*, V, 117.

the modern innovation of popular initiative; it boldly proclaimed Montesquieu's celebrated doctrine of the separation of powers in the first paragraph—only to utterly disregard the doctrine in the articles that followed; it vested legislative authority in a unicameral assembly, elected by an almost universal suffrage; it provided for compulsory voting; it based representation in the assembly upon the size of the electorate and upon "trade"; and it set up a plural executive. These and other unusual features may best be explained by a survey of the Constitution as a whole in comparison with the other Constitutions adopted during the same period.[20]

Regarded objectively, Georgia's Constitution of 1777 is a comparatively brief document, covering some sixteen printed pages, divided into sixty-three paragraphs, with little coherence between them. The most fundamental principle incorporated in the document was the declaration of the sovereignty of the people, the source "from whom all power originates, and for whose benefit all government is intended." The oppressive acts of Great Britain toward the Colonies were denounced as "repugnant to the common rights of mankind." The Americans, as freemen, had been forced "to oppose such oppressive measures, and to assert the rights and privileges they are entitled to by the laws of nature and reason."

Such justifying clauses were common in the early State constitutions. Including Vermont, which began to assume and assert statehood in the period under review, eight States went further and adopted a specific "bill of rights." [21] Georgia's Constitution of 1777 contained no

---

[20] Copies of Georgia's Constitution of 1777 may be found in *Ga. Rev. Rec.*, I, 282–298, or McElreath, *op. cit.*, 229–241. An early copy printed at Savannah by William Lancaster in 1777 is in the De Renne Collection.

[21] William C. Webster, "A Comparative Study of the State Constitutions of the American Revolution," *Annals of the American Academy of Political and Social Sciences*, IX (May, 1897), 385.

## Early State Government

separate bill of rights, but four concluding paragraphs were devoted to guaranties of personal liberty. These included freedom of religion and the press, the right of *habeas corpus,* trial by jury, and protection against excessive fines and bails. If there had been any basis in fact for the myth later to arise making Georgia in its origin a refuge for imprisoned debtors, her first Constitution would probably have contained provisions similar to those in the Constitutions of Pennsylvania, Vermont, and North Carolina against the confinement of the person of debtors, but one must look to later constitutions in Georgia to find such provisions. The Constitution of 1777 made no reference whatever to the imprisonment of debtors. Drawing together the four concluding paragraphs of the document safeguarding personal liberties and connecting them with the enunciation of popular sovereignty found in the opening paragraph, one has a fairly comprehensive bill of rights. None of these statements in Georgia's Constitution were original either in form or content. The evidence is not conclusive as to whether the members of the Convention in Georgia had before them any of the eight State constitutions already adopted, but the familiar statement that the framers of Georgia's first Constitution were "unaided and untrammeled by precedent" is clearly too strong. As for the part of the Constitution protecting individual rights, it was obviously influenced by the earlier declarations in other States, by the Declaration of Independence, by the resolutions of the First Continental Congress of 1774, by the resolutions of the Stamp Act Congress of 1765, and by the various declarations of individual rights in the colonial charters, including the Georgia Charter of 1732. "The bill of rights of the American Revolution is only a link in a long chain of institutional development, running back through the English Bill of Rights and Petition of Right to Magna Charta, and all these formal expressions were only crystallizations of previous institutional development." [22]

Next to the sovereignty of the people, the most fundamental principle of government enunciated in the early State constitutions was that of the separation of powers. "The Legislative, Executive, and Judiciary Departments, shall be separate and distinct, so that neither exercise the powers properly belonging to the other," declared the very first sentence of Article I of Georgia's Constitution of 1777. Similar statements had appeared in the Constitutions of Virginia, Maryland, and North Carolina adopted the previous year. The framers of the Georgia Constitution may have taken the statement from one of these earlier Constitutions, or from any one of many other available sources, Montesquieu's classic *Esprit des lois* not excepted. But whatever the source of its statement, the principle of the separation of powers was to have little actual place in the first Constitution of Georgia.

## A. The Legislature

THE House of Assembly in which the Constitution of 1777 vested most extraordinary powers closely resembled the Commons House of Assembly of Colonial days. There was provision for an executive Council, a majority of which should constitute "a board to examine the laws and ordinances sent them by the House of Assembly." But whereas the Council had constituted the Upper House of the General Assembly under the royal government, with powers concurrent with the Commons House in the passage of legislation, the Council could now only recommend amendments to proposed laws. Full power of

---

[22] Webster, *Comparative Study of the State Constitutions, loc. cit.* 384.

## Early State Government

enactment rested with the House of Assembly. This adoption of a unicameral legislature is one evidence of the democratic temper of the framers of the Constitution. The representatives of the people would need no check to insure adequate deliberation. Tom Paine, not John Adams, had advocated this plan.

Provision for a unicameral legislature is also found in two other State Constitutions of the Revolutionary period, those of Pennsylvania and Vermont (if we may take the instrument drawn up at Windsor in July of 1777 as the constitution of a state). The Pennsylvania Constitution could possibly have been of some influence in Georgia, but from the records as a whole it appears that Georgia's Constitution of 1777 was primarily a reduction to writing of the plan of government which had evolved through the experience of the Colony and State.

Although not a legislative body in a strict sense of the term, Georgia's first Assembly called by the Trustees in 1751 was composed of a single house. During the period of royal control, the Governor was the most influential legislative power in the Colony, and his Council, as we have seen, served as an upper house. But January of 1775 witnessed the last session of the bicameral royal legislature. The Provincial Congress which took over the legislative function was a unicameral body, and the legislature under the Constitution of 1777 was clearly a continuation of the Provincial Congress. The Convention framing this Constitution seems to have engaged in little philosophical discussion relative to the merits of various forms of government. A page of history is worth more than several volumes of logic to one seeking the origin of the provisions of this frontier State's first written constitution.

Representation in the House of Assembly was to be by counties, eight in number, carved out of the old par-

## A Constitutional History of Georgia

ishes.[23] This is one respect in which the action of all the States was the same. "In all cases existing territorial divisions (counties in the Middle and Southern States, and towns in New England) were made the units of representation in the lower house." [24] The colonial grievance of the continuation of the same membership in the legislature for many years should not be repeated in Georgia. Article III of the Constitution made it an unalterable rule that the House of Assembly should expire yearly on Monday before the first Tuesday in December, upon which Tuesday elections were to be held for a new Assembly to convene in January. The total number of representatives for the time being was fixed at seventy-two,

[23] The names chosen for the counties are of interest. William B. Stevens comments upon these names as follows: "It was a striking indication of the grateful feeling of the Georgians for those who had so warmly defended the cause of America in the British Parliament, that the fourth article of this Constitution changed the designation of the old parishes by striking out their former names and substituting therefor, with one exception, the names of the English apol ists for America. Thus the old parish of Christ Church, in which was Savannah, and a part of the parish of St. Phillip, were set off as a new county and called CHATHAM, in honor of elder Pitt, the venerable Earl of Chatham. The parishes of St. David and St. Patrick, were erected into one county and called GLYNN, after the eminent counsellor of that name. The parishes of St. Matthew and the upper part of St. Phillip, were to be known by the name of EFFINGHAM, after Lord Effingham, who had refused to employ his sword against the Americans, and resigned the Colonelcy of the 22d Regiment rather than serve with it in the war of the Revolution. To the parish of St. Paul, in which Augusta was situated, was given the name of RICHMOND, in honor of the Duke of Richmond who had boldly advocated the cause of America in the House of Lords. The parish of St. George was named BURKE, after that great commoner and wise statesman. The parishes of St. John, St. Andrew, and St. James, were to form one county under the name LIBERTY: a distinction awarded to the parish of St. John for its early and steady devotion to the cause of freedom. The parishes of St. Thomas and St. Mary, were to constitute another county by the name of CAMDEN, after the distinguished Lord Chancellor of England, and firm friend of America. The ceded lands north of the Ogeechee was constituted a county, taking the name of WILKS (sic), the name of that political demagogue who payed his court to liberty only that he might gain notoriety and wealth." *History of Georgia*, II, 299–300.

[24] Webster, *Comparative Study of the State Constitutions*, loc. cit., 391.

*Early State Government*

but after the election of the Governor's Council from the Assembly the membership would be reduced to sixty. Five counties (Wilkes, Richmond, Burke, Effingham, and Chatham) were given ten representatives each, and Liberty County, made up of three parishes, was given fourteen. The two other counties, Glynn and Camden, were given only one representative for the present, but they and any new county which the Assembly might lay out should in the future have representation based upon the size of their electorate, progressing from one representative for ten electors to ten representatives for one hundred electors. The port and town of Sunbury was allowed two members and the port and town of Savannah four, "to represent their trade."

The introduction of representation based upon the size of the electorate rather than the number of inhabitants is of particular interest. So also is the avowed representation of "trade" in the house of representatives. The Constitution of 1777 was ultra-democratic, and this provision for the representation of property interests is not in keeping with the spirit of the document. The Abbé de Mably who visited America at the time based his disapproval of the representation of trade in the Georgia Assembly upon a basis which would have had a greater appeal to a later generation. *"Je l'avoue, Monsieur, je sens un attrait particulier pour la République de Georgie,"* declared the Abbé, and proceeded to give reasons against the industrialization of the charming region along lines similar to those to appear later in the platforms of leaders in the agrarian movement.[25] The framers of the State's first Constitution would have been more logical if they had omit-

---

[25] Gabriel Bonnot de Mably, *Observations sur le gouvernement et les lois des Etats-Unis d'Amerique, par M. l'Abbé de Mably* (Amsterdam, chez J. F. Rosard et Comp. M. DCC. LXXIV). Copy in De Renne Collection. Reference to Georgia on pages 64–72.

ted the provisions relative to the trade of Sunbury and Savannah and declared for representation of man alone.

## B. *The Electorate*

THE qualifications for voting were liberal for the period. "All male white inhabitants," provided Article IX, "of the age of twenty-one years, and possessed in his own right of ten pounds value, and liable to pay tax in this State, or being of any mechanic trade, and shall have been resident six months in this State, shall have a right to vote at all elections for representatives, or any other officers, herein agreed to be chosen by the people at large." The Constitution did not stop even with this broad extension of the franchise; a further provision placed a fine of £5 upon any person qualified to vote who should fail to exercise the privilege. Voting should be by ballot, after a procedure which has been little improved upon since that date. Justices of the peace, in charge of elections in the several counties, should provide convenient boxes for receiving the ballots. To the end that elections should be "free and open," no military officer or soldier should appear at any election, nor should any process be served upon or other hindrance given to a person while going to or returning from an election. After the closing of the polls, the result of the vote should be computed in public and the result immediately declared.[26]

The two other States adopting a unicameral legislature also adopted low suffrage qualifications. In Pennsylvania the only property qualification was that the elector be a taxpayer, no amount being specified.[27] In Vermont there

---

[26] Articles X, XII, and XIII.
[27] Article VI. See Benjamin Perley Poore, *The Federal and State Constitutions, Colonial Charters, and Other Organic Laws of the United States* (Washington, 1877), I, 1542.

## Early State Government

was no property qualification whatever, the vote being extended to all freemen. The Constitutions of these States did not distinctly prescribe any property qualifications for members of the legislature, but in Pennsylvania as in New York this qualification was inferred from the electoral qualification. In Georgia representatives were required to be possessed in their own right of two hundred and fifty acres of land, or some property to the amount of two hundred and fifty pounds, to have resided in the State at least twelve months and in the county from which chosen for three months, to be of the Protestant religion, and twenty-one years of age. Qualifications of sex, race, residence, religion, and property were, with slight variations, common to most of the Constitutions of the period, but it is interesting to note that Georgia and Maryland were the only States definitely to specify an age qualification for representatives.

## C. *The Executive*

FROM its own membership the Assembly should choose a Governor, and in him and a Council executive authority was nominally vested. With the exception of New Hampshire, all of the State Constitutions of 1776–1777 made provision for at least a titular chief executive, elected in a majority of the States by the legislature, as was the case in Georgia.[28] Under her Rules and Regulations of 1776, Georgia had had a plural executive, the President and Commander-in-Chief being but the head of the Council

---

[28] In only five states (Rhode Island, New Hampshire, Connecticut, Massachusetts, and New York) was the Governor elected by the people. In Pennsylvania the "President" was elected by joint ballot of the Assembly and executive Council. Morey, *The First State Constitutions*, loc. cit. 225; Richard Frothingham, *The Rise of the Republic of the United States* (tenth edition, Boston, 1910), 567.

of Safety. The executive under the Constitution of 1777 was in large measure a continuation of this plural executive, for the Governor could act only upon the advice of the executive council.

The similarity of the Constitutions of Georgia, Pennsylvania, and Vermont in respect to a unicameral legislature has sometimes led to an erroneous classification of other features as common to the three. The executive Council in Georgia was elected by the legislature from its own membership, not by a direct vote of the people as in Pennsylvania and Vermont.[29] All of the States provided for an executive council, styled variously as the "council," "executive council," "supreme executive council," "council of state," "council to the governor," or "privy council."[30] The number of councilors varied among the several States from three to twelve. In Georgia the number was not fixed permanently but was twelve for the time being. Two members were to be chosen from the representation of each county having ten representatives in the House of Assembly, and the Councilmen thus chosen should lose their seats in the Assembly. It was laid down that one Councilman from each county should "always attend where the Governor resides, by monthly rotation, unless the Members of each county agree for a longer or shorter period." This was not intended to exclude the attendance of any Councilor should he desire to attend, but voting in the Council was to be by counties, not by individuals.[31]

In those States where a bicameral legislature was established, the functions of the old colonial council were differentiated and divided between the newly created senate

---

[29] Art. II, par. 2.
[30] Morey, "The First State Constitutions," *loc. cit.*, 227; Fletcher M. Green, *Constitutional Development in the South Atlantic States, 1776–1860* (Chapel Hill, 1930), 90.
[31] Art. II and Art. XXV.

*Early State Government*

and executive council. In Georgia a shadow of the legislative authority of the Council of the royal government was preserved in the provisions giving the new Council power to review legislation, propose amendments, and delay the final enactment of laws by the Assembly for five days. The judicial functions of the colonial Council disappeared entirely; the Council was now limited to executive and administrative functions, and *limited* indeed in the exercise of these.

The executive under the first State Constitutions was in general made a puppet of the legislature rather than a coördinate branch of government. The experience of the Colonists had led them to fear executive authority and to look upon their legislative assemblies as guardians of their rights. The executive under the early Constitutions was either deprived altogether or greatly limited in the exercise of its powers of appointment, pardon, veto, and revision. "The reconstruction of the political institutions of the original states was in the main the achievement of a tidal wave of insurgency, which sought expression through the state legislature." [32]

Election of the executive by the legislature was itself a violation of the spirit of the principle of the separation of powers. Provision for a short term strengthened the subserviency of the governors. New York, Delaware, and South Carolina were the only States to provide for a term of more than one year. Maryland, Virginia, North Carolina, and South Carolina fixed limits to the eligibility for reëlection. With a zeal for limited executive power described by an authority as "fanaticism carried to the highest degree of absurdity," [33] the Constitution of Georgia provided that "The Governor shall be chosen annually

---

[32] Holcombe, *State Government*, 69.
[33] Webster, "Comparative Study of the State Constitutions," *loc. cit.*, 396.

*A Constitutional History of Georgia*

by ballot, and shall not be eligible to the said office for more than one year out of three. . . ."

This control of the personnel of the executive by the legislature was not considered a sufficient safeguard to warrant vesting it with full executive powers. Not only was the Governor denied a veto, he was even forbidden to preside over the executive Council, as he was ordinarily to do, when that body was perusing acts offered to it by the Assembly. The Council itself was not to exercise a veto. It was, stated the Constitution, to constitute "a board to examine the laws and ordinances sent them by the House of Assembly; and all laws and ordinances sent to the Council shall be returned in five days after, with their remarks thereon." [34] The Governor was not given the customary right of chief executives to address the Assembly; he could communicate with it only through message transmitted by the secretary of the Council. Other provisions further emphasized the emasculated position of the executive. The Assembly itself was to exercise several executive functions, including the appointment of justices of the peace and registers of probate for the several counties, and the passage of final judgment upon pardons and remission of fines.[35] The Constitution shows that the Framers recognized these two functions to be executive in character; yet it specifically forbade the executive to exercise them. At the particular period, the most important executive power lay in the control of the military forces. While the Governor was made commander-in-chief, the limiting phrase "for-the-time-being" accom-

---

[34] Art. XXVII.

[35] Many other officers not named in the Constitution were in practice chosen by the Assembly, among them the Superintendent of Indian Affairs, Linguist, Commissary of Military Stores, State Surgeon, Surveyor General, Register of Grants, Commissioners of Sequestered and Confiscated Estates, Collectors for the Town and Port of Savannah and for Sunbury, Treasurer, Auditor of Accounts, and the Director General of Hospitals.

panied this grant of power. Lest some desired limitation upon the executive had been forgotten or omitted, a blanket clause made "every officer of the State . . . liable to be called to account by the House of Assembly." [36]

## D. *The Judiciary*

IF THERE were any conservatives present in the Convention of 1776–1777, they must have been disheartened when the provisions were adopted giving a unicameral legislature elected by an almost universal manhood suffrage a position of domination over the executive; they probably gave up in despair at the provisions made for the judiciary. The first State Constitutions in general said very little about the judiciary, leaving details to statutory arrangement. The existing courts were generally continued with few changes in form; but not so in Georgia. Under the royal government there had been a General Court at Savannah which tried all cases other than minor disputes settled by justices of the peace in Courts of Conscience throughout the Colony. The Governor's Council had served as a Court of Appeals, and under certain conditions, as set forth in detail above, appeal lay to the King's Privy Council, sitting at Westminster. This centralized judiciary was well adapted to the needs of a province with a small population. Viewing the scene retrospectively, one is impressed with the folly of the provisions for the judiciary under the Constitution of 1777.

There was to be no supreme court, nor was the executive Council to serve as a court of errors. A Superior Court of final jurisdiction was set up for each county, thus beginning the system of diversity in the interpretation of law which in the succeeding decades was to prove

---

[36] Art. XLIX.

the most serious defect of Georgia's government, a defect not remedied until the establishment of a supreme court in 1845. In practice, some uniformity was maintained for the moment by appointing one chief justice for the whole State, and setting the dates for terms of the Superior Courts in the several counties at such intervals as would permit the chief justice to ride circuit and attend all the Courts. The Courts of Conscience, or justice courts, were to be continued. In addition, the Assembly was also to appoint a register of probates in each county for proving wills and granting letters of administration. Captures both on land and sea were to be tried in special sessions of the Superior Courts just as any other case, except that in these cases a right of appeal to the Continental Congress was recognized.

The Constitution specifically provided for the election of justices of the peace and registers of probate by the House of Assembly. Its silence upon the method of choice of other judicial officers has given rise to considerable misconception. No judges were elected by the people in Georgia under the Constitution of 1777. In keeping with the spirit of the Constitution, the House of Assembly chose a chief justice for the whole State and four assistant justices for each county.[37] The chief justice was named annually; assistant justices and justices of the peace held office at the pleasure of the legislature. All were dependent upon the legislature for their salaries. The Constitution thus went far toward making the legislature omnipotent, but not completely so. The preamble proclaimed popular sovereignty, and ultimate control lay in the hands

---

[37] Most secondary sources are in error on this point. A reliable statement is made by William M. Reese in "The Constitution of Georgia" in *The Annual Report of the Georgia Bar Association, 1885,* p. 97. For documentary evidence, see the *Journal of the House of Assembly,* Vol. III of the *Revolutionary Records of Georgia, passim* (15, 75, and 550 for examples of specific acts); Watkins' *Digest,* 354, 315, 538.

of the people through trial by jury and the right to amend the Constitution.

## E. *The Amending Process*

ARTICLE XLIII of the Constitution established the following procedure for amendments:

> No alteration shall be made in this Constitution without petitions from a majority of the counties, and the petitions from each county to be signed by a majority of voters in each county within this State; at which time the Assembly shall order a convention to be called for that purpose, specifying the alterations to be made, according to the petitions preferred to the Assembly by the majority of the counties as aforesaid.

Professor Dodd is justified in criticizing this amending process as "cumbersome" and "unworkable." [38] One does not wonder that it was never used. Nevertheless, it is of great interest because it is the first provision for the use of popular initiative for constitutional revision.

## *Independence Achieved*

THE Convention itself declared the Constitution to be adopted. Soon thereafter the State suffered a great loss in the death of Archibald Bulloch, the foremost patriot of the time, who as President of the Council of Safety had called together the Convention. The Council of Safety next elevated Button Gwinnett to its Presidency, and he in turn issued a proclamation ordering elections for an Assembly to meet in Savannah on May 8 (1777). The House of Assembly elected John Adams Treutlen as Gov-

---

[38] Walter F. Dodd, *The Revision and Amendment of State Constitutions* (Baltimore, 1910), 42.

*A Constitutional History of Georgia*

ernor, and proceeded to inaugurate a new government under the Constitution.[39]

"Scarcely had this instrument been published," declares Georgia's most colorful historian, "when an alarm was again sounded on the southern frontier. The king's troops and the Florida banditti were in motion, and the present incursion assumed formidable proportions."[40] An annual descent upon St. Augustine had become a habit with Georgians during the Spanish War when Oglethorpe was in the Colony. The opening of another war with Florida again in the hands of an enemy brought a renewal for three years of the old comic, yet tragic, spectacle of troops sallying back and forth along the coast in attacks and counter-attacks between Georgia and Florida. But in the latter part of 1778 the British, having failed to cope with the Revolution in the North, transferred the War to the South. On December 19, 1778, Savannah was taken, and within a few months most of the State other than Wilkes County was overrun. Governor Wright, Chief Justice Stokes, and other members of the former royal government returned to Georgia; James Johnston, a Whig or Tory according to his interests of the hour, resumed publication of his newspaper under the reinforced title, *"The Royal Georgia Gazette;"* many lukewarm "patriots" now returned to the loyalist fold; and a royal government was reëstablished which remained in control of the lower region of the State until the British evacuation of Savannah in July, 1782.[41]

---

[39] *Ga. Rev. Rec.*, I, 305–306.

[40] Jones, *History of Georgia*, II, 260.

[41] The facts of the running account inserted here as a connective may be verified from any general history of Georgia. Jones, *op. cit.* gives the fullest treatment of the Revolution. Major Hugh M'Call's *History of Georgia* is of particular value on the Revolutionary Period because of the early date of its publication, 1816.

The date of Governor Wright's arrival at Savannah in 1779 was July 14th. *Ga. Col. Rec.*, XXXVIII, Part II, p. 168.

## Early State Government

After the fall of Savannah, the seat of the Whig government was Augusta, except at periods when that city, too, was in the hands of the British, in which case Heard's Fort or some other spot in the backwoods became the capital. The expiration of the term of John Houstoun as Governor in January, 1779, and the inability to assemble a quorum of the Assembly left the patriots without any chief executive during most of that year, although before the year closed there were two claimants to the title: John Wereat, representing one faction, and George Walton, another. Dissension between rival leaders was sometimes carried to extremes, as is exemplified in the duels between Button Gwinnett and Lachlan McIntosh in 1777, and between James Jackson and George Wells in 1780.

In one notable case, from a consideration of the "calamitous situation" of the State and the need for instantaneous action by a strong executive, the Council vested in Governor John Houstoun the authority to act without consulting it; but during most of the Revolutionary Period it was the executive Council, much like the earlier Council of Safety, which provided such government as that portion of the State under Whig control enjoyed.[42] The courts were closed, and in fact a condition of semi-anarchy prevailed. With the people divided and fighting among themselves, and the whole State harrowed by guerrilla bands, the condition of Georgia at the close of the war was deplorable.

Georgia had paid a great price for independence, and had achieved it through a union with her sister States. She readily ratified the Articles of Confederation which, with the final ratification by Maryland on March 1, 1781, became the written constitution upon which the already *de facto* union should rest. The weakest and most vulnerable of the thirteen original States, Georgia had never

---

[42] The Minutes of the Executive Council appear in *Ga. Rev. Rec.*, II.

had any desire for a separate and independent status. She was willing, indeed anxious, to strengthen the union among the States, and welcomed the opportunity offered for this by the Federal Convention of 1787. No amendments were made to Georgia's Constitution of 1777 prior to the adoption of the Federal Constitution, but then the whole governmental structure in Georgia was reorganized under a new constitution which, if compared with the Federal Constitution, will be found to be, as expressed by a contemporary, "as near a copy thereof as the interests of the State will admit." [43]

---

[43] *The Georgia State Gazette,* Jan. 10, 1789.

CHAPTER VI

## The Federal Union

"THE Constitution of the United States," declares Professor McPherson, "is one of the most significant facts of the modern world."[1] Georgia's history prior to the Revolution was so intimately related to that of England that it may well be studied as a chapter in English history; the constitutional development of the period since the gaining of independence must be studied in terms of a federal dualism.

Certain factors in the colonial experience tended to draw the Colonies apart, to give them a spirit of individualism, and to develop in them a passionate attachment to local self-government. One by one they were established, each growing up in practical isolation, each working out its own local laws and political practices. They were all united, it is true, under one central authority, the Crown; but the Crown found it advantageous to emphasize their separateness. There were marked differences in the economic and social life and in the political organization between the plantation States of the South and the farming and trading States of the North. Men

---

[1] J. H. T. McPherson, "The Making of the Constitution," *Studies in Social Progress*, ed. by Chester M. Destler, (Athens, Georgia, 1935), II, 165.

spoke proudly of themselves as Virginians or Carolinians. A firm basis was laid for a future State allegiance.

Yet in this same colonial experience are found other factors tending to draw the Colonies together. When the thirteen Colonies had been formed, lying as they did between the Appalachians and the Atlantic, they formed a geographic unity. There was an ethnic unit too, for in spite of the infusion of "foreigners," the population was predominantly English, eighty-two per cent according to the most reliable estimate.[2] The common religion was Christianity, and largely Protestant. The English common law furnished a firm background for the legal experience of all the Colonies. The basic concept of government was the representative system as developed at Westminster. In short, the Colonists possessed all of the essential elements of nationality, including the consciousness of a common political aspiration engendered by strife against a common foe. The foe was first of all the Indians, then the French, and finally the British Government itself. "A nationality," remarks Professor Le Fur, "is above all a state *en germe*"; so just as the colonial and revolutionary experience furnished on the one hand a solid basis for a future State loyalty, it paved on the other the way toward the second predominant characteristic of the American constitutional structure, namely, a union of the States under a strong national government. Eleven years after the Declaration of Independence, William Pierce, a delegate from Georgia to the Federal Convention, declared: "State distinctions must be sacrificed so far as the general government shall render it necessary—without, however, destroying them altogether. Although I am here as a representative from a small state, I consider myself a

---

[2] Bureau of the Census, *A Century of Population Growth from the First Census of the United States to the Twelfth, 1790–1900* (Washington, 1909), 121.

## The Federal Union

citizen of the United States, whose general interests I will always support." [3]

The progress toward union may be traced in a number of steps, the more important among the earlier ones being the New England Confederation, 1643–1664, in which the four Colonies of Massachusetts, Plymouth, New Haven, and Connecticut formed a league of mutual defense against the Indians; the short-lived Dominion of New England whereby James II sought to place all of New England, New York, and the Jerseys under the administration of Governor Andros; the unrealized scheme of William Penn in 1697 for a league of all the Colonies; and the Albany Conference of 1754, called by the Board of Trade in an effort to solidify the Colonies for the impending struggle with France. In the Albany Conference, Benjamin Franklin's famous plan for a permanent union of the Colonies was presented. It foreshadowed and in many respects was superior to the Articles of Confederation. But the Colonies quite as unanimously rejected Franklin's plan on the score that it was too dependent upon the Crown as that authority did on the score that it was too little so.

The progress of the next twenty years whereby the ties of loyalty to the mother country were weakened and finally broken was traced in some detail, particularly in regard to Georgia, in the previous chapter. Georgia, it will be recalled, had no representation in either the Stamp Act Congress of 1765 or the First Continental Congress of 1774, although an observer was sent to New York in 1765 to bring back a report on what the Congress should do. The Puritans of Midway, in St. Johns Parish, became so exasperated at the lack of action on the part of Georgia that they sent Lyman Hall as their delegate to

---

[3] Yates' "Notes," in Max Farrand's *Records of the Federal Convention of 1787* (New Haven, 1911), I, 474.

*A Constitutional History of Georgia*

the Second Continental Congress in March, 1775. Then within the brief space of six months, as outlined above, the radicals gained the upper hand, completely defied the royal government, set up a revolutionary government, and sent delegates to the Continental Congress. From this time onward the radicals, or patriots (as one pleases), took such a bold stand that even South Carolina soon lost her contempt for the former "laggard Colony." Congress welcomed the new Georgia and not only rescinded the resolution which it had passed setting all of Georgia except St. Johns Parish outside the pale of commercial intercourse, but also ordered the recruiting of a battalion of continental troops for Georgia's defense. Within the next year Congress voted $60,000 to be used in raising and maintaining additional troops in Georgia and in constructing two forts and building four galleys for protecting her coast.[4] Georgia's independence was declared by a union Congress; her independence was won through a united effort.

## *Georgia Favors a Strong Union*

SEVERAL influences caused the people of Georgia to be particularly favorable toward maintaining a strong union of the States. The horrible warfare between Whig and Tory neighbors during the Revolution showed the desirability of a united home front in dealing with outside powers. Her geographic position was the most exposed of all the States. Established in 1732 as "a frontier to His Majesty's southern dominions," Georgia still held this frontier position. Florida was inhabited largely by Spaniards, and, at the close of the War, was to return to Spanish control. Within Georgia's own borders, occupying

---

[4] Coulter, *op. cit.*, 124.

## The Federal Union

five-sixths of the State, were the powerful Creek and Cherokee Indians, with whom the Spaniards were ever conniving, and who were determined in their own minds to keep the territory they then possessed. If Georgia were to survive, she must have the support of a strong union government.[5]

During the War when the extreme South was in the hands of the British, a rumor spread that peace was about to be made on the basis of Britain's retention of South Carolina and Georgia as colonies. A lively anxiety developed in Georgia for a preservation of the union. On January 8, 1781, George Walton, William Few and Richard Howley, her delegates to the Continental Congress, published at Philadelphia their *Observation upon the Effect of Certain Late Political Suggestions,* containing weighty argument against the scheme. They enumerated the various commodities produced by Georgia, emphasizing the value of her timber for ship building, and pointed out the strategic value of Georgia to the Union of the American States. "From all these considerations," concludes the pamphlet, "it inevitably follows that the State of Georgia is a material part of the Union, and cannot be given up without affecting its essential interests, if not endangering its existence." [6]

## The Articles of Confederation

THE anticipation of greater security through a perpetual union with her sister Colonies had been the prominent cause for Georgia's entrance into the Revolution. She was anxious to strengthen the union of the States and on July

---

[5] Ulrich Bonnell Phillips, *Georgia and State Rights* (Washington, 1902), 16.
[6] White's *Historical Collections,* 106–110.

24, 1778, readily confirmed the Articles of Confederation which became effective as the first written constitution of the United States on March 1, 1781. The scope of this monograph does not include a detailed study of the Articles, but a general view of this constitution is appropriate. The style of union established was "a firm league of friendship" between the thirteen States. One of its chief features was the complete and unchallenged sovereignty of the States. "Each state," proclaimed Article II, "retains its sovereignty, freedom, and independence, and every other Power, Jurisdiction and right, which is not by this confederation expressly delegated to the United States, in Congress assembled."[7] A second notable feature was the simplicity of the machinery of government set up. For carrying on the national government, the Articles provided a single organ, a Congress composed of delegates appointed annually by the States, in such manner as their legislatures might direct. Irrespective of population or wealth, each State was given one vote in Congress, and all important measures required a vote of nine States. Each year Congress elected one member to preside, but he was simply a moderator, the president of the Congress, not the president of the United States. Executive and judicial matters were managed by committees, and civil officers were appointed and directed by Congress. A third characteristic was the rigid limitation upon the powers of the union government. A list of the nineteen powers enumerated appears at first glance to be formidable, including as it does the power to determine on peace and war, to send and receive ambassadors, to make treaties, to fix standards of weights and measures, to regulate the alloy and value both of coins struck off by authority of Congress and by authority of the States, to regulate the trade

---

[7] *Documents Illustrative of the Formation of the Union of the American States* (House Doc. No. 398, 69th Congress, 1st Session), 27–37.

and manage all affairs with the Indians, to establish post-offices, to borrow money, to build and equip a navy, and to agree upon the number of land forces and make requisitions upon the several States for their respective quotas. Yet in the exercise of these powers the national government was dependent upon the State governments, for the Congress operated not upon individuals but upon the States in their corporate capacity. In brief, it was not a government at all, but rather the central agency of an alliance, "a diplomatic assembly," as John Adams described it. Two very important powers were not bestowed upon the central agency at all; i.e., the power to regulate commerce and the power to levy taxes. Congress was authorized to supply its treasury by requisitions upon the States in proportion to the assessed value of their lands, but these requisitions could only bear the stamp "please," not "must." Congress had no authority to compel the States to honor the requisitions, and as experience showed, the States vied with one another in disregarding its humble pleas. The absence of a central power to regulate commerce permitted the States to erect barriers destructive of trade and commercial progress.[8] The powers withheld from Congress remained with the States; that is to say, with their legislatures. As Professor Corwin points out, "The evil thence resulting was thus a double one. Not only was a common policy impracticable in fields where it was most evidently necessary, but also the local legislatures had it in their power to embroil both the country as a whole with foreign nations and its constituent parts with each other. So the weakness of the Confederacy played directly into the chief defect of government within the states themselves—an excessive concentration

---

[8] See Watkins' *Digest*, 280–282, 325, 351, for the tariff acts adopted by the legislature of Georgia. Georgia also passed laws relative to citizenship. *Ibid.*, 303, 306–307.

## A Constitutional History of Georgia

of power in the hands of the legislative department."[9] A final defect of the Confederation lay in its inflexibility. The Articles could be amended only by a unanimous vote of the States. To secure unanimity among the thirteen jealous, suspicious, and increasingly unfriendly commonwealths was out of the question.

The Articles were defective in themselves, to be sure, but the real cause for their failure is found more in the temper of the times and the abuse in their use than in any inherent weakness. The actual working of the government in Brazil and in the United States today is vastly different, albeit their written constitutions are close parallels. Local jealousies prevented the establishment of a strong national government for the decade of the 'Eighties; the same jealousies rendered the government established impotent. Had the people throughout America been as nationalistic as were the Georgians of the period, the history of the Confederacy would be a different story. Georgia was willing to amend the two notable defects of the Articles relative to commerce and taxation; she enabled the United States "to commence and prosecute actions or suits in any of the courts in this State, for the recovery of their common rights and interests;" she sought to carry into execution the recommendations of the national Congress; and she was conspicuously honest in meeting the requisitions levied upon her.[10] In 1783 she set up a sinking fund in the amount of £108,859, to be derived from the disposal of property confiscated from loyalists, from which to pay the State's quota of the national debt. At the same time she made special provisions toward paying her quota of the debts owed to France and

---

[9] E. S. Corwin, "The Progress of Political Theory between the Declaration of Independence and the Meeting of the Philadelphia Convention," *American Historical Review*, XXX (April, 1925), 527.

[10] Watkins' *Digest*, 327, 331, 337, 363, 370; *Ga. Rev. Rec.*, III, 386, 500.

## The Federal Union

Holland.[11] It is true that the end of the Confederacy found Georgia far in arrears with her payments to the central government, but this is an indication of her inability to pay rather than an unwillingness. "Desirous of adopting every measure which can tend to promote the interest of the United States" was a common phrase in the laws adopted in Georgia during this period. *Georgia and State Rights*[12] is an absorbing study, but the subject relates distinctly to a later period.

The decade of the 'Eighties when the Articles were in effect is familiarly described as the "Critical Period" of American history. In this transitional period following a war of extended duration, readjustments in politics, society, commerce, and industry were to be expected; but the accompanying disorganization and depression was accentuated. There was disaffection in the army, economic chaos, impotence on the part of the central government, and in Rhode Island and Massachusetts, open resistance to governmental authority.

## The Federal Convention

THE inability to get national action upon vital questions of general concern led a few of the States to seek to adjust by joint conference some of the difficulties existing among them. From as far back as 1777, Virginia and Maryland had been trying to arrive at an understanding concerning the navigation of the Potomac River. The success gained in this matter in 1785 led to a hope both of gaining new commercial agreements and extending the sphere of the agreements to include other States. The

---

[11] Watkins' *Digest*, 219, 227–230, 276, 337, 756–757.
[12] Ulrich Bonnell Phillips, *Georgia and State Rights* (Washington, 1902).

upshot was that in January, 1786, James Madison got through the legislature of Virginia a resolution appointing delegates to meet such commissioners as should be appointed by the other States, at a time and place to be agreed on, to take into consideration the condition of the union. A formal invitation was thereupon issued to all the States to send delegates to Annapolis the following September. Nine States responded to this invitation, but at the designated time, delegates appeared from only five States. Under the circumstances it was impolitic to proceed with any important negotiations. Notwithstanding, Madison and Hamilton took advantage of the occasion to have the delegates present adopt a report calling attention afresh to the critical situation of the country and proposing another convention to meet in Philadelphia on the second Monday of the following May.

Georgia had been one of the States failing to appoint delegates to the Annapolis Convention, but she responded readily to the invitation to send delegates to Philadelphia, being the fifth State thus to act. On February 10, 1787, the Georgia Assembly named William Few, Abraham Baldwin, William Pierce, George Walton, William Houstoun, and Nathaniel Pendleton, as "commissioners" to the Federal Convention.[13]

Of these six delegates, four were members of Congress, two of whom (Few and Pierce) were actually attending its sessions in New York. The legislature probably made these appointments with the view of making sure that some of the delegates would attend. It is interesting to note that the two (Walton and Pendleton) not then members of Congress never attended the Convention.[14]

---

[13] Watkins' *Digest*, 365.

[14] William Pierce wrote the following pithy and somewhat facetious sketches of the delegates from Georgia:

"Mr. Few possesses a strong natural Genius, and from application has acquired some knowledge of legal matters;—he practices at the

## The Federal Union

When judged by either the number, length, or content of their speeches, Georgia's delegates played little part in the debates of the Convention; for while several members from other States spoke more than a hundred times, the largest number of speeches recorded by Madison for any delegate from Georgia is eight by Baldwin, and all of these so short that their total length would be less than that of any one of the several long speeches by more influential members. William Few seems never to have spoken before the Convention; Houstoun spoke seven times; Pierce four times.

> bar of Georgia, and speaks tolerably well in the Legislature. He has been twice a Member of Congress, and served in that capacity with fidelity to his State, and honor to himself. Mr. Few is about 35 years of age.
> "Mr. Baldwin is a Gentleman of superior abilities, and joins in a public debate with great art and eloquence. Having laid the foundation of a compleat classical education at Harvard College [sic], he pursues every other study with ease. He is well acquainted with Books and Characters, and has an accommodating turn of mind, which enables him to gain the confidence of Men, and to understand them. He is a practicing Attorney in Georgia, and has been twice a Member of Congress. Mr. Baldwin is about 38 years of age.
> "Mr. Houstoun is an Attorney at Law, and has been a Member of Congress for the State of Georgia. He is a Gentleman of Family, and was educated in England. As to his legal or political knowledge he has very little to boast of. Nature seems to have done more for his corporal than mental powers. His Person is striking, but his mind very little improved with useful or elegant knowledge. He has none of the talents requisite for the Orator, but in public debate is confused and irregular. Mr. Houstoun is about 30 years of age of an amiable and sweet temper, and of good and honorable principles.
> "My own character I shall not attempt to draw, but leave those who may choose to speculate on it, to consider it in any light that their fancy or imagination may depict. I am conscious of having discharged my duty as a Soldier through the course of the late revolution with honor and propriety; and my services in Congress and the Convention were bestowed with the best intention towards the interests of Georgia, and towards the general welfare of the Confederacy. I possess ambition, and it was that, and the flattering opinion which some of my Friends had of me, that gave me a seat in the wisest Council in the World, and furnished me with an opportunity of giving these short Sketches of the Characters who composed it."
> *Documents Illustrative of the Formation of the Union*, 108.

## A Constitutional History of Georgia

The fundamental problem facing the Convention was to provide a constitution "adequate to the exigencies of the Union." The weakness of the existing constitutional structure was, as pointed out above, an inefficient central machinery and its cognate, too much local authority. The task was to draw a new line of division between national and local authority, and to provide adequate governmental machinery for the national government.

It is customary to classify the delegates attending the Convention as advocates of the small States' (or New Jersey) plan of union or of the large States' (or Virginia) plan. The large States favored a general reconstruction of the Constitution, involving the creation of a national government consisting of an executive, legislature, and judiciary. Voting in the national legislature would be proportioned among the States more equitably than before. The powers of the national government would be greatly increased. According to the plan as introduced by Randolph on May 29th, the national government would be empowered "to legislate in all cases to which the separate States are incompetent, or in which the harmony of the United States may be interrupted by the exercise of individual Legislation; to negative all laws passed by the several States, contravening in the opinion of the National Legislature the articles of Union; and to call forth the force of the Union agst. any member of the Union failing to fulfill its duty under the articles thereof." [15] The small States looked only to a removal of the most glaring defects of the Articles. Their plan, as presented by William Paterson of New Jersey on June 15th, provided for an executive in the form of a council chosen by Congress and "a federal Judiciary . . . to consist of a supreme Tribunal." The unicameral legislature of the Articles was to be continued, and the equality of the States was to be

---
[15] *Documents Illustrative of the Formation of the Union*, 117.

## The Federal Union

scrupulously preserved. Congress was to have power "to pass acts for the regulation of trade and commerce as well with foreign nations as with each other." It might also raise revenue by import duties, stamp taxes, and postage charges. But the enforcement of these acts would be dependent upon actions brought originally in State courts, whence an appeal would be possible to the federal judiciary.

The Georgia delegation supported the plan of the large States for forming a strong central government. Early in the Convention, Gunning Bedford, Jr., a delegate from Delaware (the only State with a smaller population than Georgia) exclaimed: "Look at Georgia. Though a small State at present, she is actuated by the prospect of soon becoming a great one." [16] William Pierce, the most perspicacious member of the Convention, delivered a brilliant speech on June 29th, in which he declared: "The great difficulty in Congress arose from the mode of voting. Members spoke on the floor as state advocates, and were biassed by local advantages.—What is federal? No more than a compact between states; and the one heretofore formed is insufficient. We are now met to remedy its defect, and our difficulties are great, but not, I hope, insurmountable. State distinctions must be sacrificed so far as the general government shall render it necessary—without, however, destroying them altogether." [17] Luther Martin, one of the most eminent lawyers of the day, but a bitter opponent of the Constitution, in an address before the House of Delegates of Maryland after the adjournment of the Convention, explained: "It may be thought surprising, sir, that Georgia, a State now small and comparatively trifling in the Union, should advocate this system of unequal representation, giving up her pres-

---
[16] Yates' "Notes," in Farrand, *Records*, I, 491.
[17] *Ibid.*, 474. Madison and Paterson also mention this speech.

ent equality in the Federal Government and sinking herself almost to total insignificance in the scale, but, sir, it must be considered that Georgia has the most extensive territory in the Union, being as large as the whole Island of Great Britain and thirty times as large as Connecticut.[18] This system being designed to preserve to the States their whole territory unbroken and to prevent the erection of new States within the territory of any of them, Georgia looks forward to when, her population being increased in some measure proportional to her territory, she would rise in the scale and give law to the other States, and hence we found the delegation of Georgia warmly advocating the proposition of giving the States unequal representation." [19]

Clearly, Georgia was an advocate of a strong union, but the emphasis placed upon this point here and in the foregoing pages is not to be taken as suggesting that Georgia would have favored discarding State distinctions altogether. Her delegates were decidedly opposed to a federal control over the institution of slavery. The delegates from Virginia and Pennsylvania, States already having plenty of rapidly multiplying slaves, spoke of the evils of the institution and advocated an extension of power to the central government to tax further importations. Ellsworth of Connecticut pointed out the weakness of this argument by stating that if the question were to be considered in a moral light, the Convention should go further and free the slaves already in the country. Simply to prohibit or to place a duty upon further importations would not be just to South Carolina and Georgia where slaves were needed and could, under the proposed plan,

---

[18] Georgia had not yet given up her western lands. Her territory today is 58,876 sq. miles whereas the area of "the island of Great Britain" is 89,030 sq. miles.

[19] Jonathan Elliot, ed., *Debates in the Several State Conventions, on the Adoption of the Federal Constitution* (Washington, 1836), I, 356.

## The Federal Union

be procured only by purchase at augmented prices from the States advocating the restrictions. At this point in the debate Baldwin came to the defense of his adopted State. "Mr. Baldwin had conceived national objects alone to be before the Convention," says Madison in his *Journal* of the day, "not such as like the present were of a local nature. Georgia was decided on this point. . . . If left to herself, she may probably put a stop to the evil." [20]

Baldwin and Few signed the Constitution on behalf of Georgia. The indications are that Pierce and Houstoun would also have signed had they been present on September 17th, the date of the signing.

Upon the completion of its labors, the Convention submitted the Constitution to Congress, in session in New York. Immediately the document was attacked by influential members, and radical amendments proposed. Soon finding this course inexpedient, Congress unanimously resolved, on September 28th, to submit the report of the Convention to the States as it had been received. Not a word of comment was added.[21]

## *Unanimous Ratification of the Constitution*

THE provision of Article VII that "The ratification of the Conventions of nine States, shall be sufficient for the establishment of this Constitution between the states so ratifying" completely ignored Section XIII of the Articles of Confederation that no amendment should be made "unless such alteration be agreed to in a congress of the United States, and afterwards confirmed by the legislatures of every state." Had the method of ratification been

---

[20] Farrand, *Records*, II, 372.
[21] Andrew Cunningham McLaughlin, *The Confederation and the Constitution* (New York, 1904), 277 ff.

by the State legislatures, or indeed by popular referendum, it is probable that the Constitution would have been rejected. As it was, ratification was not achieved without a herculean effort upon the part of friends of the document, known by the name of Federalists.

The Anti-Federalists, opponents of ratification, subjected the Constitution to the most searching criticisms. The document was declared to be ungodly, because it failed to mention the Deity; the centralization of power filled many minds with forebodings; the powers over taxation and commerce given to Congress were feared by small farmers, backwoodsmen, and pioneers; the absence of a bill of rights was viewed with alarm generally. Victory for the Federalists was gained only after a bitter struggle, and by a very narrow margin, especially in the two important States of Virginia and New York.

There was no counterpart of this struggle in Georgia. William Pierce sailed from New York on the sloop *Friendship* on October 3rd, bringing with him a dispatch from Congress relative to the Constitution. He arrived in Savannah on October 10th.[22] Three days later a copy of the Constitution appeared in *The Georgia State Gazette or Independent Register,* published at Augusta, then the Capital. Within a week the legislature was convened, and promptly, on Friday, October 26th, passed a resolution calling a convention to meet in Augusta on the fourth Tuesday in December to adopt or reject the proposed federal constitution. Each county was authorized to elect three delegates to this ratifying convention.[23]

---

[22] *Pierce's Reliques,* MSS. in Connecticut State Library, published in part in the *American Historical Review,* III (July, 1898), 311 ff.

[23] From the manuscript minutes of the ratifying Convention. This manuscript, beautifully written by the Convention's Secretary, Isaac Briggs, is preserved in the Georgia State Archives. Dr. E. Merton Coulter has edited it in the *Georgia Historical Quarterly,* X (September, 1926), 224–237.

## The Federal Union

At this time Georgia was divided into eleven counties. Thus her ratifying convention would have consisted of thirty-three members had each county sent the full quota to which it was entitled, but only twenty-nine delegates actually participated. William Few alone of the four delegates to the Philadelphia Convention was present, and it is probable that he took an active part. Among the other prominent delegates were George Mathews, then Governor, John Wereat, Edward Telfair, and Nathan Brownson, all former Governors, George Handley and Jared Irwin, destined to be future Governors, John Milton, Joseph Habersham, William Stephens, James McNeil, and Christopher Hillary.

The ratifying convention was called to meet at Augusta on the fourth Tuesday in December, but as this happened to be Christmas, a quorum was not present to proceed to business until Friday, December 28th. John Wereat, from Richmond County (in which Augusta is located), was elected President of the Convention, and Isaac Briggs was named Secretary. The Convention lasted for a week, but with Sunday and the New Year's holiday intervening, little time was actually spent in session. The *Minutes* of the Convention indicate no division of opinion. On Monday (December 31st) it was "resolved, Unanimously, that the proposed Federal Constitution be now adopted." On Wednesday (January 2, 1788), twenty-six delegates representing ten counties signed the act of ratification. "As the last name was signed to the Ratification, a party of Colonel Armstrong's regiment . . . proclaimed the joyful tidings outside the State-house by thirteen discharges from two pieces of artillery." [24]

Georgia was the first State in the South and the fourth in the Nation to ratify the Constitution. She was a small State, but her action was significant. When it was learned

---

[24] *Georgia State Gazette or Independent Register*, January 5, 1788.

## A Constitutional History of Georgia

that Georgia had unanimously ratified the Constitution without proposing any amendments, "the hearts of many Antifederalists failed them."[25] Great enthusiasm must have been kindled in the hearts of Washington, Madison and Hamilton.

---
[25] J. B. McMaster, *A History of the People of the United States* (New York, 1884), I, 476.

CHAPTER VII

## Constitutional Revision and Land Frauds

GEORGIA had now entered a strong federal union. She would revamp her government in such a manner as to bring it into harmony with the federal system and remedy the defects experienced in the practical working of the Constitution of 1777.

The early State constitutions had all been drawn up under unfavorable conditions, and in general they were hastily devised. The time and energies of the first constitutional conventions were largely taken up by problems of war demanding immediate attention. The stability of the Massachusetts Constitution of 1780, the last constitution of the strictly Revolutionary period, is a tribute to the wisdom of the founding fathers of that State. Before the close of the century most of the immature documents originally adopted had given way to constitutions with a better balance of power. By 1800 the sixteen States composing the Union had adopted twenty-six constitutions. "In general, it was found that the crude early constitutions were most workable in those features in which they followed the colonial governments, and least practical where they departed from them."[1]

In view of what was said in previous chapters, it is not

---
[1] Nevins, *The American States During and After the Revolution*, 171.

*A Constitutional History of Georgia*

surprising to find that Georgia and Pennsylvania took the lead in the process of reformation. In 1790, without express authority, the legislature of Pennsylvania called a constitutional convention which abolished the hopeless Council of Censors and set up a government modeled largely after that of Massachusetts, although notably more democratic in suffrage requirements. A year earlier Georgia had adopted her second constitution, or third if the Rules and Regulations of 1776 be given that denomination.

## Constitutional Conventions of 1788–1789

ON JANUARY 31, 1788, less than a month after Georgia ratified the Federal Constitution, the House of Assembly proceeded to appoint "three fit and discreet persons for each County," as the House *Journal* records, "to be convened . . . by the Executive as soon as may be after official information is received that nine States have adopted the federal Constitution, to take under their consideration the alterations and amendments that are necessary to be made in the Constitution of this State. . . ."[2] This action, it should be noted, was made with entire disregard for the cumbersome amending process set forth in the Constitution of 1777.

Whereas the Constitution of 1777 had been drawn up and adopted without any reference to the people by a convention which served also as the State legislature, the framing and adoption of the Constitution of 1789 required three special conventions. Upon receipt in October of an official letter from the Secretary of Congress stating that the requisite nine States had ratified the Federal Constitution, Governor George Handly called the

---

[2] *House Journal, 1788,* 155–156.

## Constitutional Revision and Land Frauds

proposed State Constitutional Convention which convened at Augusta on November 4, 1788. No journal of this Convention has been preserved, if indeed any were ever kept, but from the manuscript copy of the constitution which it framed and a note attached thereto now deposited in the State Archives, we know that the Convention sat for but sixteen days, and that it used the Federal Constitution as a model upon which to base its work. Governor Handly, appointed by the Assembly as a delegate from Glynn County, himself served as President of the Convention, and James M. Simmons acted as Secretary. Other prominent figures among the twenty-seven delegates who signed the constitution then framed were William Few, George Walton, Edward Telfair, John Milton, and Henry Osborne. Since William Few had served in the Federal Convention, it is likely that he played a leading role in this State Convention as it proceeded to use the former's handiwork as its guide.

According to the legislative act calling it, this Convention had no authority to frame a new constitution for the State, but was merely to propose amendments which should "be printed and sent by the Executive to the different Counties and distributed among the Justices and field officers of the militia to be communicated to the people for their consideration."[3] The Convention exceeded its designated authority, as any constitutional convention is likely to do, in going beyond the letter of the law and drawing up an entirely new document.

There is no universally accepted theory or practice defining the extent of power of a constitutional convention. According to one theory, "the Convention is *a strictly representative body,* acting for and in the name of the sovereign, and possessed, by actual transfer, of all the powers inherent in that sovereign. . . . It is 'A virtual

---
[3] *Ibid.,* 139–143.

assemblage of the people,' of whom, by reason of their great numbers and remoteness from each other, an actual assemblage, imagined by political speculatists, is impossible—the most that can be effected being a gathering together in convenient numbers of deputies, empowered to represent the people, and clothed with all the power the sovereign itself would have were it assembled *en masse*." A second theory holds that "the Convention is a *collection of delegates* appointed by the sovereign, through the agency of one or more branches of the existing government, to perform certain determinate duties in relation to the formation or revision of the fundamental law; what those duties are, depending upon the tenor of the commission under which it convenes, or when that is silent, upon sound constitutional principles and precedents. . . ." In other words, in its last analysis, a convention, according to this second theory, is a mere committee, sitting for a specified purpose, under the express mandate of the sovereign, and possessed of such powers only as are expressly granted, or as are necessary and proper for the execution of powers expressly granted. This theory evidently discards the notion, so much cherished by advocates of the former, that the convention is clothed with sovereign attributes, though doubtless intrusted to some extent, under strict regulations, intended to secure responsibility, with their exercise. A third theory, which seems to be more generally accepted than the other two, holds the convention to be subject like the regular legislature to the constitution of the State, but not subject to any other legislative body. According to this theory, the terms of the vote actually adopted by the people in sanctioning the call of the convention constitute the evidence of the extent of powers of the convention, and the legislature may impose no additional restraints. All such theories of the extent of power of constitutional conventions

## Constitutional Revision and Land Frauds

are subject to criticism. In practice the extent of power is likely to be a political question determined by the circumstances of time and place.[4]

Georgia's Constitutional Convention of 1776–77 was only an extraordinary legislative body—and extraordinary only in the sense that President Bulloch had denominated the next session of the assembly as a "convention . . . where business of the highest consequence to the government and welfare of the State" would be opened for consideration. The Constitution of 1777 was adopted by the Legislature (or Convention) without submission to a vote of the people. There were few provisions of this Constitution which had not been violated during the course of the Revolutionary War. The Assembly of 1788 had wholly disregarded the Constitution in calling the Convention of that date. Why should this Convention have scrupled about the extent of its powers? Was it not but following the recent precedent of the Federal Convention in drawing up an entirely new constitution rather than altering a few specific defects of the existing inept document? The Convention did follow the legislative mandate in submitting its work to the people for their study, with the choice of adopting or rejecting it through a second convention made up of delegates of their own choice, but in doing this the delegates were probably following more the dictates of their consciences on justice and expediency than any binding legislative enactment.

Elections to the second Convention were held on the first Tuesday in December, and the delegates chosen assembled at Augusta on January 4, 1789. Among the better known of the thirty-one members were Elijah Clarke,

---

[4] For a study of the theories mentioned, see John Alexander Jameson, *A Treatise on Constitutional Conventions* (Chicago, 1887), 301–490, *passim*, and Holcombe, *State Government*, 123–128.

## A Constitutional History of Georgia

John Wereat, George Mathews, George Handly, David Emanuel, Henry Osborne, James Gunn, Benjamin Lanier, and Thomas Stafford. Only five of them had served in the previous Convention. Ex-Governor Handly who had served as President of the first Convention was among these five, but the new Convention passed over him and named Henry Osborne, a delegate from Camden County, as its President. It also named a new Secretary, Daniel Longstreet. This tends to indicate that there had been opposition to the work of the first Convention.[5] This second Convention, like the first, did not abide by the legislative act which declared it to be "vested with full power, and for the sole purpose of adopting and ratifying or rejecting" the changes proposed by the first Convention. Its *Journal*[6] discloses that instead it proceeded as a committee of the whole to consider the proposed constitution paragraph by paragraph and to formulate amendments. Chief among these were an abolition of the property qualification for voting (a modest requirement of the ownership of taxable property valued at £50 had been written into the Constitution proposed in November), a reduction in the property qualifications for members of the legislature, a reduction of the term of judges of the superior courts from seven to three years, and a provision that the governor should be elected by an electoral college in which the counties should have equal voice, rather than by the legislature.[7] At the end of a sixteen day session, the Convention submitted the amended Constitution to the people for their further consideration, and adjourned until the second Tuesday in June.

---

[5] The contemporary press indicated a divided opinion. Compare, for example, the article by "Hotspur" and that by "Casca" in the *Georgia State Gazette*, Jan. 10, 1789.

[6] *MSS.* in State Archives.

[7] Compare the Constitution of Nov., 1788, with that of Jan. 1789. Both *MSS.* in State Archives.

## Constitutional Revision and Land Frauds

The thirty-one members of this second Constitutional Convention of 1788-89 were with only five exceptions members of the House of Assembly which then numbered ninety-four.[8] Nevertheless, the Assembly was impatient with the drawn-out process of constitutional revision adopted by the second Convention. By an act of February 4th (1789) it "earnestly recommended" that the freemen of each county select delegates on the first Monday in April to a third convention which, "without any further alterations or attempts of amendment thereto," should consider the proposed constitution and amendments, and "fully ratify and adopt the said Constitution with such parts of the proposed amendments as they think most proper."[9] This act, if complied with, would put a stop to further alterations and additional conventions. Nevertheless, the Assembly itself proposed one further amendment and authorized the third Convention to adopt it; namely, "that no monies be drawn from the public funds of this state except by appropriation made by law." This amendment appeared in the Constitution of 1789 as finally adopted, and has remained in Georgia's written constitution down to the present day, although recent administrations have demonstrated that the provision has a very limited application.

The people were either disgusted with the methods adopted by the first two Conventions or else they believed in rotation in office, for of the twenty-four members serving in the third Convention, convened in Augusta on May 4th, only ten had served in either of the two former Conventions. William Gibbons, of *Gibbons vs. Ogden* fame, served as President, and Daniel Long-

---

[8] Compare the *MSS. Minutes* of the Convention of January, 1789, with the *House Journal, 1789*. Representation in the Assembly from the eleven counties varied from six to twelve at this time.

[9] *House Journal, 1789*, 160-163.

street was named Secretary.[10] The members were ready for action, so after one day spent in organization and another in deliberation, on the third day (May 6th), by a vote of twenty to three, a constitution, largely as drawn up the previous November, was adopted.[11]

## The Constitution of 1789

THE new Constitution, announced the *Augusta Chronicle*, was "an assimilation to the Federal Constitution," [12] and this was indeed its most striking feature. Instead of following the precedent of the Constitution of 1777 wherein the doctrine of the separation of powers was proclaimed in a preamble and then disregarded in the articles following, the Constitution of 1789 firmly established this basic principle of the American constitutional system by vesting the legislative, executive, and judicial powers in three distinct branches of government by Articles I, II, and III respectively. As the legislature under the model Constitution consisted of two houses, so now Georgia's unicameral legislature gave way to a General Assembly, composed of two separate and distinct branches, a Senate and a House of Representatives. The unit of representation was the county; so following closely the federal pattern, each county was given equal representation in the Senate. Representation in the House was fixed at from two to five members per county, the number for each being designated in the Constitution itself, with a total of thirty-four members for the eleven existing counties. In practice this designation of a specific number of representatives for the various counties was to prove the

---

[10] The *MSS. Minutes* of this Convention are preserved in the State Archives.
[11] This Constitution is preserved in the safe of the Secretary of State.
[12] Issue of May 9, 1789.

## Constitutional Revision and Land Frauds

most objectionable provision of the Constitution of 1789, and was to constitute the subject of prolonged and intense controversy between the seaboard and rapidly growing up-state counties. Further provisions of the Constitution set a property qualification of 200 acres of land or property valued at £150 for members of the House, and 250 acres of land or property valued at £250 for members of the Senate. Georgia had permitted a practically universal manhood suffrage from the very establishment of her state government. This tradition was continued under the Constitution of 1789 through the extension of the franchise to any citizen twenty-one years of age who paid a tax, no amount being specified. A literal construction of this electoral qualification would have permitted women to vote, although, of course, no one had this in mind.

Jefferson must have been pleased with the trend of constitutional development in Georgia. The retention of a broad electorate was accompanied by a much more effective division of powers than had existed under the Constitution of 1777. The newly created Senate would be a salutary check against hasty legislation. Most statesmen of the day shared the view of Adams that "a people cannot be long free, nor even happy, whose government is in one assembly." But more significant in effecting a better balanced government was the redivision of powers between the legislature and executive in favor of the latter.

The plural executive of the Constitution of 1777 gave way to a single chief executive. The Constitution of 1789 did not so much as mention an executive council. "The executive power," declared Article II, "shall be vested in a Governor." The legislature was still to choose the Governor, but a degree of independence was insured through the increase of the Governor's term from one to two years, and the constitutional guarantee that his salary should not be diminished during his continuance in office. The Senate was to choose the Governor from a list of three names submitted by the lower house. The Governor's authority was made far more extensive. Whereas formerly he could not even communicate with the legislature except through a group of its members serving as an executive council, he could now address it at any time upon the state of the republic, and recommend for its consideration such measures as he should deem necessary. He was empowered to convene the Assembly on extraordinary occasions, and in case of a disagreement between the two houses with respect to the time for adjournment, to prorogue them until such time as he should think proper. But most important of all was the veto power. Following the Massachusetts formula which had been written into the Federal Constitution, the Governor was given a veto upon all legislation which could be overridden only by a two-thirds vote of both houses of the General Assembly.[18]

These provisions of the Constitution of 1789 strengthening the executive are concrete evidence of a reaction against legislative omnipotence. Concentration of authority, simplicity in organization, and flexibility in procedure are qualities that add strength to government. Legislative supremacy under a written constitution had proved ill adapted to Georgia's needs during the War of the Revolution. Both the House of Assembly and the Executive Council had of necessity given over at critical moments many of their constitutional functions to the commander-in-chief. Even after the restoration of peace the legislature in Georgia, as in the other States, failed to inspire public confidence. Bent upon fostering local advantage, State legislatures pampered the public interest through their restrictions on trade. The people of Geor-

---
[18] Art. II, Sec. 10.

## Constitutional Revision and Land Frauds

gia were nationalistic in their outlook, but the House of Assembly took a narrow view of the public interest in adopting tariff barriers. Nor did the unrestrained House of Assembly manage the internal affairs of the State in such a manner as to avoid censure. Special acts for the benefit of private individuals were the order of the day, and acts in favor of one person were likely to be at the expense of another, or at the expense of the public. The reaction against legislative omnipotence in 1789 was but natural.

Unfortunately the new Constitution left the judiciary just as it had been with a Superior Court of final jurisdiction in each county. The only improvement lay in the provision that the judges should have a competent salary established by law which should not be diminished during their continuance in office (a provision obviously copied from the Federal Constitution), and that they should hold office for three years rather than during the pleasure of the Assembly, as before.

This, the briefest of Georgia's eight constitutions, contained no separate bill of rights; but freedom of the press, the most necessary of all civil liberties for the preservation of a democracy, together with trial by jury, *habeas corpus,* and the free exercise of religion were guaranteed by the Fourth Article. The framers of this Constitution bore no illusion that their handiwork should prove immortal. They wrote into the document itself provision for a convention to be held after the expiration of five years for effecting such alterations as should then appear appropriate.

## *Convention of 1795*

THE Constitution of 1789 provided that at the election for members of the General Assembly in 1794 the electors

## A Constitutional History of Georgia

in each county should select three persons to represent them in a convention to consider needed alterations in the Constitution. Noting that representatives had already been chosen, by an act of December 25, 1794, the General Assembly designated Louisville as the place for the convention and set the date as the first Monday in May, 1795.[14] Representatives from all twenty of the existing counties assembled in convention at the appointed time, and organized by electing Noble Wymberly Jones as President and Thomas Johnson as Secretary. Among the fifty-five other delegates attending were Lachlan McIntosh, William Neel, Thomas Gibbons, Josiah Tattnall, Joseph Clay, John Wereat, David Emanuel, Stephen Heard, Silas Mercer, and Solomon Wood. The Convention lasted only two weeks, spending most of this time in debate upon the apportionment of representatives, the contest being between the coastal region and the fast-growing frontier counties of the Piedmont. The total membership of the House was fixed at fifty-one, and the representation of each county designated, two counties (Chatham and Liberty) receiving four representatives each, seven counties three representatives each, and the remaining eleven counties two representatives each. This reapportionment was a distinct gain for the Piedmont region, for seven of the nine new counties now given representation for the first time lay in that region.

No change was made in the representation in the Senate where each county continued to have one representative, but the term of Senators was reduced from three to one year. Elections by the Assembly were changed to joint ballot of the two houses rather than nomination by the House and election by the Senate as before. Meetings of the Assembly would continue to be annual, but the date of convening was changed from the first Monday in

---

[14] Watkins' *Digest*, 545–46.

### Constitutional Revision and Land Frauds

November to the second Tuesday in January. Louisville was designated as the permanent seat of the State government, and the Governor and principal officers were directed to locate their offices there. On May 16th the Convention adjourned, having made provision for another constitutional convention in 1798. The amendments adopted were declared to be in full force after the first day of October, next, without any submission to a vote of the people for ratification.[15]

The Convention of 1795 might have accomplished more but for the agitation that existed at the time over the recent Yazoo land sale. On this subject, it resolved "That it is the opinion of this Convention, that from the number, respectability, and ground of complaint stated in the sundry petitions laid before them, that this is a subject of importance well meriting legislative deliberation."[16]

## The Yazoo Land Fraud

THE most exciting political event in the decade of the 'nineties was the Yazoo Land Fraud of 1795, involving the sale of over thirty million acres of Georgia's western

---

[15] The *MSS.* records of this convention are preserved in the State Archives. The amendments adopted and a list of the delegates to the Convention appeared in *The Augusta Chronicle,* May 23, 1795.

Some light is shed upon the power considered at this period of Georgia history to be vested in a constitutional convention by the following quotation from an article of May 16, 1795, in the *Augusta Chronicle* addressed to the Convention then in session: "To define your powers would be to depart from the known maxims exercised in modern times; you have only to look back to the Convention who revised the confederation of the United States . . . Again, recur to the late convention who revised the constitution of this state. . . . The constitution sets bounds to the legislature; and therefore it follows that the framers of the constitution form the highest and greatest court, because they draw the line beyond which legislative, executive, and judicial powers shall not extend."

[16] *The Augusta Chronicle,* May 23, 1795.

lands. Repercussions of this fraud were felt in Georgia politics for two decades, and the subject was one of controversy in both the United States Supreme Court and Congress. The term "Yazoo" is taken from the Yazoo River in Alabama which lies within the region sold.

The territory of Georgia was fixed by the Charter of 1732 as the land between the Savannah and Altamaha Rivers, and westward from the headwaters of these rivers to the South Seas. After the Peace of Paris in 1763 the southern boundary was designated as the St. Marys River, and from its headwaters in a straight line westwardly to the juncture of the Flint and Chattahoochee Rivers, thence along the 31st parallel to the Mississippi River. Thus upon becoming an independent state in 1783 Georgia included as part of her territory not only the present limits of the State, but also most of what is today Alabama and Mississippi.

The State had early adopted a land policy liberal enough to permit any industrious settler to acquire a homestead. The land act of 1777 was designed to encourage immigration, and its main provisions were continued under succeeding acts which established the headright land system. Under this system the head of a family was entitled to two hundred acres for himself and fifty acres for each member of his family (including his slaves), but no family could thus acquire more than one thousand acres. There was no cost except office and surveying fees for the first two hundred acres, but additional land should cost from one to four and one-half shillings per acre, depending on the amount purchased. Not content with acquiring land for use under these generous terms, speculators wanted to acquire hundreds of thousands of acres for profiteering. Governors Walton, Telfair, Mathews and Irwin disregarded the provision of the law limiting grants to one thousand acres, and between 1789

## Constitutional Revision and Land Frauds

and 1796 grants were signed for three times as much land as existed in the twenty-four counties that had been laid off at that time.[17]

But even more dazzling in the eyes of the speculators than securing hundreds of grants of a thousand acres each was the possibility of purchasing for a song millions of acres of Georgia's domain west of the Chattahoochee River. A company called "The Combined Society" was organized in secret with this view in mind in 1788, but nothing came of it. In 1789 three companies, the South Carolina Yazoo Company, the Virginia Yazoo Company, and the Tennessee Company, succeeded in pushing through the legislature a measure preempting for them a total of fifteen and one half million acres of Georgia's western lands for which they should pay the sum of $207,000.[18] These companies attempted to pay even this paltry sum in depreciated currency, but Georgia refused to accept it, thus causing the transaction to fall through. The passage of the Eleventh Amendment to the Constitution prohibiting suits against a State prevented these companies from prosecuting suits against Georgia already entered in the United States Supreme Court.

When the General Assembly met in November, 1794, four new land companies presented proposals for the purchase of Georgia's western domain. These were the Georgia Company, headed by James Gunn, Matthew M'Allister, and George Walker; The Georgia-Mississippi Company, headed by Nicholas Long, Thomas Glascock, Ambrose Gordon, and Thomas Cumming; the Upper Mississippi Company, headed by John B. Scott, John C. Nightingale, and Wade Hampton; and the Tennessee Company, headed by Zachariah Cox and Matthias Ma-

---

[17] Coulter, *Short History of Georgia*, 184; S. G. McLendon, *History of the Public Domain of Georgia* (Atlanta, 1924), 65.
[18] Stevens, *History of Georgia*, II, 466.

her. By bribing members of the legislature the companies succeeded in pushing through both houses a bill that sold to them the coveted territory. On December 29th Governor Mathews vetoed the bill on the ground that the time was not appropriate for the sale, the sum offered was inadequate, the quantity of land reserved to the citizens of Georgia was too small in proportion to the extent of the purchase, and the disposal of such extensive tracts to individuals would operate as a monopoly and retard settlement.[19] These objections were substantial and sound, but, nonetheless, the speculators were able after consultation with the Governor to push another bill of sale, with minor alterations, through the legislature and have him sign it on January 7, 1795. In its generosity the legislature included in the Yazoo Act a provision exempting the territory sold from taxation until it should be given representation in the General Assembly.[20] More than 30,000,000 acres of land were involved in the sale, but the exact amount was not known for the boundaries described in the Act had not been surveyed. The Georgia Company, headed by Senator James Gunn, received the largest share of the spoils, for which it was to pay $250,000. The total amount to be paid by the four companies was $490,000, approximately a cent and a half per acre! The Act reserved two million acres in the regions sold for citizens of Georgia not members of the companies, from which any citizen could subscribe for five thousand acres on the same terms as the original purchasers and thus become a member of one of the companies.

The sale was a flagrant case of wholesale legislative corruption. Practically all of the legislators were given shares in one or more of the companies, and many of them accepted cash bribes. As the people heard of the

---
[19] *Ibid.*, 469–70.
[20] Watkins' *Digest*, 566.

## Constitutional Revision and Land Frauds

sale, discussed its merits, and learned of the way in which the speculators had bought over the legislators, "their indignation rose higher and higher, and vented itself in presentments of grand juries, in violent newspaper warfare, in stinging personal invective and insult, in threats of corporal violence, and in scenes of actual bloodshed and death." [21] Even before the Governor had signed the bill, he received a remonstrance against it from William H. Crawford and other citizens of Columbia County. James Jackson, Georgia's senior United States Senator, soon began a series of articles over the signature of "Scillius" exposing the fraud and showing the enormous loss to the State. One citizen, writing for the *Augusta Chronicle* on March 28, 1795, expressed his indignation in verse:

> *The Dishonorable Situation of Georgia*
> How much thy real friends with horror view
> The hellish fraud of that infernal crew
> Of speculators: who in spite of right
> Insult thine honor and defy thy might.
> See! this black host of cheating knaves now vieing,
> Who shall exceed in villainy and lying;
> See! some with prying search the state ransacks,
> To find out rascals who will sell them tracts.

The people, thoroughly aroused, elected members to the legislature pledged to repeal the obnoxious Act. When the General Assembly convened at Louisville, the new Capital, in January, 1796, the House appointed a committee of nine, headed by General Jackson, to examine the validity and constitutionality of the Yazoo Act. Within a week this committee reported that the Act had been passed by corruption, that the rights of posterity had been bartered away, that the Act was un-

---
[21] Stevens, *History of Georgia*, II, 478.

## A Constitutional History of Georgia

constitutional, and that the testimony before the committee of the fraud practiced to obtain the passage of the Act made it null and void. Believing that a declaration by legislative authority of the nullity of the Yazoo Act would check the "rapacious and avaricious spirit of speculation which has overleaped all decent bounds," the committee reported a bill to that effect. This Rescinding Act of February 13, 1796, set forth at length the reasons for the invalidity of the Yazoo sale, declaring it, among other things, to be contrary to specific provisions of both the Federal and State Constitutions, undemocratic, against the public interest, and fraudulent.[22] It provided that the evidence of the fraud should be spread upon the legislative journal and that the Yazoo Act should be expunged and burned. Tradition has it that in the ceremony at which the record of the Yazoo Act was burned, fire from heaven was brought down by means of a sun glass.

By the Rescinding Act and subsequent legislation the State made provision for refunding the money that had been paid into the treasury for the purchase of the western lands, but many of the speculators denounced the Rescinding Act as retroactive and unconstitutional and refused to give up their bargain. Several pamphlets were written on both sides; suits at law were entered in various courts; and the controversy between the companies and Georgia was agitated for years. The removal of Spain's claim to a portion of the territory by an agreement with the United States in 1795 greatly increased the value of the land, and the companies sold much of it at a profit to people in the Northern States, particularly New Englanders.[23]

Most of the States had relinquished their claim to

---
[22] Watkins' *Digest*, 577–585.
[23] Stevens, *History of Georgia*, II, 495.

## Constitutional Revision and Land Frauds

western lands during the Revolution or soon thereafter; Georgia was the only State that had not taken this action by the end of the eighteenth century. In 1788 Georgia offered to cede her western lands to the United States, but Congress rejected the terms. In 1798 Congress voted to set up a territory in the disputed region, and authorized the President to appoint three commissioners to treat with a like number from Georgia for a final settlement of Georgia's claims to the region. Action was delayed until Jefferson became President, but in 1802 an agreement was reached whereby Georgia ceded both her jurisdiction and soil claims to the territory west of the Chattahoochee to the United States for the sum of $1,250,000. The Commissioners for the United States in this agreement were James Madison, Albert Gallatin, and Levi Lincoln; those for Georgia, James Jackson, John Milledge, and Abraham Baldwin. The United States bound itself to confirm the titles of all actual settlers within the region who were there prior to October, 1795, and also to extinguish all Indian titles to land remaining within the boundary of Georgia. The removal of the Indians from Georgia proved to be a difficult undertaking, involving a cost of approximately $10,000,000; but the United States derived $32,000,000 from the sale of public land in Alabama and Mississippi, carved out of the former Georgia territory.

The problem of the Yazoo claims was thus transferred from Georgia to the United States. The agreement of 1802 provided that five million acres should be set aside to satisfy the Yazoo claimants, but a group in Congress known as the Quids, led by John Randolph of Roanoke, blocked all legislation for indemnifying these claimants. In the case of *Fletcher vs. Peck,* decided in 1810,[24] the Supreme Court declared that the grants made under the

---
[24] 6 Cranch 87.

Yazoo Act of 1795 constituted a contract, and that the Georgia legislature of 1796 had been without power to invalidate this contract. The validity of the Rescinding Act, declared Chief Justice Marshall, might well be doubted had Georgia been a single sovereign power; but as a State in the Federal Union, bound by the provision of the Federal Constitution declaring that no State should pass any law impairing the obligation of contract, the Court was of unanimous opinion that the Act was void. This is one of the notable examples of an expansion of the Constitution by Marshall to protect vested property rights. The questions of whether the contract clause of the Constitution extended to executed as well as executory contracts, and whether the clause was applicable to contracts to which a State was a party as well as to contracts between individuals, were both answered affirmatively by Marshall. Finally, in 1814, with Randolph temporarily out of Congress, four million dollars was voted for the settlement of the Yazoo claims.[25]

---

[25] Coulter, *Short History of Georgia*, 192.

CHAPTER VIII

# The Constitution of 1798

THE Constitutional Convention of 1795 met at a time of intense excitement occasioned by the recent passage of the Yazoo Land Act. It remained in session only two weeks, and made relatively few changes in the Constitution. As Georgians of this epoch were accustomed to frequent alterations in their governmental structure, this Convention was in keeping with the spirit of the times when it made provision for another constitutional convention to assemble three years later. To prevent the recurrence of the recent experience of a year's delay in the meeting of the convention, the time and place were fixed as the second Tuesday in May, 1798, at Louisville. Each county should select three delegates to the convention at the time of electing members of the General Assembly in 1797.

The Convention of 1798 assembled according to schedule and was well attended. Jared Irwin, the late Governor who had signed the Rescinding Act of 1796, was elected President, and James M. Simmons, Secretary. Many of the delegates had records of service in the Revolutionary War, in the State government, or in both. Prominent among them were James Jackson, Governor of the State; Jesse Mercer, ardent Baptist preacher and politician for whom Mercer University was later named; John Couper and Thomas Spalding, prominent planters from Glynn County; Joseph Elay, an honor graduate of Princeton University; Jonas Fouché, distinguished Indian fighter from Green County; Robert Watkins, of Richmond County, a leader of the up-country in its struggle for equal representation in the legislature; and Dr. George Jones, of Chatham County, son of Noble Wymberly Jones.[1]

The dominant leader in the Convention was James Jackson (Sept. 21, 1757–March 19, 1806). Born in England, he came to Georgia at the age of fifteen and studied law in the office of Samuel Farley, in Savannah. He is said to have possessed a deep-seated prejudice against the hereditary distinctions of British aristocracy even before coming to America, and to have readily espoused the cause of freedom. His Revolutionary record was of such distinction that the legislature of Georgia, on July 30, 1782, unanimously voted to give him a house and lot in Savannah in recognition of his military service. After the war he practiced law and served in the General Assembly. Elected Governor in 1788, he declined on the ground of his youth and inexperience. The following year he entered Congress as a member of the House of Representatives, and in 1793 was elevated to the Senate. The most notable events of his life were in connection with the Yazoo Fraud of 1795. Upon learning of the fraud, he resigned his seat in the Senate, returned to Georgia, won a seat in the General Assembly, and took the lead in passing the Rescinding Act of 1796 whereby Georgia reasserted her claim to her western lands. He became the most popular man in the State, and was both Governor

---

[1] Jean A. Garrett, *Amendments and Proposed Amendments to the Constitution of 1798*. M.A. thesis, University of Georgia, 1944. Chapter I, *passim*.

## The Constitution of 1798

and the leading figure in the Constitutional Convention of 1798. His greatest interest was in securing a definition of Georgia's boundaries in the Constitution, a declaration that the Yazoo sale was void, and a guarantee against future wholesale disposals of the public lands to speculators. He felt so keenly on this subject that, as Governor, he removed from office a justice of the peace for merely witnessing a protest against the definition of the State boundary found in the first article of the Constitution, and refused to allow Robert Watkins to be paid for his labor in compiling, by legislature sanction, *A Digest of the Laws of the State of Georgia* because Watkins had included the Yazoo Act.[2]

The Convention spent the month of May studying the Constitution, article by article, sometimes referring a particular section to a special committee, and frequently debating provisions in committee of the whole. James Powell of Liberty County served as chairman of a committee on style which arranged the provisions of the Constitution under proper articles. On May 30th sixty-eight delegates, representing twenty-four counties, signed the finished document, and this event was celebrated by a banquet given by the Governor and the firing of fifteen rounds of artillery.[3] Two delegates, James Gunn, of Camden County, and Thomas Glascock, of Richmond, elected to the Convention despite their connections with the Yazoo Fraud, refused to sign the Constitution. Robert Watkins signed only after calling upon the Con-

---

[2] *Dictionary of American Biography*, IX, 545; T. U. P. Charlton, *Life of General James Jackson* (Augusta, 1809); *Executive Minutes* (MSS), *1798, 1799; The Georgia Gazette*, Feb. 14, 1799.

[3] Stevens, *History of Georgia*, II, 500. For a list of the signers of the Constitution, see *The Augusta Chronicle and Gazette of the State*, June 30, 1789. *The Columbian Museum and Savannah Advertiser* published a short extract from the proceedings of the Convention on May 22, 1789. The original manuscript Constitution is preserved in the safe of the Secretary of State, as are also the Constitutions of 1789, 1865 and 1877.

157

vention to bear testimony that he did not consider himself bound to support any part of the document "which may be intended to operate retrospectively in contravention of the eternal principles of natural justice, or, of any principles of the federal constitution." [4]

Since no constitution of Georgia had ever been submitted to the people for ratification, the Convention itself declared that the new Constitution should be effective from the date of the signing thereof.

## Provisions of the Constitution

IN FORM the Constitution of 1798 followed the pattern of the Constitution of 1789 which it replaced, both being divided into four articles and numerous sections of one paragraph each, but the new Constitution was almost twice as long, covering sixteen printed pages. The first section of Article I established the principle of the separation of powers by the provision that "The legislative, executive, and judiciary departments of government shall be distinct, and each department shall be confined to a separate body of magistracy." This principle was further guarded by a clause in Section II of the same Article making a member of the General Assembly ineligible for appointment to any office having emolument during the time for which he was elected to the legislature. There was no preamble or separate bill of rights, but freedom of the press, freedom of religion, trial by jury, and *habeas corpus*, the four freedoms of the Constitution of 1789, were continued and supplemented by a guaranty against *ex post facto* laws and imprisonment for debt, except in cases involving a strong presumption of fraud. The further importation of slaves from Africa "or any foreign

---

[4] *Augusta Chronicle and Gazette of the State*, June 30, 1798.

## The Constitution of 1798

place" was forbidden, and any person who should maliciously dismember or deprive a slave of life should suffer the same punishment inflicted in case a like offence were committed on a free white person.

The composition of the legislature remained largely as before, the greatest change being that the number of representatives from each county was not specifically designated in the Constitution but was to be determined by the population according to a census to be taken every seven years. Each county was to have at least one representative, and no county more than four; counties with a population of three thousand were to have two representatives; counties with seven thousand or more inhabitants, three representatives; and counties with twelve thousand or more, four representatives. In determining the population, the federal-ratio should be used, counting all free white persons and three-fifths of the Negroes. Representation in the Senate remained as before, each of the twenty-four counties having one member. The term of both Representatives and Senators was one year, and the annual meeting of the legislature should commence on the second Tuesday in January, unless the legislature set another date. The Constitution included most of the provisions of the Federal Constitution on such matters as the privileges of members of the legislature, impeachment, the origin of money bills in the House, each house being the judge of the qualifications of its members, and the three readings of bills. The most notable limitation placed on the power of the General Assembly was a lengthy statement of the boundary of the State and a prohibition against the sale of the public lands to individuals or private companies before the land had been laid off into counties and the Indian rights extinguished. Provisions similar to those of the Rescinding Act of 1796 were incorporated in the Constitution, declaring the Yazoo sale void and providing for refunding the Yazoo money still in the State Treasury. Because of the misleading title of the infamous Yazoo Act, the clause "No law or ordinance shall pass containing any matter different from what is expressed in the title thereof" was inserted in the new Constitution.[5] In other respects the legislative power was made the broadest possible. The General Assembly was to pass all measures deemed necessary and proper for the good of the State, including the laying off of new counties and altering the boundaries of the existing ones. The legislature was specifically directed to promote the arts and sciences in one or more seminaries of learning, to give as soon as possible "such further donations and privileges to those already established as may be necessary to secure the objects of their institution," and "to provide effectual measures for the improvement and permanent security of the funds and endowments of such institutions."[6]

Executive power was vested in a Governor, elected by the General Assembly for a term of two years. His legislative powers included the right of convening special sessions of the Assembly, recommending legislation, and exercising a veto that could be overridden only by a two-thirds vote of both houses. His executive powers were general, including command of the armed forces of the State, filling vacancies in any office until a successor should be chosen, and granting pardons and reprieves, except in cases of murder and treason, in which cases he could grant a respite, pending action by the legisla-

---

[5] The Supreme Court of Georgia has not been inclined to invalidate legislation upon a technical violation of this clause. "This salutary restriction was never intended to embarrass but was designed to prevent vicious and fraudulent legislation," said the Court in upholding an act whose title indicated the prohibition of the sale of spirituous liquors but contained in its body a prohibition of the sale of Plantation Bitters or other intoxicating bitters. *Howell vs. The State*, 71 Ga. 224.

[6] Art. IV, Sec. 13.

## The Constitution of 1798

ture. But unification of executive policy was hampered by constitutional provisions for the election by the Assembly of the Secretary of State, the Treasurer, and the Surveyor-General.

"The judicial power of this State," provided Article III, "shall be vested in a superior court, and in such inferior jurisdictions as the legislature shall, from time to time, ordain and establish." The term *"a* superior court" is misleading, for at the time this Constitution was written Georgia was divided into three judicial districts with a Superior Court of final jurisdiction in each, and the framers of the new Constitution did not intend to establish a single superior court—indeed, the number of Superior Courts was soon to be increased to ten, each a court of final jurisdiction holding sessions in each county within its circuit twice a year, with no supreme court to review its decisions. To these Superior Courts the Constitution gave exclusive jurisdiction in all criminal cases and in such other cases as the legislature should direct. The Constitution was silent upon the method of selecting judges of the Superior Courts, but they had always been elected by the General Assembly, and this method was continued in practice. It did insure that the salaries of the judges should not be diminished during their continuance in office.

To the Inferior Courts the Constitution gave jurisdiction in all civil cases except those involving titles to land. The powers of a court of ordinary, or register of probate, were also vested in the Inferior Courts, and their clerks were empowered to grant marriage licenses.[7] Judges of these Courts were to be appointed by the General Assembly to hold office as long as they maintained good behavior and resided in the county for which they were appointed. They were eligible to membership in the legisla-

---
[7] Article III, Sec. VI.

ture. The Inferior Courts were authorized to appoint two justices of the peace for each captain's district, with jurisdiction in civil cases where the amount in controversy did not exceed thirty dollars.

Clerks of the several courts and Sheriffs were to be appointed in such manner as the legislature should direct. Clerks were to hold office during good behavior, but to insure a rotation in the office of Sheriff, their term was set at two years and no person could be twice elected Sheriff within any term of four years.

From the very origin of the State, Georgia had had a practically universal manhood suffrage, and this policy was continued under the Constitution of 1798. All male citizens of the State twenty-one years of age who had paid such taxes as were required and had resided in a county six months were eligible to vote. Strange to say, the Constitution of 1798 departed from the method of voting by ballot established under the earlier Constitutions and provided that in all elections by the people the electors should vote *viva voce* until the legislature should direct otherwise.[8] Ownership of property was made a requirement for holding office: Representatives had to own an estate valued at two hundred and fifty dollars or taxable property to the amount of five hundred dollars; Senators were required to own twice this amount; and the Governor had to own five hundred acres of land within the State and other property to the amount of four thousand dollars.

The method of amendment was unusual. Proposed amendments to become effective had to pass both houses of the General Assembly by two-thirds vote, be published at least six months before the next ensuing annual election for members of the Assembly, and again pass both houses by a two-thirds vote. This method had the ad-

---
[8] The legislature provided for voting by ballot by an Act of 1799.

## The Constitution of 1798

vantage both of being democratic and of insuring a thorough consideration of proposed changes in the fundamental law.

It is curious to note that Georgia never used the provisions of her Constitution of 1777 calling for popular initiative of constitutional amendments, but that the referendum was used several times while the Constitution of 1798 was in effect, although the Constitution made no provision for it. In 1832 and in 1838 the General Assembly in calling constitutional conventions provided for submission of the amendments proposed by the conventions to popular referendum. In both instances the people rejected the proposed changes. In 1840 the General Assembly itself submitted to popular vote the question of annual or biennial sessions. The people voted in favor of the latter, and the next two sessions of the Assembly enacted a constitutional amendment embodying their will.

## Amendments

As WALTER MCELREATH has pointed out, "It is an interesting fact that the Constitution of 1798 is the only constitution ever adopted by the people of Georgia at a time when there was not a virtual revolution of the government itself."[9] The dates of the first seven constitutions of Georgia, except that of 1798, are easily remembered when associated with prominent events in our national history: The Constitution of 1777 followed the Revolution, that of 1789 resulted from Georgia's entrance into the Federal Union, those of 1861 and 1865 marked the limits of the Southern Confederacy, that of 1868 was

---

[9] *Treatise on the Constitution of Georgia* (Atlanta, 1912), 114. The revision of 1945, if considered a new constitution, is of course an exception.

the Reconstruction Constitution, and the Constitution of 1877 represented the fall of the Carpetbag Regime and the return of political control to the people of the State. The Constitution of 1798 was adopted in a period of relative tranquillity and brought to a close the Revolutionary and Formative Period of constitution-making and constitution-breaking. With only twenty-three amendments, this document served as the fundamental law of the State for a period of sixty-three years.

The provisions of all these amendments except five are given below in the discussion of the evolution of the legislative, executive, and judicial branches of the government. These five deal with miscellaneous matters not lending themselves easily to classification. Two of them related to divorces. The early practice in Georgia was for the legislature to grant divorces, and this method was continued in the Constitution of 1798, but with the limitation that the legislature could not grant a divorce until the parties had had a fair trial before a Superior Court, and a verdict had been obtained authorizing a divorce upon legal principles.[10] Because of the annoyance and expense involved in having the legislature consider frequent applications for divorce, an amendment of 1833 authorized the Superior Courts, after two concurrent verdicts of two special juries, to grant final divorces, "upon legal principles." In 1847 the Supreme Court of Georgia ruled[11] that upon legal principles meant only such grounds as existed under the ecclesiastical law of England, and did not permit divorces to be granted upon any additional or discretionary grounds. Because of this decision, the Constitution was again changed in 1849 so as to authorize divorces "upon such legal principles as the General Assembly may by law prescribe."

---
[10] Article IV, Sec. IX.
[11] *Head vs. Head*, 2 Ga. 191.

## The Constitution of 1798

Two amendments of 1843 provided, first, for the election of major generals and brigadier generals by their respective divisions and brigades, allowing all persons subject to military duty to vote; and second, for the trial of cases involving promissory notes of which the maker and endorser resided in different counties in the county which was the domicile of the maker of the notes. The last of the miscellaneous amendments, adopted in 1855, provided "The legislature shall have no power to grant corporate powers and privileges, except to Banking, Telegraph and Railroad Companies, nor to change names, nor to legitimate persons, nor to make or change precincts, nor to establish bridges or ferries, but shall by law prescribe the manner in which said power shall be exercised by the Superior or Inferior Courts, and the privileges to be enjoyed." [12]

## The Legislature

UNDER the Constitution of 1798 the legislature continued to be the dominant branch of the government. It appointed most of the executive officers, as well as the judges and officials of the courts. Among the numerous officials elected by it were the Governor (until 1825), Secretary of State, Treasurer, Comptroller General, Adjutant General, Major Generals of the several divisions of the militia, the Keeper of the Penitentiary, Directors of the Bank of Augusta, the Planter's Bank of the State of Georgia, and the Bank of Darien, Trustees of the University of Georgia, and of various academies, vendue masters, health officers, lumber measurers, notaries public, justices of the Supreme Court (after 1846), judges of

---

[12] *Acts of 1853–54,* p. 24; *Acts of 1855–56,* p. 105.

## A Constitutional History of Georgia

the Inferior Courts (until 1812), and judges of the Superior Courts.[13]

An element of stability was added to the government by the practice of the General Assembly of reëlecting executive officials already in office. Only eight persons held the position of Secretary of State under the Constitution of 1798, their average length of service being eight years. The average length of service of the Treasurer was five years; of the Comptroller General, six years; the Adjutant General, thirteen years.[14] Much of the legislature's time was spent in passing local and special laws and in such matters as authorizing a toll bridge, changing a person's name, enabling a certain person to practice law, granting a divorce, or incorporating an insurance company.

In view of the important executive functions which the General Assembly performed in addition to its legislative duties, its sessions were surprisingly short, especially so since the members were paid on a *per diem* basis. Meeting in November, it always adjourned in December, except for the first four sessions in the decade of 1850 when pressing national problems extended one session into January, two sessions into February, and one into March. Sessions were held annually, except for the period from 1843 to 1857 when they were held biennially. There

---

[13] "A friend to Merit," writing in the *Augusta Chronicle*, on September 26, 1795, charged that it was common for a candidate for the legislature to promise "fifteen or twenty, of such as he thinks may be serviceable to him, that if he gets elected they shall be justices of the peace; he also appoints collectors and receivers of tax returns, in the same manner, without the least respect being paid to their qualifications; provided they answer his purpose.... I conceive that the legislature, having the appointment annually of county officers to be one main root of the evil of which we complain (*i.e.*, the low quality of the legislators)." The better class of men, he concluded, would not engage in such practices; hence they were at a disadvantage in a legislative race.

[14] *Georgia's Official Register, 1923*. Compiled by Lucian Lamar Knight, State Historian (Atlanta, 1923), 162–163, 169–172.

*The Constitution of 1798*

were only seven extra sessions during the sixty-three years that the Constitution of 1798 was in effect. All of these were in the spring, the longest, in 1825, being of only eighteen days duration.[15]

The amendments to the Constitution of 1798 showed a definite trend away from legislative dominance toward a better balance of power between the branches of the government. Most significant among the changes made in this direction were the provisions for the popular election of the Governor and the creation of a Supreme Court. Other indications of the same trend are found in the removal of the power to grant final decrees of divorce from the legislature and vesting it in the Superior Courts, and in the amendments for popular election of judges of the Inferior Courts and the Courts of Ordinary, justices of the peace, the Attorney General and solicitors of the several judicial circuits, and clerks of both the Superior and Inferior Courts. The constitutional provision permitting justices of the Inferior Courts to serve in the legislatures was a clear violation of the principle of the separation of powers, and the practice was the subject of widespread criticism, charges being made that judges were inclined to abuse their judicial posts to maintain popularity in order to secure election to the legislature; yet no amendment forbidding the practice was ever passed.[16]

The first of the five constitutional amendments relating to the General Assembly, passed in 1835, dropped the property requirements as a qualification for membership

---

[15] *Georgia's Official Register, 1925.* Compiled by Ruth Blair, State Historian (Atlanta, 1925), 273–274. The General Assembly met annually, 1777–1843; biennially, 1843–47; annually, 1857–77; biennially adjourned, 1878–91; annually, 1892–1925; biennially, 1925–1943; biennially adjourned, 1943–date.

[16] *The Augusta Chronicle,* Dec. 9, 1808; *The Georgia Journal,* July 18, 1810.

in both the House and Senate. Georgia had always had property qualifications for membership in the legislature, but their retention in the era of Jacksonian democracy was inconsistent. Within a few years the property qualifications for the Governor were also to be abolished.

Two amendments related to sessions of the Assembly. The large number of members made sessions of the legislature excessively expensive, and several proposals for biennial sessions were introduced in the decade of 1830–40. In 1839 a resolution to submit the question to the people passed the legislature, and in the election of 1840 the people expressed their approval of biennial sessions. In his annual message in November, 1841, Governor McDonald stated that "the immense expense of the legislature of Georgia, being more than double that of any other state in the union, . . . [had] doubtless been a powerful agency in influencing the popular decision on this measure." [17] Finally in 1843, a constitutional amendment became effective providing for biennial sessions. The number of representatives having meanwhile been somewhat reduced, an amendment of 1857 restored the annual session as provided in the original Constitution, but with meetings in November rather than January, and limited to forty days, unless extended by a two-thirds vote of the General Assembly. The other two amendments to the first article, adopted in 1843 and 1852, dealt with the number of representatives in the General Assembly and their apportionment among the counties.

The Piedmont region was not ceded to Georgia by the Indians until 1773, but due to the liberal head-right laws adopted by the State and the rapid immigration from Virginia and North Carolina, before the close of the

---

[17] L. E. Roberts, "Sectional Factors in the Movement for Legislative Reapportionment and Reduction in Georgia, 1776–1860," *Studies in Georgia History and Government* (Athens, 1940), 120.

*The Constitution of 1798*

eighteenth century the center of population had shifted from the tidewater to the up-country. The excellence of the Piedmont soil for cotton culture by Negro slaves caused central Georgia to become a "black belt," richer and more populous than any other part of the State during the first half of the nineteenth century. The shift in population and accompanying divergence in social and economic patterns brought sectionalism into play as a vital force in Georgia politics.

A cleavage between the rapidly expanding frontier and the stable coast was apparent before the end of the eighteenth century. The first clash between the two sections occurred over the location of the capital.[18] In 1786 the seat of government was moved to Augusta, in 1795 to Louisville, and in 1807 to Milledgeville (where it remained until transferred to Atlanta in 1868).

A more extensive controversy ensued over the basis of representation in the legislature. The Constitution of 1789, it will be recalled, named the eleven counties then existing and specified the number of representatives for each. By 1795 the number of counties had increased to twenty, partly through laying out counties from new territory and partly through divisions of the older counties. The constitutional convention meeting that year carried out a reapportionment of representation, fixing the total membership of the house at fifty-one and designating the representation of each county. The Constitution of 1798 provided for the apportionment of from one to four representatives among the counties according to population, using the federal-ratio of three-fifths in counting Negroes. The rapid increase in the number of counties—49 by 1820, 78 by 1830, and 92 by 1840—soon resulted in a large and expensive legislature. There was dissatisfaction with the equal representation of the counties in the Sen-

---
[18] Coulter, *Short History of Georgia*, 163.

ate from the beginning, and by 1821 the General Assembly was sufficiently impressed by the need for a general revision of the basis of representation to submit to a referendum the question of calling a constitutional convention. But the people voted 18,569 to 5,080 against a convention.[19]

Finally, after twelve more years of continuous agitation for reform, a constitutional convention assembled in the House of Representatives at Milledgeville, May 6 to 15, 1833—a time at which there was still much controversy over the issue of the nullification of Federal tariffs. A note of discord pervaded the gathering from the beginning. Several delegates did not meet the qualification of seven years' residence in the State, as prescribed by the legislative Act calling the Convention, and by a vote of 132 to 102 the Convention refused to seat them. Many delegates thought the legislature had exceeded its authority both in prescribing this residence qualification and in limiting the purposes of the Convention by an oath of its members "not to change, or attempt to change or alter any other section, clause or article of the constitution other than those touching the representation of the General Assembly." [20]

James M. Wayne, a delegate from Chatham County, was elected President and empowered to appoint a committee consisting of three members from each of the State's nine judicial circuits "to report some plan" to the Convention. The plan submitted and finally approved provided for a reduction of the membership in the General Assembly by almost half, but it did little toward equalizing representation. The Senate was to be com-

---

[19] Roberts, *loc. cit.*, 100–102.
[20] *Journal of a General Convention of the State of Georgia to Reduce the Membership of the General Assembly . . . held at Milledgeville . . . in May, 1833* (Milledgeville, 1833).

## The Constitution of 1798

posed of forty-five members elected from districts composed of two counties, as named in the plan, without regard to population. If a new county were created, it should be attached to some contiguous senatorial district, thus preventing any increase above forty-five in the number of Senators. The House of Representatives was to consist of one hundred and forty-four members, apportioned as follows: to the fifteen counties having the largest number of free white persons according to a septennial census, three Representatives each; to the twenty-five next largest counties, two Representatives each; to the remaining forty-nine counties, one Representative each.[21] When a new county should be established, it would receive one Representative taken from those of the county with the smallest population among the fifteen having three Representatives, thus keeping the total membership at one hundred and forty-four.

The most interesting feature of this proposal was the abolition in Georgia, as had already been done in Alabama and Mississippi, of the federal-ratio of three-fifths in the enumeration of slaves for apportioning representatives. The "free whites" clause was adopted in the Convention by the narrow margin of one hundred twenty-six to one hundred twenty-two. The vote was strictly along sectional lines, but no longer was the sectional struggle between the coast and up-country. The counties along the Savannah River from Chatham to Elbert and inland for about one hundred miles, comprising the middle of the State where the slave population was largest, voted to retain the three-fifths clause, while the northern, western, and southern counties voted

---

[21] The principle of representation here proposed in Georgia for the first time was adopted in 1868 and is in effect today. It is the principle of representation not only for the General Assembly but also for the county unit system used in nominating the Governor and other State officials.

## A Constitutional History of Georgia

against it. The vote on the proposal for senatorial districts to be composed of two counties was 163 to 83, the opposition centering in the middle counties, but not being as strong as on the three-fifths issue. In Richmond, Baldwin, Jones, Liberty, Glynn, Camden, and other counties where the delegates had been divided on the three-fifths clause, the vote was decidedly for the new plan for the Senate.

The minority at the convention issued a protest against the proposed amendments, viewing with alarm a departure from the three-fifths ratio as "calculated to invite a change in our Federal relations." The majority, it was declared, has "resolved to propose to the people of Georgia an amendment which as to reduction falls short of what we think the public will require, without gaining anything on the score of equalization, but with an eye . . . to party ascendency." [22] A polemic brochure entitled *From Bad to Worse* branded as "palpably false" the assertion that the old system of representation put the poor man upon an equal footing with the rich man's slave. The poor man's vote counts as much as the rich man's vote, explained the writer, and to reduce the representation from a district would reduce the poor man's vote.[23]

The legislature in calling the Convention of 1833 had provided for submission of the amendments which it should propose to a referendum. Citizens of middle Georgia who had worked hardest for a reduction and reapportionment of representatives now worked hardest to defeat the proposed amendments, and in this they were successful. The people rejected the amendments by a

---

[22] *Journal of the Convention*, 45.
[23] Copy in the De Renne Collection. See also *Poor Richard to the Free Working Men of the Eastern District of Georgia* (Pole Hall, Sept. 20, 1833).

## The Constitution of 1798

majority of approximately five thousand votes.[24] Yet the need for reform continued.

By 1838 the number of counties had increased to ninety-two and the number of Representatives to two hundred and eight. In that year the legislature called another constitutional convention to meet in Milledgeville in May, 1839. The act of the legislature repeated the restrictions imposed on the Convention of 1833, and added the further provision that the Senate should be composed of forty-six members only, from senatorial districts made up of two contiguous counties, and that the "Federal basis" in apportioning representatives in the General Assembly should not be disturbed.

The procedure in this second convention was similar to that of the first. James M. Wayne was again elected President, and another committee of three members from each of the judicial districts (then numbering ten) was appointed to prepare a plan of representation. The plan proposed, and with minor changes adopted by the Convention, provided for forty-six senatorial districts composed of two counties each (except for the forty-sixth, which included three counties), as designated, with one Senator from each. In the House of Representatives each county was to have one member; counties with a population of 6,000 (counting three-fifths of the slaves), two members; and counties with a population of 12,000, three members. A somewhat ambiguous clause provided that the legislature should fix the number of Representatives under this scheme according to the last census, and the number of Representatives thus determined should not be increased "except when a new county is created; and it shall be the duty of the legislature, at that session, to be holden next after the enumeration provided for by law, so to regulate the ratio of representatives, as to

---

[24] Roberts, *loc. cit.,* 117.

## A Constitutional History of Georgia

prevent such increase."[25] No less than twenty substitute plans were submitted to the Convention, among them one by Alexander H. Stephens according to which each county would be given one member only in the House of Representatives, but this member would be given one vote for every thousand "representative population" in his county.

The Whig leaders were again dissatisfied with the amendments proposed, and condemned them as the corrupt handiwork of Union Democrats. When submitted to the people, the proposed changes were rejected by a vote of almost two to one.

The convention method having twice failed, the General Assembly, under the leadership of Governor McDonald, passed an amendment in 1842 and 1843 dividing the State into forty-seven senatorial districts, each composed of two contiguous counties, with one Senator from each, and fixing the total membership of the House at one hundred and thirty, every county to have one Representative, the thirty-seven largest counties, two Representatives, and no county more than two. This fixed number of Representatives and fixed ratio could not both be maintained if new counties were admitted, so an amendment effective in 1851 dropped the fixed number. The following year the senatorial districts were abolished and each county again given one Senator.[26]

Thirty-nine new counties were created from 1850 to 1858, with the result that the legislature again approached the unwieldy size it had reached in 1843. Governor Joseph E. Brown pointed out the need of reform in 1859, but no further action was taken before the Civil War.

---

[25] *Journal of the Convention to Reduce and Equalize the Representation of the General Assembly . . . Assembled in Milledgeville . . . 1839* (Milledgeville, 1839), 20.

[26] McElreath, *op. cit.*, 105.

*The Constitution of 1798*

## The Executive

ONLY three amendments were made in Article II of the Constitution of 1798. The first of these, that of 1818, dealt with succession to the executive office. The original provision was that succession should pass to the President of the Senate until the legislature should fill the vacancy. The amendment simply provided that in case of the death, resignation, or disability of both the Governor and the President of the Senate, the Speaker of the House should temporarily exercise the executive power. The second amendment, of 1824, one of the two most important changes ever made in the Constitution of 1798, provided for popular election of the Governor. As early as 1810 the House of Representatives had voted forty to twenty-five in favor of an amendment providing for the election of the Governor by popular vote, but this was short of the two-thirds vote for amendments required by the Constitution.[27] The need for the proposed amendment was stated forcefully in an editorial in the Savannah *Georgia Journal* on September 30, 1822:

> "The violence of the contest for seats in the legislature, whenever a Governor is to be elected, is to be deprecated. In the midst of it the great interests of the State are lost sight of; and in many instances, men are elected on no other account than because they will vote for some particular individual as Governor. This will continue to be the case as long as this officer is elected by the Legislature. Give his election to the people, and let us have a Legislature elected on account of their qualifications to discharge their duties as law makers. We have always been in favor of this change in the Constitution, and are so still." [28]

[27] The (Savannah) *Georgia Journal*, December 5, 1810.
[28] See also the issues of the same newspaper for October 14, 1822 and November 18, 1823, and the *Augusta Chronicle*, January 17, 1824.

## A Constitutional History of Georgia

The amendment finally received the necessary vote of the legislature in 1823, and, as required to make it effective, again in 1824. A majority of the popular votes cast was made necessary for election, and in case no candidate received a majority the General Assembly was to choose a Governor from the two persons having the highest number of votes. The third and last amendment to Article II, adopted in 1847, dropped all property qualifications from the office of Governor. Under the original Constitution a candidate for Governor was required to own five hundred acres of land in the State, other property to the amount of four thousand dollars, and an estate over and above this amount adequate to discharge his debts.

In the period before 1825 when the Governor was elected by the General Assembly, he was inaugurated within a few days after his election. After the constitutional change providing for popular election, he was inaugurated when the Assembly met early in November following his election in October. Due more to their personalities than to the constitutional structure, the Governors exercised great influence upon legislation.

Because of the short term of two years, a total of twenty men occupied the position of chief executive of Georgia during the sixty-three years that the Constitution of 1798 was in operation. Six of these men were born in Georgia, six in Virginia, two in North Carolina, two in South Carolina, one in Pennsylvania, one in Maryland, one in Scotland, and one in England. Only two Governors (David B. Mitchell and George R. Gilmer) had the honor of returning to the office of chief executive after having left it (Jared Irwin and George Mathews had served as Governors under earlier Constitutions), but nine Governors (John Milledge, Jared Irwin, John Clark, George M. Troup, Wilson Lumpkin, Charles J. McDonald, George

## The Constitution of 1798

W. Crawford, Herschel V. Johnson, and Joseph E. Brown) were reëlected for a second consecutive term. The youngest Governors (Josiah Tattnall, Howell Cobb, and Joseph E. Brown) were thirty-six years of age when inaugurated; the oldest (William Schley) was forty-nine.[29] The average age of the Governors was forty-three.[30] Georgia at this period was a land of opportunity, and her Governors were as a rule self-made men. With the exception of John Clark, all of them had had legislative experience, either in the General Assembly of Georgia or in Congress, or, as was true in most cases, in both. Almost all of them had studied law; four (Peter Early, George M. Troup, John Forsyth, and George W. Crawford) were graduates of Princeton, two (Howell Cobb and Herschel V. Johnson) were graduates of the University of Georgia, one (Joseph E. Brown) a graduate of Yale, and one (Charles J. McDonald) a graduate of South Carolina College. Among the more prominent of the Governors were James Jackson, John Milledge, David B. Mitchell, John Clark, George M. Troup, John Forsyth, George R. Gilmer, Wilson Lumpkin, William Schley, Howell Cobb, Herschel V. Johnson, and Joseph E. Brown.

## The Judiciary

THE weakness of the judicial structure as provided in the Constitution of 1798 is apparent from a casual reading of Article III. Further evidence of this weakness is found in the fact that ten of the twenty-three amendments to the Constitution related to the judiciary. Moreover, the

---

[29] Matthew Talbot was fifty-three when, upon the death of Governor Rabun in 1819, he, as President of the Senate, became Governor for a period of one month.

[30] The age of David Emanuel is not known.

Judiciary Act of 1799, the basic judicial act of the ante bellum period, was amended at almost every session of the General Assembly. It is difficult today to reconstruct a clear picture of Georgia's complicated judiciary of the early nineteenth century. One is led to doubt if even the contemporaries had too clear a view of their system of courts; certainly members of the legal profession held it in low esteem. A brief historical review of the judiciary from the beginning of statehood proves helpful in studying the system under the Constitution of 1798.

The Constitution of 1777 set up a Superior Court of final jurisdiction for each county, but some uniformity in the interpretation of the law was provided temporarily by the practice of appointing one Chief Justice for the whole State, and setting dates for terms of the Superior Courts in the several counties at such intervals as would permit the Chief Justice to ride circuit and attend all courts. The colonial practice of having the Governor and Council serve as a court of appeals appears also to have been continued temporarily, although there was no constitutional authority for this.[31] The Chief Justice was named annually by the Assembly, and the associate justices for each county were appointed by the Assembly and held office at its pleasure. There were also justices of the peace in each captain's district for minor cases.

In addition to their judicial functions, the Superior Courts of this period also exercised extensive administrative functions. An act of 1786 gave them supervision of roads, ferries, and bridges, and a year later they were empowered to appoint commissioners of courthouses and jails.[32]

The Constitution of 1789 contained very few provi-

---

[31] *Georgia State Gazette,* July 28 and Dec. 1, 1787, Apr. 26 and Oct. 4, 1788.
[32] Watkins' *Digest,* 346-47, 375.

*The Constitution of 1798*

sions pertaining to the judiciary. It simply provided that a Superior Court should be held in each county twice a year, with jurisdiction over all cases, civil and criminal, except such as might by law be referred to "inferior jurisdiction." The Judiciary Act of December 23, 1789, made specific provisions for the Superior Courts and established an inferior court for each county and two justices of the peace for each captain's district. From year to year new acts were passed affecting the judiciary, but the court structure established in 1789 remained substantially the same for the next half century. The office of Chief Justice provided for under the Constitution of 1777 gave way to two judges, elected by the General Assembly for a term of three years. The State was divided into two judicial districts, the Eastern District, composed of the Counties from Burke to Camden (the Coastal Region), and the Western District, composed of the remaining counties. One of the Superior Court judges should hold court in each county in the State at least twice a year, dates for court sessions in the counties being so arranged as to permit the judges to ride circuit. There was no appeal from a decision by a Superior Court, except for a new trial in the same court. The law provided for a retrial under certain conditions by a jury designated as special, because, although a trial jury, its twelve members should be drawn from the grand jury list.[33] An act of 1797 divided the State into three circuits and increased the number of Superior Court judges to three, with the provision that they should rotate in the three circuits, called the Eastern Circuit (Camden, Glynn, McIntosh, Liberty, Bryan, Chatham, Effingham, and Bulloch Counties), the Middle Circuit (Screven, Burke, Montgomery, Washington, Warren, Richmond, Columbia, and Jefferson Counties) and the Western Circuit

---
[33] Watkins' *Digest*, 389 ff.

## A Constitutional History of Georgia

(Greene, Jackson, Franklin, Hancock, Olgethorpe, Elbert, Wilkes, and Lincoln Counties.) [34]

The Inferior Courts, provided for each county by the Act of 1789, were to be held by the first five justices named by the General Assembly in the commission of the peace for the county, any three of them to constitute a quorum. The Act provided that the Inferior Courts should meet every three months, but this provision was changed in 1791 to meetings twice a year. The Inferior Courts were given jurisdiction in all cases at common law, except those affecting land titles, but with the right of the defendant in any case involving more than £50 sterling to remove his case to the Superior Court.[35] The Act of 1789 made it the duty of the Inferior Courts to make provision for the care of the poor in their respective counties. For this purpose they were authorized to levy a tax equal to one-fifteenth of the general property tax. Subsequent legislation required them to levy a further tax sufficient to pay the fees of sheriffs and jailers not provided for otherwise.[36] In addition to supervising the care of the poor, the Inferior Courts exercised other executive functions, including the appointment of tax receivers and the issuance of licenses for taverns, liquor stores, and billiard tables.[37] Judges of the Inferior Court were authorized to appoint two constables for each captain's district for a term of one year to serve processes of the court.

Courts of Conscience, held by justices of the peace in each community, dated from the Trustee Period, and had always handled the bulk of minor cases. The Constitution of 1777 extended the jurisdiction of the Courts of Conscience to cases amounting to as much as ten pounds. The

---

[34] *Ibid.*, 619.
[35] *Ibid.*, 396. This right of removal was omitted in the Judiciary Act of 1797.
[36] *Ibid.*, 602.
[37] (Savannah) *Georgia Gazette*, May 25 and July 19, 1798.

*The Constitution of 1798*

judiciary acts passed during the operation of this Constitution provided that these courts should proceed in "the old and usual manner." An Act of February 13, 1786, provided that the senior justice in each county should call a conference of justices annually to make provision for the care of the poor, and empowered the justices to levy a tax of six pence per hundred pounds of taxable property for this purpose. These courts were continued under the Judiciary Act of 1789, but as explained above, care of the poor was then vested in the Inferior Courts. The number of justices of the peace was not limited under the Constitutions of 1777 and 1789, and there were complaints that the legislature appointed too many for some counties.[88]

In providing for Superior Courts with original jurisdiction in all criminal cases and in cases involving land titles, and appellate jurisdiction in other cases, for Inferior Courts with jurisdiction in civil cases other than those involving land titles, and for justice courts with jurisdiction in civil cases involving not more than thirty dollars, it is apparent that Article III of the Constitution of 1798 was largely a continuation of the judicial structure that had evolved during the past two decades.

The Judiciary Act of 1799 gave the Superior Courts concurrent jurisdiction with the Inferior Courts in all civil cases.[89] Constitutional amendments of 1811 and 1818 redefined the jurisdiction of the Superior and Inferior Courts. By the original provisions of the Constitution of 1798, the Superior Courts had exclusive and final jurisdiction of all criminal cases. In 1811 exception to this was made in cases relating to persons of color, neglect of duty, contempt of court, violation of road laws, and obstruction to water courses, any of which cases could be

---
[88] *Augusta Chronicle*, Sept. 26, 1795.
[89] Watkins' *Digest*, 689.

## A Constitutional History of Georgia

vested in such courts as the legislature might provide. To this list of exceptions the amendment of 1818 added "all other minor offenses committed by free white persons, and which do not subject the offender or offenders to loss of life, limb, or member, or to confinement in the penitentiary." These minor offenses were to be tried in "corporation courts" in incorporated seaports.

The objective of four other amendments to Article III was the extension of the election of judges or other court officials to the people. The first amendment to the Constitution, that of 1808, provided for election by the people of clerks of both the Superior and Inferior Courts. Under the original Constitution the legislature selected the justices of the Inferior Courts and they named two justices of the peace for each captain's district. Amendments of 1812 and 1819 extended to the people the election of both the judges of the Inferior Courts and justices of the peace, and in 1855 popular election was extended to the State's Attorney and to the Solicitors.[40]

Election by the people was also a feature of the amendment of 1851 creating a Court of Ordinary, or Register of Probates, for each county. The Ordinary was to be elected for a four-year term. In addition to registering wills and granting letters of administration, he was also empowered to issue marriage licenses. Under the Constitution of 1777 the functions of a Court of Ordinary had been vested in a Register of Probates appointed by the Assembly for each county.[41] From 1789 to 1851 the probation of wills had been vested in the Inferior Courts.

Since early in the Nineteenth Century some incorporated cities had corporation courts for the trial of relatively minor offenses. These courts were recognized for

---
[40] The solicitor general of the circuit which embraced the seat of government was *ex officio* Attorney General of the State. *Code of 1860*, 79.
[41] *Revolutionary Records of Georgia*, III, 53.

## The Constitution of 1798

incorporated seaports by the amendment of 1818 defining the jurisdiction of the courts of State, and an amendment of 1855 authorized the creation of corporation courts in any incorporated city.

Far more important than any of these minor changes was the constitutional amendment for a Supreme Court in 1835, and its final establishment ten years later.

## A Supreme Court Established

THE striking feature of the judiciary before 1845 was the trial of all cases in the county where the case arose with no provision for appeal to a court outside the county. The Constitution of 1798 stated that "all criminal cases . . . shall be tried in the county wherein the crime was committed and . . . all cases respecting titles to land . . . shall be tried in the county where the land lies . . . All other civil cases . . . shall be tried in the county wherein the defendant resides, except in cases of joint obligors, residing in different counties, which may be commenced in either county. . . ."[42] Several amendments to the Constitution and numerous judicial acts passed by the General Assembly during the next three decades give evidence of a settled policy of maintaining this practice of determining finally all cases in the county of their origin.[43]

An effort to lend a degree of uniformity to decisions of the several courts was found in the annual conference of judges. Section LIX of the Judiciary Act of 1799 provided that the judges of the Superior Courts, the Attorney General, and the Solicitors should convene annually at

---

[42] Article III, Sec. I.
[43] See, *e.g.*, the Amendment to Art. III adopted in 1811 and the Judiciary Act of December 19, 1823, in Oliver H. Prince, *A Digest of the Laws of the State of Georgia* (Athens, 1837), 455, 909.

## A Constitutional History of Georgia

the State capitol for the purpose of forming rules for the governance of the Superior Courts, "determining on such points of law as may be reserved for argument and may require a uniform decision, and for giving their opinions on such constitutional and legal points as may be referred for their consideration by the executive department." [44] Liberally construed, this act might have been used by the judges as statutory authority for a supreme court. But, "This attempt to create a statutory Supreme Court was strangled in its infancy by the repeal in 1801 of so much of the Judiciary Act as provided that the judges should, while in convention for the purpose of making rules, determine cases reserved for argument. The repealing act provided that, 'All points reserved for argument, and now awaiting a decision at the seat of government are hereby directed to be sent back to the respective counties from which they have been sent, to be there decided by the presiding judge.' " [45]

Nonetheless, the judges used their annual conference as best they could to give uniformity to their decisions, and were inclined toward making it something of a supreme court by deciding there doubtful points involved in cases pending in their respective courts. Legislative opposition to a decision of the conference of judges in 1815 declaring unconstitutional certain laws recently enacted for the alleviation of debtors (explained more fully below) led to a suspension of the judicial conferences, but an act of December 24, 1821, reëstablished the conferences and made it the duty of the judges to attend them.[46]

It is indeed unfortunate that so few records have been preserved of the decisions in the early Superior and Inferior Courts. Judge Orville A. Park provides us with an

---

[44] Watkins' *Digest*, 621.
[45] McElreath, *op. cit.*, 112.
[46] G. M. Dudley's *Reports*, vii.

## The Constitution of 1798

account of an amusing, though tragic, case tried in the Superior Court of Washington County in 1779. The defendant, John Mobley, was indicted for "high treason against the State, horse-stealing, hog-stealing, and other misdemeanors." The jury returned a verdict of not guilty, whereupon the prosecuting attorney moved that he be sent to Augusta for further trial! The Court denied this motion, but the next day granted a motion of the prosecuting attorney that the case be reheard, as the attorney had more evidence against Mobley. In the second trial Mobley was found guilty of treason and sentenced "to be hanged by the Neck till dead." [47]

Many proposals for a supreme court were introduced in the legislature before securing in 1834 and 1835 the required two-thirds vote adopting an amendment to the Constitution for this purpose. The hostility of Georgians to a supreme court has sometimes been attributed to their satisfaction with the method of granting new trials before special juries in local courts and to the unfortunate experience with the United States Supreme Court in the Chisholm Case and the cases relating to the Indian lands. A judge of the Superior Courts summarized the arguments advanced against a supreme court in 1823 as, first, the difficulty of the people in going to such a court; second, the delay incident to a court of appeals; and third,

---

[47] "The Military Record of the Georgia Bar," in the *Annual Report of the Georgia Bar Association, 1918* (Macon, 1918), 62.

A description of the courts of the period is given in the Preface to Thomas U. P. Charlton, *Report of Cases in the Superior Courts of the Eastern District of Georgia, 1805–1810* (New York: Stephens Gould & Son, 1824) and also in the Preface to Thomas U. P. Charlton, *Report of Cases in the Superior Courts of the Eastern District of Georgia (by Judges Berrien, T. U. P. Charlton, Wayne, Davies, Law, Nicoll, and Robert M. Charlton; and in the Middle Circuit, by Thomas U. P. Charlton), 1811–1837* (Savannah: Thomas Purse & Co., 1837). Considerable insight on the judiciary of the period is given in the following biographies: John Donald Wade, *Augustus Baldwin Longstreet* (New York, 1924); Alexander A. Lawrence, *James Moore Wayne, Southern Unionist* (Chapel Hill, 1943).

the expense of such a court.[48] The judges led the movement to establish a supreme court, and by 1835 the entire press of the State was backing the movement, which was not a party issue.[49] A constitutional amendment of 1835 provided for a Supreme Court to consist of three judges, elected by the legislature for such terms as it should prescribe. The Supreme Court should have no original jurisdiction, but should be a court for the correction of errors in the Superior Courts. The State was to be divided by the legislature into five judicial circuits, and the Supreme Court was to sit in each circuit at least once a year.

Despite the passage of the constitutional amendment, there was still much opposition to the creation of a Supreme Court and ten years elapsed before the General Assembly made provision for establishing the court. An act of 1841 provided for submission to popular vote the question of "court or no court." At the general election the next year, 13,813 voted for a Supreme Court and 19,904 voted "No." Governor McDonald insisted that this small vote in which not one-half of those who attended the polls cast their vote for or against the measure could not be taken as decisive evidence of the opinion of the people. Finally, on December 10, 1845, an act passed the legislature setting up the Court in accord with the constitutional amendment adopted a decade earlier.[50]

## Early History of the Supreme Court

THE constitutional amendment of 1835 authorizing the Supreme Court had been a compromise, and two of its

---

[48] (Savannah) *Georgia Journal*, December 9, 1823. See also the issue of August 19, 1823.
[49] *Augusta Chronicle*, March 24, 1824, and June 15, 1825; *Federal Union*, October 31, 1835.
[50] Bond Almand, "The Supreme Court of Georgia: An Account of Its Delayed Birth," *Georgia Bar Journal*, VI (November, 1943), 105.

## The Constitution of 1798

provisions hampered the efficiency of the Court until they were abolished in 1868. In the first place, the Supreme Court was to be a circuit court in that it was to "sit at least once a year . . . in each of five judicial districts," and, secondly, it was to "dispose of and finally determine . . . every case on the docket . . . at the first term after such writ of error was brought," a provision that necessitated dismissal of many cases before they could be adjudicated. The Act of 1845 divided the ten existing superior court circuits into five districts and designated nine cities at which the Supreme Court should sit at specified dates. "Assuming that the members of the court started each year to hear cases in Savannah and traveled all the circuits and ended in Milledgeville in November, they would have traveled more than 1,000 miles at their own expense. And of this travel, only about 300 miles would have been by railroad."[51]

In view of the widespread opposition to its establishment, it is fortunate that the Supreme Court started with three excellent judges: Lumpkin, Warner, and Nisbet. Joseph Henry Lumpkin (1799–1867) had studied at the University of Georgia and at Princeton, served in the General Assembly, and been a prominent attorney in Lexington and Athens for twenty years. Reëlected to the Supreme Court three times without opposition, he served as the first Presiding Justice, and as Chief Justice after the creation of that position in 1863.[52] Hiram Warner

---

[51] The cities were as follows: Savannah, Hawkinsville, Talbotton, Americus, Macon, Decatur, Cassville, Gainesville, and Milledgeville. *Georgia Bar Journal*, VI (February, 1944), 177–183. *The Code of 1863* provided that the Supreme Court should sit twice each year in each district. The places fixed by statute as seats for the Court were Savannah, Athens, Macon, Atlanta, and Milledgeville. *Georgia Bar Journal*, VI (May, 1944), 270.

[52] The *Code of 1863*, Sec. 206, provided that "the oldest Judge in commission is the Chief Justice . . . but without greater powers than his associates."

## A Constitutional History of Georgia

(1802–1881) was born in Massachusetts, but came to Georgia as a teacher at the age of seventeen. Having served in the General Assembly and as a Superior Court judge, he was elected to the Supreme Court without opposition. Eugenius A. Nisbet (1803–1871), a graduate of the University of Georgia and of Judge Gould's law school at Litchfield, Connecticut, a former member of the Georgia legislature and of Congress, and a prominent lawyer in Madison and Macon, was also elected to the Supreme Court without opposition.

The Supreme Court met for its first session on January 26, 1846, at Talbotton. During the first year it reversed the trial courts in forty-four cases and affirmed them in twenty-eight. Most of the cases before it during the period before the Civil War involved contracts, notes, property rights, construction of wills, transactions involving slaves, and relations between debtors and creditors.[53] The Judiciary Act of 1845 provided that when the judges were not unanimous in their opinion, they should deliver their opinions *seriatim*, but few dissenting opinions were written in the early years.[54]

## Judicial Review of Legislation

IN VIEW of the important practice of judicial review by federal courts and the position of this principle of judicial supremacy in the American constitutional system, one is naturally curious to know if the judges in Georgia in this early period set themselves up as guardians of the State Constitution and invalidated legislative acts. A study of the extant records reveals that in the period prior to

---

[53] *Georgia Bar Journal*, VI (May, 1944), 206.

[54] This requirement was repealed in 1858. "Thereafter, if the decision were not unanimous, the opinions were to be delivered *seriatim*, but they were not required to be written." *Georgia Bar Journal*, VI (May, 1944), 276.

## The Constitution of 1798

establishment of the Supreme Court in 1845 the courts in Georgia followed a practice closely akin to that followed by the United States Supreme Court since 1936, that is, a practice of judicial self-restraint, with deference to the opinion of the legislature that enables the courts to sustain laws of doubtful constitutionality. All doubtful questions, stated many decisions of the early Georgia courts, should be resolved in favor of the legislature. But the *dicta* of the court records leaves no doubt that the judges felt they had authority to invalidate legislative acts, even though they usually refrained from enforcing it. In invalidating a city ordinance of Savannah, Judge T. U. P. Charlton declared in 1809: "I will not sit here and suffer the constitution to be violated; no, not by the legislature, and certainly not by a small body of men, clothed with a *'little brief authority,'* and exercising a puny legislation upon matters of city policy." [55] In invalidating a soldiers' relief law in 1815 as violating the obligation of contract, Judge Harris of the Putnam County Superior Court gave a lengthy defense of the practice of judicial review, stating that the legislature of Georgia had "virtually given its assent to the existence of such power" in amending the Constitution to take care of the situation that arose when the courts declared void a legislative act giving inferior courts jurisdiction in a type of case placed exclusively under the jurisdiction of superior courts by the Constitution.[56]

---

[55] *State vs. Corporation of Savannah,* in Charlton's *Reports,* 235. See also *Grimball vs. Ross* (1808), in Charlton's *Reports,* 175; *Smith vs. Oliver* (1833), in Dudley's *Reports,* 190; and *State vs. Tassels* (1830), in Dudley's *Reports,* 230.

[56] The reference is to the amendment of 1811 empowering the General Assembly to vest jurisdiction in certain designated cases, formerly exclusively under jurisdiction of the Superior Courts, in such courts as the General Assembly might provide. (Savannah) *Georgia Journal,* April 19, 1815. This newspaper supported the position of the judiciary at this period. See the issue of March 15, 1815 and August 19, 1823.

## A Constitutional History of Georgia

The notable example of the exercise of judicial review in Georgia during this period is found in the gratuitous opinion rendered by a conference of Superior Court judges held at Augusta in January, 1815, declaring two alleviating laws unconstitutional. In November, 1812, the General Assembly passed one act to alleviate the condition of debtors, and in 1814 another affording temporary relief to soldiers while in the service. The first act made it unlawful for any civil officer whatever to issue any civil "precept or process" during the continuance of the act for the collection of a debt, but exempted from its operation, among others, the Planters Bank of the State of Georgia, the Bank of Augusta, landlords whose tenants refused to give possession after the expiration of their terms, the University, academies, and private schools. The period of this suspension of civil process was at first indefinite, but by an amendment of 1813, limited to December 25, 1814. The judges unanimously held the acts void as a violation of the contract clause of the Federal Constitution, "the fundamental principle which is inherent in every free constitution which requires that justice shall be administered equally to every denomination of citizen, without respect to persons," and the Constitution of Georgia. In a long opinion, citing precedents from both the United States Supreme Court and the courts of neighboring States, the judges showed conclusively that the Act impaired the obligation of contract by making it impossible to collect valid debts, and that it did not afford equal protection of the law to all citizens. "The privilege of resorting to the courts of justice for the redress of his violated rights is indeed the constitutional inalienable right of every free citizen of this republic," declared the opinion. "Its preservation is entrusted to the judicial department—and we will not shrink from the solemn duty which is committed to our charge." In holding void the relief to soldiers, the judges declared themselves "not insensible of the merits of our brethren in arms; our constitutional power will always be cheerfully exerted for their protection, who are engaged in protecting us. But this is an inequality forbidden by the Constitution; and we yield an unqualified obedience to its injunctions." [57]

The facts in this case are analogous to the Minnesota Mortgage Moratorium of 1933, sustained by the United States Supreme Court in *Home Building and Loan Association vs. Blaisdell.*[58] The people of Georgia in 1812 viewed "with deep concern the distressed situation of a number of the good people . . . unable to pay their just debts, owing to the fall of the staple commodity . . . as well as the confined and convulsed state of . . . public affairs, events which no human mind could foresee, and of course unknown to them at the time of their contracts." [59] The wisdom of the judges in invalidating the alleviating law is debatable. This action brought forth such opposition that it temporarily suspended the conference of judges. At the next session of the General Assembly, in November, 1815, the House passed a resolution denying the power of the judges to assembly in such conventions, and expressed hope that in the future this expression of public opinion would be obeyed. The Senate, on November 16, 1815, divided nineteen to nineteen, the presiding officer casting the deciding vote in the negative, on a resolution that a committee be appointed to prepare an address to the Governor for the purpose of removing from office John M. Berrien, Robert Walker, Young Gresham, and Stephen W. Harris, judges of the Superior Courts, "for usurping a power not given

---

[57] *Augusta Chronicle,* February 10 and 17, 1815.
[58] 290 U. S. 398.
[59] (Milledgeville) *Georgia Journal,* September 9, 1812.

them by the Constitution of this State, in declaring certain acts of the Legislature unconstitutional, at a convention held at Augusta on the 13th January, 1815, as well as subsequent Judicial proceedings."[60]

The case of *Hammond vs. Whitaker*[61] is a notable example of judicial restraint upon executive power. In 1822 Governor John Clark removed Abner Hammond from the office of Secretary of State and appointed Simon Whitaker in his place. The Governor charged that Hammond, who had been Secretary of State since 1811, was inefficient, "often . . . unable, for various causes, to sign his name," and that in leaving the seat of Government without notifying the Governor he had vacated his office. Judge Augustin S. Clayton of the Western Circuit Superior Court issued a *writ of mandamus* directing Whitaker to turn over the office of Secretary of State to Hammond, which court order was obeyed. At the next session of the General Assembly the House of Representatives appointed a committee to investigate the removal and subsequent reinstatement of Hammond. The report of the majority of this committee, composed of members of the Troup political party, found that Hammond had been improperly removed by Governor Clark, and stated that while it was true that Hammond had been sometimes unable to sign his name, he was aged, infirm, and often affected with rheumatism. He had been seen somewhat intoxicated on a number of instances, but never so in his office. A minority report vindicated the action of the Governor.[62] When the Clark party

---

[60] *Senate Journal, 1815,* p. 16.

[61] (Milledgeville) *Georgia Journal,* October 22, 1822.

[62] (Milledgeville) *Georgia Journal,* December 31, 1822. Taking notice of this case, the Grand Jury of Hancock County in its *Presentment* for the term of October, 1822, stated: "Whatever indignation we may have felt upon the removal of Col. Hammond from an office, to which he had been called by the representatives of a free people, by his fellow-servant of the same people, himself elected by their representatives, in the prompt

*The Constitution of 1798*

gained control of the legislature in 1825, Judge Clayton was not reëlected.

In the case of *Forsyth vs. Marbury* [63] decided in 1830, Judge Law declared invalid as conflicting with the contract clause of the United States Constitution a Georgia law of 1832 when applied retroactively. The law in question prohibited enforcement of a judgment by sale of real or personal estate which the defendant had sold to a third party without notice of such judgment if the third party had been in peaceable possession of the real estate for seven years and the personal estate for four years.[64]

But the actions of the judicial conference in 1815 and of Judge Law in 1830 were unusual. The typical action of the judges in this early period may be illustrated by their decisions upholding laws apparently in violation of the strict constitutional provision resulting from the Yazoo fraud to the effect that no law should pass containing any matter different from that expressed in its title. In the case of *Green vs. the Mayor of Savannah* [65] the court ruled that it was not necessary that the title of an act should particularize the several provisions and

---

restoration of that office by the proper arm of the government, we have much to solace us. A Governor has removed a Secretary of State, and appointed another in his station. The expelled officer appeals to the law for redress and restitution. No terrible throes shake the State to its centre. Blood does not copiously flow in civil strife. The ardour of discussion and the zeal of investigation is all that announces a wrong to have been committed. Our constitution was known to have been formed in the spirit of salutary jealousy, and in the full light of experience.... The calm and steady look of the State towards the judiciary for the solemn and effectual adjustment of the contest has at length been satisfied by the quiet reinduction of Col. Hammond into his office; this is a memorable instance of the strength and beauty of our institutions. It proves that ours is not a paper constitution alone; but is armed with the living principles of its own preservation, and pregnant with blessings to us all." *Georgia Journal*, November 5, 1822.

[63] R. M. Charlton's *Reports*, 324 ff.
[64] *Ibid.*, 355.
[65] *Ibid.*, 368.

## A Constitutional History of Georgia

amendments contained in the body of the act. Later the courts ruled that if the title specified some of the provisions of an act and contained the inclusive phrase, "and for other purposes therein contained," portions of the act not specifically indicated in the title but related thereto were valid under this general clause.[66]

At the first session of the Supreme Court, held in 1846, an act of 1837 designed to "protect the citizens of Georgia against the unwarrantable and too prevalent use of deadly weapons" was declared void when applied to bearing arms openly as conflicting with the second amendment of the Constitution of the United States.[67] In subsequent years a large number of statutes were invalidated by the court.[68]

The Court won such popular favor that the legislature resolved in 1858 that "a decision of the Supreme Court . . . made by a full court, and in which all three of the judges . . . concur . . . shall be considered as the law of this state . . . as if the same had been enacted in terms by the General Assembly" [69]—a striking contrast to the action of the legislature in 1815 censuring the judges for usurping power. This unanimous decision act carrying the doctrine of *stare decisis* beyond the English concept of strict adherence to precedent and caution in reversals was confirmed by the section of the *Code of 1863* providing that "A decision concurred in by three Judges cannot be reversed or materially changed, except by a full bench, and then after argument had, in which the

---

[66] *Mayor of Savannah vs. The State*, 4 Georgia, 26; *Martin vs. Broach*, 6 Georgia, 21; *Howell vs. The State*, 71 Georgia, 224.

[67] *Nunn vs. The State*, 1 Kelly 250. This Georgia decision was not in accord with the interpretation of the United States Supreme Court.

[68] See *Tift vs. Griffin*, 5 Georgia, 185; *Young vs. Harrison*, 6 Georgia, 130; *Brewer vs. Bowman*, 9 Georgia, 37; *Parham vs. The Justices*, 9 Georgia, 361; and *Winter vs. Jones*, 10 Georgia, 190.

[69] *Georgia Laws*, 1858, 74. The Constitution of 1877 expressly authorized the courts to invalidate unconstitutional acts.

## The Constitution of 1798

decision by permission of the Court is expressly questioned and reviewed, and after such argument the Court in its decision shall state distinctly whether it affirms, reverses, or changes such decision." [70] This provision was continued in subsequent codes. Nonetheless, reversals of previous decisions by the Supreme Court of Georgia have not been infrequent.[71]

---

[70] Section 210.

[71] In *Ellison vs. Georgia Railroad and Banking Co.*, Chief Justice Bleckley declared that when a serious error in a previous case "competes with truth in the struggle for existence, the maxim for a Supreme Court, supreme in the majesty of duty as well as in the majesty of power, is no *Stare decisis* but *Fiat justicia ruat coelum.*" 87 Ga. 691, overruling *Martin vs. The Gainesville, J. & S. Railroad* (78 Ga. 307). Other illustrations of reversals of earlier decisions during the period after the Civil War are found in *Catts & Johnson vs. Hardee* (38 Ga. 350) overruling *Aycock vs. Martin* (37 Ga., 127); *Weems, Trustee, vs. Coker* (70 Ga. 746) overruling *Iverson vs. Saulsbury, Respess & Co.* (68 Ga. 790); *Brown vs. Moughon* (70 Ga. 756) overruling *Williams & Co. vs. Hart* (65 Ga. 201). For reversals in a later period, see *Railroad Commission vs. Palmer Hardware Co.* (124 Georgia 633) overruling *Gibson vs. Thornton* (99 Georgia 647); *Carr & Co. vs. Roney* (118 Georgia 634) overruling *Columbus Iron Works vs. Pou* (98 Georgia 516); *Josey vs. State* (148 Georgia 468) overruling *Rainey vs. State* (100 Georgia 82); *Wheatley vs. Glover* (125 Georgia 710) overruling *Chatham Bank vs. Brabston* (99 Georgia 801); and *Pitts vs. Maier* (115 Georgia 281) overruling *Pirkle vs. Equitable Mortgage Co.* (99 Georgia 524); *Byrd vs. Piha* (165 Ga. 397) overruling *Brandon vs. Pritchett* (126 Ga. 286); *Slaton vs. Hall* (168 Ga. 710) overruling a forty-three-year-old decision on conflict in law on common law.

CHAPTER IX

# Empire State Politics

DURING the first half of the nineteenth century Georgia progressed from the position of a frontier of the Union to that of "Empire State of the South." As indicated in a previous chapter, the population of Georgia was small during the colonial period, numbering only 50,000 at the time of the Revolution. The early inhabitants came from Europe and settled on the seacoast and along the navigable rivers. During the administration of the last Royal Governor immigrants began to come to Georgia from the colonies further north. Encouraged by the liberal land policy of Georgia, they came in increasingly large numbers after the Revolution and during the first part of the nineteenth century. These new settlers, though chiefly of English, Scottish, and Irish extractions, had already been Americanized before entering Georgia, having come by way of Virginia and North Carolina instead of through Savannah. They were principally engaged in growing tobacco under a system of culture that rapidly exhausted the fertility of the soil, thus necessitating migration. Barred by the Allegheny Mountains from westward expansion, these frontiersmen gradually moved into the Piedmont Region of the South, and soon turned to planting cotton. In 1796 the twenty-four counties that

*Empire State Politics*

had been laid out in Georgia stretched along the seaboard and up the Savannah River; by 1835 their number had increased to eighty-seven, embracing the entire area of the State.[1]

In 1800 the population of Georgia numbered but 162,686; by 1850 it had increased to 906,185, including 384,613 Negroes. Of the 521,572 whites, only 6,478 were foreign born.[2] The rapid increase in population was accompanied by spectacular economic progress.

A dramatic statement of Georgia's claim to the title of Empire State of the South was given by Alexander H. Stephens in a debate in the House of Representatives in 1854 with Representative L. D. Campbell, of Ohio, in which Stephens sought to prove that Georgia was wealthier and more prosperous than Ohio. He pointed out that

---

[1] Phillips, *Georgia and State Rights*, 87–88.

[2] The foreign born population in Georgia in 1900 was only 12,403. Bureau of the Census, *A Century of Population Growth in the United States, 1790–1900*, pp. 87, 128.

For information on the population, see *Georgia Facts in Figures* (University of Georgia Press, 1946), 17–44. The following table gives the population by decades. The difference between the total indicated and the sum of the figures under the headings Black and White for the decades after 1850 represents the number of persons of other races in Georgia. In 1940 this included 106 Indians, 326 Chinese, 31 Japanese, and 55 persons of other classifications.

| YEAR | TOTAL | WHITE | BLACK |
|---|---|---|---|
| 1800 | 162,686 | 102,261 | 60,425 |
| 1810 | 252,433 | 145,414 | 107,019 |
| 1820 | 340,985 | 189,566 | 151,419 |
| 1830 | 516,823 | 296,806 | 220,017 |
| 1840 | 691,392 | 407,695 | 283,697 |
| 1850 | 906,185 | 521,572 | 384,613 |
| 1860 | 1,057,286 | 591,550 | 465,698 |
| 1870 | 1,184,109 | 638,926 | 545,142 |
| 1880 | 1,542,180 | 816,906 | 725,133 |
| 1890 | 1,837,353 | 978,357 | 858,815 |
| 1900 | 2,216,331 | 1,181,294 | 1,034,813 |
| 1910 | 2,609,121 | 1,431,802 | 1,176,987 |
| 1920 | 2,895,824 | 1,689,114 | 1,206,365 |
| 1930 | 2,908,521 | 1,837,021 | 1,071,125 |
| 1940 | 3,123,723 | 2,038,278 | 1,084,927 |

## A Constitutional History of Georgia

by the Census of 1850 Georgia had thirteen colleges with 1,535 enrolled, this being one college student for every 339 of her white population. "In this particular," Stephens contended, "Georgia . . . is . . . ahead . . . of every State in the Union, and of any and every State or nation in the civilized world!" Her agricultural products, he continued, amounted to $38,414,168 in the year 1850. Chief among these were cotton and Indian corn, each exceeding $15,000,000, and wheat, oats, rice, peas, beans, sweet potatoes, and sugar cane. The annual product of her thirty-five cotton mills and three woolen mills was placed at $7,086,526. The State possessed 1,862 churches, of an average value of $679, and 553 miles of railroad, "all but one-twelfth paid for!" [3]

The economic leadership of Georgia was often conceded by her sister States in the decade before the Civil War. "Georgia will soon be a model state," observed the *Knoxville* (Tennessee) *Register*. "Because of her press, factories, and railroads, she is indisputably in advance of any other southern state in enterprise and success," remarked the *Raleigh* (North Carolina) *Star*. "Georgia makes more cotton and corn—has more railroads—more manufactures—more shipping (except perhaps for New Orleans)—pays less taxes—has more schools—has more diversified mineral wealth—is nearly ready to furnish her own citizens and those of sister states with flour to eat, clothes to wear, iron to work—she has a smaller public debt—a finer climate or climates (as she has them by assortment)— . . . than most (may we not say, than any) of her sister states of the South," boasted an enthusiast in *De Bow's Review*.

Similar praise was sometimes heard in the North.

---
[3] Alexander H. Stephens, *More of Georgia and Ohio* (Washington, 1855), 9-12.

## Empire State Politics

James M. Crane, of Virginia, speaking before the American Institute of New York, described Georgia as "the New England of the South, with $55,000,000 invested in railroads and manufacturing." Frederick L. Olmsted, the Yankee peripatetic, declared: "It is obvious to the traveler and notorious in the stock-market that there is more life, enterprise, skill and industry in Georgia than in any other of the Southern Commonwealths. It is the Yankee-Land of the South."[4]

In this ante bellum period of prosperity Georgia could well be proud of the prominence of her statesmen in national affairs: William H. Crawford was Secretary of the Treasury from 1816 to 1824, and almost reached the Presidency; John McPherson Berrien was Attorney General from 1820 to 1832, and perhaps the ablest constitutional lawyer in the Senate from 1841 to 1852; John Forsyth was Minister to Spain, 1819–22, and Secretary of State, 1834–41; Howell Cobb served as Speaker of the House of Representatives in 1849, and Secretary of the Treasury, 1857–60; James M. Wayne was a Justice of the Supreme Court, 1835–67; Herschel V. Johnson was nominated for Vice-President on the ticket with Stephen A. Douglas in 1860; Alexander H. Stephens, in the House of Representatives, 1843–59, and Robert Toombs, in the House, 1845–53, and in the Senate, 1853–61, were acknowledged national leaders.

Issues of national politics had much influence in shaping the course of political development within the State, but there were local issues as well, and during most of the ante bellum period political strength in Georgia was fairly evenly balanced between opposing political parties.

[4] Richard Harrison Shryock, *Georgia and the Union in 1850* (Durham, 1926), 27–29.

# A Constitutional History of Georgia

## Troup and Clark Parties

THERE had been no distinct organization of political parties in Georgia during the Colonial Period, but the events leading to the Revolution divided the people into two hostile groups known as Loyalists and Patriots, or as Whigs and Tories. Independence from British rule brought doom to the Loyalists who either left the State or changed their colors. The struggle over ratification of the Federal Constitution led to the organization of Federalist and Anti-Federalist parties in most of the States, but in Georgia where everyone felt keenly the need of protection against the Indians on the west and the Spaniards in Florida, there was no opposition to entering a stronger union of the States. But this did not mean that in the years to follow Georgia would be a one party State in the Federalist fold. The Republican Party, organized by Jefferson, a Southerner, appealed to frontiersmen everywhere. Influenced by the peculiar course of Indian affairs and the reaction to the Chisholm Case, the majority of the people of Georgia adopted the views of the Republican Party. Some of the Federalist leaders were prominently connected with the Yazoo Fraud, which tended to discredit them. Remnants of Federalism lingered in the State as late as the War of 1812, but the bulk of the people were always Republicans.[5] The electoral vote of Georgia was cast three times for Jefferson (1796, 1800, and 1804), twice for Madison, and twice for Monroe. As a general rule, in the period before the Civil War, as Georgia went, so went the Nation in presidential elections, the two exceptions being the elections of 1824 and 1836.

---

[5] Phillips, *Georgia and State Rights*, 90–93. Coulter, *Short History of Georgia*, 223–24.

## Empire State Politics

It is interesting to note the contradiction between the composition of the Republican Party in Georgia and in the nation as a whole. Whereas the Republican Party in general was made up of the democratic element in the nation, in Georgia it was composed largely of the aristocratic element. The first quarter of the nineteenth century was really a period of personal politics in Georgia, with political differences centering more around personalities than questions of policy, either national or local. The political leaders were usually men of great physical vigor. That the people liked fighters is evidenced by the many duels between prominent figures, such as the duel between William H. Crawford and John Clark, in 1806. It was James Jackson, "Prince of the Duelists," who organized the Republican Party in Georgia. He served as Governor from 1798 to 1801, and as United States Senator until his death in 1806. Among his strongest supporters were William Harris Crawford and George Michael Troup.

Crawford was a Virginian by birth, but came to Georgia in his boyhood. After some experience as a school teacher, he studied under Moses Waddell and entered the practice of law. In 1807 he was elected to the United States Senate, and entered upon a career that makes his biography belong more to the history of the United States than to Georgia. With Crawford in Washington, the mantle of leadership of the Jackson-Crawford-Troup party fell to Troup, and the party became known by his name.

Opposed to the Troup Party was the Clark Party, led by John Clark, and his brother Elijah, sons of General Elijah Clarke of Revolutionary fame. "Educated as much on the Indian warpath as in the log-cabin school, with more to fear from arrows and bullets than the schoolmaster's rod, and perfectly fearless of either," John Clark "developed into an adroit Indian fighter, carried his rough and ready principles into politics, and so became a politician of the extreme Andrew Jackson type."[6] Prominent among the supporters of the Clark Party were W. J. Hobby, owner of the *Augusta Chronicle* and brother-in-law of John Clark, Wilson Lumpkin, and Judge Murray Dooly. Vague issues did not prevent Georgians of this period from showing a lively interest in elections. With an apology to Pope, the (Savannah) *Georgia Journal* explained that, "Fire in each eye, and paper in each hand, they read and calculate throughout the land."[7]

Inasmuch as both the presidential electors and the Governor were chosen by the legislature prior to 1825, it is difficult to ascertain the relative strength of the two parties, or factions, as they might more properly be designated. "The slave owners, who constituted the well-to-do class in Georgia, were as a rule members of the Troup Party, and the poorer whites, who tended to be more numerous on the edge of settlements, were as a rule in the Clark Party."[8] The aristocratic element held an advantage in the election of prominent officers, such as Governor and representatives to Congress, since most of the better known men of the State lived in the eastern counties and were allied with the Troup Party. Commencement day at the State University in Athens was a favorite time for party caucuses to nominate candidates. Occasionally groups of trustees of the University acted as executive committees for the two parties.[9]

In 1824 Georgia cast her electoral vote for William H. Crawford, her own favorite son, who had received the nomination of the Congressional caucus; but a stroke of

---
[6] Phillips, *op. cit.*, 97.
[7] October 23, 1821.
[8] Phillips, *op. cit.*, 105.
[9] *Ibid.*, 125; E. Merton Coulter, *College Life in the Old South* (New York, 1928).

paralysis defeated his chance of election. No one of the four candidates for President received a majority vote that year, so the election passed to the House of Representatives, which chose John Quincy Adams. Near the end of his administration the Tariff of Abominations was passed. Georgia had favored a moderate protective tariff at an earlier period, but the burden upon an agricultural region resulting from the sale of raw materials on a world market and the purchase of manufactured goods on a protected domestic market was not long in making itself felt. In December, 1827, the Joint Committee of the General Assembly of Georgia on the State of the Republic made a lengthy report that was adopted for transmission to Congress as a protest against the protective tariff, asserting that the question of a protective tariff was not one of expediency, but one of constitutionality.[10]

## The Tariff Controversy

THE adoption of the Tariff of Abominations in 1828 with its excessively high rates called forth fiery denunciation throughout the South and resulted in the well-known nullification controversy. All groups in Georgia opposed the tariff, but there were many different views as to the proper remedy to be applied. Some advocated manufactures for the South; others called for united action by a convention of the Southern States; still others thought the State of Georgia should itself nullify the federal tariff law. Under the leadership of John M. Berrien and Judge A. S. Clayton, a resolution was adopted at a political rally in the University Chapel during commencement exercises in August, 1832, calling for a State convention on

---

[10] *Senate Journal, 1827;* U. S. House Doc. No. 120, 20th Congress, 1st Session, 9–10.

the subject of the tariff, to be held at Milledgeville the following November. Delegates to the convention should be chosen at the time of the regular election of members of the legislature in October, while in the meantime preliminary meetings were to be held in all counties. Most of the county meetings failed to declare for nullification, holding this too extreme a remedy. The convention assembled at Milledgeville on November 12th with one hundred and thirty-one delegates present, representing sixty counties. Disagreement on policy soon led to the withdrawal of John Forsyth and fifty other delegates. Vehement denunciations of the tariff were adopted, but it was not clear whether the resolutions by this extra-legal body went so far as to recommend nullification. Wilson Lumpkin, then Governor of the State, opposed nullification, and the legislature adopted resolutions against this radical doctrine. President Jackson was popular in Georgia and in the South generally, and South Carolina alone went so far as actually to nullify a federal law.[11]

## Removal of the Indians

THE people of Georgia were much more concerned at this period with the problem of getting rid of the Creek and Cherokee Indians than with the tariff controversy. By the terms of the settlement of 1802 whereby Georgia sold her western lands the United States agreed to remove the Indians, then occupying three-fourths of Georgia's remaining territory, as soon as this could be done peaceably. But the United States was slow in executing its promise, and Georgians, hungry for new land and seeing the Indians removed from other regions while remaining in Georgia, became impatient. George M. Troup, Governor from 1823 to 1827, pursued a militant course, accused the

---

[11] E. Merton Coulter, "The Nullification Movement in Georgia," *Georgia Historical Quarterly*, V (March, 1921), 3-39; Phillips, *op. cit.*, 123 ff.

United States of bad faith, became embroiled with Presidents Monroe and Adams, and threatened to make war if the United States interfered with his Indian policy. Finally, in 1827, the United States secured a treaty with the Creeks ceding the last vestige of their Georgia land.

But getting rid of the Creeks was a solution to only half the problem: the Cherokees still occupied the northwestern section of the State, and the United States seemed to be using more effort in civilizing these Indians than in inducing them to move west of the Mississippi. By 1827 the Cherokees had invented an alphabet, begun printing a newspaper, and framed a constitution. Acting upon the advice of Governor John Forsyth, in 1828 the Legislature of Georgia extended its laws to the Cherokee country, and two years later "forbade the Indians to play longer with their make-believe government." A number of interesting decisions from the Supreme Court of the United States followed, including *The Cherokee Nation vs. Georgia*,[12] and *Worcester vs. Georgia*.[13] In the latter case Chief Justice Marshall ruled the Georgia laws relating to the Cherokee territory null and void, but the Indians soon found Georgia stronger in this situation than the Court. Governor Wilson Lumpkin ignored Marshall's decision, and President Jackson refused to give the Court any support. Finally, in 1835, the Cherokees bowed to the inevitable and agreed to a treaty with the United States whereby they gave up the last of their Georgia lands in exchange for $5,000,000 and territory in the west.[14]

---

[12] 5 Peters 1.
[13] 6 Peters 515.
[14] Coulter, *Short History of Georgia*, Ch. XVII, *passim*. For a review by a State Rights Democrat of the cases involving controversy between Georgia and the Supreme Court of the United States, see the eighty-two page opinion by Justice H. L. Benning in *Padelford vs. Savannah*, 14 *Georgia Reports*, 438. A summary account is found in John W. Parks, "Historical Sketch of Georgia as Litigant in the Supreme Court of the United States." Ga. Bar Association's *Annual Report, 1896*, pp. 106–146.

# A Constitutional History of Georgia

## State Rights (Whig) and Union (Democratic) Parties

THE period of Adams and Jackson witnessed much shifting in the organization of political parties in Georgia and the substitution of new party names. Members of the Clark Party felt that even though the belligerent policy adopted by Governor Troup in dealing with the Indians had gained him the material part of his contention against President Adams, such radical action was not admissible as a policy. The tariff issue was another ground for political division. In general members of the Troup Party were for nullification, and the Clarkites were opposed to such extreme action. The way seemed opened for the substitution of measures for men as the chief consideration in party alignment. John Clark accepted an appointment from President Adams as Indian Agent and moved to Florida in 1827. The plan was suggested that the Clark Party change its name to the Union Party, and this appellation was gradually effected. The Troup leaders answered the challenge by avowing States' rights as their principle and using it as their slogan. The years 1829 to 1832 may be taken as rough limits for the period of transition from the Clark and Troup Parties to the State Rights and Union Parties.[15] The administration of Jackson was also a period of transformation in national party lines. The Republican Party divided into two branches: the Democrats, supporters of Jackson, and the National-Republicans, his opponents. By 1836 the opposition to "King Andrew" adopted the name Whig.

Georgia was almost solid in its support of Andrew Jackson in 1828 and again in 1832, thanks to his faithful discharge of the expectations of Georgians regarding the

---
[15] Phillips, *op. cit.*, 111–112.

Indian lands. Yet his sanction of the principle of a protective tariff, threat to coerce South Carolina in the nullification controversy, and high-handed methods in general bred opposition. "The common opposition of Clay and Calhoun and Berrien and Troup and Gilmer to Andrew Jackson led in time to a coalition of all of them against Jackson and his friends. The breach of the State Rights party with Jackson had become complete in July, 1834, when Mr. Troup in a semi-public letter denounced the administration as vicious and corrupt. A further lapse of time was necessary, however, before the force of common enmity to a foe could completely reconcile and combine the extreme anti-tariff men of the South with the champions of the American system elsewhere." [16]

In the election of 1836 the State Rights leaders in Georgia still claimed that their organization was a part of the true Democratic Party, but they were at complete loggerheads with Jackson and Van Buren. The Union Party supported Van Buren, but the State Rights leaders carried Georgia for Judge Hugh L. White of Tennessee. The Whigs did not nominate a national candidate, hoping that with various sections of the country supporting local favorites the election would be thrown into the House of Representatives, as had been the case in 1824.

As a whole the Whigs represented the aristocrats of the nation, and in this respect a union between the national Whig Party and the State Rights Party of Georgia was logical. This element agreed that executive tyranny should be checked. The Whigs in general thought this should be done by strengthening the powers of Congress; the State Rights group in Georgia concurred in this point of view, and added that much could be achieved through respecting the constitutional position of the States. Clay's American System of a protective tariff and internal

---
[16] Phillips, *op. cit.*, 138.

## A Constitutional History of Georgia

improvements was not popular in Georgia, but the Whigs never pressed these points forward in the South, and Georgia Whigs were willing to support a moderate protective tariff. The Whigs won the electoral vote of Georgia in 1840 and 1848; they lost the State in 1844 because of Clay's equivocal stand on the annexation of Texas. The political strength of the Georgia Whigs and Democrats was about equal in the decade of the 'forties. After the adoption of the district system for the election of representatives to Congress in 1844, the eight districts of the State were at first evenly divided between the two parties. In 1848 the Whigs permanently lost one of their districts, and in 1850 another; but the seventh and eighth districts, composed of the central counties of the State and extending eastward to the Savannah River, represented by Stephens and Toombs, remained Whig until the final overthrow of that party. The Democrats elected most of the Governors of the State, but the Whig opposition was always vigorous, and frequently controlled the legislature.[17]

---

[17] The close division in political strength between the political parties in ante bellum Georgia is illustrated by the vote in gubernatorial races. In *High Lights of a Decade, 1936-46*, a pamphlet published in 1946, Miss Ella May Thornton, State Librarian, gives the election statistics quoted below, compiled from the Legislative Journals. A similar summary is given in Stephen F. Miller's *Bench and Bar of Georgia* (Philadelphia, 1858), I, 267-68.

| 1825 | | 1827 | |
|---|---|---|---|
| Geo. M. Troup | 20,545 | John Forsyth | 22,220 |
| John Clark | 19,862 | Scattering | 9,072 |
| 1829 | | 1831 | |
| Geo. R. Gilmer | 12,316 | Wilson Lumpkin | 24,731 |
| Wm. H. Crawford | 6,798 | Geo. R. Gilmer | 23,428 |
| 1833 | | 1835 | |
| Wilson Lumpkin | 28,814 | William Schley | 31,122 |
| Joel Crawford | 27,379 | Chas. Dougherty | 28,520 |
| 1837 | | 1839 | |
| Geo. R. Gilmer | 34,179 | Chas. J. McDonald | 34,634 |
| William Schley | 33,417 | Chas. Dougherty | 32,807 |

## Empire State Politics

There were about forty newspapers in the State at this period, and their editors took a leading part in political affairs. Each town of any size had two journals, one Democratic and the other Whig. Circulation was small, most of the papers reaching but a few hundred readers. The *Savannah News,* a new venture in the cheap newspaper, was the only daily in the State whose patrons exceeded 1,000 in 1850. In the same year the weekly *Augusta Chronicle* (Whig) had by far the largest circulation of any paper in the State, about 5,400, save that of its own agricultural monthly, *The Soul of the People,* which reached about 8,000 subscribers.[18] Other than newspapers, the chief influences upon public thinking were discussions at county caucuses, district conventions, public barbecues, and courthouse gatherings. The even balance in the strength of the parties and subtlety of the issues involved added excitement to the campaigns. A tendency to vote independently in important elections was a characteristic of the democracy of the day, and there was much shifting of party allegiance.

The Whigs inclined more and more toward nationalism during the decade of the 'forties, and the Democrats in-

| 1841 | | 1843 | |
|---|---|---|---|
| Chas. J. McDonald | 37,847 | Geo. W. Crawford | 38,502 |
| W. C. Dawson | 33,703 | Mark A. Cooper | 35,061 |
| 1845 | | 1847 | |
| Geo. W. Crawford | 41,059 | Geo. W. Towns | 43,220 |
| H. M. McAllister | 39,140 | Duncan L. Clinch | 41,931 |
| 1849 | | 1851 | |
| Geo. W. Towns | 46,514 | Howell Cobb | 57,397 |
| Edward Y. Hill | 43,322 | Chas. J. McDonald | 38,824 |
| 1853 | | 1855 | |
| H. V. Johnson | 47,638 | H. V. Johnson | 53,478 |
| Chas. J. Jenkins | 47,128 | Garnett Andrews | 43,228 |
| 1857 | | B. H. Overby | 6,284 |
| Jos. E. Brown | 57,067 | 1859 | |
| Benj. H. Hill | 46,295 | Jos. E. Brown | 63,784 |
| | | Warren Akin | 41,830 |

[18] Shryock, *Georgia and the Union in 1850,* 117.

clined more towards particularism, with the result that by 1846 the old party names of State Rights (Whig) and Union (Democratic) had become misleading. The Calhoun Democrats, former members of the Whig Party who followed the lead of Calhoun in returning to the Democratic Party in 1840 after the nomination of Harrison, had a great influence in directing the Democratic Party toward localism.[19]

It is interesting to note that the political parties in Georgia continued during the ante bellum period to be affiliated with a national rather than a sectional party organization. Though frequently described as a separate socio-economic entity, the South never even approximated a political unity. The theories of John C. Calhoun were not typical. "Howell Cobb, Georgia's leading Democrat of the decade and a half before the Civil War, scored his greatest triumphs as an opponent of Calhoun's political theories." The Southern leaders realized that the aristocratic element which they represented constituted a minority of the population. "Thus it was that the Southern 'system' came to rest on a national political entente, composed of planters and non-planters. . . ."[20]

## Constitutional Union Party

THE territorial gains resulting from the Mexican War renewed in national politics the vexing problem of slavery in the territories and brought the tension between the North and South nearly to a breaking point; but cooperative action on the part of real statesmen produced the Compromise of 1850 and preserved the Union for another decade. This compromise met with widespread

---
[19] *Ibid.*, 93.
[20] Horace Montgomery, *Party Development in Georgia, 1846–1861.* Ph.D. dissertation at the University of Georgia, 1939.

*Empire State Politics*

opposition in Georgia until Cobb, Stephens, and Toombs came home from Congress in September and stumped the State in support of the measure. The Legislature had called a convention to determine what course the State should follow. Meeting at Milledgeville in December, 1850, it adopted by the surprising vote of 237 to 19 the now celebrated Georgia Platform. The substance of this document was that although not entirely content with the compromise recently adopted by Congress, Georgia was willing to remain in the Union under its provisions, but in case of the slightest further encroachment by the North, the attitude of Georgia would at once be reversed and disruption of the Union would probably ensue.[21] Professor Richard Harrison Shryock emphasizes the influence of economic factors causing Georgia to accept this compromise. The renowned prosperity of Georgia at this period was proof that progress could be made in the national union, despite northern tariffs and criticisms. Georgia's decision to accept the Compromise of 1850 was a cardinal factor in the preservation of the Union.[22]

The Convention of 1850 was the occasion of the forming of a new political party in Georgia. During the previous decade there had been much shifting of votes, with control of the State passing back and forth between the Whig and Democratic Parties. George M. Troup continued to be the prophet and honored advisor of the local Whigs and Wilson Lumpkin the leader of the Democrats. Howell Cobb had formerly belonged to the Democratic Party, but at a caucus during the Convention of 1850 joined forces with Stephens and Toombs, both Whig leaders, in forming a new Constitutional Union Party.[23] Practically all Georgians agreed that the rights of

---

[21] *Journal of the Convention of 1850*, pp. 19-23.
[22] *Georgia and the Union in 1850*, pp. 5-8.
[23] Phillips, *op. cit.*, 166.

the South had been encroached upon by the Compromise; the point of difference was upon the advisability of resistance. The Constitutional Unionists appealed to all friends of the Union to support the Compromise under the doctrine of the Georgia Platform. Charles J. Jenkins of Augusta, J. B. Lamar of Macon, H. R. Jackson of Savannah, Hopkins Holsey of Athens, and many other prominent men joined the Cobb-Toombs-Stephens triumvirate in backing the Compromise. Those who felt that the Compromise involved too much sacrifice and that the South should hold out for greater concessions rallied under the name State Rights Party. Leaders in this group were Herschel V. Johnson, C. B. Strong, Charles J. McDonald, H. L. Benning, and Joseph E. Brown. They considered the issue as one of resistance or submission, not union or disunion. Recalling the early means of resistance to Britain's obnoxious measures of taxation in the period before the Revolution, they suggested non-intercourse or discrimination in trade as suitable means of resistance.[24]

## Ascendancy of the Democratic Party

THE Constitutional Union Party elected Howell Cobb as Governor in 1851 by a large majority, and for several years thereafter Georgia was strongly in favor of maintaining the Union; but as there was no special need of a party with such a platform, a tendency set in toward the former arrangement of parties. In an address to the people issued on August 10, 1852, the Executive Committee of the Constitutional Union Party declared that the Party had accomplished its purpose, and was thereby disbanded.

---

[24] Montgomery, *Party Development in Georgia, 1846–1860*, p. 50.

*Empire State Politics*

The party of Toombs and Stephens, largely the former Whig Party, thereafter called itself the Union Party, and the opposition soon resurrected the name Democratic Party. The Constitutional Union Party had been formed to meet an emergency and in this it had succeeded. The vote in the Presidential election of 1852 was divided between four candidates in Georgia, but Franklin Pierce, the Democratic candidate, received by far the largest popular vote, and consequently the electoral vote of the State.

The Whig Party had never had any platform other than opposition to Jacksonian methods upon which members of the Party in all sections of the country could agree. The Wilmot Proviso and Compromise of 1850 dealt the Party a telling blow, and the Kansas-Nebraska struggle of 1854 split it asunder. The following year Toombs finally left the Party and entered the ranks of the Democrats, and Stephens followed his example.[25] The logical development would have been for the whole of Georgia to have combined in one organization following the renewal in 1854 of the struggle over the extension of slavery in the territories. That this did not actually occur was due in part to the fundamental classification of the people upon economic and social lines and to personal antagonisms. With the passing of the Constitutional Union Party, many of the former Georgia Whigs entered the newly formed American, or Know-Nothing Party, with Benjamin H. Hill and Eugenius A. Nisbet as leaders. There was no real fear of the influence of foreigners in Georgia, but the former Georgia Whigs wanted an alliance with some national party. The old Whig Party degenerated into a mere opposition element, adopting in-

---

[25] Ulrich Bonnell Phillips, *The Life of Robert Toombs*, (New York, 1913), 169.

consistent positions from time to time as the best chances of victory seemed to advise.[26] Yet Whig inertia lived long after that Party's national organization had fallen apart. An important agency in keeping alive the spirit of partisan conflict in Georgia was the "county officer" influence. "In each county . . . the local party organization was kept in training by the county elections, which, if won, paid attractive dividends in the form of county offices, legislature seats and a modicum of patronage."[27]

In the presidential campaign of 1856 most of the political leaders in Georgia, including such prominent ex-Whig-Constitutional, Union-Know-Nothing leaders as E. A. Nisbet, C. J. Jenkins, and F. H. Cone, and the veterans Troup and Lumpkin, who wrote public letters from their retirement, supported James Buchanan, the Democratic candidate, thus assuring him an easy victory. In 1860 a remnant of the old Whig Party, acting under the name of the Constitutional Union Party, still existed in Georgia, but the Democratic Party clearly controlled the State. Hope of maintaining the union of the States rested upon the ability of the Democratic Party to continue its control of the National Government.

## The Election of 1860

IN VIEW of the intensity of the sectional differences over slavery, it is not surprising that the presidential election of 1860 resulted in a cleavage of the one remaining national party. Stephen A. Douglas, an advocate of popular sovereignty in the territories, and popular in the Northwest, was the strongest candidate in the Democratic Party, but he was not acceptable to the Southern leaders

---

[26] Phillips, *Georgia and State Rights*, 170.
[27] Montgomery, *Party Development in Georgia, 1846–1860*, p. 287.

who demanded a positive guarantee of slavery, and refused to compromise on a moderate platform.

The Democratic members of the General Assembly of Georgia held a caucus during the session of the legislature in December, 1859, at which delegates to the Democratic National Convention were selected and Howell Cobb was endorsed as a candidate for President.[28] The State Democratic Executive Committee protested the authenticity of this action, and issued a call for a convention to meet in Milledgeville the following March. The press of the State was divided over the wisdom of holding a convention. Cobb demonstrated his interest in the public welfare by urging delegates to attend the March convention. "If the people were for him it would be a plain and simple duty to affirm and approve the action of the December Convention; if they were against him, then they could adopt a new platform and select new delegates." [29] On March 14th two hundred and three delegates representing ninety of the one hundred thirty-two counties of the State assembled at Milledgeville in the hall of the House of Representatives. This Convention passed a resolution stating that only the Executive Committee of the Party could call a convention and named delegates to the National Convention, largely the same delegates that had been named in December. Many members of the March Convention supported Alexander H. Stephens for President, so the resolution of the legislative caucus endorsing Cobb was not reaffirmed.

The Democratic National Convention meeting at Charleston in April, 1860, seated the delegates from Georgia named by both the December caucus and the March convention. A division of the Charleston Conven-

---
[28] *The Federal Union*, Dec. 20, 1859.
[29] Jack N. Averitt, *The Election of 1860 in Georgia*. M.A. Thesis, the University of Georgia, 1945, p. 40.

tion over the platform to be adopted led the delegates of several Southern States, including a majority of those from Georgia, to withdraw and thus break up the Convention. Another convention was held in Georgia on June 4th, attended by three hundred and four delegates representing one hundred and five counties. This convention appointed twenty of the former delegates to Charleston to attend the Baltimore Convention called by the rump of the Charleston Convention. Another convention of the same month in Georgia also named delegates to attend the Baltimore Convention, and in the event of failure of the Party to act harmoniously there, to proceed to the convention called by the bolters of the Charleston Convention to meet in Richmond. At the Baltimore Convention, only one of the delegations from Georgia was seated, and it soon withdrew in protest over the refusal of the Convention to seat the delegation from Alabama.

The Baltimore Convention nominated Stephen A. Douglas for President and Herschel V. Johnson for Vice-President. The Richmond Convention nominated John C. Breckenridge of Kentucky and Joseph Lane of Oregon on a platform demanding federal protection of slavery in the territories. During the interval between the adjournment of the Charleston Convention and the assembling of the one at Baltimore, a coalition of remnants of the Whig and Know-Nothing parties, adopting the name Constitutional Union Party, met in convention at Baltimore and nominated John Bell of Tennessee and Edward Everett of Massachusetts. This new party evaded the issue of the campaign by enunciating the profound doctrine that it was the part of patriotism to recognize "no political principle other than the Constitution of the country, the Union of the States, and the enforcement of the laws!"

*Empire State Politics*

With Alexander H. Stephens and Herschel V. Johnson supporting Douglas; Howell Cobb and Joseph E. Brown supporting Breckenridge; and Benjamin H. Hill supporting Bell, three conventions were held in Georgia in August to select candidates for the electoral college. Douglas spoke in Atlanta on October 30th, only to lose many votes by his assertion that there was no right of secession under the Constitution. In the presidential election the popular vote in Georgia was: Breckenridge, 51,893; Bell, 42,855; Douglas, 11,580. No candidate having a majority, the selection of electors passed to the General Assembly, which named the Breckenridge group. With the opposition throughout the nation hopelessly divided between three candidates, the Republican Party, a sectional party first organized in 1854 upon a platform of uncompromising hostility to the extension of slavery, was able to elect its candidate, Abraham Lincoln.

## Summary

IN RETROSPECT, the principal facts in the history of political parties in Georgia during the ante bellum period are as follows: James Jackson, famed for his opposition to the Yazoo Land Act of 1795, formed at the opening of the nineteenth century a strong political organization backed by the conservative element within the State. This local faction allied itself with the national party of Thomas Jefferson. Notable among Jackson's supporters were William H. Crawford and George Michael Troup. Jackson died in 1806, and Crawford soon entered upon a national career, leaving Troup as the head of the local organization which gradually became known as the Troup Party. Its membership included most of the large slave owners and prominent men, and it usually controlled the public offices of the State during the first quarter of the Century. Among its supporters were: Thomas U. P. Charlton, Jesse Mercer, John Milledge, William Rabun, and John Forsyth. An opposition party developed, known by the name of its leader, John Clark, and supported by W. J. Hobby, Murray Dooly, and Wilson Lumpkin. The two parties were differentiated more on economic and social grounds than any other, the aristocrats tending to be in the Troup Party. Personalities rather than principles decided most elections.

The division of the Jeffersonian-Republican Party into two wings during the period of Andrew Jackson was paralleled in Georgia by the rise of a State Rights and a Union Party, the former largely a continuation of the Troup Party and the latter made up principally of Clarkites. By 1840 the State Rights Party, formed largely in opposition to the high-handed methods of Andrew Jackson, allied itself with the national Whig Party, and the Union Party in Georgia allied itself both in name and principles with the national Democratic Party. Most of the eminent statesmen of the day, including Toombs, Stephens, and Berrien, were Whigs, but they were never fully in accord with the program of the national party. In 1850 Howell Cobb, formerly a Democrat, joined Toombs and Stephens in forming a Constitutional Union Party in Georgia, advocating acceptance of the Compromise of 1850. After the Kansas-Nebraska Controversy in 1854, Toombs, Stephens, and most of the former Whigs went over to the Democratic Party. Factional differences prevented the State from uniting in one party at this time, as would have been logical. A portion of the former Whigs, now under the leadership of Benjamin H. Hill, organized a Know-Nothing Party in Georgia and allied itself with the national party of that name. By 1860 most Georgians belonged to the Democratic Party.

CHAPTER X

# The Civil War

THE most distinctive feature of the constitutional system established by the Federal Convention of 1787 was a geographic division of the powers of government between the central government and the State governments, the great federal dualism, with a dual citizenship and dual government. The Constitution specifically delegated certain powers to the national government. In theory these "delegated," or "enumerated" powers, and those powers necessary and proper for their execution, were the only powers bestowed upon the national government. "The powers not delegated to the United States by the Constitution, nor prohibited by it to the States, are reserved to the States respectively, or to the people," declared the Tenth Amendment. This wording was similar to that of Article II of the Articles of Confederation which proclaimed that "Each State retains its sovereignty, freedom, and independence, and every power, jurisdiction and right which is not by this confederation expressly delegated to the United States in Congress assembled." The framers of the Constitution meant to create a system of government lying somewhere between the confederate and unitary systems. The central government was to be supreme within its sphere of delegated authority, but this sphere was to be decidedly limited. James Madison explained that the term "national" when used in the Federal Convention was not equivalent to "unlimited" or "consolidated," but was used because there was "no technical or appropriate denomination applicable to the new and unique system."[1] Alexander Hamilton, the strongest advocate of centralization in the period of the formation of our national government, argued that the inclusion of a bill of rights expressing limitations on the powers of the national government would be superfluous. "Why," he asked, "declare that things shall not be done which there is no power to do?"[2] Clearly, the national government was in theory one of limited powers. Matters of national interest such as war and peace, the regulation of commerce, and the coinage of money were placed under its authority; matters of local interest were left to the control of the States. In this combination of national unity with local autonomy lay the advantage of the federal system.

Georgians were deeply attached to the Union of the States, but the doctrine of States' rights played its part in the history of Georgia from the very formation of the Union. Georgia early set herself up as a guardian of States' rights in refusing to accept the decision of the United States Supreme Court in the case of *Chisholm vs. Georgia*. The Court was probably mistaken in its opinion that the Constitution conferred jurisdiction on the federal courts to hear suits against a State by a citizen of another State.[3] In any event, there was a general agitation throughout the Union against the decision of the

---

[1] Madison to Stephens, March 25, 1826, in *Documentary History of the Constitution* (House Doc. No. 529, 56th Congress, 2nd Session. Washington, 1894), II, 322.

[2] *The Federalist*, No. LXXXIV.

[3] Contrast the opinions in *Chisholm vs. Georgia*, 2 Dallas 419, with that in *Hans vs. Louisiana*, 134 U. S. 1.

## The Civil War

Court, and in 1798 the Eleventh Amendment was added to the Constitution denying such power to the federal courts.

The year 1798 also brought forth the Virginia and Kentucky Resolutions, one of the earliest notable statements of the compact theory of the federal union. These Resolutions, written by Jefferson and Madison, maintained that the Constitution was a compact between equal and sovereign States, that the central government in the exercise of powers delegated to it by the States was answerable to the States both for these powers and the means used in exercising them, and that if the central government assumed powers not delegated to it, its acts were unauthoritative, void, and of no force. Nullification of such unauthorized acts by the sovereign States, the Resolutions held, was the proper remedy. These Resolutions were passed by the legislatures of Virginia and Kentucky only; in most other States they received a cool reception. The journals of the legislature of Georgia for 1799 have not been preserved; other sources do not indicate that these Resolutions received much attention.

Theories of States' rights and opposition to acts of the national government considered as usurpations, while more frequently voiced in the South, were not restricted to any one geographic area of the United States. Opposition to the War of 1812, "Mr. Madison's War," as they called it, led the five New England States to hold a Convention in Hartford in 1814 for the purpose, as it was stated, of uniting "in such measures for . . . safety as the times demand and the principles of justice and the law of self respect will justify." This Hartford Convention published an address declaring that when there were "deliberate, dangerous, and palpable infractions of the Constitution," it was the duty of the States to "interpose their authority for the preservation of their liberty." It proposed a number of amendments to the Constitution, including a two-thirds vote of Congress to declare war or to establish commercial non-intercourse, and a relinquishment of the provision for counting three-fifths of the slaves in apportioning representation, and provided that if the Federal Government did not take adequate steps for the protection of the New England States, a second convention should be assembled with such powers and instructions as the exigencies of the crisis might demand.[4] The Treaty of Ghent brought an end to the War of 1812 and prevented the assembling of the second New England convention, but the Hartford Convention has been the stock example of Southerners in proving that the doctrine of secession was no Southern innovation.

An account of the friction between Georgia and the central government over removal of the Creek and Cherokee Indians from Georgia was given in the previous chapter. In his determination to survey the Indian lands, despite the opposition of President Adams, Governor Troup acted upon what the *Augusta Chronicle* described as "wild ideas of State Rights."[5] When the United States Supreme Court sought to restrain the State of Georgia in its dealings with the Cherokees, Governor Lumpkin ignored the Court. President Jackson had little sympathy for the Indians, and is reported to have remarked soon after the case of *Worcester vs. Georgia*,[6] "Marshall has made his decision; now let him enforce it." Georgia openly defied the Supreme Court and nothing was done about it. The Indians saw that the only course open to them was to accept western lands and move out of the State.

---

[4] Asa Earl Martin, *A History of the United States* (New York, 1928), I, 263–264.

[5] Issue of November 26, 1825.

[6] 6 Peters 515.

## The Civil War

The Tariff Controversy, Calhoun's *Exposition of 1828*, the Hayne-Webster Debate of 1830, nullification of the federal tariff by South Carolina in 1832, President Jackson's determination to enforce the federal law, and the compromise tariff of 1833 are chapters in our national history too well known to be taken up here. The federal union was strong enough to survive the tariff controversy. Slavery was the issue that brought secession. The causes of secession were similar in the cases of all of the Southern States, but they are presented here in terms of Georgia history.

The social and economic order of Georgia was dependent upon slavery. Georgia's four hundred and sixty thousand slaves, some of them selling for as much as two thousand dollars each, were more valuable than her lands and cities combined. The cotton culture, in which most of the people were engaged, and the agricultural life in general were organized on the basis of slave labor. The editor of the Milledgeville *Georgia Journal* stated on January 9, 1821, that "there was not an editor in the Southern States who dared advocate slavery as a principle"; but as the attack upon the institution of slavery grew in the North, defense of it grew in the South. Poor whites and wealthy planters alike came to accept slavery as natural and wholly justified. According to Ulrich Bonnell Phillips, "The first direct and conscious connection between slavery and State rights by a prominent Georgian was probably in the inaugural address of Governor Gilmer, delivered in November, 1837. In it he said that on account of slavery and its products, 'our true position is to stand by the powers of the States and the people as the surest safeguards of our rights, of liberty, and of property.' " [7]

Secession as a remedy for the ills of the South had considerable support in Georgia in 1850, but the prosperity of

---
[7] *Georgia and State Rights*, 182.

the State, her attachment to the union, and her willingness to accept Clay's Compromise on the basis of the Georgia Platform accounted in no small measure for the preservation of the union. Georgia was equally as prosperous in 1860 as she had been in 1850. Why did she then secede from the union for which she still had a strong attachment? There are numerous contemporary answers to this question, but they have more meaning when read in connection with a statement of the occasions that produced them and the characters who made them. Prominent among the many able statesmen in Georgia during the Civil War period were Stephens, Toombs, and Brown.

Alexander Hamilton Stephens (February 11, 1812—March 4, 1883), whom Georgia today honors as her most illustrious statesman by a statue in the nation's Hall of Fame, was born on a Wilkes County farm. Both parents died when the youth was only fourteen, but a patron sent him to an academy in Washington, Georgia, and a Presbyterian educational society later lent funds for his study at the University of Georgia, in nearby Athens. He was graduated in 1832 at the head of his class and during the next two years taught school and read law. In 1834 he was admitted to the bar and began practicing at Crawfordville, within a few miles of his birthplace. He subsequently served several terms in the State legislature where his outstanding advocacy was the project of the Western and Atlantic Railroad. In 1843 he entered Congress as a member of the lower house and served there until 1859. In the conflict between North and South over slavery in the territories, Stephens used strong words at Washington and soft counsel at home. After his retirement from Congress, as previously between sessions, he plied a lucrative practice in the Georgia courts, and in leisure kept open house at Liberty Hall, in Crawford-

## The Civil War

ville, with a widowed sister presiding in the absence of a wife. Known by his contemporaries as "Little Ellick," he was of average stature, but in weight seldom if ever attained a hundred pounds. "A shrill voice, a sallow complexion, recurrent illness, and occasional melancholia gave evidence of organic defects; but his mind was not often morbid, and his will was always robust." [8]

Robert Augustus Toombs (July 2, 1810–December 15, 1885) was born in Wilkes County in the uplands of eastern Georgia, the son of a well-to-do planter. He attended the University of Georgia, and the community of Athens still treasures a number of traditions concerning him, best known of which is the legend of his commencement speech under "Toombs' Oak." As the story runs, Toombs had been expelled from the University for some conflict with the authorities, but lingered on the campus during commencement exercises in August. When faculty, guests, and students assembled in the Chapel to hear addresses from the students chosen for places of honor by the faculty, Toombs began speaking from an improvised rostrum under a large oak tree directly in front of the Chapel. His loud voice penetrated the open windows and doors of the Chapel, and soon his eloquence and wit had the crowd coming out to listen to him. Before his address was completed, the speakers inside the Chapel had only empty seats before them.[9] Toombs completed his education at Union College, Schenectady, New York, in 1828. Returning to Georgia he began his career by practicing law and serving in the General Assembly where he advocated, above all other things, a sound financial policy. In 1845 he entered Congress as a member of the House of

---
[8] *The Dictionary of American Biography*, XVII, 574.
[9] Ulrich Bonnell Phillips, *The Life of Robert Toombs* (New York, 1919), 13.

Representatives, and in 1852 was elected to the Senate. A talented, forthright, high-spirited individual, he became a champion of Southern rights and was second to none in influencing the secession of the Southern States and the formation of the Confederacy.

Joseph Emerson Brown (April 15, 1821—November 30, 1894), Georgia's Civil War Governor, and the only Governor of Georgia to serve eight consecutive years, was born in South Carolina. During his youth his parents moved to Union County, in the mountainous section of North Georgia, where he worked as a day laborer on the farm and attended a rural school. Later he taught school and read law. In 1846 he was graduated from the Yale Law School. Returning to Georgia, he served in the State Senate and was subsequently judge of the Blue Ridge Circuit. His election to the governorship was the result of a deadlock in the Democratic State Convention in 1857 when no one of five prominent candidates could gain the two-thirds vote necessary for nomination. After more than twenty ballots, extending over three days, no candidate had a majority and Brown was accepted as a compromise. Not the least curious circumstance in this remarkable nomination was the fact that Brown was tying wheat on his farm in far-off Cherokee County at the very hour he was nominated and the news was brought to him at sundown by a friend who rode up on horseback from Canton. Toombs, then in Texas, upon hearing of the nomination asked, "Who in the hell is Joe Brown?" [10]

But soon everyone would know Joe Brown. Just before he came into office, the banks of the State suspended specie payment. In his inaugural address Governor Brown denounced the suspension as unnecessary and unjustified, and announced his intention to suspend the charters of

---

[10] Avery, *History of Georgia*, 39.

## The Civil War

offending banks. A fight with the legislature ensued in which that body passed a measure suspending forfeiture proceedings against the banks over the Governor's veto. The money interests and, momentarily, most of the newspapers denounced Brown as a woefully ignorant man; but when the fight was carried to the people they sided with the Governor. He became the people's champion and the moving power in the public life of the State. The next convention of the Democratic party nominated him for reëlection by acclamation.

Governor Brown took the lead in the movement for secession in Georgia. In a special message to the legislature on November 7, 1860, he advised against the appointment of delegates to a Southern convention, holding that unless the Southern States were generally represented little would be accomplished. In the event of Lincoln's election to the Presidency, the Governor recommended that the legislature call a State convention. In his opinion the constitutional rights of the people of Georgia and of the other slave-holding States had been violated to an extent that would justify them, in the eyes of all civilized nations, in adopting any measures necessary for the restoration and future protection of their rights. The time for decisive action was at hand. He showed how Massachusetts and other Northern States had violated the Federal compact through their aid to fugitive slaves, and argued that these States would have less interest in slaves if the Southern States were not in the federal union. "If the fifteen Southern States of the Union should meet in convention, and determine to secede . . . there would be no war, no bloodshed," he argued. The Northern people were held to be too dependent upon Southern cotton and trade for employment. Great Britain, he predicted, would go to war before she would let a single crop of cotton be cut off. He concluded by recommending that the legislature appropriate a million dollars for putting the State into a defensive condition as fast as possible.[11]

While deliberating upon a course of action, the General Assembly invited several of the State's most distinguished men to address it on the state of the Republic. Among these, Toombs and Thomas R. R. Cobb spoke in favor of immediate secession; Stephens, in an appeal to reason above passion, warned against hasty action. In his judgment the election of no man to the Presidency was sufficient cause to justify a State to separate from the Union. Lincoln had been elected in a constitutional manner. The South, and especially Georgia, should not be the first to prove untrue to national engagements. "Let us not anticipate a threatened evil," he pleaded. If Lincoln violated the Constitution, then would be the time to act. He did not anticipate that Lincoln would attempt to jeopardize the safety and security of the South, and even if he should, the system of checks and balances established in the Constitution would prevent him. The President of the United States was no emperor, no dictator—he was clothed with no absolute power. Lincoln could do nothing unless backed by Congress, and the Democratic Party controlled the House of Representatives by a comfortable majority and the Senate by a majority of four votes. Stephens would not submit to aggression upon the constitutional rights of the South, but he believed that the South, standing upon the Georgia Platform of 1850, could maintain its rights in the Union. Twenty years before the tariff question had been agitated almost as fearfully as the slave question was in 1860. Reason had triumphed, and a moderate tariff, supported by both Massa-

---

[11] Allen D. Candler, editor, *The Confederate Records of the State of Georgia* (Atlanta, 1909), I, 19–57, *passim*. Brown's address of November 7th was printed in full in *The Federal Union*, November 13, 1860.

chusetts and South Carolina, had come to prevail. The truth is omnipotent, maintained Stephens; when properly wielded, it wins. Granting that the administration of the Federal government had its faults, under its operation the South had grown great, prosperous, and happy. Georgia should be careful before discarding a proven government in favor of a rash experiment. She should participate in a convention of all Southern States to secure united action. Yet if Georgia, through a convention, should determine to secede, Stephens promised to bow to the will of the people.[12]

This speech ably expressed the convictions of the most conservative element in the State, but the legislature agreed with Brown, Cobb, and Toombs that the time for action had arrived. It voted the million dollars requested by the Governor for putting Georgia in condition to defend herself, and, on November 17, 1860, directed the Governor to call a convention of the people to consider the grievances affecting the State as a member of the federal union and the proper mode and time of redress. It directed that the election of delegates should be held on the first Wednesday in January, and that the convention should assemble at the State Capitol on January 16th. Counties entitled to two representatives in the House of Representatives were authorized to send three delegates to the Convention; counties having one representative should send two delegates. Four days after the legislative authorization, Governor Brown issued the call for the convention.

During the period intervening between the election and assembling of the Convention a series of statements were issued influencing the cause of secession. On December 7th Governor Brown published a letter in which he

---

[12] Alexander H. Stephens, *A Constitutional View of the Late War Between the States* (Philadelphia, 1870), II, 279–307.

## A Constitutional History of Georgia

held that submission to the inauguration of Lincoln would bring utter ruin to the South. A letter from Howell Cobb, dated at Washington, December 6th, reached the people of Georgia, together with the news of Cobb's resignation from President Buchanan's cabinet, soon after the publication of Brown's letter. It proclaimed that the union of justice and equality would be supplanted on March 4th by a union of sectionalism and hatred. On December 19th the legislature approved a series of resolutions explaining the grievances of the Southern States which, it was held, would justify them in seceding and forming a Southern confederacy. On Christmas day the newspapers carried a letter from the Southern Congressmen to their constituents stating that all hope of preserving the union was gone. On January 1st the Milledgeville *Federal Union* published a telegram from Senator Toombs, who had returned to Washington, stating that all hope for security in the union was abandoned. Wilson Lumpkin wrote from his retirement advising secession, and Thomas R. R. Cobb urged the legislature to take Georgia out of the union without waiting for a convention.[13]

In the election of delegates to the Convention the foremost citizens stood as candidates, and people voted with little regard to shattered party lines. In most counties there were candidates in favor of immediate secession and others opposed to hasty action. Realizing the seriousness of the moment, the people sought to elect their best men. The delegates assembled at the State Capitol on January 16, 1861. George W. Crawford, a former Governor of the State, was elected President of the Convention, and Albert R. Lamar, Secretary. Ulrich Bonnell Phillips describes the gathering as "without doubt the most distinguished body of men which had ever assembled in Georgia. . . . Of the 297 delegates, there were not four whose

---
[13] Phillips, *Georgia and State Rights,* 199–201.

## The Civil War

names were not of pure English, Scotch, or Irish origin. It would not have been possible to assemble in one hall, by any method of selection, a more truly representative body of the best intelligence of Georgia." [14] Among the delegates were Alexander H. Stephens, Robert Toombs, Herschel V. Johnson, Thomas R. R. Cobb, A. H. Colquitt, Benjamin H. Hill, E. A. Nisbet, Hiram Warner, Augustus Reese, Henry L. Benning, Francis S. Bartow—in fact, all of the prominent political leaders of the State except Governor Brown, Howell Cobb, and Charles J. Jenkins. These three leaders, together with the judges of the State Supreme Court, the judges of the Superior Courts, T. L. Guerry, President of the Senate, C. J. Williams, Speaker of the House, and the delegates from Georgia to Congress were invited to seats in the Convention.

After two days spent in organizing and in hearing communications from the already seceded States of South Carolina and Alabama, the Convention was brought directly to the question of immediate secession from the federal union by the following resolution offered by Eugenius A. Nisbet: "Resolved: That in the opinion of this Convention, it is the right and duty of Georgia to secede from the present Union, and to coöperate with such of the other States as have or shall do the same, for the purpose of forming a Southern Confederacy upon the basis of the Constitution of the United States." [15]

In an effort to forestall immediate secession and to secure united action by the Southern States, a lengthy substitute for Nisbet's motion was offered by Herschel V. Johnson, proclaiming Georgia's attachment to the Federal Union and her desire to preserve it if this could be done consistent with her rights and safety. But recogniz-

---
[14] *Ibid.*, 202.
[15] *Journal of the Public and Secret Proceedings of the Convention of the People of Georgia, Held in Milledgeville and Savannah in 1861* (Milledgeville, 1861), 15.

ing the imminent danger confronting the State, the resolution provided for a convention of the Southern States in Atlanta on February 16, 1861, to consider the whole subject of their relations with the Federal Government, and to devise such course of action as their interests, equality, and safety might demand. The resolution specified certain indispensable amendments to the federal Constitution designed to safeguard the interests of slaveholding States, and declared that Georgia was unalterably determined not to remain in a union with States maintaining laws for the aid of fugitive slaves. If the united efforts of the Southern States failed to secure their rights in the union, concluded the resolution, then Georgia, "reluctantly compelled to resume her separate independence . . . will promptly and cordially unite . . . in the formation of a Southern Confederacy upon the basis of the Constitution of the United States." [16]

An elaborate discussion followed in which Nisbet, Toombs, T. R. R. Cobb, Reese, and Bartow, advocates of immediate secession, were opposed by Stephens, Johnson, Hill, and Means. Unfortunately these speeches have not been preserved, but Stephens later stated that the keynote of the secessionist, as condensed by T. R. R. Cobb in a discourse of remarkable power, was, "We can make better terms out of the Union than in it." After these speeches, a yea and nay vote was taken on the original motion of Nisbet, the result being one hundred sixty-six to one hundred thirty in favor of immediate secession. The closeness of the vote on so important a matter as withdrawing from the Federal union is worthy of note. A subsequent motion to submit the secession ordinance to a vote of the people for ratification was defeated; [17] so it is difficult to ascertain precisely what percentage of the peo-

---

[16] *Conf. Rec. of Georgia*, I, 230–235.
[17] *Journal of the Convention. . . ,* 46.

*The Civil War*

ple in Georgia favored immediate secession in January, 1861. According to Avery, "A pretty fair criterion of the disunion sentiment in Georgia before the election of Lincoln and Hamlin was the Breckenridge vote. The union element voted for Douglas and Bell. The Breckenridge platform naturally attracted the most pronounced Southern rights men who were for making an unqualified issue for slavery. The vote showed a majority against disunion. . . . The vote taken in the election for members of the (secession) convention showed an aggregate of 50,243 for secession and 37,123 against, giving a majority of only 13,120 for immediate disunion, out of 87,366." [18]

On January 19th a committee of the Convention appointed by President Crawford presented an ordinance of secession which declared that "the ordinance adopted by the people of the State of Georgia in Convention on the second day of January in the year of our Lord seventeen hundred and eighty-eight, whereby the Constitution of the United States of America was assented to, ratified and adopted; and also all acts and parts of acts of the General Assembly of this State ratifying and adopting amendments of said Constitution, are hereby repealed, rescinded, and abrogated." This ordinance was adopted at two o'clock in the afternoon by a vote of 208 to 89, whereupon President Crawford declared Georgia to be a free, sovereign, and independent State.[19] On January 21st Nisbet moved that inasmuch as the lack of uniformity in the Convention indicated a difference of opinion due not so much to the rights that Georgia claimed or to the wrongs of which she complained as to the remedy and its application, that all members of the Convention should sign the ordinance of secession in order to show a unanimous determination to sustain the State in her chosen remedy,

---

[18] *History of Georgia*, 135.
[19] *Journal of the Convention.* . . , 39.

whereupon all but six of the delegates signed the ordinance. These entered in the record their protest against the immediate secession of Georgia, but pledged their lives, if necessary, to defend the State from hostile invasion.[20]

A statement written by Robert Toombs was adopted on January 29th to accompany and justify the ordinance of secession. This twelve page document set forth the following as causes leading Georgia to withdraw from the Federal Union: For the past ten years there had been numerous and serious causes for complaint against the North with reference to slavery, and with the election of Lincoln, administration of the Federal Government would pass into the hands of an admittedly anti-slavery party. Prohibition of slavery in the territories, hostility to it everywhere, equality of the black and white races, and disregard of all constitutional guarantees in favor of slavery had been boldly proclaimed by the Republican leaders; yet the people of the North had voted this party into office. The North had sought to exclude slavery from all of the territory acquired by the Mexican War, and thus appropriate to itself territory won by the joint efforts of the whole country. The claim itself was less arrogant than the reason by which it was supported. That reason was a fixed purpose to limit, restrain, and finally to abolish slavery in the States where it existed. The South declared her determination to resist the principle of prohibition to the last extremity, and this particular question, together with a series of questions affecting the same subject, was disposed of in 1850 by the defeat of prohibitory legislation. The Presidential election of 1852 resulted in a total overthrow of the advocates of restriction. Immediately the anti-slavery portion of the defeated party resolved to

---

[20] Phillips, *Georgia and State Rights*, 204.

## The Civil War

unite all elements in the North opposed to slavery and to stake their future and political fortunes upon their hostility to slavery everywhere.

The right of Southerners to carry slaves into the territories was good under the Constitution, and was fortified by the practice of the Government from the beginning, Toombs continued. The Northwest Ordinance of 1787 excluded slavery from the territory northwest of the Ohio River, to be sure; but this Ordinance was adopted under the old Articles of Confederation, with the assent of Virginia, who owned and ceded the territory. This case was a special one. In all other territory claimed and acquired by the United States, the uniform policy of the Government prior to 1820 had been to open it to the settlement of all citizens of all States of the Union. Emigrants to the territories were protected by public authority in their persons and property, including slaves, until they were sufficiently numerous to form their own government, and then they were admitted into the Union with whatever republican constitution they might adopt for themselves. James Madison had declared the Missouri Compromise of 1820 unconstitutional at the time of its adoption, and Jefferson had predicted that it would result in the dissolution of the Union. Exclusion of slavery from the territories was unconstitutional, Toombs reiterated, pointing to the judgment of the United States Supreme Court as the highest authority.

There had always been opposition to slavery in the Northern States, continued the statement, but a distinct abolition party had not been formed for more than half a century after the United States Government went into operation. "The main reason was, that the North, even if united, could not control both branches of the Legislature during any portion of that time. Therefore, such an

## A Constitutional History of Georgia

organization must have resulted, either in the utter failure, or in the total overthrow of the Government. The material prosperity of the North was greatly dependent on the Federal Government; that of the South not at all. In the first years of the Republic, the navigating, commercial and manufacturing interests of the North began to seek profit and aggrandizement at the expense of the agricultural interests." The navigation interests had been guarded against competition, and the Government had borne the expenses of lighthouses, buoys, and other legitimate burdens of business. Manufacturers had received protection through tariffs, but, fortunately, the tariff act of 1846 had resulted in a gradual reduction of rates.

The conduct of the Northern adversaries, continued Toombs, was not confined to such acts as might aggrandize themselves or their section of the Union; they found contentment in merely injuring the South. The provisions in the Constitution for the return of slaves and fugitives from justice were clear and unmistakable. Without these provisions it was historically true that the South would have rejected the Constitution. Because of a lack of coöperation on the part of local magistrates in the North in enforcing the fugitive slave law of 1793, Congress, in 1850, had passed an act providing for complete execution of this duty by Federal officers; but the non-slaveholding States had made of this law a dead letter. "We have their covenants, we have their oaths, to keep and observe it, but the unfortunate claimant, even accompanied by a Federal Officer, with the mandate of the highest judicial authority in his hands, is everywhere met with fraud, with force, and with legislative enactments, to elude, to resist and defeat him; claimants are murdered with impunity; officers of the law are beaten by frantic mobs, instigated by inflammatory appeals by persons holding the highest public employment in these States,

## The Civil War

and supported by legislation in conflict with the clearest provisions of the Constitution, and even the ordinary principles of humanity. In several of our confederate States, a citizen can not travel the highway with his servant, who may voluntarily accompany him, without being declared by law a felon, and being subjected to infamous punishments. It is difficult to perceive how we could suffer more by the hostility, than by the fraternity of such brethren." [21]

The public law of civilized nations requires every state to restrain its citizens from committing acts injurious to the peace and safety of other states; yet for twenty years past the Abolitionists and their allies in the Northern States had been engaged in constant efforts to subvert Southern institutions, and to incite insurrections and servile war. The people of Georgia had struggled to maintain the union, but knowing the value of parchment rights in treacherous hands, they refused to submit to the rulers offered by the North. The reason, concluded Toombs, is because these Republican leaders, "by their declared principles and policy, . . . outlawed three thousand millions of our property in the common territories of the Union, put it under the ban of the Republic in the States where it exists, and out of the protection of Federal law everywhere; because they give sanctuary to thieves and incendiaries who assail it to the whole extent of their power, in spite of their most solemn obligations and covenants; because their avowed purpose is to subvert our society, and subject us, not only to the loss of our property, but the destruction of ourselves, our wives, and our children, and the desolation of our homes, our altars, and our firesides. To avoid these evils, we resume the powers which our fathers delegated to the Government of the United States, and henceforth will seek new safe-guards

---
[21] *Conf. Rec. of Ga.*, I, 358–359.

for our liberty, equality, security and tranquility."[22]

This explanation of the causes of secession in terms of a broken compact and disregard of constitutional obligations on the part of the North, as well as long-suffered economic grievances on the part of the South, had a universal appeal. In the early stages of the Civil War the South enjoyed the sympathy of the British Government and received considerable aid, short of recognition, from it. But in the end most people outside the South came to view the moral issue of slavery rather than constitutional principles as the basic issue in the struggle. The most masterful statement of this issue ever given was by none other than Alexander H. Stephens in his "Cornerstone Speech" delivered at Savannah on April 21, 1861. His thesis added to the popularity of Stephens at home, but it was destined to weaken the cause of Southern independence in the judgment of the world. "It narrowed the issue from the broad domain of political independence founded upon a contract that had been violated, and upon which the sympathy of the world was with us, to the untenable foothold of the intrinsic righteousness and supreme good policy of slavery, in which civilized mankind stood immutably against us."[23]

The Confederate Constitution, explained Stephens, "has put at rest forever all the agitating questions relating to our peculiar institution—African slavery as it exists among us—the proper status of the negro in our form of civilization. This was the immediate cause of the late rupture and present revolution. Jefferson . . . had anticipated this as the 'rock upon which the union would split. . . .' He was right. But whether he fully compre-

---
[22] *Conf. Rec. of Ga.*, I, 360–361. Contrast the argument of Mr. Chief Justice Warner of the Supreme Court of Georgia in the *Central Railroad and Banking Co. vs. Ward*, 37 *Ga. Reports* 515, delivered after the Civil War, holding that a State had no legal right to secede.
[23] Avery, *History of Georgia*, 196.

## The Civil War

hended the great truth upon which the rock *stood* and *stands*, may be doubted." Jefferson and his contemporaries had looked upon slavery as socially, morally, and politically wrong, and trusted that somehow or other in the order of Providence the institution would pass away. This idea, though not incorporated in the Constitution, was the prevailing idea of the time, but it was fundamentally wrong. It rested upon the assumption of the equality of races. The government under the Constitution was built upon this sandy foundation; so when the storm came and the wind blew, it fell. "Our new government," explained Stephens, "is founded upon exactly the opposite idea; its foundations are laid, its cornerstone rests upon the great truth that the negro is not equal to the white man—that slavery, subordination to the superior race, is his natural and moral condition. I recollect once of having heard a gentleman from one of the Northern States, of great power and ability, announce in the House of Representatives . . . that we of the South would be compelled, ultimately, to yield upon this subject of slavery, that it was as impossible to war successfully against a principle in politics as it was in physics and mathematics. That the principle would ultimately prevail. That we in maintaining slavery . . . were warring against . . . a principle founded in nature, the principle of the equality of man. The reply I made to him was, that upon his own grounds we should succeed. The truth announced . . . I admitted, but told him it was he and those acting with him, who were warring against a principle. They were attempting to make things equal which the Creator had made unequal. . . . The great objects of humanity are best attained when conformed to His laws and decrees, in the formation of governments as well as in all things else. Our Confederacy is founded upon principles in strict conformity with these laws. This stone which was rejected by the first builders, 'is become the chief stone of the corner' in our new edifice. I have been asked what of the future? It has been apprehended by some, that we would have arrayed against us the civilized world. I care not who or how many they may be, when we stand upon the eternal principles of truth we are obliged and must triumph."[24]

Withdrawing from a union of which Georgia had been a member for three quarters of a century presented many problems, some of which the Secession Convention sought to meet. It defined as citizens all persons (meaning white persons, of course) born in Georgia, or born of a father who was a citizen of Georgia, citizens of the United States who should come to Georgia within one year, and men serving in the armed forces of Georgia for three months. For naturalization procedure, the former laws of the United States were adopted.[25] Postmasters, collectors of customs, and other Federal civil officers were directed to continue to discharge the duties of their offices in accordance with regulations heretofore governing them. The United States pension agent for Georgia in particular was singled out and by special resolution requested to continue to exercise the usual functions of his agency.[26] The courts of the United States in Georgia were transformed into State courts, and the Governor was empowered to appoint and commission the judges.[27] Governor Brown was congratulated for having occupied Fort Pulaski, at the

---

[24] *The Federal Union*, April 2, 1861.
[25] *Journal of the Convention*. . . , 88.
[26] *Ibid.*, 114.
[27] Governor Brown tendered the office of judge of the District Court of the independent State of Georgia to Edward J. Harden, but he declined the position, and no appointment was ever made. The Confederate Government organized a district court for Georgia, and it not only occupied the court rooms and chambers of the former United States district courts of Georgia, but also used the dockets and tried the unfinished business pending in 1861. A Confederate Supreme Court was never organized. Warren Grice, "The Confederate States Court for Georgia," in *The Georgia Historical Quarterly*, IX (June, 1925), 131–158.

## The Civil War

mouth of the Savannah River, on January 3rd, and authorized to raise and equip two regiments of soldiers and to purchase three steamers for the defense of the Georgia coast. Provision was made whereby officers of the United States Army and Navy entering the service of Georgia should be given the same rank and pay they had formerly received. The lands in Georgia formerly ceded to the United States, including the Federal arsenal at Augusta, were repossessed with the understanding that compensation would be made to the United States in the settlement of claims between the two governments.

The Convention sent the following delegates to the Convention of Southern States scheduled to meet in Montgomery in February: Robert Toombs, who came near to being elected President of the Confederacy; Alexander H. Stephens, who was elected Vice-President of the Confederacy; Howell Cobb, who served as President of the Montgomery Convention; his brother, Thomas R. R. Cobb, who was largely responsible for the writing of the Confederate Constitution; Eugenius A. Nisbet, Benjamin H. Hill, Francis S. Bartow, Martin J. Crawford, Augustus R. Wright, and Augustus H. Kenan. Four of these delegates (Stephens, Hill, Kenan, and Wright) had not been secessionists at the opening of the Georgia Convention. The delegation to Montgomery was given plenary powers to enter a provisional union of the Southern States based upon the Constitution of the United States for a period of twelve months, and power to join in the work of framing a permanent government. Upon receipt of the Constitution of the Confederacy, the Georgia Convention, following the precedent of 1788, unanimously ratified it, on March 16th. Thus Georgia was out of a union with her sister States for a period of only fifty-five days, January 19th–March 16th.[28]

The Constitution of the Confederacy was in the main

---
[28] *Conf. Rec. of Ga.*, I, 458.

*A Constitutional History of Georgia*

very similar to that of the United States. The main differences were in the provisions added to safeguard slavery, to make clear the sovereign character of the States, and to institute certain changes in the machinery of government suggested by experience under the old Constitution. No federal law denying the right of property in Negro slaves was to be passed, and Congress was to protect slavery in the territories. There were to be no protective tariffs. The term of the President was fixed at six years, with ineligibility for reëlection, and he was empowered to veto items in appropriation bills. Congress was authorized to permit the heads of executive departments to have seats in either house, with the privilege of discussing any measure affecting their departments.[29] Regarding this change in the direction of cabinet government, Stephens, in his famous Cornerstone Speech said: "I should have gone farther, and allowed the President to select his constitutional advisers from the Senate and House of Representatives. That would have conformed entirely to the British Parliament, which, in my opinion is one of the wisest provisions of that body."

## *The Constitution of 1861*

AMONG other things, the Secession Convention also framed a new constitution for Georgia. One of the five standing committees named on January 18th was entitled The Committee on the Constitution of this State and the Constitution of the United States.[30] The *Journal* of the

---

[29] The original Permanent Constitution of the Confederate States of America and also an early manuscript draft of the Provisional Constitution are now in possession of the Library of the University of Georgia.

[30] The twelve members appointed were: Thomas R. R. Cobb, Richard H. Clark, Linton Stephens, J. N. Ramsey, N. M. Crawford, B. H. Hill, Augustus Reese, T. H. Trippe, Simpson Fouche, A. H. Kenan, G. D. Rice, and La Fayette Lamar.

*The Civil War*

Convention gives the impression that Thomas R. R. Cobb, as Chairman, was the most active among its members. While this committee was given functions in addition to the revision of the State Constitution, it was not entrusted fully with that responsibility. Perceiving that it was then more than ever the duty of Georgia to husband her resources, the Convention adopted a resolution that a committee be appointed on the reduction of membership of the General Assembly. Two days later President Crawford named sixteen members to this committee, and within a week the Convention was debating various plans of reduction.[31] The Convention adjourned on January 29th, but reassembled on the call of its President at Savannah on March 7th. Both the Committee on the Reduction of the Membership of the General Assembly and the Committee on the Constitution remained active. On March 14th, following a report of the former committee, it was agreed that the Senate should in the future consist of forty-four members chosen from forty-four senatorial districts, each to be composed of three counties. This provision was accepted by the Committee on the Constitution.

The Convention received reports on the several articles of the Constitution from the Committee on Revision and debated them on March 21st and 22nd. On March 23rd it adopted the revised Constitution, largely as reported by the Committee, provided for its submission to popular ratification on the first Tuesday in July, and adjourned, *sine die*. This, Georgia's fourth Constitution, was the first one to be submitted to the people for ratification. The vote was 11,499 to 10,704, in favor of ratification. Thus by the narrow margin of 795 votes, with only 22,203 voting, a new Constitution was adopted. It was proclaimed effective on August 20th. Governor Brown explained the

---
[31] *Journal of the Convention.* . . , 55, 81–82

## A Constitutional History of Georgia

small vote on the ratification of the Constitution as "owing doubtless to the fact that the thoughts of our people were so much engrossed with the war that little attention was given to any other subject; and as the Constitution had received the sanction of the Convention, composed as it was of so many of the brightest intellects and best men of the State, the people were, it would seem, generally willing to ratify their action without serious opposition." [32]

The long bill of rights in the Constitution of Georgia dates from 1861. The earlier constitutions had enumerated only four or five personal liberties. Thomas R. R. Cobb presented to the Convention of 1861 a *Declaration of Fundamental Principles* which it adopted as Article I of the new Constitution. This *Declaration* consisted of twenty-eight paragraphs, embodying Cobb's conservative philosophy of government. All of the provisions of the Bill of Rights of the Federal Constitution were included, along with many other safeguards. "Protection to person and property is the duty of Government; and a Government which knowingly and persistently denies, or withholds from the governed such protection, when within its power, releases from the obligation of obedience," proclaimed Georgia's new Bill of Rights. Suspension of the writ of *habeas corpus,* save in case of rebellion or invasion, *ex post facto* laws, laws impairing the obligation of contracts, and retroactive legislation injuriously affecting the rights of the citizen, were prohibited. No citizen was to be deprived of life, liberty or property without due process of law. Legislative acts in violation of the fundamental law were void, "and the Judiciary shall so declare them," provided Paragraph Seventeen. "This declaration," concluded the last paragraph, "is a part of this Con-

[32] Message to the legislature, November 6, 1861.

## The Civil War

stitution and shall never be violated on any pretence whatever."

The basis of representation in the legislature under the Constitution of 1861 represented largely a reversion to the system adopted in 1843. In the lower house the thirty-seven largest counties were given two representatives each; other counties,[33] one representative. The Senate was to consist of one member from each of forty-four senatorial districts, each composed of three contiguous counties. The constitutional provision against a bill containing subject matter different from that expressed in its title was reenforced by the additional provision, "Nor shall any law or ordinance pass which refers to more than one subject matter." Paragraph Nineteen of the Bill of Rights was a safeguard against special legislation: "Laws shall have a general operation; and no general law shall be varied in a particular case by special legislation; except with the consent of all persons to be affected thereby." Profiting by experience, the framers of this Constitution forbade the legislature "to make or change election precincts, . . . to establish bridges and ferries, . . . to change names, or legitimate children"; it should by law prescribe the manner in which such powers could be exercised by the courts. Nor was the legislature to authorize the suspension of specie payment by any bank, nor grant any donation or gratuity, except by a two-thirds vote. Otherwise, the General Assembly was given the broad power "to make all laws and ordinances, consistent with this Constitution and not repugnant to the Constitution of the Confederate States, which they shall deem necessary and proper for the welfare of the State."[34]

Executive power was vested in a governor, elected by

---

[33] The total number of counties in 1861 was 131.
[34] Art. II, Sect. V, Par. I.

## A Constitutional History of Georgia

popular vote for a term of two years. His powers were similar to those under the existing Constitution, except that his power of appointment was extended to the judges of both the Supreme Court and the Superior Courts. The Secretary of State, Treasurer, Comptroller General, and Surveyor General were still to be elected by the legislature.

The judiciary remained as before, except in the manner of selecting judges of the Supreme and Superior Courts. A Supreme Court, consisting of three judges appointed by the governor, was to sit in each judicial circuit at least once a year for the correction of errors from the lower courts. The Superior Courts continued to have exclusive jurisdiction over the principal criminal cases, cases of divorce, and cases involving land titles. The judges of the Superior Courts, as noted above, were now to be appointed by the governor. Judges of the inferior courts and courts of ordinary were still to be elected in each county; and justices of the peace continued to be elected by the people in their district.

Universal white male suffrage was continued, the only requirement for voting being citizenship in Georgia, twenty-one years of age, payment of all taxes, and residence within a district or county for six months. Voting by ballot, already used in practice, was to continue unless the General Assembly should direct otherwise. The Constitution provided that amendments could be made only by a convention of the people called for that purpose, and no amendment was ever made.

In addition to this revision of the Constitution, Thomas R. R. Cobb left a lasting imprint upon the law of Georgia through his work in publishing the State's first *Code*. There had been a number of earlier compilations of the statutory laws, but here for the first time appeared a summary of the substantive common law as well

*The Civil War*

as the statutory law. An act of December 9, 1858, had provided for a commission of three members "to prepare for the people of Georgia a code, which should as near as practicable, embrace in a condensed form, the Laws of Georgia, whether derived from the Common Law, the Constitutions, the Statutes of the State, the decisions of the Supreme Court, or the Statutes of England, of force in this State."[35] The Commission consisted of Cobb, Richard H. Clark, and David Irwin. The code that they prepared, and revised before publication to conform to the condition of the State as a member of the Confederacy, was a remarkable work. By legislative act, it became effective on January 1, 1863.[36]

---

The people of Georgia responded whole-heartedly to the war effort, and sent to the fields of battle 120,000 soldiers, this being 20,000 more than the voting population at the beginning of the war.[37] During the War the legis-

---

[35] "Georgia was the first English speaking commonwealth to codify the whole body of the law in force in the State," according to the "Introduction" in Parks, *Code*, Vol. I. "Georgia was also a pioneer in annotating her Code, the Code of 1873 being among the first, if not the first, annotated Code." *Ibid.*

There were two earlier codes of penal law in Georgia, the *Penal Code of 1817*, prepared by Charles Harris and T. U. P. Charlton, and the *Penal Code of 1833*, prepared by Wm. Schley, John A. Cuthbert, and Joseph Henry Lumpkin. Both were adopted by the General Assembly.

A list of compilations of Georgia laws is given below in the bibliography. The place of publication (Savannah, Augusta, Milledgeville) shown on the title page of some of the early compilations is probably inaccurate. The preface to Cobb's *Digest* (1851) directed attention to the fact that this "was the first book of the kind ever entirely printed and bound at home." Joseph R. Lamar, "Georgia Law Books," Ga. Bar Association's *Annual Report, 1898*, p. 127.

[36] The *Code* was first adopted to become effective on January 1, 1862, but by subsequent act it was suspended until 1863. Even so, it did not contain the revisions in the State Constitution made in 1861. See note in the *Code*, p. 81.

[37] Avery, *History of Georgia*, 331.

## A Constitutional History of Georgia

lature sought to encourage the production of food by placing limitations on the production of cotton. To preserve grain, a prohibition was adopted against the manufacture of whiskey. Brown was elected for a third term in 1861, thus breaking all precedents in the State's history, and for a fourth term in 1863. He was a vigorous war governor, but his attention centered too much on Georgia and not enough upon the needs of the Confederacy as a whole. His obsession to maintain a Georgia army was frustrated by progressive extension of the age limits of conscription by the Confederate Government, with the result that Brown became a bitter enemy of President Davis. Toombs and Stephens also disapproved of much of the President's policy. In addition to conscription, the chief points of disagreement between this group, the "anarchists," and President Davis were impressment of property and suspension of the writ of *habeas corpus*. The most prominent supporters of Davis in Georgia, the "monarchists," were Benjamin H. Hill and Howell Cobb.[38]

The occupation and burning of Atlanta in November, 1864, followed by the destructive march of Sherman's army through the heart of Georgia during the next month, marked the closing phase of the War. The Georgia legislature was in session in Milledgeville at the time of the fall of Atlanta. On November 23rd Governor Brown received a telegram at the dinner hour informing him that Sherman had left Atlanta and was on his way through the country to Savannah. The news brought panic to Milledgeville, in the line of march. Bills and other matters before the legislature at the time of its adjournment for dinner were left lying on the desks while members paid fabulous prices for conveyances to carry them home. Governor Brown, General Ira A. Foster, and

---

[38] Coulter, *Short History of Georgia*, Ch. XXIV, *passim*.

## The Civil War

a few heads of departments remained in the City in an effort to preserve the State records and as much property as possible. The railroads were still in operation, and a portion of a train of cars was detained at Milledgeville to be loaded with State property, including the furniture of the executive mansion. In desperation for workers, Governor Brown went to the State penitentiary, gave a spirited talk to the prisoners, and offered pardons to all, except a few serving life terms for murder, who would aid in the removal of State property and enlist in the defense of the Confederacy. The convicts responded unanimously, and did good work in loading the train. They were then formed into a military company and most of them subsequently rendered faithful military service and received honorable discharges. The Federal Army burned only the penitentiary at Milledgeville, but it sacked the Capitol and left the State records that had not been carried away scattered over the floor with the result that many important documents were irreparably lost. In a mock session of the legislature, the Union soldiers repealed the ordinance of secession. Sherman reached Savannah by Christmas.

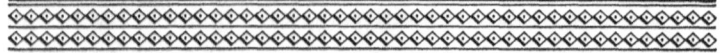

CHAPTER XI

Reconstruction

THE surrender of Robert E. Lee at Appomattox on April 9, 1865, followed by the surrender of Joseph E. Johnston at Durham on April 26th, Richard Taylor at Citronelle on May 4th, and Kirby Smith at New Orleans on May 26th marked the transition of the war for Southern independence into the "Lost Cause." By a proclamation of December 8, 1863, President Lincoln had already offered pardon, with certain exceptions, to the adherents of the Confederacy who would take an oath to support "the Constitution of the United States and the Union of the States thereunder." At the same time he announced his plan of reconstruction for the South. Whenever in any State a loyal nucleus equal to one-tenth of the voters in the presidential election of 1860 should take the oath to support the Constitution and establish a State government with the abolition of slavery, Lincoln promised executive recognition of such government. This generous plan was carried out in Tennessee, Louisiana, and Arkansas, to the satisfaction of the President, but the leaders in Congress did not share Lincoln's view that reconstruction was a matter to be handled by the President, and representatives from the States reconstructed under his plan were not admitted to seats in Congress. In July, 1864,

*Reconstruction*

Congress set forth its own terms of readmission into the Union in the Wade-Davis Bill. This measure made Congress instead of the executive the ultimate authority on reconstruction and imposed more stringent conditions, notably the requirement that a majority of the white people must take an oath of allegiance. Lincoln gave this bill a pocket-veto, but by executive proclamation offered it as a possible alternative to his own plan. Had he lived, Lincoln might have been able to carry through a moderate plan of reconstruction by compromising with the radical element in Congress. On April 14th, five days after Lee's surrender, he held a cabinet meeting at which he expressed the hope that there would be no persecution or bloodshed after the war. The next day he lay dead, the victim of a shot fired by John Wilkes Booth.[1] The new President, Andrew Johnson, while honest, fearless, and committed to Lincoln's generous plan of reconstruction, was ill-fitted by temperament and training to assume the reins of government at this critical juncture.

## *Presidential Reconstruction*

News of the cessation of hostilities reached Georgia on April 30th through a dispatch from General Johnston to Governor Brown. At this time Federal authority was already established in Savannah and Macon, and from these points as centers, military occupation was extended over the whole State during the next two months. On June 27th the Military Department of Georgia was established as part of the Military Division of Tennessee, Major General G. H. Thomas commanding. The Department of Georgia was subdivided into four districts with

---

[1] J. G. Randall, *The Civil War and Reconstruction* (New York, 1937), 683.

*A Constitutional History of Georgia*

headquarters in Atlanta, Macon, Savannah, and Augusta. Military rule supplanted the State government, but most local officials were authorized to continue to perform their duties.[2]

Governor Brown issued a call for the General Assembly to meet in Milledgeville on May 22, 1865, but Brown, Alexander H. Stephens, Howell Cobb, Benjamin H. Hill, and other prominent Confederate leaders were arrested and the legislature was forbidden to assemble. Brown was taken to Washington, but after an interview with President Johnson, he was released on parole. Returning to Georgia, on June 29th he resigned his office as Governor to remove any impediment that he might personally interpose to the problem of reconstruction. At the same time he advised the people to acquiesce in the abolition of slavery and to support President Johnson's program.[3] Already, on June 17th, President Johnson had appointed as Provisional Governor of Georgia James Johnson, a member of Congress from 1851 to 1853 and a respected lawyer of Columbus, who had opposed secession and taken no part in the government of the Confederacy. Provisional Governor Johnson took office on July 13th and stated that the sole purpose of his appointment was to enable the people of Georgia to form a government. Following instructions from the President, he issued a proclamation for an election on the first Wednesday in October to select delegates to a constitutional convention to convene at Milledgeville on the fourth Wednesday in October. The thirty-seven counties formerly having two representatives in the General Assembly should each elect three delegates to the convention; the remaining counties, two delegates each. To qualify as an elector or mem-

---

[2] C. Mildred Thompson, *Reconstruction in Georgia* (New York, 1915), 136.

[3] Avery, *History of Georgia*, 340.

*Reconstruction*

ber of the convention, a person had to meet the qualifications for voting that had prevailed in Georgia on January 19, 1861 (the date of the Secession Ordinance), and also take the amnesty oath of loyalty to the Constitution and laws of the United States and to the proclamation of the emancipation of slaves.[4] County ordinaries were authorized to administer this oath.

President Johnson was in the main successful in throwing control of the work of restoring civil government in Georgia into the hands of those who had opposed secession in 1861. Of the two hundred and ninety-four delegates who assembled in convention at Milledgeville in October, 1865, twenty-one had been members who voted against secession in the Convention of 1861, and fourteen had been defeated candidates in 1861 on an anti-secession platform.[5]

Most of the State's distinguished leaders were ineligible for membership in the Convention by virtue of having held high offices, civil or military, in the Confederacy. Conspicuous by their absence were Alexander H. Stephens, Robert Toombs, Joseph E. Brown, Benjamin H. Hill, and Eugenius A. Nisbet. Some of the delegates elected were ineligible, but President Johnson granted them pardons in order that they might participate.[6] The Convention extended an honorary seat to Brown, but he took no part in its deliberations. Responding to a petition of the Convention, President Johnson released Alexander H. Stephens who was being held prisoner at Fort Pulaski.[7]

Despite the ineligibility of many stalwart political figures, the Convention of 1865 was not without able lead-

---

[4] *Conf. Rec. of Ga.*, IV, 12, 14.
[5] Thompson, *Reconstruction in Georgia*, 149.
[6] *Conf. Rec. of Ga.*, IV, 144.
[7] *Ibid.*

253

## A Constitutional History of Georgia

ers. Herschel V. Johnson, one of the able statesmen in Georgia who had opposed secession in 1861 but who had bowed to the decision of the majority, was elected President of the Convention, and J. B. Waddell, Secretary. The President was authorized to appoint a committee consisting of one member from each of the sixteen judicial circuits in the State to "report business for this Convention," and this committee, headed by Charles J. Jenkins, was responsible for most of the work carried out.[8]

The principal work of the Convention of 1865 was the repeal of the Ordinance of Secession, abolition of slavery, repudiation of the war debt, and framing of a new State constitution. On October 30th Chairman Jenkins of the Committee of Sixteen introduced a resolution repealing the Ordinance of Secession of January 19, 1861, the ordinance of March 16th of the same year whereby Georgia joined the Confederacy, and all other ordinances and resolutions of the Convention of 1861 "subversive of, or antagonistic to the civil and military authority of the government of the United States of America." [9]

On November 7th, W. W. Thomas, a delegate from Coweta County, introduced a resolution proclaiming "the institution of slavery as consistent with the dictates of humanity and the strictest principles of morality and religion." It averred that the abolition of slavery would prove both injurious to the white race and a curse to the Negro, but that inasmuch as the only two alternatives presented were "a compliance on our part with the requirement of the Federal Government in demanding a formal prohibition of slavery in our Constitution, or perpetual military rule, with its consequent evils and bur-

---
[8] The other members were: Davis Irwin, J. C. Nichols, A. H. Chappell, J. F. B. Jackson, R. A. T. Ridley, E. G. Cabiness, C. B. Cole, W. M. Reese, Augustus H. Kenan, J. L. Wimberly, J. L. Seward, Henry Morgan, W. F. Wright, T. C. Lloyd, and J. P. Simmons.

[9] *Conf. Rec. of Ga.*, IV, 145–146.

thens and perhaps total loss of our civil and constitutional rights," Georgia would in good faith accept the former.[10] This resolution was promptly tabled, but the following wording adopted for the provision of the Constitution of 1865 abolishing slavery signifies the feeling of the delegates on this subject:

> The Government of the United States having, as a war measure, proclaimed all slaves held or owned in this State emancipated from slavery, and having carried that proclamation into full practical effect, there shall henceforth be, within the State of Georgia, neither slavery nor involuntary servitude, save as a punishment for crime, after legal conviction thereof; provided, this acquiescence in the action of the Government of the United States is not intended to operate as a relinquishment, waiver, or estoppel of such claim for compensation of loss sustained by reason of the emancipation of his slaves, as any citizen of Georgia may hereafter make upon the justice and magnanimity of that Government.[11]

The most difficult task confronting the Convention was settlement of the State war debt, amounting to approximately eighteen million dollars. The subject of repudiation had been widely discussed before the assembling of the Convention and was the greatest bone of contention during the whole session. Perceiving that the Convention was opposed to repudiation, Provisional Governor Johnson telegraphed to President Johnson: "We need some aid to reject the war debt. Send me some word on the subject. What should the Convention do?"[12] President Johnson's reply was that repudiation of the war debt was an absolute condition for the reconstruction of Georgia. Confronted with this situation, finally, on November 7th, next to the last day of the Convention, an ordinance in-

---
[10] *Ibid.*, 343–44.
[11] Art. I., Par. XX.
[12] *Conf. Rec. of Ga.*, IV, 239.

troduced by A. H. Chappell, "to render null and void all debts of this State created for the purpose of carrying on the late war against the United States," was adopted by a vote of one hundred thirty-five to one hundred seventeen.[13]

## The Constitution of 1865

THE Constitution drawn up by the Convention of 1865 was so similar to the Constitution of 1861 that it is misleading to label it as a new constitution. The long bill of rights was continued, with the elimination of some of the broader generalizations, such as the statement that "The fundamental principles of Free Government cannot be too well understood, nor too often referred to," and the addition of a section prohibiting slavery. No changes of importance were made in the legislature. The precedent against a third term for the Governor, broken by Joseph E. Brown in 1861, was made a constitutional limitation. "Each Governor subsequently elected shall hold the of-

---

[13] *Ibid.*, 335-39; 402-04. Much litigation ensued during the next decade from the repudiation of war debts. The Georgia Supreme Court ruled that those who had paid taxes to the *de facto* government while it was supreme had no means of recovery, but that those who had not paid were under no obligation to pay (*O'Byrne vs. Savannah,* 41 Georgia 331). The rule, "contracts made in pursuance of the Rebellion are void," was easier to state than to apply. A note having as a consideration service as a substitute in the Confederate Army was held invalid (*Chancelry vs. Bailey,* 37 Georgia 352). Bonds issued by a county in 1862 to raise money to support indigent families of Confederate soldiers were held valid (*Bartow County vs. Newell,* 64 Georgia 700). A railroad transporting soldiers and receiving compensation therefor from the State or Confederacy was held to come under the rule *in pari dilecto* and hence not liable for negligence because both the soldiers and the railroad were engaged in an illegal transaction, but the same railroad was held liable for injury to one of the soldiers who had been forced to pay the fare of a slave who accompanied him (*Redd vs. Muscogee Rr. Co.,* 48 Georgia 101).

fice for two years, and until his successor shall be elected and qualified, and shall not be eligible to reëlection, after the expiration of a second term, for the period of four years," stated the first section of the third article.

The most significant changes in the Constitution related to the composition of the judiciary—a chronic defect in the constitutional structure of Georgia in the nineteenth century. The Constitution of 1861 had vested the appointment of judges of both the Supreme Court and the Superior Courts in the Governor. In an address delivered to the Convention of 1865 at its opening meeting, Provisional Governor Johnson stated: "Within the past few years we have made several experiments on our judicial system. These experiments . . . have demonstrated that the Judges should be independent of the Executive; and that sound policy and the wholesome administration of law require that the Governor be deprived of the appointment of all judicial functionaries."[14] By a vote of two hundred eight to sixty-one, the Convention placed the selection of judges of both the Supreme Court and the Superior Courts in the hands of the legislature. Judges of the inferior courts, courts of ordinary, and justices of the peace continued as under the old Constitution to be elected by the people. In the address referred to above, Provisional Governor Johnson earnestly recommended "the propriety of ordaining that the Supreme Court shall hold its sessions at one place, and that one place shall be the seat of government. . . . The advantages resulting from it," he pointed out, "will be many and great. It will better secure the convenience of suitors, and approximate more nearly in distributing justice at each man's door. It will add consequence to our Capitol, give more dignity to the Court, and more authority to their decisions." The Convention approved this point of

---

[14] *Conf. Rec. of Ga.*, IV, 41.

*A Constitutional History of Georgia*

view and wrote into the Constitution a provision that the Supreme Court should sit at the seat of government.

An interesting new clause in the Constitution of 1865 was that prohibiting "the marriage relation between White persons and persons of African descent."[15] The concluding Article of the Constitution contained a section on "the laws of general operation now of force in this state" which the reader will recognize as the source of Article XII of the present Constitution of Georgia.

## *Congressional Reconstruction*

BROWN and Stephens refused to let their names be used; so the only candidate for Governor in the election of November 15, 1865, was Charles J. Jenkins, who received 37,200 votes.[16] Most of the people were for accepting the new order, and when the General Assembly convened on December 4th, it speedily ratified the Thirteenth Amendment to the Federal Constitution. On December 14th Jenkins was inaugurated as Governor. "That," said Bill Arp, "was a proud and glorious day, when that great and good man was makin' his affectin' speech. We all felt happy, and Captain Dodd, the member from Polk, remarked that he would like to die then, for he never expected to feel as heavenly again."[17] Five days later James Johnson was relieved of his position as Provisional Governor and directed by Secretary of State Seward to turn over the papers and property relating to that trust to Gov-

---

[15] Art. IV, Par. III.

[16] Avery, *History of Georgia*, 351.

[17] Charles Henry Smith, *Bill Arp So-Called* (New York, 1866), 155. The writings of Charles Henry Smith, or "Bill Arp" (1826–1903), country lawyer, politician, farmer, journalist, homely philosopher and humorist, who lived in Lawrenceville, Rome, and Cartersville, furnish an excellent source for the life and thought of Georgians of the last half of the Nineteenth Century. Miss Annie May Christie, of Decatur, is writing a biography of Bill Arp.

ernor Jenkins. Reconstruction, it appeared, was at an end in Georgia. Reassembling in January, 1866, the General Assembly elected Alexander H. Stephens and Herschel V. Johnson to the United States Senate. During the year 1866 the government of Georgia functioned normally, except for the presence of Federal troops and the Freedmen's Bureau, and considerable progress was made toward reëstablishing the economic life of the people. In striking contrast to the doctrine of secession that had been so elaborately expounded in Georgia seven years earlier, in determining legal rights acquired from contracts and judgments under the Confederacy, the State Supreme Court ruled that Georgia had continued to be one of the States of the Union during the war. "It is to be regretted," wrote Chief Justice Warner, "that the political heresy of peaceable State secession from the Union . . . should ever have found lodgment in the minds of our people. It finds no legal support either in the Federal Constitution or in the decisions of the Supreme Court, the recognized interpreter and expounder of that instrument." [18]

President Johnson's whole plan of reconstruction was based upon the theory that the Southern States never had been out of the Union, but that their attempt to secede had placed them in a condition of suspended vitality. This theory was consistent with the theory of Lincoln that the war had been waged not against the States as such but against combinations of individuals too powerful to be dealt with by the ordinary processes of law. From this

---

[18] *Central Railroad and Banking Co. vs. Ward*, 37 Georgia 515. The Court held invalid title to stock acquired under a judgment of a Confederate Court confiscating the property of alien enemies. In a concurring opinion in *Hardeman vs. Downer*, 39 Georgia 425, sustaining the validity of the homestead and exemption provisions of the Constitution of 1868, Justice Brown held that in 1868 Georgia was "under the dictation and control of Congress," and hence was not a State. *Ga. Bar Journal*, VI (May, 1944), 291, 296–297.

## A Constitutional History of Georgia

it logically followed that the problem of reconstruction was a matter to be adjusted by the Federal executive. But Senator Charles Sumner of Massachusetts advocated a theory of State suicide according to which the seceded States had reverted to the condition of a territory and were therefore under the exclusive jurisdiction of Congress. Somewhat similar was the conquered-province theory advanced by Thaddeus Stevens, leader of the radicals in the House of Representatives. In December, 1865, Congress set up a joint committee of fifteen to inquire into the conditions of the Southern States and to report whether they were entitled to representation in Congress. In April, 1866, this Committee reported that the States lately in rebellion were disorganized communities, without civil government by virtue of which political relations could legally exist between them and the federal government, that they were hostile to the North, to freedmen, and to Unionists, and that before readmitting them to Statehood the main features of the Civil Rights Bill, recently passed by Congress over the President's veto, should be incorporated into the Federal Constitution and ratification of this amendment made a condition of readmission. The radicals controlled Congress and pushed through this program.

Following President Johnson's advice, the legislatures of every Southern State rejected the Fourteenth Amendment. In a message of January 16, 1866, Governor Jenkins pointed out the inconsistency of the Federal Government in forcing a State to ratify an amendment as a condition of readmission to the Union: If a State was not already a member of the Union, how could it legally ratify an amendment? In rejecting the Fourteenth Amendment in November, 1866, the General Assembly adopted a report containing the following unanswerable propositions:

1. If Georgia is not a State composing part of the Federal Government known as the Government of the United

## Reconstruction

States, amendments to the Constitution of the United States are not properly before this body.

2. If Georgia is a State composing part of the Federal Government . . . , then these amendments are not proposed according to the requirements of the Federal Constitution, and are proposed in such a manner as to forbid the legislature from discussing the merits of the amendments without an implied surrender of the rights of the State.[19]

President Johnson attempted an appeal to the nation in the Congressional election of 1866, but, unfortunately for him and for the South, the radicals carried both houses of Congress by sweeping majorities, thus assuring defeat of the President's program of reconstruction.

By an act of March 2, 1867, supplemented by acts of March 23rd and July 19th, Congressional reconstruction was established. Military rule was to be resumed with the South divided into five military districts, each under the command of an officer of the United States Army not below the rank of brigadier general, appointed by the President with the consent of the Senate. This officer duly supported by an adequate military force should register the legal voters of each State, excluding those who had ever been disfranchised for disloyalty, and admitting Negroes on the same basis as whites. This done, he should arrange for the election of delegates to a convention to draw up a new constitution providing for Negro suffrage. If on submission to the people this constitution should receive a majority vote, the general in charge should order the necessary elections to put it into effect. If Congress then approved the new constitution and the legislature elected under it should ratify the Fourteenth Amendment so as to make it a part of the National Constitution, the reconstructed State should be considered eligible for readmission to both houses of Congress and military rule would be withdrawn. These harsh measures were passed over

---
[19] *House Journal, 1866*, p. 67–68.

## A Constitutional History of Georgia

the vigorous opposition and veto of President Johnson; there was no course open to him other than to enforce them.

General John Pope assumed control of Georgia as part of the Third Military District on April 1, 1867, and reconstruction began all over again. The State was divided into eight military districts with headquarters in Savannah, Augusta, Atlanta, Dahlonega, Rome, Athens, Columbus, and Macon. General Pope was understood to be a conservative in politics, and for several months after his arrival a fair degree of harmony prevailed between him and the civil officers of the State, nearly all of whom retained their posts.

The people of Georgia had willingly submitted to the Presidential program of reconstruction at the end of the War, but they were not psychologically prepared in 1867 to be reconstructed a second time under a punitive scheme. The advice of Brown, who managed to be on the winning side in most political questions, was: "Agree with thine adversary quickly." Delay, he maintained, would but make the terms harder. For taking this position, the press of the State denounced him bitterly as a traitor. Notable among the vigorous denunciations of Brown and the military regime was a series of articles entitled "Notes on the Situation" by Benjamin H. Hill, published in the *Augusta Chronicle and Sentinel,* beginning June 19, 1867.[20] Governor Jenkins opposed submission to the Congressional demands, and sought to have the Reconstruction Acts tested before the Supreme Court of the United States; but the Court dismissed his plea in the case of *Georgia vs. Stanton et. al.* for want of jurisdiction in a political question.[21] Robert Toombs returned

---

[20] For a summary of the argument of Hill, see Haywood J. Pearce, Jr., *Benjamin H. Hill* (Chicago, 1928), 149.

[21] 6 Wallace 50.

## Reconstruction

from Europe in the summer of 1867 ready to organize the anti-reconstruction feeling. In retaliation for criticism of his administration by a student in a commencement oration, General Pope closed the University of Georgia for a short period. Two of his orders issued in August requiring that Negroes be placed on jury lists and that all official publications be confined to newspapers that had not opposed reconstruction under the acts of Congress added to the bitterness toward him. Judge Augustus Reese, of the Ocmulgee Circuit, refused to admit Negroes to the jury list and was summarily removed from office.

General Pope proceeded to carry through the reconstruction program outlined by Congress. A registration of the people was conducted in April, 1867, under the supervision of Colonel Edward Hulbert. Illiterate Negroes were puzzled over the meaning of registration and the extent of their new political rights, but they were herded to the polls. The conservative whites who were not excluded by the strict test oath registered in the hope of defeating the radical reconstruction program. The registration resulted in a white majority of less than two thousand, the figures being: whites, 95,214; colored, 93,457. At the election held on October 29th, 30th, 31st, and November 1st and 2nd, the electors were asked to vote for or against a convention, and for delegates thereto. Inasmuch as the Congressional Act of March 23rd provided that a constitutional convention should be held only in case a majority of those registered voted for a convention, the conservatives abstained from voting, hoping that the required majority would not be secured. Of the total vote of 106,410 cast, three-fourths of the voters being Negroes, 102,283 were in favor of the convention. Thus it would have been far better if the conservatives had taken part in the selection of delegates.[22]

---
[22] Thompson, *Reconstruction in Georgia,* 186.

## A Constitutional History of Georgia

The Constitutional Convention assembled in Atlanta on December 9, 1867, and remained in session until March 11th of the following year. J. R. Parrott, of Bartow County, was elected President, and P. M. Scheibley, Secretary. Of the one hundred sixty-nine delegates attending, the great majority were Scalawags, nine were Carpetbaggers, thirty-seven were Negroes, and about a dozen were conservative whites. The delegates in general were obscure men with little experience in public affairs. The contempt in which they were held by the better element was recognized by the President of the Convention in his opening address when he said: "Many of us have come here from amongst a people who have spurned us and spit upon us. . . . The bitter and proscriptive spirit manifested toward us by our neighbors . . . should not influence our action. . . . We should form a State Government for an unwilling people, based upon the soundest principles of justice. . . ." [23] Prominent among the Negroes were Bradley, Campbell, and Turner. Investigation proved that Bradley, who boasted the given name Aaron Alpeoria, had served a jail sentence in New York for seduction and had been stricken from the roll of attorneys in Massachusetts for malpractice and contempt of court. He proved particularly obnoxious, and was expelled from the Convention by unanimous vote for "malicious mouthing." [24] Tunis G. Campbell, whose record was also black, had come to Georgia from New Jersey soon after the War and set up a so-called republic on St. Catherines Island with himself at its head. H. M. Turner, a better sort, had served as a chaplain in the Union Army and later entered missionary work for the African Methodist Church; but at this period he saw a greater oppor-

---

[23] *Conf. Rec. of Ga.*, VI, 216.
[24] *Ibid.*, 580.

*Reconstruction*

tunity in politics than in religion. He later became a bishop.

The Carpetbaggers included men from Vermont, Ohio, New York, and other Northern States who had come South seeking their fortune and had been in Georgia for only two or three years. For example, there was J. E. Bryant, of Maine, who had served in the Union Army and settled in Georgia after the War, and C. H. Prince, also of Maine, who had come to Georgia with the Freedmen's Bureau. These Carpetbaggers, like the Negroes in the Convention, were largely controlled by Rufus Bullock and radical Republicans. But the Convention of 1867 in Georgia was not dominated by Negroes and Carpetbaggers, as was the case in some of the Southern States. Its principal leaders—Rufus B. Bullock, Benjamin F. Conley, Amos T. Ackerman, and N. K. McCay—though not natives of Georgia, were men who had resided in the State long enough to establish permanent interest.[25]

The relief of debtors occupied more attention than any other subject in the proceedings of the Convention. A stay law of December 13, 1866, that gave temporary relief from judgments for the levy or sale of property to fulfill liabilities contracted before June 1, 1865, had already been held unconstitutional by the Supreme Court of Georgia.[26] Rufus Bullock, supported by the radical Republicans, Negroes, and Carpetbaggers, was champion of the relief measure before the Convention. This group had less to gain from relief than those who opposed it, and apparently the measure was sponsored for political rather than economic motives. An ordinance for a temporary stay of executions on debts was adopted soon after

[25] Thompson, *Reconstruction in Georgia*, 192.
[26] *Aycock vs. Martin*, 37 Georgia 124.

## A Constitutional History of Georgia

the Convention assembled. The Constitution as finally adopted by the Convention deprived the courts of jurisdiction to enforce most debts contracted before June 1, 1865, and authorized the legislature to levy a twenty-five per cent tax on creditors for debts contracted before that date unless the creditor should abandon his claim. In addition a homestead of realty and personalty to the value of $3,000 which should be free from judgment was allowed to each head of a family, guardian, or trustee of a family of minor children. Congress accepted the homestead provision, but required as a condition of the readmission of Georgia into the Union annulment of the other relief clauses in the Constitution of 1868, except as they applied to debts contracted for the price of slaves or contracts made with the intention of aiding rebellion.[27]

The Convention passed an ordinance directing that the State Treasurer pay forty thousand dollars to the Convention's disbursing agent to meet incidental expenses and to pay the *per diem* compensation of its members. Treasurer John Jones responded that he could not disburse money except upon a warrant of the Governor sanctioned by the Comptroller General. General Pope then asked Governor Jenkins to issue a warrant for this money, but the Governor refused, saying that he found nothing in the Federal law to indicate an intention "to saddle the Treasury of Georgia with the cost of this novel experiment."[28] General George G. Meade, who replaced General Pope in Georgia on December 28, 1867, inherited this quarrel. A week after his arrival he removed Governor Jenkins and Treasurer Jones and appointed in

---

[27] McElreath, *op. cit.*, 165, 340, 348–350; *Conf. Rec. of Ga.*, VI, 921–924. Under the leadership of Joseph E. Brown, Chief Justice from December, 1868, to June, 1870, the Supreme Court of Georgia took a liberal view of questions involving economic matters. A relief act of 1868 was sustained in *Catts & Johnson et. al. vs. Hardee*, 38 Georgia 350.

[28] Avery, *History of Georgia*, 379

*Reconstruction*

their places Brigadier General Thomas H. Ruger and Captain Charles F. Rockwell. A few days later he removed Comptroller General John T. Burns and Secretary of State N. C. Barnett on charges of obstruction to the fulfillment of the Reconstruction Acts, and detailed Captain Charles Wheaton to fill both offices. After hiding the Great Seal of the State, Governor Jenkins fled with $400,000 of the State's funds which he deposited for safety in a New York bank. He sought without success to bring suit against Ruger and Rockwell in the Supreme Court of the United States.

## *The Constitution of 1868*

ADDITIONS made in the bill of rights by the Convention of 1867–68 expanded the first article of the Constitution to the length of four and a half pages, divided into thirty-three sections. Among the new provisions, all logical products of the time and circumstances, were the following: "The social status of the citizen shall never be the subject of legislation;" "Whipping as a punishment for crime is prohibited;" "Mechanics and laborers shall have liens upon the property of their employers for labor performed or material furnished. . . ." The substance of the first paragraph in the Fourteenth Amendment of the Federal Constitution was inserted in the new bill of rights.

The electoral franchise had been the subject of one of the paragraphs on miscellaneous matters at the end of the former Constitutions of Georgia. It was now elevated to the second article, entitled Franchise and Elections. The phrase "free white male citizens of this State" used in earlier Constitutions in defining the electorate was replaced by the phrase, "male citizens of the United

States." The residence qualification for voting was reduced to only six months in the State and thirty days in the county.

The composition of the Senate remained as it had been under the previous Constitution—one member elected from each of forty-four senatorial districts, each composed of three contiguous counties. The composition of the House of Representatives was changed by the introduction of a system of representation which, with slight alterations, was retained in the Constitution of 1877 and continues to this day: The six counties largest in population were given three representatives each; the thirty-one next largest counties, two representatives each; and the remaining ninety-five counties, one representative each. The Constitution of 1868 provided that the General Assembly might alter the apportionment among the counties after each decennial census by the United States Government, but that in no event should the aggregate number of Representatives be changed. The qualification of residence in the State for three years formerly required of both Senators and Representatives was reduced to two years in the case of a Senator and to one year for Representatives. The term of Senators was increased to four years. The powers of the General Assembly remained largely as before, including that of electing the Secretary of State, Treasurer, and Comptroller General.

The Governor's term was increased to four years, and there was no prohibition against reëlection. The power of granting pardons, formerly given to the General Assembly in cases of capital offenses, was vested in the Governor alone and was unqualified, except in cases of impeachment. The Governor was granted authority to appoint judges of the Supreme, Superior, and District Courts, the Attorney General of the State, solicitors of the

*Reconstruction*

Superior Courts, attorneys of the District Courts, and the State School Commissioner. Otherwise, his powers remained as they had been under the previous Constitution.

The judiciary, ever a subject of new experiments in Georgia, was made simpler under the Constitution of 1868 than it had ever been. A Supreme Court of three judges, appointed by the Governor for terms of twelve years, was established for the correction of errors made by the lower courts. A Superior Court, consisting of one judge appointed by the Governor for a term of eight years, was provided for each judicial circuit in the State. The Superior Courts were given jurisdiction as before over both civil and criminal cases, with exclusive jurisdiction in cases of divorce, in cases where the offender was subject to the loss of life or confinement in the penitentiary, in cases respecting titles to land, and in cases of equity. The Inferior Courts that dated from the Constitution of 1798 were expressly abolished and their books, papers, and proceedings transferred to the Courts of Ordinary. In their place the new Constitution set up a District Court for each of the forty-four senatorial districts. Judges of the District Courts, appointed by the Governor for a term of four years, assisted by district attorneys, appointed in like manner for the same term, were to hold court not less than once a month in each county. These District Courts were given jurisdiction over all criminal cases not punishable with death or imprisonment in the penitentiary, and in such civil cases as the legislature might direct. Trial in the District Courts should be without jury, except upon demand of the accused, and then the jury should consist of seven members. A Court of Ordinary for each county, and a Justice of the Peace and a Notary Public for each militia district were continued as before.

## A Constitutional History of Georgia

The Constitution directed the General Assembly to provide "a thorough system of general education, to be forever free to all children of the State." The office of State School Commissioner was established, the Commissioner to be appointed by the Governor for a term of four years. The poll tax, taxes on shows, exhibitions, and the sale of spirituous liquors, and the proceeds from commutations for military service (provided especially for conscientious objectors) were set aside for the support of the common schools. The funds from these sources were to be supplemented, if necessary, by a general property tax.

The general provisions of Article VII, Homestead and Exemption, were outlined above, but one further provision in this article deserves notice, namely: "All property of the wife, in her possession at the time of her marriage, and all property given to, inherited, or acquired by her, shall remain her separate property, and not liable for the debts of her husband." Under the statute law of Georgia prior to 1866, the control of a husband over his wife's property was even greater than that existing under the common law. The Married Women's Act of 1866 gave a wife control of her property and freed it from liability for the debts of her husband. This principle has remained a part of the constitutional law of Georgia since 1868.[29]

Article VIII provided for organizing a militia. Article IX fixed the term of county officers at two years. Article X made Atlanta the seat of government. Article XI listed the order of supremacy in the laws of general operation in the State (including *Irwin's Code* and the laws passed by the General Assembly during the period of the War, except those in aid of rebellion or in conflict with the Constitution and laws of the United States or the Georgia

---

[29] See McElreath, *op. cit.*, 166–168, for a fuller treatment of the subject.

Constitution of 1868). Article XII reverted to the method of constitutional amendment that had prevailed under the Constitution of 1798 (*i.e.*, passage of an amendment by a two-thirds vote of two successive legislatures), but added the requirement of submission of amendments to popular vote before final ratification.

## The Bullock Regime

GENERAL MEADE set April 20-24 (1868) as the date for voting to ratify or reject the new State Constitution and to elect officers. Profiting from the experience of their error in refusing to vote in 1867, the conservatives tried to perfect an organization and control the election of 1868 in order to prevent the State from falling under the control of Negroes, Carpetbaggers, and Scalawags. Rather than submit to this, they preferred to continue under military rule. After Judges Augustus Reese and David Irwin had been declared ineligible by the commanding General, the Democratic Executive Committee nominated, with General Pope's approval, General John B. Gordon as their candidate for Governor. The strategy of the Democrats was to elect Gordon but defeat the new Constitution. The Republicans in the Constitutional Convention had nominated Rufus Bullock, and in the campaign they used the new Constitution as their platform, emphasizing in particular the provisions for the relief of debtors. In the election it was charged that droves of Negroes were brought in from South Carolina, and that many were carted about from county to county and voted more than once. Bullock won by a majority of 7,172.[30]

---

[30] Thompson, *Reconstruction in Georgia*, 204. The act of Congress rejecting the provisions of the Georgia Constitution of 1868 for the relief of debtors was not passed until June 25, 1868.

## A Constitutional History of Georgia

In order to facilitate the reëstablishment of civil government, General Meade named Bullock as Provisional Governor before the convening of the General Assembly on July 4, 1868. The Assembly ratified the Fourteenth Amendment to the Federal Constitution and gave its assent to the elimination from the State Constitution of the relief provisions that had been objected to by Congress. On July 22nd Bullock was inaugurated, and eight days later reconstruction in Georgia was for a second time declared at an end, albeit a considerable number of Federal troops still remained in the State. The end was not yet; more bitter experience with reconstruction lay ahead.

General Meade was out of sympathy with the radical Republicans in Georgia and refused to support Governor Bullock in having members of the General Assembly declared ineligible when it assembled. A test of strength in the legislature was shown in the election of United States Senators. A coalition of conservatives, moderate Republicans, and independents—in general, the anti-Bullock element—elected Joshua Hill and H. V. M. Miller, in opposition to Joseph E. Brown and Foster Blodgett, who were supported by Bullock. Friction between Bullock and the legislature, and the fact that the conservatives in Georgia gained control too quickly to please the radicals in Congress, was soon to place Georgia again under military rule. In September, 1868, the legislature, over the protest of Governor Bullock, expelled its Negro members, twenty-five from the House and three from the Senate, on the ground that under the Constitution of Georgia Negroes were ineligible to hold office.[31] In a case decided the next year, the Supreme Court of

---

[31] The infamous Aaron Alpeoria Bradley had been expelled earlier. Four members included in the expulsion resolution as originally introduced were permitted to retain their seats because they were so nearly white that their race was indeterminate. Thompson, *Reconstruction in Georgia*, 213–214.

*Reconstruction*

Georgia ruled that Negroes were eligible to hold office.[32] Even worse in the eyes of the Republican Congress than expulsion of the Negroes from the legislature was the fact that Georgia chose Democratic electors in the presidential election of 1868. The effect of the Ku Klux Klan in this election was unmistakable. This secret organization of the whites used nocturnal costume parades and other weird acts to play upon the superstitious nature of the Negroes and keep them in subordination. The original mistake had been made by Congress in attempting to extend the franchise to illiterate freedmen. At this period when legal remedies could not be had, the Klan served a wholesome purpose in convincing ignorant Negroes that voting was not meant for them, and it was more effective than the courts in preventing Negro men crazed with their new freedom from making attacks upon white women.

Viewing with alarm the course of events, in December, 1868, Senator Charles Sumner introduced a bill for a further reconstruction of Georgia. The Senate had never admitted Georgia's members, Hill and Miller. The House of Representatives had seated the members from

---

[32] *White vs. Clements*, 39 Georgia 232, decided in June, 1869. White, a Negro, had been elected clerk of the Superior Court of Chatham County, and Clements, his opponent, sought to have him removed through *quo warranto* proceedings on the ground that he had one-eighth or more of African blood. The majority of the Court, Justices H. K. McCay and Joseph E. Brown, held that since Negroes had been made citizens, they were entitled to hold office in the absence of any law that specifically disqualified them. Justice Hiram Warner dissented. The decision raised the question of whether the General Assembly should re-seat the Negroes who had been expelled. Many prominent men supported the position of the *Atlanta Constitution* that the decision of the Court should be obeyed, but that the parliamentary method would be to have an election to fill the vacancies. Avery, *History of Georgia*, 415. In another decision of 1869, *Scott vs. The State of Georgia*, 39 Georgia 232, Justice Brown wrote the unanimous opinion of the Court that marriage between Whites and Negroes was illegal. *Ga. Bar Journal*, *VI* (May, 1944), 296.

## A Constitutional History of Georgia

Georgia elected in 1868, but they were not seated after March 4, 1869. The Joint Committee on Reconstruction, to which Sumner's bill for the further reconstruction of Georgia was referred, heard extensive, conflicting evidence on conditions prevailing in the State. The most damaging witness for Georgia was none other than Governor Bullock who contended that federal troops were needed to preserve order. He wanted the legislature of Georgia reorganized under the test oath that would exclude a number of white members and reinstate the Negroes who had been expelled. The indications were that Bullock, while openly supporting the Fifteenth Amendment to the Federal Constitution, used his influence to have the legislature of Georgia reject it in March, 1869, in order to support his bid for federal troops. Congress was equivocal on the stand to take in regard to Georgia until it developed that her vote was needed for the passage of this Amendment. On December 22, 1869, the Georgia Bill remanded the State to military jurisdiction under the Reconstruction Acts of 1867, with the added requirement that the Fifteenth Amendment be ratified as a condition of her readmission to the Union. General Alfred H. Terry was placed in command of Georgia.

Rufus Bullock, the central figure in the reconstruction of Georgia, is described by Avery as "a large, handsome, social specimen of a man, pleasant-mannered, and well-liked." [33] He was not a Carpetbagger in the true sense of the word, for he came to Georgia from New York in 1859, was connected with the Southern Express Company in Augusta, and held a minor post in the Quartermaster Corps of the Confederate Army. Supported by radical Republicans, Negroes, and the debtor class, he rose to power in 1868. The abuses of his regime were severe, but not as extreme as the reconstruction abuses

---

[33] *History of Georgia*, 384.

in most of the other Southern States. Bullock's worst offenses as Governor arose from his association with Hannibal I. Kimball, his intimate friend and financial adviser, whose chief enterprise was the construction of railroads with State aid. In 1870 a large hotel, the Kimball House, was built in Atlanta, and it was commonly believed to have been financed with State bonds. A scandal of widespread denunciation was Governor Bullock's payment of $31,000, without legislative authorization, to Kimball for heating and lighting an abandoned opera house used as the State capitol, albeit the sum involved in this deal was small when compared with many of the railroad transactions between Bullock and Kimball. The notoriety of Kimball's financial dealings led the Negroes to concoct a refrain:

> H. I. Kimball's on de floor,
> 'Taint gwine ter rain no more.[34]

In January, 1870, Provisional Governor Bullock reconvened the General Assembly upon the basis of the election of 1868, before the Negroes had been expelled. A test of eligibility of members conducted under appointees of the Governor assisted by General Terry—Terry's Purge, it was called—resulted in re-seating the Negroes and debarring a sufficient number of conservative whites to give Bullock's Republicans a strong majority in both houses. The new legislature promptly ratified the Fifteenth Amendment, and re-ratified the Fourteenth. As members to the United States Senate it named Foster Blodgett for the term ending in 1877, H. P. Farrow for the 1873 term, and R. H. Whiteley for the short term, 1871.[35]

Feeling that Georgia had been tinkered with long

---

[34] Thompson, *Reconstruction in Georgia*, 217.
[35] *Ibid.*, 267.

enough, on July 15, 1870, Congress passed an act declaring Georgia entitled to representation. The question then arose as to who were the properly accredited Senators, Hill and Miller, elected in 1868, or Farrow and Whiteley. After investigating, Hill and Miller were seated. Representatives in the lower house of Congress had in the meanwhile already been seated. Georgia was again in the Union.

## The Democrats Regain Control

BULLOCK had had a difficult time remaining in power even with the support of Federal troops; now that Georgia was back in the Union, his fall could not be long delayed. The election of members to the State legislature in December, 1870, resulted in a large Democratic majority for both houses. Foreseeing that he would be impeached when the legislature met in November, 1871, Bullock filed his resignation on October 23rd to become effective two days before the meeting of the legislature. Ben F. Conley, President of the Senate at its last session, and an ally of Bullock, was secretly sworn in as Governor in the hope that he would be able to hold office until the expiration of Bullock's official term, which would last more than another year. But the legislature passed a bill over Conley's veto ordering a special election for Governor on the third Tuesday in December. Of special interest during the short administration of Governor Conley were the receipt and subsequent sale for ninety cents per acre of the 272,000 acres of land which Georgia received for educational purposes under the Morrill Act of 1862. James M. Smith, a Columbus lawyer, and Speaker of the House of Representatives, was elected Governor in December, without opposition, the Repub-

## Reconstruction

lican nominee, James Atkins, declining to run. He was inaugurated on January 12, 1872, and thus for the first time since April, 1867, the Democrats were in full control of the State government. Ex-Governor Jenkins returned the great seal of the State which had "never been desecrated by the grasp of a military usurper's hand," and in appreciation the Legislature of 1872 authorized Governor Smith to present to him a gold facsimile with the inscription, *In arduis fidelis*. In the regular election of 1872, Governor Smith, Democratic nominee for reëlection, won over Dawson A. Walker, the Republican nominee, by a vote of 104,256 to 45,812. Horace Greeley, candidate of the Liberal Republicans and Democrats, received the largest popular vote for President in Georgia that year, but as he died before the date of the meeting of the electoral college, Georgia's electoral vote was split between Greeley, B. Gratz Brown, and Charles J. Jenkins.[36] The opposition of Alexander H. Stephens to the fusion of Democrats and Liberal Republicans placed him in opposition to the dominant element in the Democratic party and led the General Assembly, by a close margin, to elect John B. Gordon rather than Stephens to the United States Senate in 1872. The Eighth Congressional District then sent Stephens to the lower house of Congress where he served until 1882.

As was to be expected, committees of the General Assembly carried out an extensive investigation of the Bullock regime, Robert Toombs volunteering his services as prosecuting attorney. Bullock was found guilty of corruption, dishonesty, and general mismanagement. Some of the charges were indictable offenses, but when Bullock returned in 1876 to stand trial he was acquitted because of insufficiency of evidence against him. The legislature of 1872 declared bonds amounting to $7,957,000 issued

---
[36] Avery, *History of Georgia*, 502–503.

## A Constitutional History of Georgia

during Bullock's regime to be fraudulent, null, and void. An amendment to the Constitution adopted in 1877, the only amendment ever made in the Constitution of 1868, verified the action of the legislature in declaring these bonds void, and also declared certain additional endorsements of railroad bonds by the State under Bullock to be illegal.[87]

[87] Act of Feb. 27, 1877; ratified May 1, 1877.

CHAPTER XII

The Constitution of 1877

As soon as the Bullock regime fell and the Democrats returned to power in Georgia, an agitation arose for a new State constitution. The method by which the Constitution of 1868 had been formed and imposed upon the people was resented, regardless of its intrinsic merits. Throughout the year 1876 the press of the State repeatedly mentioned the need of a new constitution, and numerous presentments by grand juries urged that a constitutional convention be called. In 1877 a bill by Allen D. Candler, then a representative from Hall County, passed the General Assembly providing for the submission of the question of holding a convention to popular vote. An election held on the second Tuesday in June resulted in 48,181 votes cast for and 39,057 against a convention.[1]

The act of the General Assembly making provision for the convention adopted senatorial districts as the unit of representation, but fixed representation on a basis of population in the ratio of one delegate to every six thousand inhabitants. Thus the representation of senatorial districts varied from one to eight, with a total

---

[1] Avery, *History of Georgia*, 529

of one hundred and ninety-four delegates for the whole State.[2]

On July 11, 1877, one hundred and eighty-five convention delegates assembled in the hall of the House of Representatives in Atlanta. Lucius J. Gartrell, a delegate from Fulton County, called the Convention to order and moved for the purpose of temporary organization that T. L. Guerry, of Quitman County, be called to the chair. In a brief address Guerry referred to the moment as an "auspicious occasion . . . , an indication that the iron heel of despotism . . . [had] been lifted from off this people. . . ." After the election of two temporary secretaries and a roll call, the Convention unanimously elected as its permanent president Charles J. Jenkins, hale and hearty despite his three score and ten years. In addressing the Convention, Jenkins stressed the distinction between constitutional and statutory law and warned against including in the constitution details subject to frequent change that should properly be left to the legislature; yet he felt that the recent experience of the State pointed to the need of constitutional restrictions in the field of finance.[3] The Convention voted down a resolution to notify the Governor that it had convened, feeling that a convention of the people should be absolutely independent of the government. This was not an indication that Governor Colquitt was unpopular with the members of the Convention, for the opposite was true.

The large number of delegates necessitated the use of a system of committees. After some debate, it was agreed that there should be thirteen standing committees of

---

[2] *Acts of 1877*, pp. 26–28. There were forty-four senatorial districts under the Constitution of 1868.

[3] Samuel W. Small, *A Stenographic Report of the Proceedings of the Constitutional Convention Held in Atlanta, Georgia, 1877* (Atlanta, 1877), 2–5.

## The Constitution of 1877

nine members each, one member to be appointed by President Jenkins from each of the nine congressional districts in the State. These committees and their chairmen were as follows:

1. Legislative Department—Robert Toombs
2. Executive Department—Lucius J. Gartrell
3. Judicial Department—Alexander R. Lawton
4. Finance, Taxation, and Public Debt—Thomas J. Simmons
5. Public Institutions—S. W. Harris
6. Bill of Rights—James L. Seward
7. Elective Franchise—A. R. Wright
8. Militia—R. B. Nisbet
9. Counties and County Officers—James M. Mobley
10. Education—A. N. Hansel
11. Homesteads and Exemptions—Pryor L. Mynatt
12. Laws of General Operation—Abda Johnson
13. Amendments and Miscellaneous Provisions— W. T. Thompson.

It will be observed that these thirteen committees represented the thirteen articles of the existing constitution (that of 1868), and that by replacing the name of the Committee on Public Institutions with "Power of the General Assembly over Taxation" one has the headings of the thirteen articles of the Constitution of 1877.

In addition there was a committee of twenty-six on Order, Consistency, and Harmony of the Constitution (commonly referred to as the Committee on Revision), made up of two members from each of the thirteen other committees. Resolutions were referred by the President to the appropriate committee without debate, which, in turn, reported to the Convention through the Committee on Revision.

Maintaining order proved a difficult task in so numerous a body. President Jenkins tried to act as an impartial moderator, but, as he himself confessed early in the proceedings, he was none too well versed in parliamentary law. At times the noise was so great that members could not hear what was being said.[4]

As chairman of the Committee on Revision, Toombs held the most strategic position in the Convention. Without waiting until all of the thirteen committees had completed their work, he reported articles on various subjects to the Convention for adoption from day to day. There was considerable complaint over this method, members holding that they could not vote intelligently upon the parts until they had seen how they would fit into the general plan of the Constitution. On July 24th the *Atlanta Constitution* reported that "General Robert Toombs . . . , by all odds the most conspicuous figure in the Convention, . . . has ideas on every subject, and no contingency finds him unprepared or unwilling to press them." Toombs was particularly interested in safeguarding the finances of the State through constitutional limitations, and is reported to have said later that he had "locked the door to the Treasury and given the key to the people." After one month the Convention had spent its $25,000 appropriation and the State Treasurer refused to honor any more drafts. He referred the matter to Governor Colquitt who accepted the ruling of the Attorney General that there were no legal means to make further payments. Toombs was in no disposition to see the Convention's work disrupted for lack of money, so he personally advanced the funds necessary to complete the Constitution—approximately $20,000, which the State later repaid.[5]

A number of members realized as the Convention pro-

---

[4] For examples, see Small's *Report*, 37, 75, 138.
[5] Kenneth Coleman, *The Constitutional Convention of 1877*. M.A. thesis at the University of Georgia, 1940.

*The Constitution of 1877*

ceeded that too many details were being incorporated into the new Constitution. For example, in opposing provisions for a definite salary for the Governor, Mr. Guerrard said: "I am opposed to the idea that all wisdom will die with us. The people were wise when they sent us here, and it shows that the people who are able to collect such an amount of wisdom, and to put it here to shine in this hall, will be wise and will remain wise after this convention has dissolved and its members gone back to mingle as indistinguishable atoms among the great mass of the people."[6] After prolonged debate over almost every paragraph of the new Constitution, the Convention completed its work on August 25 (1877), and submitted the document to the people. Both Senators Gordon and Hill supported the new Constitution, but Governor Colquitt gave it only a passive approval as the best available at the time. On December 5th the people approved the document by a vote of 110,442 to 40,947. At the same time they selected Atlanta in preference to Milledgeville as the State Capital by a vote of 99,147 to 55,201, and approved the homestead provisions of the Constitution of 1877 over those in the Constitution of 1868 by a vote of 94,722 to 52,000. On December 21st (1877) Governor Colquitt proclaimed the new Constitution to be in effect.[7]

## *Provisions of the Constitution of 1877*

ARTICLE I of the Constitution, the Bill of Rights, continued to be an elaborate list of personal rights, most of them dating from the Constitution of 1861, now divided into five sections covering five printed pages. "The enumeration of rights herein contained as a part of this

---
[6] Small's *Report*, 115.
[7] Coleman, *loc. cit.*

Constitution, shall not be construed to deny to the people any inherent rights which they may have hitherto enjoyed," concluded the last paragraph.

Article II, the Elective Franchise, remained largely as under the previous Constitution. The franchise was extended to male citizens of the United States, twenty-one years of age, who had resided in the State for one year and in the county six months before the election, and paid all taxes required. The residence qualification under the Constitution of 1868 had been six months in the State and thirty days in the county. Election returns for members of the General Assembly and officers commissioned by the Governor were to be made to the Secretary of State.

Article III left the composition of the General Assembly largely as before, the Senate to consist of forty-four members elected from forty-four districts, composed of counties as previously arranged; the House of Representatives to consist of one hundred seventy-five members, the six largest counties having three Representatives each, the twenty-six next largest counties, two Representatives each, and the remaining one hundred five counties, one Representative each. The term of Senators had previously been four years, but by the new Constitution the term of both Senators and Representatives was fixed at two years.

As a reaction to abuse of power during the Reconstruction period, the Convention of 1877 wrote into the Constitution numerous restrictions on legislative power. Two new articles, Articles IV and VII, were devoted to this object, but several notable restrictions were also placed in Article III. The general appropriation bill should contain nothing except appropriations fixed by previous laws and the ordinary expenses of government; all other appropriations should be made by separate bills,

## The Constitution of 1877

each embracing but one subject. On the passage of any bill appropriating money, the yeas and nays in each house should be recorded. Clerical expenses were limited to sixty dollars per day in the Senate and seventy dollars per day in the House of Representatives. The General Assembly should not authorize the construction of any street passenger railway in any city without consent of the corporate authorities. All special or local bills should originate in the House of Representatives and be referred to a committee of fifteen on local legislation whose duty it would be to consolidate local bills on the same subject for the consideration of the House. The House could not consider local or special bills other than those reported by this committee, except by a two-thirds vote.

Article IV, The Power of the General Assembly over Taxation, appeared in the Constitution for the first time. The right of taxation was declared to be a sovereign, inalienable right, belonging to the people in all republican governments, and the General Assembly was forbidden "to irrevocably give, grant, or restrain this right." The renewal or amendment of any existing charter was to be made only on the condition that the charter be subject to the provisions of the Constitution. The General Assembly was directed to pass laws for fair freight rates, preventing monopolies and rebates.

Article V vested the executive power in a Governor, elected for a two year term, ineligible to succeed himself after a second term for a period of four years. His powers remained substantially as before, including the broad pardoning power, but he was required to inform the General Assembly of each case of a reprieve or pardon, stating the name of the convict, the offense for which he had been convicted, and the reason for his pardon. The Secretary of State, Comptroller General, and Treasurer, formerly elected by the General Assembly, were made elective by the people for the same term as the Governor. The salary of each of these officers was limited to $2,000, and their clerical expenses, as well as those of the Governor, were limited.

The chief changes made in the judiciary, Article VI, were the abolition of the District Courts that had been erected in 1868 and a return to the practice of selecting most judges by the General Assembly rather than by the Governor, as provided under the Constitution of 1868. The Supreme Court should consist of three judges, selected by the General Assembly for terms of six years. It was given no original jurisdiction, but was to correct errors made in the lower courts. The Superior Courts continued to be the principal courts of original jurisdiction for both civil and criminal cases. The General Assembly should appoint one judge for each judicial circuit for a term of four years, and the Superior Court should sit in each county not less than twice a year. It was given exclusive jurisdiction in cases of divorce, in criminal cases where the offender was subject to the loss of life or confinement in the penitentiary, in cases involving land titles, and in equity cases. A Court of Ordinary and of Probate was continued for each county, with a judge elected by the people for a term of four years. The Ordinary was vested with most of the administrative duties that had been exercised by the Inferior Courts prior to 1868, and thus became the principal administrative officer of the county. "The Courts of Ordinary," stated the Constitution, "shall have such powers in relation to roads, bridges, ferries, public buildings, paupers, county officers, county funds, county taxes, and other county matters as may be conferred on them by law." The Constitution made provision for one justice of the peace for each militia district, to be elected by the people of the district for a period of four years, with power to

## The Constitution of 1877

try cases involving not more than one hundred dollars. It also authorized not more than one notary public for each militia district, with the same power as a justice of the peace, to be appointed by the judge of the Superior Court upon recommendation of the grand jury. The Attorney General of the State was to be elected by the people for a term of two years, and a Solicitor General for each judicial circuit was to be selected by the General Assembly for a term of four years. Low salaries were fixed in the Constitution for most judicial officers, but they were subject to change by a two-thirds vote of the General Assembly.

Article VII, Finance, Taxation, and Public Debt, was designed to prohibit a recurrence of financial abuses such as those the State had suffered during the Reconstruction Era. The only purposes for which the General Assembly might levy taxes were to support the State government and public institutions, promote education, pay the principal and interest on the public debt, defend the State, and supply artificial limbs to Confederate soldiers. The purposes of county taxes were likewise enumerated. All taxation should be uniform upon the same class of subjects, and *ad valorem* on all property within the territorial limits of the authority levying the tax. Neither the State nor a county nor a municipality should become a joint stockholder, and the State should issue no new bonds. No debts should be contracted by the State, other than for military defense or to supply casual deficiencies of revenue, and debts created to supply deficiencies in revenue could not exceed, in the aggregate, two hundred thousand dollars. The debt that might be incurred by any county, municipality, or other political subdivision of the State was limited to seven per cent of the assessed value of the taxable property therein, and subject to approval of two-thirds of the qualified voters in such sub-

## A Constitutional History of Georgia

division. Moreover, any political subdivision incurring a bonded indebtedness was required to make provision for repayment of the principal and interest of such debt within a period of thirty years. Proceeds from the sale of any State property and income derived from the rental of railroads held by the State were to be applied to paying the public debt. Furthermore, the General Assembly should provide for the payment of a hundred thousand dollars annually into a sinking fund to retire the public debt. Finally, in order that the people might be informed on the state of public finances, the Comptroller General and Treasurer were required to furnish the Governor with a quarterly report on the financial condition of the State, and the Governor was directed to publish an abstract thereof.

Article VIII provided that there should be a thorough system of common schools "for the education of children in the elementary branches of an English education only," and a State University. There was also authorization for one college for Negroes, separate schools being required for the white and colored races. A State School Commissioner, with a salary of two thousand dollars *per annum,* was to be appointed by the Governor for a term of two years. Certain specified taxes, including the poll tax, a special tax on shows and exhibitions, taxes on the sale of spirituous and malt liquor, taxes on commutation for military service, and "all taxes on such domestic animals as, from their nature and habits, are destructive to other property" were set apart for the support of the common schools. Counties and municipalities might be granted authority to establish public school systems and levy taxes for their support, but no such local law should become effective until approved by a two-thirds majority of those qualified to vote in the district concerned.

## The Constitution of 1877

Article IX, Homestead and Exemptions, provided that the property of the head of a family, and certain others, to the extent of sixteen hundred dollars, should be exempted from levy and sale by virtue of any process whatever except for taxes, for the purchase money of the property, for labor done thereon, or materials furnished thereon, or removal of the incumbrance thereon. The debtor should have the right to waive or renounce in writing his right to this benefit, except for property to the value of three hundred dollars. The provisions of this article were made optional with the existing homestead laws, the debtors having the right to take either, but not both, of the exemptions.

Article X authorized the General Assembly to provide by law how the militia of the State should be organized, officered, trained, armed and equipped. The officers and men of the militia were not to receive compensation except when in active service by authority of the State.

Article XI, Counties and County Officers, provided that county officers should be elected by the people for a term of two years. No new counties should be created, but any county could be "dissolved and merged with contiguous counties, by a two-thirds vote of the qualified electors of such county, voting at an election held for that purpose."

Article XII listed the laws of general operation in the State, and Article XIII provided for amendments to the Constitution. The method of amendment was made easier than under previous Constitutions. An amendment could be proposed by a two-thirds vote of those elected to both houses of the General Assembly, advertised in one or more newspapers in each congressional district for two months previous to the time for holding the next general election, and ratified by a majority of the people voting on the amendment. The General As-

*A Constitutional History of Georgia*

sembly might, by a two-thirds vote, call a convention to revise the Constitution, and representation in such a convention should be based on population.

## *Amendments to the Constitution of 1877* [8]

### ARTICLE I, THE BILL OF RIGHTS

THIS article was never amended until the new Constitution was adopted in 1945.

### ARTICLE II, THE ELECTIVE FRANCHISE

Article II was amended three times: in 1908 by the introduction of the "grandfather clause," in 1931 by dropping the requirement of the payment of all taxes due as a requirement for voting (leaving only the requirement of payment of all poll taxes due), and in 1943 by lowering the age qualification for voting to eighteen years.

### ARTICLE III, THE GENERAL ASSEMBLY

Article III was amended twenty-five times. Seven of these amendments related to the number of members in the House and Senate, six to the date and length of sessions of the General Assembly and the term of members, two to the compensation of members, two to legislative procedure in passing local bills, two to the granting of corporate powers, five to zoning laws for counties and

---

[8] A summary of the amendments to the thirteen articles of the Constitution of 1877 is given in the remaining portion of this chapter. A more detailed study of these amendments, in chronological order, occurs in the chapters that follow. Citations to page references in the *Georgia Laws* for the proposal of these amendments, except those of 1943, and exact dates of their ratification, are given in the appendix to *The Constitution of the State of Georgia, 1877, as Amended Through 1941*, compiled by Ella May Thornton, State Librarian (Atlanta, 1942), 60–69. An annotated copy of the Constitution as amended through 1943, based largely on the annotated Constitution in *The Code of Georgia, 1933*, was published by the State Department of Law in 1945.

## The Constitution of 1877

cities, and one to preferences to veterans in civil service laws.

By an amendment of 1918, the number of senatorial districts was increased from forty-four to fifty-one, and in 1937, following the consolidation of Milton, Campbell, and Fulton Counties, an amendment was added making Fulton County alone the fifty-second senatorial district of the State. The number of counties constituting a senatorial district was thus brought to range from one to five, three being the usual number. There were three districts composed of two counties each, forty-one composed of three counties each, six composed of four counties each, one (the sixth) composed of five counties, and one composed of one county (Fulton).

Recognizing that an excessively large membership in the House of Representatives had in the past been a defect in the structure of the government, the framers of the Constitution of 1877 provided that no new counties should be created, and that in no event should the aggregate number of representatives be increased. These provisions were maintained for a quarter of a century, but constitutional limitations can always be overridden by constitutional amendments; so between 1904 and 1920, a series of amendments brought the number of counties to 160 and the membership of the House of Representatives to 206. The amendment of 1904 increased the number of representatives from 175 to 183; that of 1908, to 184; of 1914, to 189; of 1918, to 193. The amendment of 1920 dropped the attempt at setting a fixed number of representatives in the Constitution, and provided that the eight largest counties should have three representatives each, the thirty next largest counties, two representatives each, and the remaining counties, one representative each. Thus the creation of Peach County by an amendment to Article XI in 1924 brought the total representation in the House to 207, but this did not necessitate an amendment to Article III. Fortunately, there was no further increase in the House membership. The consolidation of Milton, Campbell, and Fulton counties in 1931 reduced the membership of the House by two members, leaving the present number of representatives at 205.

Meetings of the General Assembly were biennial under the original provisions of the Constitution of 1877, annual by an amendment of 1891, and again biennial by an amendment of 1924. Sessions were to begin in November under the provisions of 1877, in October under the amendment of 1891, in July under the amendment of 1893, in June under the amendment of 1924, and in July under the amendment of 1931. The length of a regular session was limited to forty days (unless extended by a two-thirds vote for a longer period) by the provisions of 1877, to fifty days by the amendment of 1891, and to sixty days by the amendment of 1924. The "split session" as adopted by an amendment of 1931 provided for a ten day session in January for the organization of the General Assembly, introduction of bills, and inauguration of the Governor, and a sixty day session, convening in July. An amendment of 1943 abolished the split session and established the provisions now in force under which the General Assembly convenes in regular session on the second Monday in January in odd numbered years. "By concurrent resolution, adopted by a majority of the members elected to both houses, the General Assembly may adjourn any regular session to such later date as it may fix for reconvening in regular session, but shall remain in regular session no longer than seventy days, in the aggregate, during the term for which the members were elected. If it shall adjourn the first regular session before the expiration of seventy days, without fixing a

## The Constitution of 1877

date for reconvening, the General Assembly shall reconvene in regular session on the second Monday in January of the next year. All business pending in the House or Senate at the adjournment of any regular session may be considered at any later regular session of the same General Assembly as if there had been no adjournment," [9] stated the amendment of 1943.

The limit on the compensation of members of the General Assembly was four dollars *per diem* under the provisions of the original Constitution of 1877, and that of the President of the Senate and Speaker of the House, seven dollars. By an amendment of 1918 the *per diem* limitation was raised to seven dollars for members, and ten dollars for the President and Speaker. An Amendment of 1943 fixed the compensation of members of the Assembly at $600 for each full term, and eight dollars *per diem* for days spent in extraordinary sessions. The President of the Senate and Speaker of the House each were to receive $900 for a full term, and twelve dollars *per diem* for days spent in extraordinary sessions.

The Constitution of 1877 provided that all local and special bills should originate in the House of Representatives, and be referred to a committee consisting of one member from each congressional district, which should consider and consolidate the local and special bills on the same subject matter and report the same to the House. No local or special bill not originating with this committee could be considered by the House, unless requested by a two-thirds vote. The whole paragraph of the Constitution containing this provision was eliminated by an amendment of 1885. The second amendment relating to local bills, adopted in 1891, simply provided that the first and second readings of each local bill and bank and railroad charter should consist of a reading of

---
[9] Art. III, Sec. IV, Par. III.

the title only, unless the bill was ordered to be engrossed.

All corporate powers were granted by the General Assembly in Georgia prior to 1855. An amendment of that year to the Constitution of 1798 divided the power of incorporation between the courts and the legislature. The Constitution of 1877 continued this division of power. The legislature retained authority to grant corporate powers to banking, insurance, railroad, canal, navigation, express, and telegraph companies. It was forbidden to grant corporate powers in other cases, but should prescribe by law the manner in which such powers should be exercised by the Courts. An amendment of 1892 transferred the authority of granting corporate powers in cases formerly reserved by the legislature to the Secretary of State. Another amendment, adopted in 1912, provided that the legislature could confer on judges of the Superior Courts in vacation authority to grant corporate powers and privileges to private companies.

The first of five amendments relating to zoning and planning laws, adopted in 1927, empowered the legislature to grant to the governing authorities of certain designated cities, and others having a population of 25,000, authority to pass such laws. Subsequent amendments added additional cities. The last of these five amendments, adopted in 1937, authorized the legislature to grant zoning and planning powers to any city or county in the State having a population of 1,000 or more.

The last of the twenty-five amendments to Article III, adopted in 1943, provided that in any civil service system maintained by either the State of Georgia or any political subdivision thereof, veterans of any war should be given the same preference as then existing under Federal Civil Service Laws.

## The Constitution of 1877

ARTICLE IV, POWER OF THE GENERAL ASSEMBLY
OVER TAXATION

The only amendment to Article IV was that of 1943 creating a constitutional Public Service Commission, to consist of five members elected by the people for terms of six years.

The Public Service Commission is an outgrowth of the Railroad Commission, established by legislative act in 1879. The regulatory powers of the Commission were considerably increased in 1907, and its jurisdiction extended to include the regulation of docks, wharves, terminal companies, cotton compress companies, railroad terminals, telephone and telegraph companies, street railroads, gas, light, and power companies. In 1931 its jurisdiction was extended further to cover transportation for hire by motor vehicles. The name Railroad Commission of Georgia was replaced by the name Georgia Public Service Commission in 1922.[10]

ARTICLE V, THE EXECUTIVE

Article V was amended seven times. Three of these amendments dealt with salaries and clerical expenses of executive officers, one with special sessions of the General Assembly, one with the term of the Governor, and two with constitutional commissions.

In 1918 the limitation upon the cost of secretarial and clerical force for the Governor was raised from $6,000 *per annum* to $10,000. Another amendment of the same year raised the limitation on the Treasurer's salary from $2,000 *per annum* to $4,800, and made provision for an increase in the clerical assistance in his office. An amend-

---

[10] Richard C. Job, editor, *Government Manual of Georgia*. Published by the State Planning Board, cooperating with the Works Progress Administration (Atlanta (?), 1938), p. 35.

## A Constitutional History of Georgia

ment of 1928 provided that the General Assembly should have power to fix salaries and clerical expenses of the Treasurer, Secretary of State, and Comptroller General, thus abolishing the constitutional limitations on expenses in these offices.

The original Constitution authorized the Governor to convene the General Assembly in extraordinary sessions. An amendment of 1937 established the following provisions whereby the General Assembly can convene itself: When three-fifths of the members of both the House and Senate certify to the Governor that in their opinion an emergency exists, it shall be mandatory upon him, within five days of the receipt of such certificates, to convene the General Assembly; should he fail in this duty, the General Assembly may convene itself in extraordinary session for all purposes. Such extraordinary, self-convened session shall be limited to thirty days, unless an impeachment trial is pending.

The term of the Governor and the other constitutional officers elected at the same time and for the same term as the Governor was changed by an amendment of 1941 from two to four years. The Governor was made ineligible to succeed himself for the next succeeding four year term, or any part thereof.

An amendment of 1943 added a constitutional State Board of Pardons and Paroles. The broad pardoning power originally vested in the Governor under the Constitution of 1877 was now vested in this Board, to consist of three members appointed by the Governor and confirmed by the Senate for terms of seven years. "The State Board of Pardons and Paroles," stated the Amendment, "shall have power to grant reprieves, pardons, and paroles, to commute penalties, remove disabilities imposed by law, and may remit any part of a sentence for any offense against the State, after conviction, except in cases

## The Constitution of 1877

of treason or impeachment, and except in cases in which the Governor refuses to suspend a sentence of death." The power of the Governor is now limited to a suspension of execution in death sentences until the Board has had time to hear an application for relief, and in cases of conviction of treason until the General Assembly has pardoned, commuted, or ordered execution of the sentence.

Another amendment of 1943 created a constitutional State Game and Fish Commission, to consist of one member from each Congressional District, and one additional member from one of the following counties: Chatham, Bryan, Liberty, McIntosh, Glynn, or Camden. Members of the Commission should be appointed by the Governor and confirmed by the Senate for terms of seven years.[11]

### ARTICLE VI, THE JUDICIARY

Article VI was amended thirty-three times. An amendment of 1896 provided for the popular election of judges of the Supreme Court, increased the number of judges to six, and authorized the Court to determine cases when sitting either as a body or in two divisions of three judges each, under such rules as the General Assembly should prescribe. In 1937 the qualified judges of the Supreme Court were authorized to designate a judge or judges of the Superior Court to preside in the Supreme Court when one or more of the judges of the Supreme Court were disqualified. This authority had formerly been vested in the Governor.

---

[11] A legislative act of 1943 abolished the Department of Natural Resources, which had consisted of five divisions: Wild Life, Natural Resources, Forestry, State Parks, and Mines, Mining and Geology. All of the functions of this Department, except those formerly vested in the Division of Wild Life, were now vested in a Division of Conservation, of which the Governor was made *ex officio* chairman.

*A Constitutional History of Georgia*

The most extensive change made in the structure of the judiciary resulted from the amendment of 1906 establishing a Court of Appeals, to consist of three judges, unless otherwise provided for by law, elected by popular vote for terms of six years. The number of judges was increased to six by legislative action in 1916, and the Court was authorized to sit in two divisions of three judges each. All laws relating to the Supreme Court, as to the qualifications and salaries of judges, procedures, time of sitting, publications of records, etc., unless otherwise provided, were made applicable to the Court of Appeals. The amendments of 1906 divided appellate jurisdiction between the Supreme Court and the Court of Appeals. The former was given appellate jurisdiction in all civil cases from the Superior Courts and in all cases of conviction of a capital felony; the latter had jurisdiction to correct errors in both law and equity in cases appealed from the Superior Courts where the Supreme Court was not given exclusive jurisdiction (i.e., in criminal cases not involving a conviction of a capital felony), in cases from the City Courts, and in such other cases as might be prescribed by law. The Court of Appeals was required to certify to the Supreme Court all questions involving the construction of the Constitution of the United States or the Constitution of Georgia, and the rulings of the Supreme Court on these questions were made binding upon the Court of Appeals.

The jurisdiction of the two high courts was altered in 1916. An amendment of that year extended the jurisdiction of the Supreme Court to cases from the City Courts involving the construction of the Constitution or treaties of the United States or the Constitution of Georgia, to all equity cases and cases involving special remedies, to cases respecting a title to land, construction of wills, *habeas corpus,* and divorce. The Supreme Court was also

## The Constitution of 1877

authorized to require by certification any case to be brought to it from the Court of Appeals. In the event of an equal division among the justices of the Supreme Court upon a question certified to it by the Court of Appeals, the Court of Appeals could decide the question.

The Supreme Court was required by the Constitution of 1877 to dispose of every case at the first or second term after the writ of error was filed. If the plaintiff in error was not prepared at the first term to prosecute the case (unless prevented by providential cause), the case was stricken from the docket and the judgment below affirmed. In the early years of the operation of this provision the Supreme Court dismissed many cases and this was considered a grievance. By Acts of 1881, 1885, and 1893 the General Assembly limited the technicalities upon which suits could be dismissed by the Supreme Court.[12] Mr. Justice Lumpkin was constrained to be critical of "the broad provisions of the Act of Dec. 18, 1893," declaring in the case of *Gregory vs. Daniel*[13] that, "with all due respect, we feel that the General Assembly has gone quite far enough in encouraging in the legal profession negligence and inattention to the forms of procedure which even slight care would be sufficient to prevent." An Amendment of 1935 provided that a case should not be stricken from the docket of the Supreme Court because of an unavoidable delay in the transmission of records by the clerk of the trial court. An Amendment of 1943 made this provision applicable to both the Supreme Court and the Court of Appeals, and provided further that no writ of error should be dismissed because of a delay in transmission of the bill of exceptions and the copy of the record "resulting from the default of the

---

[12] *Ga. Bar Journal*, VII (August, 1944), 12; *Ibid.*, November, 1944, 109, 123.

[13] 93 Georgia 795. The justice quoted here is Samuel Lumpkin.

## A Constitutional History of Georgia

clerk or other cause," unless it should appear that the plaintiff in error or his counsel caused the delay.

Fourteen of the amendments to Article VI related to the Superior Courts. The first of these, adopted in 1898, provided for the popular election of judges of the Superior Courts. (They were formerly elected by the General Assembly.) Under the original Constitution of 1877 the terms of judges of the Superior Courts were to begin on January 1st, unless changed by the General Assembly. Another amendment of 1898 removed the power of the General Assembly to alter the date for the beginning of the judges' terms, and provided that any vacancy in a judgeship should be filled by appointment by the Governor "until the first day of January after the general election held next after the expiration of thirty days from the time such vacancy occurs," at which election a successor for the unexpired term should be chosen. An amendment of 1906 authorized the General Assembly to create additional judges in any judicial circuit of the Superior Courts.

Amendments of 1917 and 1920 raised the amount of the limitations on salaries of judges of the Supreme Court, the Court of Appeals, and the Superior Courts. Eight amendments (adopted in 1910, 1914, 1916, 1918, 1922, 1926, 1928, and 1939) made special provisions for increasing the salaries of the Superior Court judges serving in Fulton, Chatham, Richmond, Bibb, Clarke, Floyd, Sumter, Muscogee, and DeKalb Counties. The last amendment relating to the Superior Courts, adopted in 1939, granted power to the judges to hear and determine cases not requiring a jury at any time, in vacation, at chambers, provided reasonable notice was given to the parties.

An amendment of 1898 provided for election of the

## The Constitution of 1877

Solicitors General of the Superior Courts by popular vote. An amendment of 1916 authorized the General Assembly to abolish fees accruing to the office of Solicitor General in any particular circuit and to prescribe a salary for this office, without regard to uniformity of salaries in the various judicial circuits.

Six of the amendments to Article VI related to justices of the peace. An amendment of 1912 authorized the General Assembly to abolish justice of the peace courts in any city, except Savannah, having a population of over twenty thousand, and to establish *in lieu* thereof such courts as the General Assembly might deem necessary. In 1914 the exception in the case of Savannah was eliminated. An amendment of 1928 further authorized the General Assembly to abolish justice courts in any county in the State having within its borders a city with a population of more than twenty thousand, except Richmond County, and to establish *in lieu* thereof such courts as the General Assembly might deem necessary. In 1932 the exception in the case of Richmond County was eliminated, and in 1943 special constitutional provision was made whereby Glynn County would come within the same category as counties having a city whose population was more than twenty thousand.

An amendment of 1937 conferred jurisdiction in all misdemeanor cases arising under the Georgia State Highway Patrol Act of 1937 on the Court of Ordinary in counties not having a City or County Court, provided the defendant waived a jury trial. This same jurisdiction was conferred upon judges of the police courts of incorporated cities for cases arising within their territorial jurisdiction.

The last amendment to Article VI, adopted in 1943, provided that any person who had been a resident of a United States Army post or military reservation within

## A Constitutional History of Georgia

the State of Georgia for one year could bring an action for divorce in any county adjacent to the post or reservation.

### ARTICLE VII, FINANCE, TAXATION, AND PUBLIC DEBT

Article VII was amended one hundred and eighty-eight times, but not more than fifteen per cent of these amendments were of general interest, the greater number of them being limited in application to a single city or county.

Among the purposes for which taxes could be levied under the strict limitations of the Constitution of 1877 was, "To supply the soldiers who lost a limb in the military service of the Confederate States with substantial artificial limbs, during life." Between 1885 and 1937 nine amendments authorized the levying of taxes for additional care of Confederate veterans. Four other amendments, of the dates indicated, added the following purposes for which the General Assembly could levy taxes: 1926, to construct and maintain a system of State highways; 1937, to provide assistance to aged persons in need, to the needy blind, and to dependent children, and for other welfare benefits; 1941, to advertise and promote the agricultural, industrial, historic, recreational and natural resources, facilities and assets of the State; 1943, to establish a teachers' retirement system.

More effective in controlling the finances of the State than the enumeration of purposes for which taxes could be levied was an amendment of 1904 limiting the total amount of taxes that might be levied by the General Assembly to five mills on each dollar of the value of taxable property.

The Constitution of 1877 provided that all taxation should be uniform upon the same class of subjects and *ad valorem* on all property. An amendment of 1937 au-

## The Constitution of 1877

thorized the classification of property for purposes of taxation into tangible property and one or more classes of intangible personal property, including money, and authorized different rates and methods in the taxation of different classes of property.

The Constitution of 1877 authorized the General Assembly to exempt from taxation all public property, places of religious worship or burial, institutions of public charity, buildings erected for and used as a college, incorporated academy, or other seminary of learning, the real and personal estate of public libraries and literary associations, books and philosophical apparatus, and paintings and statuary kept in a public hall—provided the property exempted was not used for profit or income. An amendment of 1912 added to this list of exemptions farm products, including baled cotton, grown in the State and retained in the hands of the producer, but this exemption was limited to a period of one year after the farm products were produced. An amendment of 1918 added all funds and property held or used as endowments by educational institutions, provided the funds were not invested in real estate, that the institution was open to the general public, and that the endowments to institutions established for white people be limited to white people and endowments to colored institutions be limited to colored people. An amendment of 1924 authorized an exemption from county and city *ad valorem* taxes for a period of five years new buildings, or expanded equipment in specified industries, provided a majority of the electors in the city or county concerned approved the exemption. An amendment of 1937 exempted from all *ad valorem* taxation (whether State, county, municipal, or school district) personal property (including clothing, household and kitchen furniture, domestic animals, and tools and implements used in trade by manual laborers, but not including motor vehicles) to the value of $300. Another amendment of the same year exempted from *ad valorem* taxation for State, county, and school (but not municipal) purposes, except to pay interest on and retire bonded indebtedness, homesteads to the value of $2,000, if occupied by the owner.[14] An amendment of 1941 exempted from taxation for a period of twenty years all coöperative, non-profit, rural electrification corporations. Another amendment of the same year authorized the city of Macon to make temporary exemptions from taxation under specified conditions. The last amendment in this category, adopted in 1943, exempted from all *ad valorem* intangible taxes the common voting stock of a subsidiary corporation not doing business in Georgia, "if at least ninety per cent of such common voting stock is owned by a Georgia corporation with its principal place of business located in this State and was acquired or is held for the purpose of enabling the parent company to carry on some part of its established line of business through such subsidiary."

An amendment of 1912 provided that all persons required to make tax returns to the Comptroller General should do so before the first day of March of each year and should pay the taxes due to the State on or before the first day of September.

The Constitution of 1877 strictly limited the purposes for which taxes could be levied not only by the State, but by the counties as well. The only purposes for which county taxes could be levied, stated the Constitution, were "for educational purposes in instructing children in the elementary branches of an English education only; to build and repair the public buildings and bridges; to maintain and support prisoners; to pay jurors and coro-

---

[14] The General Assembly was authorized to lower this exemption to $1,250.

## The Constitution of 1877

ners, and for litigation, quarantine, roads, and expenses of courts; to support paupers and pay debts heretofore existing." For thirty-one years no changes were made in this paragraph; but during the past thirty-seven years a total of fifteen amendments have been made, seven of them applying to only one or two counties. The six amendments of statewide application, adopted on the date indicated, added the following governmental functions that might be supported financially by the counties: 1910, county police and sanitation; 1926, records of births, deaths, disease, and health; 1937, agricultural and home demonstration agents; 1937, assistance to aged persons, the needy blind, and dependent children; 1938, fire protection of forest lands and conservation of natural resources; 1938, medical care and hospitalization for the indigent sick.

The only debt authorized to be contracted on behalf of the State by the Constitution of 1877 (other than to repel invasion, suppress insurrection, and defend the State in time of war) was an amount not to exceed $200,000 "to supply casual deficiencies of revenue." An amendment of 1912 substituted for "casual deficiencies of revenue" the words "such temporary deficit as may exist in the treasury in any year from necessary delay in collecting the taxes of that year," and raised the amount of permissible loans to $500,000, but required that any loan made should be repaid out of taxes levied for the year in which the loan was made. An amendment of 1926 authorized a loan of $3,500,000 to pay public school teachers, but provided that the principal of any amount borrowed for this purpose should be repaid each year out of the common school appropriation, and interest thereon should be paid each year out of the general funds of the State. The original Constitution prohibited the State from assuming the debts of a city, county, or other political subdivision. An amendment of 1931 made an exception in the case of debts incurred by counties in the construction of highways under specified conditions. A further amendment of 1939 made provision for refunding highway bonds.

Paragraph I, Section VII, of Article VII, limited the debt of a county, city, or other political subdivision of the State to seven per cent of the assessed value of its taxable property, and required the approval of two-thirds of the qualified voters for any new debt (except a loan to supply casual deficiencies in revenue, not to exceed one-fifth of one per cent of the assessed value of the taxable property). This paragraph was the subject of more amendments than any other in the Constitution, being amended one hundred and thirty-five times, but all of these amendments except two were authorizations for specific debts by a particular city or county. The two of statewide application were adopted in 1918 and 1943. The first required that the two-thirds vote necessary to approve a new loan should constitute a majority of the registered voters and forbade special registrations for votes on bond issues. The amendment of 1943 provided that revenue anticipation obligations for revenue producing facilities issued by any city, county, or other political subdivision under authority of the Revenue Certificate Law of 1937, as amended on March 14, 1939, should not be deemed as debts within the meaning of the Constitution, and that the power of taxation should not be used for the purpose of paying the interest or principal of such obligations.

An amendment of 1941 authorized cities or counties to contract, with each other or with any public agency, for a period not exceeding thirty years for the use of any facilities or services that cities or counties are authorized to undertake. Any city or county was empowered to con-

## The Constitution of 1877

vey to such public corporation or agency its existing facilities, provided they be used for the same purpose that they had been operated for by the city or county, and provided also that they would not be mortgaged or pledged to secure obligations of the public agency. The same amendment authorized any city or county to contract with any public corporation or agency for the care and hospitalization of indigent sick.

### ARTICLE VIII, EDUCATION

Article VIII was amended a total of fourteen times. Eight of these amendments dealt with taxation for school purposes, and of these, four were applicable to one county only. The Constitution of 1877 provided that counties and municipal corporations might be authorized to maintain schools by local taxation, but no such local law was to take effect until approved by a two-thirds vote of the qualified voters in the county or municipality affected. An amendment of 1904 extended this provision to include militia districts and school districts as well as counties and municipal corporations, and provided that local laws for this purpose should be submitted to the qualified voters of the district concerned and approved by a two-thirds majority of those voting at such election. Under the original wording of the Constitution, education supported in the common schools by taxation should be "in the elementary branches of an English education only." This restrictive clause was eliminated by an amendment of 1912, thus implying authorization for the support of high schools.[15] Restrictions on the amount of local taxes to be levied for school purposes were adopted in 1920. The amendment of that year authorized the proper county authorities, on recommendation of the board of

---

[15] Authorization of the support of high schools by local governments had been implied by an amendment to Article VII in 1910.

education, to levy a school tax of not less than one nor more than five mills on all taxable property outside of independent local school systems. An additional levy, not to exceed five mills, was authorized for independent local systems, municipalities, or school districts, on a two-thirds vote of those voting.

An amendment of 1932 authorized the consolidation of two or more local school districts upon a majority vote in each of the districts, the bonded indebtedness of either to be assumed by the entire new district. An amendment of 1943 changed this provision so as to require a two-thirds majority of the qualified voters in a district not having a bonded indebtedness to consolidate with a district having a bonded indebtedness.

Two amendments related to the State School Superintendent. The original Constitution provided for a State School Commissioner, appointed by the Governor and confirmed by the Senate for a term of two years. An amendment of 1896 provided for popular election of the State School Commissioner, and limited his salary to not more than $2,000 per year. An amendment of 1941 changed the name of this officer to State School Superintendent and provided that he should be elected for the same term as the Governor, *i.e.*, four years. The $2,000 limitation on his salary was continued.

An amendment of 1920 eliminated the provision originally appearing in this Article for the support of not more than one Negro university. The same amendment added specific authorization for the support of high schools.

The last amendment to this Article, adopted in 1943, created a constitutional Board of Regents of the University System of Georgia, composed of one member from each Congressional district and five members from the State-at-large, appointed by the Governor and confirmed by the Senate for terms of seven years.

## The Constitution of 1877

### ARTICLE IX, HOMESTEAD AND EXEMPTION
This article was never amended.

### ARTICLE X, THE MILITIA
This article was never amended.

### ARTICLE XI, COUNTIES AND COUNTY OFFICERS

Article XI was amended thirty-two times. Twenty of these amendments, an average of one per year for the period from 1904 to 1924, provided for new counties. Most of the other amendments were restricted in application to only a designated county. Among the amendments of statewide application, one of 1914 extended the term of county officers to four years. Another of the same year empowered the General Assembly to abolish the office of treasurer in any county, or to fix the compensation of county treasurers without regard to uniformity in the various counties. An amendment of 1924 authorized the General Assembly to consolidate the functions of tax receiver and tax collector in the hands of a new officer to be known as the county tax commissioner, and to fix the compensation of such new officer without regard to uniformity among the counties. Another amendment of 1924 authorized the consolidation of city and county governments.

### ARTICLE XII, THE LAWS OF GENERAL OPERATION
No amendments.

### ARTICLE XIII, AMENDMENTS
No amendments.

CHAPTER XIII

# Late Nineteenth Century

THE interval between the restoration of home rule in the 'seventies and the rise of the Populist movement in the 'nineties is generally known in Georgia history as the regime of Bourbon Democracy, the term Bourbon implying a ruling class secure in power and essentially conservative. This was essentially a businessman's regime, characterized by remarkable developments in industry and commerce. Between 1870 and 1890 the amount of capital invested in manufacturing enterprises is estimated to have more than quadrupled, railway mileage to have nearly trebled, and total property values to have risen from two hundred fifteen to eight hundred twenty million dollars.[1]

The dominant philosophy of the period was best expressed by Henry W. Grady, editor of *The Atlanta Constitution* from 1880 until his death in 1889. Few addresses in American history have received such widespread applause as his entitled "The New South" delivered before the New England Society in New York City on December 22, 1886. "We have found out that in the general summary the free negro counts more than he did as a

---

[1] Alex Mathews Arnett, *The Populist Movement in Georgia* (New York, 1922), 47.

slave," said Grady. "We have sowed towns and cities in the place of theories and put business above politics. We have challenged your spinners in Massachusetts and your iron-makers in Pennsylvania. . . . We have learned that one northern immigrant is worth fifty foreigners, and have smoothed the path to southward, wiped out the place where Mason and Dixon's line used to be, and hung our latch-string to you and yours. . . . We have let economy take root and spread among us as rank as the crab grass which sprung from Sherman's cavalry camps. . . . The old South rested everything on slavery and agriculture, unconscious that these could neither give nor maintain healthy growth. The new South presents a perfect Democracy, the oligarchs leading in the popular movement—a social system compact and closely knitted, less splendid on the surface but stronger at the core—a hundred farms for every plantation, fifty homes for every palace, and a diversified industry that meets the needs of this complex age." [2]

The triumvirate of the Bourbon Democracy consisted of Alfred H. Colquitt, John B. Gordon, and Joseph E. Brown. Colquitt and Gordon together held the governorship for ten of the eighteen years between 1872 and 1890; either Gordon or Brown held one of the United States Senatorships throughout the period, and Colquitt held the other after the expiration of his term as Governor in 1882. The only other members from Georgia in the United States Senate for any considerable length of time during the period were Thomas M. Norwood, 1871-77, and Benjamin H. Hill, 1877-1882.

Following his break with the Radical Reconstructionists in 1870, Brown turned his attention to business interests. As President of the Western and Atlantic Railroad,

---

[2] Raymond B. Nixon, *Henry W. Grady, Spokesman of the New South* (New York, 1943), 240-50.

## A Constitutional History of Georgia

the Southern Railroad and Steamship Association, the Walker Iron and Coal Company, and the Dade Coal Company (where he worked 350 convicts leased from the State), he became Georgia's most prominent industrialist and a noted philanthropist. Among his gifts to numerous institutions were $53,000 to the Southern Baptist Theological Seminary and $50,000 to the University of Georgia. The latter gift was designated as a loan fund for deserving young men, and the elaborate and wise instructions that he set forth for its preservation and use were more impressive than the sum of money.[3] Georgians could never forget their love for Brown as War Governor, and his active support of Tilden in the campaign of 1876 went far toward restoring him to favor in the Democratic Party.

The second of the Bourbon Triumvirate, John Brown Gordon (February 6, 1832–January 9, 1904), the most distinguished soldier that the State has ever produced, was born in Upson County. He attended the University of Georgia and subsequently studied law and entered the bar, but there was nothing of distinction in his early life. At the beginning of the War he was located in the extreme northwestern part of the State and came down to Atlanta to volunteer his service at the head of a picturesque company of mountaineers, the "Racoon Roughs." Blessed with unusual military ability, he advanced rapidly to fame, being one of three Georgians to gain the rank of lieutenant-general. He fought at Manassas, Malvern Hill, Seven Pines, Antietam (where he was wounded several times), Chancellorsville, Gettysburg, Spottsylvania, Petersburg, and led the last charge at Appomattox. A man of impressive physique and courtly manner, he became

---

[3] Herbert Fielder, *A Sketch of the Life and Times and Speeches of Joseph E. Brown* (Springfield, 1883), 570–575.

*Late Nineteenth Century*

the idol of the people. He was commander-in-chief of the United Confederate Veterans from 1890 until his death in 1904.[4]

The other member of the triumvirate, Alfred Holt Colquitt (April 20, 1824–March 26, 1894), eldest son of Walter T. Colquitt, United States Senator from Georgia, 1843–48, was born in Walton County. He was graduated from the College of New Jersey (Princeton), studied law, and was admitted to the bar. Entering the State Senate with Joseph E. Brown in 1849, he went to Congress as a States' Rights man in 1853, and supported secession in 1860. Having gained some military experience in the Mexican War, he advanced to the rank of major general in the Confederate Army. After the War he became a prosperous farmer, producing a thousand bales of cotton per year, and a successful businessman as well.

Colquitt was elected Governor in an uneventful campaign of 1876. The Republicans ran Jonathan Norcross, but he polled only 33,443 votes, while the vote for Colquitt was 111,297.[5] Once inaugurated, Colquitt found that far too many people had worked zealously for his election in expectation of being rewarded by appointment to State offices. As Governor he had only about thirty appointments to fill; yet several thousand of his friends sought jobs. There were over a hundred applications for the office of Principal Keeper of the Penitentiary, and as many for the office of State Librarian. Under the circumstances, in appointing one, the Governor of necessity offended many. Disappointed office-seekers took the lead in a campaign of hostility to the Colquitt administration. Widespread murmurings led him to ask

---

[4] The equestrian statue of General Gordon located on the Capitol plaza was unveiled on May 25, 1907.

[5] Avery, *History of Georgia*, 519.

## A Constitutional History of Georgia

the General Assembly to investigate his motives and conduct in endorsing bonds of the North-Eastern Railroad to the extent of $260,000. The legislative committee was unanimous in vindicating the Governor, but this did not allay popular feeling. Having made a start, the General Assembly appointed committees to investigate all branches of the executive department. The Comptroller General, W. L. Goldsmith, was impeached and found guilty of illegal discriminations in matters of taxation, illegal issuances of wild land executions, and other malpractices. The Treasurer, J. W. Renfroe, was impeached on a charge of taking interest on public deposits, but profiting from the mistake of the Comptroller in trying to contest the jurisdiction of the Senate, Renfroe admitted the charge against him, and was acquitted. Investigations of the other departments revealed only minor irregularities. The School Commissioner, Gustavus J. Orr, was found to have paid his own expenses when traveling in the interest of the public schools. The Secretary of State, N. C. Barnett, it was jocularly declared, had used several cents' worth of wax in affixing the great seal of the State to public documents.[6]

A more serious challenge to the Democratic Party organization than the legislative investigation of executive departments was the appearance of Independent Democrats in the mountainous region of North Georgia where the Negro population was too small for the white solidarity appeal to carry the weight it evidenced elsewhere in the State. The revolt began in the Seventh District when the Democratic Convention nominated L. N. Trammell for congressman. The objection was both to the candidate and to the method by which he was chosen, the contention being that under the convention system a central machine in Atlanta operating through local

---

[6] Avery, *History of Georgia*, 546–550.

courthouse rings controlled the entire political life of the State.

The revolt was led by William H. Felton, a graduate of both the University of Georgia and the State Medical College, a farmer, a country doctor, Methodist preacher, and speaker of singularly effective eloquence. He was ably assisted by his wife, Rebecca Latimer Felton, a tireless worker, who largely managed his campaigns. Traveling in a buggy, he attracted large crowds from the countrysides to applaud his fiery attacks upon the courthouse rings.[7] First elected to Congress in 1874 as an Independent Democrat, he was reelected in 1876 and 1878, despite all opposition the Democratic party organization could bring against him. Defeated in the congressional election of 1880, he subsequently served in the General Assembly of Georgia where he advocated educational improvements, prison reform, and restrictions on the liquor traffic. Meanwhile, in the adjacent Ninth District, Emory Speer was elected to Congress as an Independent in 1878 and again in 1880.

The insurgents seized upon Governor Colquitt's appointment of Joseph E. Brown to the Senate in 1880 as a basis for charges of bargain and corruption. The General Assembly had only recently reelected John B. Gordon to the Senate, who resigned with the explanation that he wanted to go into business to build up his private fortune. Brown was glad of an opportunity to reënter public life. The opposition to the Colquitt administration charged that a bargain had been made whereby Gordon was to give his seat in the Senate to Brown, who was to extend favors to him in the railroad industry, including the Presidency of the State Railroad which Brown then held, and that both Brown and Gordon were to aid Colquitt in the next gubernatorial campaign.

---

[7] Arnett, *Populist Movement in Georgia*, 35.

*A Constitutional History of Georgia*

Gordon did return to Georgia and enter the railroad business, but he did not become president of the State Railroad.

In the Democratic Convention of 1880 the insurgents sought to use the two-thirds rule to prevent Colquitt's renomination. This rule had been used in Georgia Democratic Conventions from 1843 to 1857, the date of Brown's first election as Governor. In the first election following the end of Reconstruction, in 1871, James M. Smith was nominated under a majority rule, and in the Convention of 1872 he was renominated under the same rule. In 1876 all contending candidates withdrew by the opening date of the Convention, and Colquitt was nominated by acclamation. His supporters controlled more than a majority of the Convention of 1880, but in caucus they decided to support the two-thirds rule. As a result, the determined opposition was able to prevent the formal renomination of Colquitt; so the majority of the Convention passed a resolution "recommending" to the people his reëlection.[8] Following the recommendation of Colquitt, the majority adopted a motion to adjourn *sine die*, but the minority remained in session and nominated Thomas M. Norwood as their candidate. Norwood, who was "cold and unelectrical," not gifted as a speaker, and lacking sympathy for the Negro, whose vote was widely sold in the election, proved an unfortunate choice to lead the insurgents against the Solid South stronghold of the Colquitt forces; yet Norwood polled 64,004 votes to Colquitt's 118,349. The victory of Colquitt was of course a victory for Brown as well, so when the General Assembly convened on November 3, 1880, it elected Brown to the Senate, thus confirming the appointment that Colquitt had made, and in 1884 Brown was reëlected to the Senate for a full term.

---

[8] Avery, *History of Georgia*, 583.

## Late Nineteenth Century

Toombs and Stephens had not approved of the prevailing trend of the organized Democracy in Georgia during the decade following the restoration of home rule, so in 1882 the Independents sought to capitalize upon the fame of Stephens by presenting his name as their candidate for Governor. This threat was so formidable that the regular Democrats hastily besought Stephens to become their candidate in the interest of party solidarity. He consented, and thus put an end to Independence in Georgia for the decade of the 'eighties.[9]

In February, 1883, Stephens went to Savannah in connection with that city's sesquicentennial. The trip proved too much for the invalid Governor and led to his death on the night of Saturday, March 4th. James S. Boynton, President of the Senate, succeeded to the governorship until a special election could be held. A convention of the Democratic Party met in Atlanta in April and, thanks to the support of Grady and *The Atlanta Constitution,* nominated for Governor Henry D. McDaniel, a banker, railroad director and member of the House of Representatives from Walton County. When the convention first assembled Augustus O. Bacon, Speaker of the House for the past eight years, was the most prominent candidate for the nomination, but Grady gave his full support to McDaniel. A few weeks after the election, Woodrow Wilson, then a young attorney in Atlanta, watched from his office window the crowd gathering for the inauguration of McDaniel, and wrote to a friend in Berlin: "They were probably not much entertained but they must have been considerably diverted, for our new governor cannot talk. . . . A Tennessean wag expressed great commiseration for . . . a State

---

[9] Arnett, *Populist Movement in Georgia,* 45. As an independent Democrat, Lucius J. Gartrell opposed Stephens in the election of 1882. The vote was: Stephens, 107,253; Gartrell, 44,896.

## A Constitutional History of Georgia

which was about to replace a governor who could not walk with a governor who could not talk. McDaniel is sound enough in other respects, . . . steady and sensible, all the harder worker, perhaps, because he can't talk."[10] During the administration of Governor McDaniel the legislature appropriated a million dollars to erect a new Capitol building.[11] The Governor served as the chairman of the Building Commission which had the distinction of completing the project within the limits of the appropriation. In general McDaniel made an able executive and was reëlected without opposition in 1884.

Two amendments to the Constitution were adopted during McDaniel's administration. The first of these, the first amendment ever made in the Constitution of 1877, eliminated the provision that all local bills should originate in the House of Representatives and be referred to a committee consisting of one member from each Congressional District, and that no special or local bill should be considered by the House without having been reported to this committee, unless brought up by a two-thirds vote.[12] The other amendment broadened the provision authorizing taxation for the support of Confederate veterans.[13] The Constitution originally authorized taxation "to supply the soldiers who lost a limb or limbs . . . with substantial artificial limbs during life." The amendment added the clause, "and to make suitable provision for such Confederate soldiers as may have been permanently injured in the Service."

---

[10] Ray Stannard Baker, *Woodrow Wilson, Life and Letters* (New York, 1927), I, 156.

[11] This measure was passed in the summer of 1883, a few weeks after the old Kimball House burned to the ground.

[12] Amendment to Art. III, Sec. VII, Par. XV. *Georgia Laws, 1884–85*, pp. 33–34. Ratified Oct. 6, 1886. For a study of local legislation and its problems in Georgia, see Chapter XI in James C. Bonner, *et. al., Studies in Georgia History and Government* (Athens, 1940).

[13] Amendment to Art. VII, Sec. I, Par. I. *Georgia Laws, 1884–85*, pp. 37–38. Ratified Oct. 6, 1886.

## Late Nineteenth Century

John B. Gordon, who had resigned from the United States Senate in 1880 in order to build up his private fortune, but was known to be in New York "somewhat out at the elbow," was brought back into public life by Grady during the gubernatorial election of 1886. Both Gordon and Jefferson Davis were scheduled to speak at the laying of the corner-stone of the Confederate Memorial at Montgomery, Alabama, in April, 1886. As the statue of Benjamin H. Hill in Atlanta was nearing completion, Grady easily persuaded the Monument Committee to invite Davis to extend his trip to Atlanta for the unveiling. Gordon accompanied Davis, and Grady managed to put him in the limelight. From Atlanta, Gordon and Davis went on to Savannah for another great demonstration, "the Chatham Artillery there having discovered conveniently that its centennial fell a few days after the unveiling ceremony in Atlanta." On May 9th Gordon announced his candidacy for Governor, Grady taking personal charge of the campaign and serving as manager. The other leading candidate was again Augustus O. Bacon. In the early stages of the campaign Bacon held an advantage through control of the party organization, but Gordon's supporters capitalized upon the support of Civil War veterans. When the Democratic Convention met in Atlanta on July 28th it nominated Gordon on the first ballot.[14]

The only amendment to the Constitution adopted during the administration of Gordon related to pensions for widows of Confederate veterans. It authorized taxation "for the widows of such Confederate soldiers as may have died in the service . . . or since from wounds received therein or disease contracted in the service; provided that this Act shall only apply to such persons as were married at the time of such service, and have re-

---

[14] Nixon, *Henry Grady*, 226 ff.

mained unmarried since the death of such soldier husband."[15]

## The Populist Movement

HENRY W. GRADY, spokesman of the New South, delivered his last speech at the annual banquet of the Boston Merchants Association on December 12, 1889. He was sick at the time, and upon his return home pleuropneumonia developed, resulting in his death on December 23rd.[16] The passing of Grady marked the end of an epoch in Georgia and Southern history. Two years earlier Charles Colcock Jones, Georgia's most colorful historian, had published a notable address, *The Old South*.[17] Elaborating his theme in another address of 1889 he called upon the people to witness that in the "epoch of commercial methods—of absorption by foreign capital of favored localities, and of the creation in our midst of gigantic corporations intent upon self-aggrandizement . . ." there was a "general and increasing poverty of the agricultural regions" and a "manifest modification, if not actual obliteration of those sentiments and modes of thought and action which rendered us a peculiar people."[18] The creed of Grady and of the decade of the

---

[15] Amendment to Art. VII, Sec. I, Par. I. *Georgia Laws, 1889*, pp. 39–40. Ratified Oct. 1, 1890.

An Amendment to increase the number of justices on the Supreme Court from three to five passed the General Assembly in 1889 but was defeated when submitted to the people. An amendment relating to the first reading of House and Senate bills passed the General Assembly in 1890, but there is no record of its submission to popular vote.

[16] Nixon, *Henry Grady*, 330.

[17] *The Old South: Addresses Delivered before the Confederate Survivors Association . . . by His Excellency, Governor John B. Gordon, and by Col. Charles C. Jones, Jr., LL.D.* (Augusta, Georgia, 1887).

[18] Vann Woodward, *Tom Watson*, 124; *Library of Southern Literature*, VII, 2851.

'eighties had been: "industrialization of the South; glorification of the capitalist and his way of life; political, economic, and cultural unity between the South and the East; rigid subordination of class conflict in the South to the maintenance of the *status quo* of a business man's regime identified with white supremacy; and the exclusion of the Negro from political life." The creed of the 'nineties, best expressed by Tom Watson, was just the reverse. It embraced: "agrarianism for the South, a glorification of the farmer and his way of life; war upon the industrial East and alliance with the agrarian West; open and relentless class conflict with the enemy classes both without and within the South; and the enlistment of the Negro in the battle for the farmer equipped with as many political weapons as Watson dared give him." [19]

"The Southern farmer had listened apathetically to preachments on diversified crops, scientific methods, and improvements from Grady and others of his sincere well-wishers ever since the War. He grudgingly acknowledged the pertinence of their advice, but he observed that Southern agriculture continued to sink lower and lower in the morass of despair." Continued discouragement inclined him to heed the admonition of Mrs. Elizabeth Lease, of Kansas, "Raise less corn and more Hell." [20]

The destitute condition of Southern farmers following the upheaval of the Civil War is well known. Negroes frequently misinterpreted their newly-won freedom as meaning freedom from work, and the unfortunate program of Congressional Reconstruction sponsored political rather than industrial activity on the part of the new freedmen. Attempts were made to continue the plantation system of farming, but hired Negroes proved no

---

[19] Vann Woodward, *Tom Watson,* 165–66. By permission of The Macmillan Co., publishers.
[20] *Ibid.,* 129, 177.

substitute for the closely supervised slave laborer of ante bellum days. Economic failures led to a rapid disintegration of plantations into smaller holdings.[21] Cotton, the chief agricultural product in Georgia, naturally dropped rapidly from the extraordinary price of $1.00 per pound prevailing at the close of the War, but the downward trend in price continued to the end of the century. Cotton sold for approximately twelve cents per pound during the decade of the 'seventies, nine cents during the 'eighties, and seven cents during the 'nineties. The amount of cotton produced annually was almost trebled by the end of the century, but the total selling price of the crop increased only slightly.[22] In addition to low prices and unstable labor, the farmer also suffered from the lack of credit. The government offered no financial assistance to agriculture, and land, the only basis of credit that most farmers owned, was not a favored form of security with banks. As early as December 15, 1866, the General Assembly of Georgia responded to the farmer's pressing need of credit by enacting a law permitting liens upon crops for provisions and materials furnished for their production. At first an attempt was made to confine the right of taking crop liens to landowners, but such restrictions proved easy to circumvent.[23] The rapid changes in the lien law reflected a contest between planters and merchants for the control of tenants. In this contest the merchant held an advantage, for tenants preferred to buy directly from the store rather than to be furnished by the landlord. Many landlords became merchants, and many successful merchants became landlords; hence the rise of the merchant-planter.

The crop lien system provided necessary credit in a

---
[21] Robert Preston Brooks, *The Agrarian Revolution in Georgia 1865–1912* (Madison, Wisconsin, 1914), Chapters II and III.
[22] Arnett, *The Populist Movement in Georgia*, 65.
[23] Brooks, *Agrarian Revolution*, 32–33.

period of emergency, but it entailed many subsequent evils. At the beginning of a year the farmer, by means of a lien upon his yet-unplanted crop, would contract with a merchant to furnish him commodities up to a certain limit. The merchant, who thus "ran" the farmer, customarily raised the price, sometimes as much as 50%, on the goods that the farmer purchased from the merchant's store, and in addition charged the farmer a high rate of interest on his account. Furthermore, the merchant usually insisted that the farmer plant most of his acreage in cotton, the money crop, if he was to secure credit. With a declining price for cotton, the farmer was fortunate to sell his crop for enough to pay out of debt, and the usual case was for him to begin the new year with a portion of the previous year's debt unpaid. There is little wonder that many became thoroughly disheartened.[24]

The lowly economic status of the farmer was by no means confined to Georgia. Farmers throughout the country suffered from hard times during the post-war period and were in a state of discontent. During the 'seventies an association of farmers, the Patrons of Husbandry, or the Grange, gained sufficient strength in the Northwest to force some governmental regulation of railroads in the interest of farmers. A branch of the Grange appeared in Georgia in 1872 and within three years had 18,000 members. It sponsored cooperative stores as buying and selling agencies for farmers, but these ventures proved short-lived. The interest stimulated by the Grange probably influenced the inclusion in the Georgia Constitution of 1877 of provisions for regulating railroads.

Similar to the Grange was the Alliance. Unions, Wheels, Alliances, and numerous associations of similar character sprang up simultaneously among farmers in

---

[24] Arnett, *Populist Movement in Georgia*, 75.

widely scattered regions throughout the United States during the 'seventies and 'eighties, and an amalgamation of various groups led in 1889 to the formation of the National Farmers' Alliance and Industrial Union. The Southern branch of the Alliance alone claimed a membership of three million by 1890,[25] and within three years after its first appearance in Georgia in 1887 there were more than two thousand lodges in the State with a combined membership exceeding a hundred thousand.

The Alliance mingled group discussions, reports, and speeches with ritualistic functions. Traveling lecturers with scientific information on improved agricultural methods were employed to address the various lodges, and each State organization established or maintained an agricultural journal. But the Alliancemen felt that improved methods of farming would not be sufficient to alleviate conditions inasmuch as the monied interests and politicians seemed to be in league to rob the toiling masses. Two general lines of attack were presented: cooperative agencies and political action. Joint agents for purchasing and selling, cooperative stores, warehouses, and gins sprang up throughout the South. Most of the cotton States organized State exchanges with stocks issued in small shares and owned by farmers. The Georgia Exchange, organized in 1887, claimed to have saved its patrons $200,000 on fertilizer alone during the first year of its existence. But true to the pattern of most cooperatives, these enterprises, under constant attack from business and banking interests, and poorly managed, began with a flourish but soon died. The Georgia Exchange survived only until the depression of 1893.[26]

Believing that the National Government had long been controlled by New England industrialists and

---

[25] *Ibid.*, 76–77, 100.
[26] *Ibid.*, 81.

*Late Nineteenth Century*

capitalists, the embattled farmers turned their attention to political action. Conventions of several branches of the Alliance met simultaneously at St. Louis in December, 1883, and adopted platforms to be used as yardsticks for measuring candidates for public office. Foremost among the planks were demands for cheaper money, including the abolition of national banks and substitution of legal tender treasury notes *in lieu* of national bank notes, and the free and unlimited coinage of silver. Other planks called for revision in the tax laws, public ownership of the means of communication and transportation, and congressional prohibition of dealing in futures on all agricultural and mechanical products. The Southern Alliance included in its platform a novel scheme whereby the National Government should establish sub-treasuries in every county that offered for sale in one year as much as $500,000 worth of farm products. Each sub-treasury should have a warehouse or elevator where farmers could store such non-perishable products as cotton, grain, and tobacco, and borrow legal tender notes up to 80% of the market price on products stored. The Alliancemen were themselves divided on the wisdom of this sub-treasury scheme, and it afforded an excellent target of attack for critics of the whole Alliance movement.[27]

By 1890 the Alliance had become so powerful in Georgia that there was no course open to the Democratic Party of the State other than to embrace its principles. It was not a question of whether the Alliancemen would capture the State Democracy; it was theirs already. "The Farmer's Alliance *is* the Democratic party," said Evan P. Howell, Grady's successor as editor of the *Atlanta Constitution*.[28] The two principal gubernatorial candidates in 1890 were William J. Northen and T. F. Livingston,

---
[27] *Ibid.*, 83–96, *passim*.
[28] Issue of July 4, 1890.

both planters with Civil War records who had served in the General Assembly and been active in Alliance work. Livingston was reported to have been a joint author of the sub-treasury plan; Northen, more conservative, was in no hurry to commit himself to this particular phase of the Alliance program. The *Atlanta Constitution* supported Northen, but the *Atlanta Journal,* an evening daily paper, founded in 1883 and gradually becoming a rival of the *Constitution,* feared that Northen would be too conservative in dealing with the railroads. Before the election Livingston withdrew as a candidate for Governor and was elected to Congress from the 5th District (including the City of Atlanta). In the 10th Congressional District (including the City of Augusta) Tom Watson was elected to Congress, thus making his first entrance into national politics. All ten of the Congressmen elected from Georgia that year supported the Alliance movement. In addition to choosing the Governor and entire Congressional delegation, the Alliance named three-fourths of the Senators and four-fifths of the Representatives to the General Assembly.

The Assembly that convened in November, 1890, was greeted by the press as the farmer's legislature. Now that the Alliancemen controlled the State Government, what would they do? As its Speaker, the House chose Clark Howell, son of Capt. Evan P. Howell, owner of the *Constitution,* and a railroad promoter. As a successor to Joseph E. Brown in the United States Senate, the Assembly elected John B. Gordon who had suddenly resigned from the Senate ten years earlier to enter the railroad business, but now felt that duty called him back to public office.

Turning its attention to legislation, the General Assembly extended the regulatory powers of the Railroad Commission to cover telegraph and express companies;

established a thirteen hour day for railway employees; expanded the inspection of banks with the view of safeguarding deposits; provided additional regulations for primaries, aimed at preventing the stuffing of ballot boxes; expanded the inspection of fertilizer and cottonseed meal; prohibited combinations or pools of insurance companies in restraint of trade; declared Labor Day a holiday, and established an Arbor Day; prohibited the sale of intoxicating drinks in the vicinity of rural schools and churches; made provision for a State Normal School at Athens to train teachers for the public schools; set up an annual appropriation of $8,000 for a school for colored youths as a department of the University; raised the rate of the general property tax by one and one-half mills to cover the increased State expenditures; and passed enough local and special laws to fill a volume of more than a thousand pages.[29]

This same Assembly passed four amendments to the Constitution that were ratified by popular vote the next year. The first provided for annual sessions of the General Assembly; the second increased the number of days in a session from forty to fifty, and eliminated the provision whereby the Assembly had formerly been able to extend its sessions; the third provided that the first and second readings of local bills, bank charters, and railroad charters should be by title only unless such bills were ordered to be engrossed; and the fourth divested the General Assembly of the power to grant corporate charters to banking, insurance, railroad, canal, navigation, express, and telephone companies, and vested this power in the Secretary of State.[30]

---

[29] *Georgia Laws, 1891*, Vol. I–II.
[30] Amendments to Art. III, Sec. IV, Par. III; Art. III, Sec. IV, Par. VI; Art. III, Sec. VII, Par. VIII; Art. III, Sec. VII, Par. XVIII, respectively. *Georgia Laws, 1891*, pp. 55–60. All ratified on Oct. 5, 1892.

*A Constitutional History of Georgia*

While this record was gratifying to some, it was disappointing to others who had hoped for extensive legislation against combinations in restraint of trade and a redistribution of the tax burden. Dissatisfaction in Georgia and throughout the South and West with the accomplishments of the Alliance through association with the old parties led to the desire for a new party. The name of the new party varied from State to State, but the name People's Party, adopted in Kansas to dramatize the battle between the people and the plutocrats, won increasing acclaim. The third party movement was retarded in the South by the Negro problem and fear of a revival of Congressional Reconstruction; but under the leadership of Westerners, the People's Party as a national organization was launched at a convention of Alliancemen at Cincinnati, in May, 1891. Tom Watson [31] in Congress had refused to be bound by the Democratic caucus. Holding that "the new wine of reform fared badly in old

---

[31] Thomas Edward Watson (September 5, 1856—September 26, 1922) was born on a farm in Columbia County, near Thomson, Georgia, of English Quaker ancestry. He attended Mercer University for two years, and spent two years as an impoverished country school teacher. After studying law privately, he entered the bar, won dramatic success as a criminal lawyer, and was soon able to move his family from their miserable shanty back to the old homestead of his grandfather. In politics he assumed the role of an agrarian avenger. "A rebel and fighter by temperament, he was made by circumstances hostile to the new order and nostalgic for the old." He challenged Grady's "New South" creed of industrialism and alliance with the East, insisting that the natural ally of the South was the agricultural West. He served one term in the General Assembly (1882), and in 1890 was elected to United States House of Representatives on the Farmers' Alliance Platform.

Watson's position in Congress was weakened by the open hostility between him and Charles F. Crisp, a conservative representative from Georgia, who was elected Speaker of the House in 1891. Watson was not placed on any important committee, and most of the bills that he introduced were never considered. An exception to this rule was his bill appropriating $10,000 for experimental free-delivery of mail in rural communities, thus giving him the proud claim to the title, "Father of the R.F.D." *Dict. of Amer. Biog.*, XVIII, 549.

bottles," he became a leader in the third party movement. On October 1, 1891, there appeared in Atlanta the first issue of Watson's *People's Party Paper* that was to appear weekly for the next eight years.

In 1892 the Populist Party entered Georgia politics by naming W. L. Peek as candidate for Governor to oppose William J. Northen, nominated by the Democrats for a second term; but the majority of Georgians could not be drawn into a third party and Northen was elected by a vote of 140,492 to 68,990. In this election the Democratic organization succeeded in defeating Watson in his race for reelection to Congress, using such corrupt practices that he contested the count, but his unpopularity with the Democratic majority in Congress caused his case to receive an unsympathetic hearing.

In 1894 the standard bearer of the Democratic Party in the gubernatorial election was William Y. Atkinson, former Speaker of the House of Representatives. The Populist candidate was James K. Hines, a member of the Atlanta bar. Stuffed ballot boxes, double voting, and purchase of Negro votes at one dollar each was the order of the day. On the face of the returns the Democrats won, but the Populists were credited with 44.5% of the votes. The Populists lost all of the Congressional contests, but elected five Senators and forty-seven Representatives in the Georgia General Assembly.[33] In the country at large the Populists polled 1,471,590 votes and elected six United States Senators, thus giving them the balance of power in Congress.

In the gubernatorial election of 1896 the Populist candidate, Seaborn Wright, polled 85,832 votes to 120,-827 for William Y. Atkinson, the Democratic candidate. This was the last campaign in which the Populist Party

---

[33] Arnett, *Populist Movement in Georgia*, 184.

was to be a formidable threat, and during the following decade it gradually faded from the Georgia scene.[34]

Populism as a party organization was largely destroyed by its merger with the Democratic Party in the presidential election of 1896. The Democratic national convention nominated William J. Bryan, an advocate of free and unlimited coinage of silver, long a plank in the platform of Alliancemen and Populists. Tom Watson was opposed to a fusion with the Democrats, holding the silver issue to be but a drop in the bucket of the Populist reform program. But leaders of the Populists' national convention persuaded Watson in the interest of harmony to accept the nomination of Vice President on a ticket with Bryan, the understanding being that the Democratic Party would withdraw the name of Arthur Sewall, an Eastern capitalist who had been named by the Democratic national convention as Bryan's running-mate. The Populist convention followed the unusual procedure of first electing Watson as their Vice Presidential candidate and then electing Bryan as Presidential candidate. Bryan denied that the Democrats had agreed to withdraw Sewall, and in most States, including Watson's home State, the Democratic candidates for the electoral college were pledged to Bryan and Sewall. But the election left no room for a contest over the Vice Presidency. The Republican Party won by 95 electoral votes over the combined Democratic and Populist candidates. It is interesting to note that Mark Hanna rented a home in Thomasville, Georgia, in 1895, and opened McKinley's campaign by entertaining visitors from various parts of

[34] The vote in succeeding campaigns in which the Populist Party entered a candidate for Governor was as follows:

|  | Democratic Candidate | | Populist Candidate | |
|---|---|---|---|---|
| 1898 | Allen D. Candler | 117,455 | J. R. Hogan | 50,841 |
| 1900 | Allen D. Candler | 90,455 | J. H. Traylor | 23,235 |
| 1902 | Joseph M. Terrell | 81,344 | Jas. K. Hines | 4,747 |
| 1906 | Hoke Smith | 76,962 | J. B. Osburn | 148 |

*Late Nineteenth Century*

the South. The support of Southern Republican bosses was an important factor in the nomination of McKinley.[85]

Defeat in the election of 1896 virtually wrecked the Populist Party. Populism in one form or another remained a vital force, but the People's Party was never again a serious factor in national politics. Prosperity returned during McKinley's administration. People were tired of the long agitation for reform. The Spanish-American War turned attention from domestic issues to foreign affairs; the platform of the Democratic Party in the 1898 gubernatorial campaign in Georgia, affirming the righteousness of our cause in the Spanish War, scarcely alluded to State affairs.

In addition to the four amendments of 1892 relating to the General Assembly noted above, five additional amendments to the Constitution were adopted during the decade of the 'nineties. Two of them had as objectives a further liberalization of the provision for pensions to Confederate Veterans.[36] Popular election of officials, in keeping with the agitation of the Populist movement, was the objective of the three other amendments: one of 1895 relating to justices of the Supreme Court (formerly elected by the General Assembly), one of 1896 relating to the State School Commissioner (formerly appointed by the Governor), and one of 1898 relating to both the judges and solicitors of the Superior Courts (formerly elected by the General Assembly).[37] The

---

[85] Many wealthy Northerners, among them the heirs of Mark Hanna, still maintain magnificent estates at Thomasville.

[36] Amendments to Art. VII, Sec. I, Par. I. *Georgia Laws, 1893*, pp. 19-20, ratified Oct. 3, 1894, and *Georgia Laws, 1899*, p. 19, ratified Oct. 9, 1900.

[37] Amendments to Art. VI, Sec. II, Par. VIII, *Georgia Laws, 1895*, pp. 15-17, ratified Oct. 7, 1895; Art. VIII, Sec. II, Par. I, *Georgia Laws, 1894*, pp. 34-35, ratified Oct. 7, 1896; Art. VI, Sec. III, Par. II and III, and Art. VI, Sec. XI, Par. I, *Georgia Laws, 1897*, p. 93, ratified Oct. 5, 1898.

## A Constitutional History of Georgia

amendment relating to the Supreme Court increased the number of judges to six and authorized it to hear cases either when sitting as a body or in two divisions.[38]

---

[38] Members of the Bar had long recognized that the Supreme Court was overworked. An Amendment of 1887 increasing the number of justices had been defeated. The resignation of Chief Justice Bleckley was an important factor in awakening the people to a realization of the need of assistance for the Court.

The Supreme Court has customarily sat in two divisions for hearing cases, but decisions have been made by the full bench. The practice has been for the Chief Justice to divide the Court into three pairs of judges, called "consulting mates," for the study of records and the writing of opinions. After an opinion is written, it is read before the full bench, desirable changes are made, and it is then voted on. The even number of judges from 1895 to 1945 sometimes led to a three to three division among the justices, as in *Harrison vs. Hardman* (169 Ga. 435) and *Norman vs. Bradley* (173 Ga. 482). For the procedure in the Court, see *The Georgia Bar Journal*, VIII (Aug., 1945), 22-23. Few justices of the Supreme Court have had opposition in campaigns for reelection. Since the Governor fills vacancies by appointment and the appointed members seldom have opposition in the ensuing election, in practice Georgia tends to have a Supreme Court appointed by the Governor, subject to confirmation by popular vote.

CHAPTER XIV

# Early Twentieth Century

THE passing of the Populist movement left to the Democratic Party a position of supremacy in Georgia politics that remained unchallenged during the first half of the twentieth century. The vast majority of Georgians, as well as other Southerners, felt obliged to stand together as members of the Democratic, or "White-man's Party," the party that would save "Anglo-Saxon civilization." "Tens of thousands of Southern men had no other political platform except 'I'm a Democrat, because my daddy was a Democrat, and I'm g'wine to vote agin the nigger!' "[1] But the presence of only one effective political party did not mean the absence of political factions. Rivalry was simply confined within the Democratic Party whose nominees for State offices, chosen in a party primary, were usually unopposed and always certain of victory in the general election. Constitutional issues were frequently involved in political campaigns, and the administration of each Governor witnessed one or more amendments in the Constitution.

---

[1] Mrs. William H. Felton, *My Memoirs of Georgia Politics* (Atlanta, 1911), 6.

*A Constitutional History of Georgia*

# Allen Daniel Candler, 1898–1902

Two amendments were made in the Constitution during the term of Allen D. Candler,[2] Governor of Georgia at the opening of the twentieth century. The first, in 1898, as noted in the previous chapter, provided for the election of judges and solicitors of the Superior Courts by the people of the whole State.[3] The second broadened the field of compensation to Confederate veterans and their widows. Under the existing provisions of the Constitution, only veterans disabled or permanently injured in

---

[2] Allen Daniel Candler (November 4, 1834—October 26, 1910), was born in Lumpkin County and graduated from Mercer University. He lost one eye during his service in the Confederate Army, and returned to Jonesboro, as he said, with "one wife, one baby, one dollar, and one eye." He taught school for five years, and then entered business as a contractor at Gainesville. After serving several terms in the General Assembly, in 1882 he was elected to Congress, defeating Emory Speer, and served four terms. From 1894 to 1898 Candler was Secretary of State of Georgia, and from 1898 to 1902, Governor. "A man of excellent reputation, conservative by nature, and inclined to view the problems of his day in the light of the business man's ideal," he gave the State an economic and efficient administration. Arnett, *The Populist Movement in Georgia*, 215; *Dictionary of Amer. Biog.*, III, 470.

[3] Amendment to Art. VI, Sec. III, Par. II and III, and Sec. XI, Par. I, *Georgia Laws, 1897*, pp. 93–95. Ratified October 5, 1898. There were 22 judicial circuits in 1898. Warren Grice, *The Bench and Bar of Georgia*, (Macon, 1931), I, 234. While voted for by the electorate of the whole State in the general election, the judges and solicitors of the Superior Courts have always been nominated in the Democratic primary by the electorate of their own circuit only. The Act of 1908 regulating primary elections by requiring the candidates to be voted for "on one and the same day throughout the State" provided that this should "not have the effect to require a primary for judges and solicitors except in their respective circuits." *Laws, 1908*, p. 56.

In retrospect, Georgia has had wide experience in the method of selecting judges and solicitors of her Superior Courts. Under her early constitutions, they were appointed by the General Assembly, but an amendment of 1855 provided for popular election of the solicitors. Under the Constitution of 1861 both the judges of the Superior Courts and the solicitors were appointed by the Governor, but the Constitution of 1865 returned to appointment by the General Assembly. The Constitution of 1868 provided for their appointment by the Governor, but the Constitution of 1877 returned to election by the General Assembly.

*Early Twentieth Century*

service were eligible for benefits. The amendment of 1900 authorized compensation to Confederate veterans who, by reason of age and poverty, or infirmity and poverty, or blindness and poverty, were unable to provide a living for themselves. The amendment also authorized aid to widows of such veterans.[4]

## James M. Terrell, 1902–1907

JAMES MERIWETHER TERRELL (June 6, 1861–November 17, 1912), a lawyer, member of the General Assembly, and Attorney General of Georgia from 1892 to 1902, succeeded Candler as Governor and served for two terms. He worked zealously for the establishment of an agricultural and mechanical school in each congressional district of the State, which was accomplished by an Act of August 18, 1906. The legislature of 1906 also appropriated $100,000 to develop the State College of Agriculture and Mechanical Arts in Athens. The University had recently purchased 500 acres of land adjoining its campus for an agricultural school. In September, 1907, Dr. Andrew M. Soule came from the Virginia Polytechnic Institute to accept the presidency of the Georgia Agricultural College.[5]

Seven constitutional amendments were adopted during Terrell's administration. Two of these, in 1903, dealt with taxation. The purposes of taxation were already strictly limited, but even more effective would be a limi-

---

[4] Amendment to Art. VII, Sec. I, Par. I. *Laws, 1899*, p. 19. Ratified Oct. 9, 1900.

[5] Clark Howell, *History of Georgia*, (Chicago, 1926), I, 687. The State Board of Health was also established during Terrell's administration. A Board of Health had been set up by an Act of 1875, but soon became inactive because of insufficient funds. It was reestablished by an Act of 1903. *Government Manual of Georgia, 1938*, p. 53.

## A Constitutional History of Georgia

tation on the amount of taxation. The first amendment of 1903 provided that "the levy of taxes on property for any one year by the General Assembly . . . shall not exceed five mills on each dollar of the value of the property taxable in the State."[6] The other amendment authorized taxation by militia districts and school districts (in addition to taxation by counties and municipal corporations already authorized) for educational purposes.[7]

Three amendments dealt with the number of counties and representation in the General Assembly. There were 137 counties in 1877, and the Constitution provided that no new counties should be created.[8] Two amendments of 1904 increased the number of counties to 145 and the membership of the House of Representatives to 183.[9] The third, adopted in 1906, created Ben Hill County, but made no provision for representation from this new county in the General Assembly, thus necessitating an additional amendment for that purpose two years later.[10]

The other two amendments adopted during Terrell's administration dealt with the judiciary. The first, of 1905, authorized the General Assembly to add one or more additional judges for any judicial circuit.[11] The other, adopted in 1906, created a Court of Appeals, to consist of three judges, until otherwise provided by law,

---

[6] Amendment to Art. VII, Sec. I, Par. II. *Laws, 1903*, pp. 21–22. Ratified Oct. 5, 1904.

[7] Amendment to Art. VIII, Sec. IV, Par. I. *Laws, 1903*, pp. 23–24. Ratified Oct. 5, 1904.

[8] Art. XI, Sec. I, Par. II.

[9] Amendments to Art. II, Sec. I, Par. II and Art. III, Sec. III, Par. I. *Laws, 1904*, pp. 47–49. Ratified Oct. 5, 1904.

[10] Amendment to Art. XI, Sec. I, Par. II. *Laws, 1906*, pp. 28–29. Ratified Nov. 6, 1906; Amendment to Art. III, Sec. III, Par. I. *Laws, 1908*, pp. 31–32. Ratified Oct. 7, 1908.

[11] Amendment to Art. VI, Sec. III, Par. I. *Laws, 1905*, pp. 66–67. Ratified October 3, 1906. The General Assembly has provided for seven judges in the Atlanta circuit and two judges for the Macon circuit. The other 31 circuits have only one judge.

*Early Twentieth Century*

elected in the same manner as justices of the Supreme Court (*i.e.*, by popular vote), for six-year terms. The Court of Appeals was given appellate jurisdiction over all cases from City Courts and criminal cases other than convictions of a capital felony from the Superior Courts.[12]

## *Hoke Smith, 1907–1909*

THE decade from 1896 to 1906 had been one of economic prosperity and Georgia had experienced an era of good feeling in politics. By contrast, the intensity of the gubernatorial campaign of 1906 was reminiscent of the days of Troup and Clark. The two leading candidates were Hoke Smith, supported by the *Atlanta Journal,* and Clark Howell, publisher of the *Atlanta Constitution.* Three other candidates, John H. Estill, Richard B. Russell, and James M. Smith also campaigned widely. Hoke Smith ran upon a reform platform, and the support that he received from Tom Watson, again coming into the foreground of Georgia politics, was logical insofar as Smith's program related to curbing ring politicians, regulating railroads, and abolishing the convict lease system. But the plank in his reform program that Smith and the *Journal* emphasized most was a constitutional amendment to disfranchise the Negro. This was the antithesis of Watson's earlier equalitarian doctrines, but as early as 1904 he had advocated an amendment to remove the "bugaboo of Negro domination." "Gradually, the Jeffersonian equalitarianism and humanitarianism of the 'nineties had been exchanged for a patchwork of the garments of Calhoun's Greek Democracy: Militant sec-

---

[12] Amendment to Art. VI, Sec. I, Par. I. *Laws, 1906,* pp. 24–28. Ratified Nov. 6, 1906. The jurisdiction of the two appellate courts was redefined by an amendment of 1916.

tionalism, fear of majority rule, racial domination, and perceptible overtones of a landed aristocracy. . . . The tenuous lines that Watson had tied between national Progressivism and Southern Agrarianism . . . snapped under the tension of the race issue."[13] Smith opened his campaign by an attack upon the railroads in an address delivered at Madison on June 29, 1905, and four months later Watson announced his support of Smith.

Clark Howell, Smith's strongest opponent, was opposed to any disturbance of the existing method of election, holding that the Democratic primary effectively eliminated the Negro vote. John H. Estill, "the South Georgia candidate," agreed with Howell's view that the white primary was Georgia's only safeguard against Negro votes. It was charged that Estill was in the race only to support Howell, but he emphatically denied the charge. He "paid his respects to the two Atlanta candidates, declaring that if what each says about the other is true, neither should be elected, and if they have been telling what is not true, both should be disqualified. . . ."[14] Judge Russell held that the less the Negro question was agitated, the better, as the Negro was already disfranchised in practice. An interesting plank in his platform was a provision for the exemption from taxation of property to the value of $300 for each person. Thirty years later this provision had a wide appeal and was written into the Constitution, but in 1906 it was denounced as merely an exemption of Negroes from the small share of the tax burden they then paid. James M. Smith, the self-styled "farmer's candidate," advocated a division of the public school funds of the State so that only the taxes paid by Negroes should be used to educate Negro children.

---

[13] Vann Woodward, *Tom Watson*, 380, 402. By permission of The Macmillan Company, publishers.

[14] *Savannah Morning News*, June 22, 1906.

## Early Twentieth Century

The Democratic Executive Committee, meeting at the Kimball House in Atlanta on April 30th, made provision for the following oath to be printed on the ticket for the primary election of 1906: "By voting this ticket I hereby declare that I am an organized Democrat, and I hereby pledge myself to support organized Democracy, both State and national." [15] Thanks to Watson's support and the popular appeal of the proposal to disfranchise the Negro legally, Smith swept the State, carrying 25,000 more votes than his four opponents combined. He was opposed to printing a pledge on the ballot, and the Democratic Convention declared that the executive committee, a "ministerial and executive body only," had exceeded its authority.[16]

The triumph of Smith [17] was due to the popular appeal of the "restoration of the government . . . to the hands of the people" and exclusion of the Negro from the ballot "by forms of Anglo-Saxon law." A tragic sequel to the election was the race riot that broke upon the streets of Atlanta a few days after the election. "It raged for four

---

[15] *Savannah Morning News*, May 1, 1906. The rules of the party for 1900, 1902, and 1904 had provided that: "All qualified white voters, without regard to past political affiliations, who desire to align themselves with the Democratic Party, and who will, upon their right to participate in the primary being challenged, agree to support the nominee of said primary, are qualified to vote therein and are invited to the same." *Newnan News*, quoted in *Atlanta Journal*, April 9, 1906.

[16] *Atlanta Journal*, Sept. 5, 1906.

[17] Hoke Smith (September 2, 1855—November 27, 1931) was born in Newton, North Carolina. He received little formal training but profited from the tutelage of his father, a professor of Greek and Latin at the University of North Carolina, before he moved to Atlanta in 1872. Hoke read law, entered politics, and in 1887 purchased the *Atlanta Journal* through which he built up a wide following for the liberal reform movement associated with his name. Partly as a reward for carrying Georgia for Cleveland against David B. Hill in the Presidential nomination of 1892, he was made Secretary of Interior in 1893 and served until 1896. Courageously, but in vain, he sought to uphold in Georgia Cleveland's effort to maintain the gold standard. Following the nomination of Bryan, Smith retired from politics for a decade. *Dictionary of American Biography*, XVIII, 280–282.

days. Innocent men and women were hunted by packs and shot down in the streets of the city. Destruction, looting, robbery, murder, and unmistakable brutality went unrestrained." [18]

The progressive legislation enacted during Smith's first administration was even more impressive than that enacted by the Populist Legislature of 1891. As a part of the reform movement of the period, the General Assembly of 1906 (during Terrell's administration) passed a pure food and drug act, restricted the use of child labor in factories, and provided for popular election of the Railroad Commission. Smith's first legislature increased the membership of the Railroad Commission to five, extended its jurisdiction to street railways, docks and wharves, terminal stations, cotton compress corporations, telephones, gas and electric power, and increased its power, particularly the authority to investigate utilities under its jurisdiction, empowering it to require a uniform system of accounting by such utilities and to supervise their issuance of stock. The same legislature prohibited traffic in narcotic drugs, created a bank bureau in the Treasury Department charged with the duty of investigating banks, and prohibited fishing on Sunday. Though not a dominant issue in Smith's campaign, a bill providing for statewide prohibition of the sale and manufacture of intoxicating liquors caught up on the wave of the reform movement, and was also swept through the legislature of 1907.[19]

In 1908 the legislature made five per cent the maximum legal limit of interest rates, established a tuberculosis sanitarium and a board of veterinary examiners, regulated primary elections, requiring that they be held on the same date throughout the State, required the pub-

---

[18] Vann Woodward, *Tom Watson*, 379. By permission of The Macmillan Co., publishers.

[19] *Laws, 1907*, pp. 72–124, *passim*.

lication of campaign expenditures, and prohibited corporations or their officers from contributing to political campaigns.[20] At a special session of 1908 the legislature abolished the convict lease system, long recognized as inhuman, and made provision for juvenile courts.[21]

Four constitutional amendments were adopted during Smith's first administration. The first made provision for representation from Ben Hill County in the House of Representatives by increasing the membership of the House from 183 to 184.[22] Another extended the enumerated purposes of taxation to cover pensions for any Confederate soldier or the widow of a Confederate soldier (formerly only disabled veterans could receive pensions).[23] A third amendment empowered the counties to collect taxes to pay county police and to provide necessary sanitation.[24] The fourth amendment was the crafty "grandfather clause."

The framers of the Federal Constitution had wisely left the question of the qualifications for voting, even for members of Congress, to be determined by the legislatures of the several States; but in 1869 the radicals in control pushed through the Fifteenth Amendment which prescribed that the right to vote should not be abridged by the United States or by any State "on account of race, color, or previous condition of servitude." This was intended to secure the right of the Negro to vote, although the language did not specifically so declare. During the

---

[20] *Laws, 1908*, pp. 54–106, *passim*.
[21] *Laws, 1908*, pp. 1107–1130. The Supreme Court of Georgia as late as March 1, 1907, followed the established precedent that the labor of a convict during his term of sentence was a property right which could be made the basis of a valid contract. *Hamby vs. Georgia Iron Company*, 127 Georgia 792.
[22] Amendment to Article III, Sec. III, Par. I. *Laws, 1908*, p. 31. Ratified Oct. 7, 1908.
[23] Amendment to Article VII, Sec. I, Par. I. *Laws, 1908*, p. 34. Ratified Oct. 7, 1908.
[24] Amendment to Article VII, Sec. VI, Par. II. *Laws, 1908*, pp. 33–34. Ratified Oct. 7, 1908.

Reconstruction period the Ku Klux Klan used intimidation and violence to keep Negroes from the polls, but this secret order soon fell into disrepute. Taking advantage of the generality of the wording of the Fifteenth Amendment, the Southern States sought legal refuge from Negro suffrage. A Mississippi law of 1890 required in addition to other suffrage tests that the voter be able to either read or give a reasonable interpretation of any part of the Constitution, a requirement few Negroes could meet. In the case of *Williams vs. Mississippi*[25] the Supreme Court found no objection to the Mississippi law. Other methods used to disfranchise the Negro were the imposition of property qualifications, the requirement that the voter not only pay his taxes but present a receipt for his tax payment at the time of voting, and the disqualification of persons convicted of any one of numerous inconsequential offenses.

The objection raised against these strict requirements for voting was that they disqualified a large number of whites as well as Negroes. To overcome this factor, Southern ingenuity evolved the "grandfather clauses" that were adopted in Louisiana, Alabama, North Carolina, Virginia, Georgia, Oklahoma, and Maryland. The "grandfather clause" written into the Constitution of Georgia in 1908 required in addition to the existing qualifications (male citizenship, twenty-one years of age, residence in the State one year and in the county six months, and payment of all taxes) that a voter pay all taxes required of him six months prior to an election and qualify for registration under one of the five following headings:

> 1. All persons who have honorably served in the land or naval forces of the United States in the Revolutionary War, or in the War of 1812, or in the War with Mexico,

---
[25] 170 U. S. 213 (1898).

## Early Twentieth Century

or in any war with the Indians, or in the War between the States, or in the War with Spain, or who honorably served in the land or naval forces of the Confederate States or of the State of Georgia in the War between the States; or,

2. All persons lawfully descended from those embraced in the classes enumerated in the sub-division next above; or,

3. All persons who are of good character and understand the duties and obligations of citizenship under a republican form of government; or,

4. All persons who can correctly read in the English language any paragraph of the Constitution of the United States or of this State and correctly write the same in the English language when read to them by any one of the registrars, and all persons who solely because of physical disability are unable to comply with the above requirements but who can understand and give a reasonable interpretation of any paragraph of the Constitution of the United States or of this State, that may be read to them by any one of the Registrars; or,

5. Any person who is the owner in good faith in his own right of at least forty acres of land situated in this State, upon which he resides, or is the owner in good faith in his own right of property situated in this State and assessed for taxation at the value of $500.00.

The right to register under the first two headings should continue only until January 11, 1915, but the amendment provided that a permanent roster of those qualifying under these headings should be kept and that a person once registered thereunder should always be permitted to vote.[26] The constitutionality of this Georgia law was never tested before the United States Supreme Court, but in *Guinn vs. United States,* decided in 1915, a similar grandfather clause in the Constitution of Oklahoma was declared null and void.[27]

---

[26] Amendment to Art. II, Sec. I, Par. I–IX. *Laws, 1908,* pp. 27–31. Ratified Oct. 7, 1908.
[27] 238 U. S. 347.

Another amendment of 1908 provided that only qualified voters could participate in a party primary or a convention of a political party.

## Joseph M. Brown, 1909–1911

IN VIEW of the energetic way in which Smith carried out his platform pledges and the precedent in Georgia of giving a successful Governor an endorsement term, it is strange that he should have been defeated in the election of 1908. Several factors contributed to this end. The national depression of 1907 brought economic distress to Georgia, and the opponents of the Governor charged that his reform program and agitation against corporations had brought on hard times. "Hoke and Hunger, Brown and Bread" became the battle cry. Smith was opposed in the gubernatorial race by Joseph M. Brown[28] whom he had suspended from the Railroad Commission in 1907. The immediate conflict leading to Brown's suspension was the issue of port rates, but there had been a long-standing breach between them. The fact that Brown was suspended three days after the adjournment of the General Assembly and thus "not given a hearing" made of

---

[28] Joseph Mackey Brown (December 28, 1851—March 3, 1931), son of Governor Joseph E. Brown, was born at Canton, in Cherokee County. Having a scholastic average of 99½, he was graduated from Oglethorpe University with first honor in 1872. He then read law, gained admission to the Georgia Bar, and attended the Harvard Law School, but trouble with his eyes caused him to give up the legal profession. After studying at Moore's Business College he began work for the Western & Atlantic Railroad, first as a clerk with a salary of forty dollars per month, and subsequently in such varied phases of railroad work as conductor on a freight train, claim clerk, claim agent, timekeeper, accountant, freight agent, ticket agent, and traffic manager. In 1904 he was appointed to the State Railroad Commission by Governor Terrell. Upon the death of Senator Alexander S. Clay in 1910 Brown, as Governor, rewarded Terrell by appointing him to the United States Senate. For a "Personal History of 'Little Joe' Brown," see the *Atlanta Constitution,* June 4, 1908.

## Early Twentieth Century

"Little Joe," son of Georgia's famous war Governor, Joseph E. Brown, a martyr who should be vindicated. And who could make more of an issue of this kind than Tom Watson? The inconsistency of Watson in supporting Smith in 1906, praising the accomplishments of his early administration, and then violently opposing his reëlection is explained by the incident of the Glover Case.

Arthur Glover, a semi-literate factory foreman of Augusta, was convicted of the murder of a woman millworker and sentenced to hang. Of his guilt there was no question. But Glover had been one of Watson's loyal apostles in the bloody battles of the workers' district back in the 'nineties, and his prosecution was made by Boykin Wright, former manager of the campaigns against Watson in Augusta. Watson promised to ask Governor Smith to commute Glover's sentence to life imprisonment. The State Prison Commission reported unfavorably on the petition, and Smith could see no way to commute the sentence. Watson, in extravagant contentions, stated in the press that Glover was a "cracked-brained degenerate" and that his execution would be murder. The law took its course and Glover was executed. Watson broke completely with Smith and urged Brown to enter the gubernatorial race against him.

Another issue in the campaign was the county unit system of election for State officials. This system was firmly established in custom, but Smith favored nomination by popular vote.

Smith spoke all over the State, waging his campaign upon the record of his first administration. "The most important of the issues raised by my candidacy have become law, and are being enforced for the benefit of the State," he declared in March, 1908.[29] Brown, the "Silent man of Marietta," made no speeches in the campaign, but

---

[29] *Savannah Morning News,* March 10, 1908.

promised that if elected he "would attend to the duties of his office" and "not be found running all over the state for weeks at a time and allowing the business of his office to take care of itself." [30] The *Atlanta Constitution* hailed the victory of Brown by a vote of 109,806 to 98,949 as a return to "sanity, justice, and conservatism." [31] The platform adopted by the State Democratic Convention declared in favor of "a return to the constitutional representative system, or county unit plan, of representation in our state conventions, with its safeguarding checks and balance." [32]

In the Presidential election of 1908 William Howard Taft was the successful candidate. He had spent several winters at Augusta, and subsequently appointed Joseph Rucker Lamar as a Justice of the United States Supreme Court.[33]

Other than two amendments of local application—one relating to the debt of Augusta and the other to the salaries of judges in Chatham, Richmond, and Fulton counties—the only change in the Constitution during Brown's administration was an amendment of 1910 which struck out the limiting clause, "in instructing children in the elementary branches of an English education only," from the paragraph authorizing counties to levy taxes for educational purposes.[34]

---

[30] *Athens Banner*, quoted in the *Atlanta Constitution*, May 11, 1908.
[31] June 5, 1908.
[32] *Atlanta Constitution*, June 24, 1908.
[33] Joseph Rucker Lamar was an Augusta lawyer, member of the General Assembly, and Justice of the Supreme Court of Georgia from 1902 to 1905. See Clarinda Pendleton Lamar, *The Life of Joseph Rucker Lamar, 1857–1916* (New York, 1926), 90–91, for citation to nine of his articles on various phases of the legal history of Georgia. These articles are the best in their field.
[34] Amendment to Art. VII, Sec. VI, Par. II. *Laws, 1910*, pp. 45–47. Ratified Oct. 5, 1910. For the local amendments, see *Laws, 1909*, pp. 76–80, and *Laws, 1910*, pp. 42–44.

*Early Twentieth Century*

## *Hoke Smith, 1911*

IN THE campaign of 1910 Hoke Smith, again opposed by Brown, was elected by a vote of 97,989 to 93,734, despite the opposition of Watson. Shortly after the date of his inauguration as Governor (July 1, 1911), Smith was elected by the General Assembly to succeed Joseph M. Terrell as United States Senator, and sent in his resignation as Governor effective November 15, 1911. Congress was in session several weeks after Smith was elected Senator, and his opponents criticized him for not proceeding forthwith to Washington; but Smith felt it his duty to continue as Governor temporarily to insure the success of his legislative program. There was also much criticism of his suspension of William J. Northen, whom Brown had appointed as Compiler of the State Records to complete the work inaugurated by former Governor Allen D. Candler. Smith contended that this task had virtually been completed, that the remaining work was of a clerical nature, and that Northen refused to visit the office of the Governor.[35]

During Smith's second administration the General Assembly passed three amendments to the Constitution that were ratified by the people in 1912. The first of these dealt with education. Article VIII of the Constitution of 1877 provided: "There shall be a thorough system of common schools for the education of children in the elementary branches of an English education only." The amendment of 1912 struck the words "in the elementary branches of an English education only."[36] The second

---

[35] Howell, *History of Georgia*, I, 695.

[36] Amendment to Art. VIII, Sec. I, Par. I. *Laws, 1911*, pp. 46–48. Ratified Oct. 2, 1912. The amendment did not strike the restrictive language, "For educational purposes, in instructing children in the elementary

amendment made minor changes in the authority of the State to contract debt. Section III of Article VII originally provided: "No debts shall be contracted by or on behalf of the State, except to supply casual deficiencies of revenue, to repel invasion, suppress insurrection, and defend the State in time of war, or to pay the existing public debt; but the debt created to supply deficiencies in revenue shall not exceed, in the aggregate, two hundred thousand dollars." The amendment of 1912 struck the words "casual deficiencies of Revenue" and substituted, "such temporary deficit as may exist in the Treasury in any year from necessary delay in collecting the taxes of that year," and in lieu of the words "two hundred thousand dollars" substituted "five hundred thousand dollars, and any loan made for this purpose shall be repaid out of the taxes levied for the year in which the loan is made." [87] The third amendment of 1912 fixed the date for the return and payment of taxes. Returns on property owned on January 1st were to be made on or before March 1st, and payment thereon was to be made on or before September 1st.[88]

## John M. Slaton, 1911–1912

JOHN M. SLATON, President of the Senate, was sworn in as Governor on November 16, 1911, and four days later issued a proclamation calling a special election for January 10, 1912. Acting Governor Slaton was not a candidate for the executive office. Instead, he gave his support to

---

branches of an English education only" of Art. VII enumerating the purposes of taxation. This clause, never enforced, remained in the Constitution until 1945. Note that the amendment of 1912 applied to the State whereas a similar amendment of 1910 applied to counties.

[87] Amendment to Art. VII, Sec. III, Par. I. *Laws, 1911*, pp. 49–50. Ratified Oct. 2, 1912.

[88] Amendment to Article VII, Sec. II, Par. VI, Act of Aug. 19, 1911. *Laws, 1911*, pp. 51–53. Ratified Oct. 2, 1912.

Joseph M. Brown who was elected and took the oath of office on January 25, 1912, to fill the unexpired term of sixteen months.

## Joseph M. Brown, 1912–1913

FIVE amendments to the Constitution were adopted during Brown's second administration, all in the year 1912. The first authorized the General Assembly to confer upon judges of the Superior Courts in vacation authority to grant corporate powers and privileges to private companies.[39] The second dealt with justices of the peace. The Constitution of 1877 provided for one justice of the peace in each militia district. The amendment of 1912 authorized the General Assembly to abolish the offices of justice of the peace and notary public *ex officio* justice of the peace in any city, except Savannah, having a population of over 20,000 and to establish in lieu thereof such courts as the General Assembly saw fit.[40] The third authorized the General Assembly to exempt from taxation "farm products, including baled cotton, grown in this State and remaining in the hands of the producer, but not longer than for the next year after their production."[41] The other two amendments created new counties, Bleckley and Wheeler.[42]

## John M. Slaton, 1913–1915

IN THE regular election of 1912, in which John M. Slaton, Hooper Alexander, of Atlanta, and Joseph Hill Hall, of

---

[39] Amendment to Art. III, Sec. VII, Par. XVIII. *Laws, 1912*, pp. 27–29. Ratified Nov. 5, 1912.

[40] Amendment to Art. VI, Sec. VII, Par. I. *Laws, 1912*, pp. 30–33. Ratified Oct. 2, 1912.

[41] Amendment to Art. VII, Sec. II, Par. II. *Laws, 1912*, pp. 36–37. Ratified Nov. 5, 1912.

[42] Amendments to Art. XI, Sec. I, Par. II. *Laws, 1912*, pp. 38–41. Ratified Nov. 5, 1912.

## A Constitutional History of Georgia

Macon, were the leading candidates, Slaton [43] was elected by a large majority.

Ten amendments were added to the Constitution during Slaton's administration, one in 1913 and nine in 1914. The amendment of 1913 simply extended to Bibb County the constitutional provisions already applicable to Chatham, Richmond, and Fulton counties, requiring these counties to pay from their treasury to the Superior Court judges of the circuit of which they were a part "such sums as will with the salaries paid each judge from the State Treasury, make a salary of $5,000 *per annum* to each judge." [44] The first four of the amendments of 1914 created new counties—Bacon, Barrow, Candler, and Evans,[45] and the fifth increased the total number of representatives in the House of Representatives from 184 to 189 in order to give representation to Bleckley and Wheeler Counties (created in 1912) and to three of the new counties, Bacon, Barrow, and Candler.[46] The sixth struck the words "except Savannah" which had been incorporated in the amendment of 1912 authorizing the General Assembly to abolish justices of the peace in any city, except Savannah, having a population of over 20,000.[47] The seventh authorized the General Assembly to abolish the office of county treasurer in any county, or to fix the compensation of county treasurers without regard

---

[43] John Marshall Slaton was born in Meriwether County, December 25, 1866. He attended the University of Georgia (M.A., 1886) and was subsequently admitted to the bar. He served in both branches of the General Assembly and was elected Speaker of the House and President of the Senate. Northen, *Men of Mark in Georgia*, VII, 412–14.

[44] Amendment to Art. VI, Sec. XIII, Par. I. *Laws, 1913*, pp. 30–31. Ratified Nov. 3, 1914.

[45] Amendment to Art. XI, Sec. I, Par. II. *Laws, 1914*, pp. 23–33. Ratified Nov. 3, 1914.

[46] Amendment to Art. III, Sec. XIII, Par. I. *Laws, 1914*, pp. 36–39. Ratified Nov. 3, 1914. The act made no provision for representation from Evans County.

[47] Amendment to Art. VI, Sec. VII, Par. I. *Laws, 1914*, pp. 39–41. Ratified Nov. 3, 1914.

## Early Twentieth Century

to uniformity. This amendment was necessitated by the provision of the Constitution requiring uniformity in county officers.[48] The eighth amendment changed the term of county officers from two to four years.[49] The ninth clarified the wording of the Constitution relative to dates for the term of office for members of the General Assembly. The original Constitution provided that members of the General Assembly should serve "until their successors are elected." The amendment substituted the words, "until the time fixed by law for the convening of the next General Assembly," so that Article III, Section IV, Paragraph I should read: "The members of the General Assembly shall be elected for two years and shall serve until the time fixed by law for the convening of the next General Assembly." [50]

An incident of unrivaled excitement occurred two months before the end of Governor Slaton's term. On the morning of April 27, 1913, the body of Mary Phagan, a fourteen-year-old girl, was discovered in the basement of an Atlanta pencil factory. "The young superintendent of the factory, Leo M. Frank, who admitted paying the girl her wages when she came to the factory alone during the holiday on which the murder took place, was at once arrested. A fateful weight of irrelevant but prejudicial facts dogged Frank's case to the end. He was a Jew, a Northerner, an employer of underpaid female labor. Mary Phagan was a Gentile, pretty, popular, and a working girl. The Atlanta press immediately assumed the guilt of Frank, and rival papers vied with each other in exploiting the sensational details of the story." In a courtroom filled to overflowing and surrounded for blocks with a

---
[48] Amendment to Art. II, Sec. III, Par. I. *Laws, 1914*, pp. 42-43. Ratified Nov. 3, 1914.
[49] Amendment to Art. XI, Sec. II, Par. I. *Laws, 1914*, p. 43. Ratified Nov. 3, 1914.
[50] *Laws, 1914*, pp. 45-46. Ratified Nov. 3, 1914.

jeering mob, Frank was sentenced to die. Hugh M. Dorsey, the prosecuting attorney, became a popular hero. The case became a *cause célèbre* in liberal circles throughout the nation.[51]

In March, 1914, the *Atlanta Journal* printed an editorial asking a new trial for Frank. Watson seized upon this editorial as an excuse for dragging the Frank case into politics. On June 20, 1915, two days before the execution date and one day before his term ended, in the face of threats by Watson and the danger of mob violence, Governor Slaton commuted Frank's sentence to life imprisonment. It became necessary to declare martial law to protect the Governor. *Watson's Jeffersonian* compared the Atlanta mobs to the liberty boys of Revolutionary days. On the night of August 16th twenty-five armed men took Frank from the State Penitentiary in Milledgeville, boldly drove one hundred and seventy-five miles across the State in eight automobiles, and hanged him on a tree near Marietta, the home of Mary Phagan.

Watson kept the Frank case alive and capitalized upon it in future years: "His influence waxed and waned. Yet there was no governor of the state between 1906 and the time of Watson's death, a period of sixteen years, who did not owe at least one of his terms, in a greater or lesser degree, to Tom Watson's support." [52]

## Nathaniel E. Harris, 1915–1917

IN 1914 Georgians were called upon to elect a Governor and two United States Senators. The seventeenth amendment to the United States Constitution, effective on May

---

[51] Vann Woodward, *Tom Watson*, 435. By permission of The Macmillan Co., publishers.
[52] *Ibid.*

## Early Twentieth Century

31, 1913, provided that Senators should be chosen by popular vote. In a special election on July 1, 1913, Senator Augustus O. Bacon, whose term had expired on March 4th of that year, was reëlected for a fourth term. He died on February 14, 1914, and Governor Slaton appointed William S. West, of Valdosta, to succeed him until a successor should be chosen by ballot. Five candidates, Congressman Thomas W. Hardwick, Governor Slaton, John R. Cooper, Thomas B. Felder, and G. H. Hutchins, entered this race. Governor Slaton, basing his campaign upon the success of his tax equalization program in Georgia, received a plurality of both the popular and county unit votes, but no candidate received a majority vote. The Democratic Convention was temporarily deadlocked over this office, but on the fourteenth ballot Felder withdrew, and Hardwick, who based his campaign largely upon his twelve years of experience in Congress, was nominated. In the race for the long term Senatorship, Hoke Smith was reëlected by a two-to-one vote over his opponent, Joseph M. Brown. The gubernatorial campaign was between Nathaniel E. Harris,[58] Dr. L. G. Hardman, of Jackson County, and J. Randolph Anderson, of Savannah, President of the State Senate. Harris, the win-

---

[58] Nathaniel Edwin Harris (January 21, 1846–September 21, 1929), son of a physician, was born in Tennessee. He served in the Confederate Army, and after the war moved to Georgia. Through the aid of a loan from Alexander H. Stephens he attended the University of Georgia where he was graduated with first honor. After a few years spent in teaching school at Sparta and in reading law, he moved to Macon and became the law partner of Walter B. Hill, his former classmate at the University. While a member of the General Assembly in 1885 he took the lead in the passage of the act establishing the Georgia School of Technology. In an autobiography of guileless candor he attaches political significance to the fact that as chairman of the Board of Trustees of Georgia Tech for thirty years, in 1914 his name appeared on diplomas of more than 15,000 graduates of the school. Despite his advanced age of sixty-nine, he delivered one hundred sixty-two speeches in the campaign for Governor. Nathaniel Edwin Harris, *Autobiography* (Macon, 1927), *passim;* Walter G. Cooper, *The Story of Georgia* (New York, 1938), III, 446.

ning candidate, supported by Tom Watson, said he was campaigning as a Confederate veteran "to arouse the present generation to the bravery of the men of the sixties."[54]

There were four amendments to the Constitution during the administration of Governor Harris, all in the year 1916. One of these redefined the jurisdiction of the Supreme Court and the Court of Appeals. Under the constitutional provisions adopted in 1906, the Supreme Court was given appellate jurisdiction over the Superior Courts in all civil cases and in criminal cases where the accused had been convicted of a capital felony. The Court of Appeals was thus by construction left appellate jurisdiction over the Superior Courts in criminal cases not involving a capital felony and over all cases in the City Courts. If the decision of a case involved the construction of the Constitution of the United States, the Constitution of Georgia, or an Act of the General Assembly, the Court of Appeals was required to certify the constitutional question involved to the Supreme Court for direction. The amendment of 1916 gave the Supreme Court appellate jurisdiction over both the Superior and City Courts, but enumerated the types of cases to be heard by the Supreme Court as follows: cases involving (1) the construction of the Constitution of the United States, or treaties of the United States, or the Constitution of Georgia, (2) land titles, (3) equity, (4) wills, (5) capital felony, (6) *habeas corpus,* (7) extraordinary remedies, and (8) divorce. The Supreme Court was authorized to call up by *certiorari* any case from the Court of Appeals, which Court was authorized to certify to the Supreme Court any question upon which it desired instruction.[55]

---

[54] *Atlanta Constitution,* June 17, 1914.
[55] Amendment to Art. VI, Sec. II, Pars. V & IX. *Laws, 1916,* pp. 19-22. Ratified Nov. 7, 1916.

*Early Twentieth Century*

The second amendment of 1916 authorized the General Assembly, without regard to uniformity, to abolish fees and establish a salary for the solicitor general of any judiciary circuit.[56] The third amendment simply added four counties (Clarke, Floyd, Sumter, and Muscogee) to the list of those required to supplement the annual salary of the judge of the Superior Court circuit of which they were a part by a sufficient sum to bring it to $5,000. While unrelated to the remainder of the amendments, a rider was added providing, "The city court of Americus shall not be abolished, nor shall the salaries of the officers thereof be increased or diminished prior to January 1, 1921." [57] The fourth and last amendment of 1916, and of Harris' administration, related to Bacon County, declaring it to be a "statutory county," empowering the General Assembly to create "local offices and local courts in the said county, other than those provided for in this Constitution," and authorizing the county to create a bonded debt, not to exceed $100,000.[58]

## *Hugh M. Dorsey, 1917–1921*

THERE were four candidates for Governor in 1916: Governor Harris, seeking reëlection; Hugh M. Dorsey,[59] famed for his prosecution of Leo Frank and campaigning

---

[56] Amendment to Art. VI, Sec. XIII, Par. II. *Laws, 1916,* pp. 24–26. Ratified Nov. 7, 1916.

[57] Amendment to Art. VI, Sec. XIII, Par. II. *Laws, 1916,* pp. 22–24. Ratified Nov. 7, 1916.

[58] Amendment to Art. XI, Sec. I, Par. II. *Laws, 1916,* pp. 17–18. Ratified Nov. 7, 1916.

[59] Hugh M. Dorsey was born in Fayetteville, Georgia, July 10, 1871, and attended the public schools of Atlanta and Hartwell. In 1893 he was graduated from the University of Georgia with the Bachelor of Arts degree, and then spent one year studying law at the University of Virginia. He began the practice of law in Atlanta in 1895. Appointed Solicitor General of the Atlanta Judicial Circuit in 1910 to fill an unexpired term, he was elected to that position in 1912 and held it until he was elected Governor.

*A Constitutional History of Georgia*

upon a platform of upholding the verdicts of the courts, charging Harris with using the executive pardon too freely; Dr. L. G. Hardman, who contended that Georgia had had enough lawyers as Governor and now needed a physician; and Joseph E. Pottle, ex-Solicitor General of the Ocmulgee Circuit.[60] Dorsey, supported by Watson, was elected by a large majority.

In the election of 1918, Governor Dorsey was unopposed for reëlection, but four candidates entered the race against Senator Hardwick who had been criticised for voting against conscription and other measures sponsored by the Wilson administration. *Watson's Jeffersonian* had been banned from the mail in 1917 because of its obstruction to the draft and other war measures. In a campaign with loyalty as the issue, William J. Harris, of Cedartown, supported by President Wilson, was elected to succeed Hardwick by an electoral vote three times that of the combined vote of his four opponents.[61]

The first session of the General Assembly during Dorsey's administration passed the Neill Primary Act, destined to be of far-reaching significance in the future political history of the State. Beginning with California in 1866, several states introduced legal regulations of primary elections soon after the Civil War, but in Georgia primaries continued to be managed by political parties with little legal restraint. An act of 1887 prohibited the giving or furnishing of liquor within a certain distance of polling places on election days and gave legal recognition to the existence of primaries,[62] and an act of 1891 prescribed several regulations, but left their use optional with the political parties.[63] Several laws on the subject were enacted during the first decade of the twentieth cen-

---
[60] *Atlanta Constitution*, Aug. 23, 1916.
[61] *Ibid.* Sept. 12, 1918.
[62] *Georgia Laws, 1887*, p. 42.
[63] *Georgia Laws, 1890-91*, p. 210.

## Early Twentieth Century

tury, including an act of 1904 making it a misdemeanor to buy votes and an act of 1908 requiring that primaries for the nomination of State officers be held on the same date in all counties. Yet primary elections continued to be governed largely by party custom and rules.

Prior to 1886 diverse methods had been used to select delegates to State conventions of political parties—mass meetings in county courthouses, meetings in militia districts to select delegates to county meetings, or appointment by county executive committees. Relatively few delegates had been chosen by actual vote of the people. In that year Henry Grady, managing Gordon's campaign for Governor, effectively offset the advantage that Augustus O. Bacon held in the party organization by an appeal to the people to revolt against the politicians and elect their own delegates to the Democratic State Convention.[64] In 1890 the State Democratic Executive Committee recommended the use of primaries in selecting delegates to the State Convention, and eight years later the Democratic Party required this procedure. Delegates from each county to the State Convention of the Party were to be chosen by the county executive committees from the friends of the gubernatorial candidate receiving the largest popular vote in the county, and they were required to vote for State officers in the convention according to the vote of the people in their county.[65]

The county unit rule, under which the number of votes of a county in the State Convention was determined by its representation in the House of Representatives, was used from the very beginning of primaries by the Democratic Party, except in 1908, as noted above. The failure of the Democratic Convention to nominate John

---

[64] Nixon, *Henry Grady*, 226; John M. Graybeal, *The Georgia Primary Election System* (M.A. Thesis, Emory University, 1932), 4.

[65] *Atlanta Constitution*, March 18, 1898. Graybeal, *loc. cit.*, 18.

## A Constitutional History of Georgia

M. Slaton for United States Senator in 1914 when he received the largest popular vote and a plurality of the county unit votes led to a movement for a second primary when no candidate for United States Senator or Governor should receive a majority county unit vote. An act for this purpose, introduced by Cecil W. Neill, passed the General Assembly in 1916, but was vetoed by Governor Harris. The next year a similar act was again passed by the General Assembly and signed by Governor Dorsey.

The principal provisions of the Neill Primary Act of 1917 were as follows: Whenever any political party should hold a primary election to nominate candidates for Governor, United States Senator, Statehouse officers, Justices of the Supreme Court, and Judges of the Court of Appeals, such election should be held throughout the State on the second Wednesday in September in the years of general elections. Candidates who received the largest popular vote in a county should be considered to have carried that county and be entitled to its county unit vote, *i.e.*, two votes for every representative the county had in the lower house of the General Assembly. If two candidates for the same office tied in popular votes in any county, the county unit vote should be divided between them. A plurality of county unit votes was sufficient to nominate a candidate for any office other than Governor or United States Senator, for which offices a majority unit vote was required. If there were only two candidates for the office of Governor or Senator and they tied in county unit votes, the candidate with the largest popular vote should be nominated; but if there were more than two candidates and none of them received a majority county unit vote, a second primary race between the two candidates with the highest unit vote should be held on the first Wednesday in October following the first primary. If the two candidates tied in unit votes in the second pri-

*Early Twentieth Century*

mary, the one receiving the largest popular vote should be the nominee. There was no provision for a run-over primary for other officers. In case no candidate received a plurality county unit vote in the first primary and there was a tie between the candidates receiving the highest unit votes, then the holder of the largest popular vote should be nominated. The State executive committee of the party was given authority to consolidate the election returns and see that the names of the nominees were placed on the ballot in the general election. No person who was not "a duly qualified and registered voter in accordance with the rules and regulations of the party holding the same" was eligible to vote in a primary.[66]

There were twenty-seven amendments to the Constitution during Governor Dorsey's administration: four in

---

[66] *Ga. Laws, 1917*, pp. 183 ff. In 1944 The United States Supreme Court ruled in *Smith vs. Allwright* (321 U. S. 649), a case arising in Texas, that Negroes could not be barred from primaries if there were State laws regulating the primary, for State regulation made the primary an integral part of the election machinery. In a subsequent case in Georgia, *King vs. Chapman*, a United States District Court ruled that the Democratic primary in Georgia was an integral part of the election machinery and thus came within the rule of *Smith vs. Allwright*. The Circuit Court of Appeals upheld the decision of the District Court, but in its opinion, written by Judge Samuel Sibley, a native of Georgia, the Court pointed out that in the absence of State laws regulating the primary, "we are advised of no statute, State or federal, which undertakes to limit the right of citizens who form a political party to select those who shall participate in it." The Supreme Court refused to grant *certiorari* in the case. Eugene Talmadge used as the principal issue in his successful campaign of 1946 a restoration of the Democratic White Primary by repealing the State laws regulating the primary. The Commission on revision had already removed from the Constitution the provisions relating to primaries. The only member to oppose this action was Mrs. Leonard Haas. Albert B. Saye, ed., *Records of the Commission of 1943–44 to Revise the Constitution of Georgia* (Atlanta, 1946), I, 112–114. Talmadge's opponent in the race for Governor, James V. Carmichael, supported by Governor Arnall, advocated letting the Negroes vote. Georgia is the only Southern State, except Arkansas, that does not have either a literacy test or a poll tax, or both, as a qualification for voting. No candidate sponsored a literacy test; hence the people were forced to choose between the two extremes of suddenly enfranchising all adult Negroes or continuing to disfranchise all of them.

1917, eleven in 1918, and twelve in 1920. These dealt with representation in the General Assembly, new counties, county and municipal debts, local school taxes, tax exemptions, salaries, pensions and municipal bonds.

The first amendment of 1917 raised the annual salary of justices of the Supreme Court and judges of the Court of Appeals to $5,000, and the annual salary of judges of the Superior Courts to $4,000.[67]

The second amendment of 1917 authorized the General Assembly to exempt from taxation "all funds or property held or used by . . . colleges, incorporated academies or seminaries of learning," provided the same were not invested in real estate, the institution was open to the public, and that endowments to institutions for white people should be limited to white people and institutions for colored people should be limited to colored people.[68]

The third and fourth amendments of 1917 created two new counties, Atkinson and Treutlen.[69]

One amendment of 1918 created another new county, Cook,[70] and two others of the same year increased the membership of the House of Representatives and the Senate. To take care of the three counties created in 1917 and 1918, and Evans County, created in 1914, the membership of the House was increased from 189 to 193.[71] The

[67] Amendment to Art. VI, Sec. XIII, Par. I. *Laws, 1917*, pp. 36-38. Ratified Nov. 5, 1918. The amendment carried forward the earlier amendments requiring certain designated counties to supplement the salary of the judge of the Superior Court circuit of which they were a part.

[68] Amendment to Art. VII, Sec. II, Par. II. *Laws, 1917*, pp. 39-41. Ratified Nov. 5, 1918.

[69] Amendments to Art. XI, Sec. I, Par. II. *Laws, 1917*, pp. 41-49. Ratified Nov. 5, 1918. An error was made in the Act of Aug. 15, 1917, defining the boundaries of Atkinson Co., and this was corrected by an Act of Aug. 17, 1918. *Laws, 1918*, pp. 106-107. Both Acts were amendments to the Constitution.

[70] Amendment to Art. XI, Sec. I, Par. II. *Laws, 1918*, pp. 102-106. Ratified Nov. 5, 1918.

[71] Amendment to Art. III, Sec. III, Par. I. *Laws, 1918*, pp. 87-89. Ratified Nov. 5, 1918.

## Early Twentieth Century

number of senatorial districts was increased from 44 to 51, and the grouping of counties in several of the districts was rearranged.[72]

A fourth amendment of 1918 raised the *per diem* compensation of the General Assembly from four to seven dollars.[73] A fifth increased the salary of the Treasurer and made provision for additional assistance in his office. The Constitution of 1877 had placed the salary of the Treasurer at $2,000 *per annum* and limited the expenses for clerical help in his office to $1,600. The amendment of 1918 raised the Treasurer's salary to $4,800, fixed a salary of $3,600 *per annum* for an Assistant Treasurer, limited clerical expenses of the Treasurer's office to $6,000 a year, and provided that the State should pay the premium on the Treasurer's bond.[74]

A sixth amendment of 1918 increased the limitation on the sum that might be expended for secretaries and clerical assistance in the office of the Governor from $6,000 to $10,000.[75] This provision became a "dead letter" in the Constitution long before it was eliminated in 1945. The Attorney General ruled that clerical expenses of the "Governor's office" were limited, but clerical expenses of the Governor were not.[76]

A seventh amendment of 1918 struck Chatham and Fulton from the list of counties required to supplement the salary of the judge of the Supreme Court Circuit of which they were a part by sufficient amount to bring the

---

[72] Amendment to Art. III, Sec. II, Par. I. *Laws, 1918*, pp. 84–87. Ratified Nov. 5, 1918.
[73] Amendment to Art. III, Sec. IX, Par. I. *Laws, 1918*, pp. 89–91. Ratified Nov. 5, 1918.
[74] Amendment to Art. V, Sec. II, Par. II. *Laws, 1918*, pp. 91–93. Ratified Nov. 5, 1918.
[75] Amendment to Art. V, Sec. I, Par. XIX. *Laws, 1918*, pp. 93–94. Ratified Nov. 5, 1918. The record of the amendment in the *Georgia Laws, loc. cit.*, states this as an amendment to Art. VI, but this is an obvious error.
[76] *Records of the Commission of 1943–44 to Revise the Constitution*, I, 264, 267–68.

annual salary to $5,000, and prescribed that Chatham County should supplement the salaries of the judges of the Eastern Judiciary Circuit by $3,000 *per annum,* and that Fulton County should supplement the salary of the judges of the Fulton Superior Court by such amount as the County Commissioners deemed advisable.[77]

The eighth amendment of 1918 liberalized the provision for pensions to Confederate veterans (1) by striking the provision that pensions should not be paid to any veteran or widow of a veteran owning more than $1,500, and (2) by making widows who were married to Confederate soldiers previous to the year 1881 eligible for pensions.[78]

The ninth amendment of 1918 placed additional restrictions upon an increase in the debt of any county, municipality, or other political division of the State. It prohibited the General Assembly from providing for a special registration for a vote on increased indebtedness, and provided further that the two-thirds vote required to increase a debt should include a majority of the registered voters.[79]

The tenth amendment of 1918 redefined the boundary of Atkinson County.[80]

The first amendment of 1920 placed limitations on the amount of local taxation for school purposes. County taxes for school purposes were limited to five mills on the dollar of all taxable property outside of independent local school systems; and independent local school systems, municipalities, or school districts were limited to a tax of ten mills for school purposes. The two-thirds vote of the electorate in the locality concerned to approve a law au-

---

[77] Amendment to Art. VI, Sec. XIII, Par. I. *Laws, 1918,* pp. 94–96. Ratified Nov. 15, 1918.

[78] Amendment to Art. VII, Sec. I, Par. I. *Laws, 1918,* pp. 96–99. Ratified Nov. 5, 1918.

[79] Amendment to Art. VII, Sec. VII, Par. I. *Laws, 1918,* pp. 99–102. Ratified Nov. 5, 1918.

[80] Amendment to Art. XI, Sec. I, Par. II. *Laws, 1917,* p. 44, *Laws, 1918,* pp. 102, 106. Ratified Nov. 5, 1918.

## Early Twentieth Century

thorizing a tax for schools, adopted by an amendment of 1903, was maintained for independent local school systems, municipalities, and school districts, but not for counties.[81]

Another amendment of the same year specifically authorized appropriations for high schools (already implied by an amendment of 1912) and removed the restriction whereby the State could appropriate money to only one college for Negroes.[82]

The third amendment of 1920 raised the annual salary of justices of the Supreme Court and judges of the Court of Appeals to $7,000, and judges of the Superior Courts to $5,000. Supplements to the salaries of Superior Court judges by designated counties were continued.[83]

A fourth amendment of 1920 broadened the provisions of the Constitution for eligibility for Confederate pensions by extending them to Confederate veterans residing in Georgia on January 1, 1920.[84]

A fifth amendment of 1920 authorized cities with a population of 150,000 or more to issue street improvement bonds under specified conditions, without regard to the amount of other outstanding debts.[85] A sixth amendment authorized flood protection bonds for the city of West Point.[86]

---

[81] Amendment to Art. VIII, Sec. IV, Par. I. *Laws, 1919*, pp. 66–68. Ratified Nov. 2, 1920.

[82] Amendment to Art. VIII, Sec. VI, Par. I. *Laws, 1920*, p. 32. Ratified Nov. 2, 1920.

[83] Amendment to Art. VI, Sec. XIII, Par. I. *Laws, 1920*, pp. 20–23. Ratified Nov. 2, 1920.

[84] Amendment to Art. VII, Sec. I, Par. I. *Laws, 1920*, pp. 23–24. Ratified Nov. 2, 1920.

[85] Amendment to Art. VII, Sec. VII, Par. I. *Laws, 1920*, pp. 25–29. Ratified Nov. 2, 1920. The amount of each such bond issue was limited to the amount assessed by the municipality upon each improvement, and the improvement involved had to be upon petition in writing of the owners of more than fifty per cent of the property abutting on the street to be paved or improved.

[86] Amendment to Art. VII, Sec. VII, Par. I. *Laws, 1920*, p. 29. Ratified Nov. 2, 1920.

## A Constitutional History of Georgia

Five amendments of 1920 created new counties (Brantley, Lamar, Lanier, Long, and Seminole).[87] The last amendment of this year made provisions for representation of these new counties in the House of Representatives by the following significant changes in the basis of representation: The "fixed" number of representatives (then 193) was dropped; the eight (formerly six) largest counties were given three representatives each, the thirty (formerly twenty-six) next largest counties were given two representatives, and the remaining counties one representative each.[88]

---

[87] Amendments to Art. XI, Sec. I, Par. II. *Laws, 1920*, pp. 34–55. Ratified Nov. 2, 1920. The amendment creating Lanier County first passed the General Assembly in 1919. The amendment was amended twice by the General Assembly in 1920 (redefining the boundary and placing the County in a different judicial circuit) before it was submitted to the people for ratification.

[88] Amendment to Art. III, Sec. III, Par. I. *Laws, 1920*, p. 55. Ratified Nov. 2, 1920.

CHAPTER XV

# Amendments and More Amendments

THE year 1920 was a busy one politically for Georgia, there being a presidential primary in the spring and an election of both a Governor and United States Senator in the summer. Early in the year Attorney General Palmer entered the presidential primary as the candidate of the Wilson administration, endorsing the League of Nations. He was opposed by Senator Hoke Smith, who took an equivocal stand on the League, and by Tom Watson, a bitter enemy of the League. Palmer, supported by the *Atlanta Constitution*, gained a majority of the county unit votes, but the popular vote was almost equally divided between the three candidates, Watson having the largest. The State Democratic Executive Committee declared that Palmer was entitled to name the delegates to the Democratic National Convention, but the State Convention repudiated this ruling and selected a Watson-Smith delegation. Rival delegations appeared at San Francisco, but the Democratic National Convention seated the Palmer delegation.[1]

---

[1] Vann Woodward, *Tom Watson*, 469–70. The Presidential preferential primary was first introduced in Georgia in 1912. It was used again in 1920, 1924 and 1932. When no primary is held the State Democratic Executive Committee has a free hand in selecting delegates to the Democratic National Convention.

365

*A Constitutional History of Georgia*

The race for the United States senatorship was between Hoke Smith, seeking reëlection, Governor Hugh Dorsey, proponent of the League, and Tom Watson. Watson, who a few years earlier had carried out an anti-Catholic crusade, chose, of all things, the American Legion as the brunt of his most fiery denunciation in this campaign. The officers, he asserted, had abused the enlisted men in France. To the amazement of many, Watson won by a landslide. His hold on the masses was a reality.

## *Thomas W. Hardwick, 1921–1923*

IN THE gubernatorial race of 1920 no one of the four candidates, Tom Hardwick,[2] Clifford Walker, John N. Holder, or Walter R. Brown, received a majority vote, so a run-over election was held to choose between the two leading candidates, Hardwick and Walker. Hardwick, allied with Watson again after ten years of enmity, won by an overwhelming majority.[3] The two Toms ruled supreme in Georgia politics.

Only three amendments to the Constitution were proposed during the administration of Governor Hardwick, and two of these were defeated. The amendment that passed was of local application only, authorizing Rich-

---

[2] Thomas William Hardwick (December 9, 1872–January 31, 1944) was born in Thomasville and attended Mercer University. He began the practice of law at Sandersville and served in the Georgia House of Representatives. From 1903 to 1919 he was a member of Congress, as Representative from 1903 to 1914, and as Senator from 1914 to 1919. After his term as Governor of Georgia, 1921–23, he was appointed special assistant to the Attorney General of the United States, but resigned this position after one year to take up the practice of law in Atlanta. *Biographical Dictionary of the American Congress* (Washington, 1928), 1060.

[3] The vote in the first primary was as follows: Hardwick, 99,210; Walker, 90,738; Holder, 37,957; Brown, 3,530; in the second primary, Hardwick, 84,257; Walker, 68,234.

*Amendments and More Amendments*

mond County to supplement the salary of the judge of its Superior Court circuit.⁴

The death of Senator Watson on September 26, 1922, from an attack of bronchitis and asthma led to a special election to fill this vacancy. Governor Hardwick named Rebecca Latimer Felton, then eighty-seven years old, to fill the vacancy temporarily, thus bestowing upon her the honor of being the first woman to serve in the United States Senate. Attempts to have the State Democratic Convention meeting at Macon nominate a successor to Watson without holding an election were hooted down. Eight candidates entered the race, but the contest was largely between Walter F. George and Governor Hardwick, George winning by an overwhelming vote. His platform stressed opposition to "a compact with European nations whereby this Republic will either assume an obligation to protect the boundaries of foreign countries or settle their international differences," limited immigration, collection of war debts, rehabilitation of American industry, and a reduction in government spending.⁵

## *Clifford M. Walker, 1923–1927*

IN THE gubernatorial election of 1922, the first in which Georgia women were enfranchised, Governor Hardwick was defeated by Clifford Walker,⁶ a lawyer and business-

---

⁴ Amendment to Art. VI, Sec. XIII, Par. I, *Laws, 1922*, 26–27. Ratified Nov. 7, 1922. One of the amendments that was rejected proposed to increase the number of senatorial districts to fifty-two; the other proposal was to authorize Muscogee County to supplement the salary of the judge of the Chattahoochee Circuit.

⁵ *Atlanta Constitution*, October 8, 1922. Walter Franklin George was born in Preston, Georgia, Jan. 29, 1878. He attended Mercer University (B.S., 1900; B.L., 1901) and began the practice of law at Vienna. He was Solicitor General of the Cordele Judicial Circuit, 1907–12, Judge of the Superior Court of the same circuit, 1912–17, a Judge of the Court of Appeals, Jan.-Oct., 1917, and a Justice of the Supreme Court, 1917–22.

⁶ Clifford Mitchell Walker was born in Monroe, Walton County, Georgia, July 4, 1877, and graduated from the University of Georgia with an

367

## A Constitutional History of Georgia

man of Monroe, whose platform called for a complete revision of the tax system.[7]

Fifteen amendments to the Constitution were adopted during the administration of Governor Walker, six in 1924 and nine in 1926.

The first amendment of 1924 authorized cities and counties to exempt from all *ad valorem* taxation for a period of five years any new building or equipment for the manufacture or processing of cotton, wool, linen, silk, rubber, clay, wood, metal, mineral, milk, or electricity.[8]

The second amendment provided for biennial sessions of the General Assembly limited to sixty days.[9] The Constitution of 1877 had originally provided for a biennial session, but this had been changed to annual sessions by an amendment of 1892.

The third amendment created the Coastal Highway District, composed of Chatham, Bryan, Liberty, McIntosh, Glynn, and Camden Counties, as a political subdivision and corporate body, and empowered it to issue bonds to the extent of $900,000, to be retired within thirty years, for the construction of the Dixie and South Atlantic Coastal Highway, extending from the Savannah River to the Florida line. Control of this project was vested in ten commissioners, to be selected by the county commissioners of the counties of the District.[10]

---

A.B. degree in 1897. He served as Mayor of Monroe, 1902–04, Solicitor General of the Western Judicial Circuit, 1909–13, and Attorney General of Georgia, 1915–20. *Georgia's Official Register, 1925*, p. 9.

[7] The vote was as follows: Walker, 122,784; Hardwick, 86,389; George Baylor, 2,830.

[8] Amendment to Art. VII, Sec. II, Par. II, *Laws, 1923*, 67–69. Ratified Nov. 4, 1924.

[9] Amendment to Art. III, Sec. VI, Par. III, *Laws, 1924*, 31–33. Ratified Nov. 4, 1924.

[10] Amendment to Art. VII, Sec. VII, Par. I, *Laws, 1924*, 35–38. Ratified Nov. 4, 1924. The State assumed this indebtedness by an amendment of 1932. See the amendments of 1939 for a new debt of $4,000,000 by the Coastal Highway District.

## Amendments and More Amendments

The fourth amendment authorized the General Assembly to consolidate with the county in which it was located the governmental functions of any city having a population of more than 52,900, and to establish governmental agencies for consolidated cities and counties without regard to the uniformity provision of the Constitution relating to city and county government, provided the offices of Clerk of the Superior Court, Ordinary, Sheriff and Coroner were preserved, and the consolidation was approved by a majority vote both in the city and in the county outside the city.[11]

The fifth amendment authorized the General Assembly to consolidate in any county the offices of Tax Receiver and Tax Collector in a new office to be known as Tax Commissioner and to authorize county authorities to fix the compensation of the Tax Commissioner, this without regard to uniformity among the various counties.[12]

The sixth amendment authorized additional indebtedness for the port at the City of Brunswick.[13]

Two local amendments were proposed in 1925 and ratified the next year, one allowing Muscogee County to supplement the salary of its Superior Court judge,[14] the other relating to the debt of Crisp County.[15]

The first four amendments of 1926 were local in application. The first authorized any county having within its borders a city with not less than 200,000 population

---

[11] Amendment to Art. XI, Sec. I, Par. II. *Laws, 1924,* 811–15. Ratified Nov. 4, 1924. This power has never been exercised.
[12] Amendment to Art. XI, Sec. III, Par. I, *Laws, 1924,* 815–17. Ratified Nov. 4, 1924.
[13] Amendment to Art. VII, Sec. VII, Par. I, *Laws, 1924,* 33. Ratified Nov. 4, 1924.
[14] Amendment to Art. VI, Sec. XIII, Par. I, *Laws, 1925,* 70. Ratified Nov. 2, 1926. This same amendment had been defeated in 1922.
[15] Amendment to Art. VII, Sec. VII, Par. I, *Laws, 1925,* 72. Ratified Nov. 2, 1926.

*A Constitutional History of Georgia*

(hence applicable only to Fulton County) to levy a one mill tax for educational purposes on all property in the county, including property within the limits of independent school districts.[16] The second authorized either the County of Lowndes or the City of Valdosta to create an indebtedness of one million dollars to aid in establishing a college.[17] The other two local amendments related to the debt of Chatham and McIntosh Counties.[18]

The first of the three amendments of State-wide application adopted in 1926 authorized counties to tax "for the collection and preservation of records of birth, death, disease, and health."[19] The second authorized the State to borrow $3,500,000 for the purpose of paying the public school teachers, but any amount borrowed for this purpose should be repaid each year out of the common school appropriation.[20] The third added to the enumerated purposes for which the State could levy taxes the construction and maintenance of a system of State highways.[21]

In 1924 Georgians seemed satisfied with their State officials, for most of them, including Governor Walker, were reëlected without opposition. There was also no opposition to six of the twelve Congressmen seeking reëlection. Tom Hardwick ran against Senator Harris, but Harris was reëlected by an overwhelming vote.

---

[16] Amendment to Art. VII, Sec. VI, Par. II. *Laws, 1926*, 20–21. Ratified Nov. 2, 1926.

[17] Amendment to Art. VII, Sec. VII, Par. I. *Laws, 1926*, 25. Ratified Nov. 2, 1926.

[18] Amendments to Art. VII, Sec. VI, Par. I. *Laws, 1926*, 22–28. Ratified Nov. 2, 1926.

[19] Amendment to Art. VII, Sec. VI, Par. II. *Laws, 1926*, 30–31. Ratified Nov. 2, 1926.

[20] Amendment to Art. VII, Sec. III, Par. I. *Laws, 1926*, 31–32. Ratified Nov. 2, 1926.

[21] Amendment to Art. VII, Sec. I, Par. I. *Laws, 1926*, 33. Ratified Nov. 2, 1926.

## Amendments and More Amendments

### Lamartine Griffin Hardman, 1927–1931

IN 1926 there were four candidates for Governor, and a run-over election was held between Lamartine G. Hardman [22] and John N. Holder, Chairman of the Highway Department. In the second race, both minority candidates, George H. Carswell and J. O. Wood, supported Hardman, who carried 228 county unit votes to 132 for Holder.[23] Hardman, a physician as well as a statesman, had as the main planks in his platform a business administration for the State and an abolition of machine politics.

In his campaign for reëlection to the United States Senate, George was opposed in 1926 by Chief Justice Richard B. Russell who denounced him as an internationalist for supporting the World Court.[24] Senator George won a sweeping victory. Eugene Talmadge entered State politics that year by election to the office of Commissioner of Agriculture.

In the campaign of 1928 Governor Hardman, opposed by E. D. Rivers, was reëlected by a comfortable majority.[25]

---

[22] Lamartine Griffin Hardman (April 14, 1856–February 18, 1937) was born in Commerce, Jackson County, Georgia. He was graduated from the Medical Department of the University of Georgia in 1876, and subsequently studied medicine in New York, Pennsylvania, and London. He began the practice of medicine at Commerce, Georgia, but combined business and farming with his professional work, and also served in the General Assembly. *Georgia's Official Register, 1929*, p. 7.

[23] The vote in the first primary was as follows: Holder, 71,976; Hardman, 67,708; Carswell, 32,484; Wood, 20,857; in the second primary, Hardman, 80,868; Holder, 60,197. After his inauguration as Governor in 1927, Hardman sought to remove Holder from the State Highway Department, but the Senate refused to confirm Hardman's appointee and Holder remained in office. Holder again opposed Hardman in the gubernatorial race of 1928, but Hardman was reëlected by a large majority.

[24] *Atlanta Constitution*, Sept. 1, 1926.

[25] The vote was as follows: Hardman, 137,430; Rivers, 97,339.

*A Constitutional History of Georgia*

Sixteen amendments were passed during the administration of Governor Hardman, eight in 1928 and eight in 1930. Only three of these amendments were of State-wide interest, one relating to justices of the peace, another to the salaries of the Treasurer, Secretary of State, and Comptroller General, and the third to zoning laws.

Five of the amendments of 1928 were of only local application. Four related to the debt of particular cities (Columbus and LaGrange) and counties (Ware, Fulton, Chatham, and Richmond),[26] and the fifth authorized Chatham County to supplement the salary of the judge of the Eastern Judicial Circuit.[27]

One of the three amendments of State-wide interest authorized the General Assembly to abolish the office of justice of the peace in any county, except Richmond, having within its borders a city with a population of 20,000 or more and to establish in lieu thereof, without regard to uniformity among the several counties, such courts as the General Assembly should deem necessary. This wordy amendment employed the same language used in the amendment of 1914 authorizing the abolition of the office of justice of the peace in cities with a population of more than 20,000.[28]

The second amendment of 1928 struck from the Constitution the provisions fixing the salary and clerical expenses of the offices of Treasurer, Secretary of State, and Comptroller General and authorized the General Assembly to prescribe the duties and salaries of these offices and to provide for necessary clerical help.[29]

---

[26] Amendments to Art. VII, Sec. VII, Par. I. *Laws, 1927*, 109, 113, 122, 124. Ratified Nov. 6, 1928.

[27] Amendment to Art. VI, Sec. XIII, Par. I. *Laws, 1927*, 111. Ratified Nov. 6, 1928.

[28] Amendment to Art. VI, Sec. VII, Par. I. *Laws, 1927*, 117–120. Ratified Nov. 6, 1928.

[29] Amendment to Art. V, Sec. II, Pars. II, III, IV. *Laws, 1927*, 121–122. Ratified Nov. 6, 1928.

## Amendments and More Amendments

The third amendment permitted the General Assembly to grant the cities of Atlanta, Savannah, Macon, Augusta, Columbus, LaGrange, Brunswick, Waycross, Albany, Athens, Rome, Darien, Dublin, Decatur, Valdosta, Newnan, Thomaston and East Thomaston, and cities having a population of 25,000, authority to pass zoning and planning laws.[30] There was really no reason why the General Assembly could not have exercised this power without special authorization, for the Constitution already provided that "The General Assembly shall have power to make all laws and ordinances consistent with this Constitution, and not repugnant to the Constitution of the United States, which they shall deem necessary and proper for the welfare of the State."[31] But in 1926 the Supreme Court of Georgia had ruled unanimously in *Smith vs. Atlanta*[32] that a zoning regulation making it unlawful to erect a store in a designated residential section denied due process of law to the property owner and was hence void under both the State and Federal Constitutions. After the amendment to the Georgia Constitution, the Court upheld zoning laws when attacked under the Federal Constitution.[33]

The General Assembly passed thirteen amendments to the Constitution in 1929, but when they were submitted to the people for ratification in 1930, five were defeated. The eight ratified were all of local application, relating to debts of particular cities and counties.[34] Only one of

---

[30] Amendment to Art. III, Sec. VII, Par. XXV. *Laws, 1927,* 127–129. Ratified Nov. 6, 1928.
[31] Art. III, Sec. VII, Par. XXII.
[32] 161 Georgia 769.
[33] *Howden vs. Savannah.* 172 Georgia 833 (1931).
[34] Amendment to Art. VII, Sec. VII, Par. I (relating to the debts of the cities of Cornelia, Elberton, and Lakeland and to the Counties of Washington and Stephens). *Laws, 1929,* 121–130, 142, 149. Ratified Nov. 4, 1930. Amendment to Art. IX, Sec. I, Par. I (relating to taxation for water and fire systems by Fulton County). *Laws, 1929,* 135–137. Ratified Nov. 4,

*A Constitutional History of Georgia*

the thirteen proposed amendments was of State-wide application. It would have authorized the General Assembly to levy an income tax not to exceed five per cent and limited the State *ad valorem* tax to two mills.[35]

## Richard B. Russell, Jr., 1931–1933

FIVE candidates ran for Governor in 1930: Richard B. Russell, Jr.,[36] George H. Carswell, John N. Holder, Eurith D. Rivers, and James A. Perry. For several years the State had been operating under a deficit and at this time was in arrears in its payments to veterans and to various State institutions, owing $4,000,000 in back salaries to teachers alone. Carswell, then Secretary of State and supported by the Hardman administration, proposed to divert funds from the Highway Department to liquidate the State debt. Russell emphasized the need of reorganizing the State administration as a means of economy and denounced the school book trust. "Russell would sell books at 10¢ each and Rivers would give them away," charged Carswell, who held that the State should pay its debts before becoming too generous. No candidate received a majority vote in the first primary, so a second was

---

1930. Amendment to Art. XI, Sec. I, Par. VI (relating to taxation by Glynn and McIntosh Counties for sanitation and other improvements). *Laws, 1929,* 137. Ratified Nov. 4, 1930. Amendment to Art. VIII, Sec. IV, Par. I (authorizing additional taxation for high schools in Pierce County). *Laws, 1929,* 139. Ratified Nov. 4, 1930.

[35] Proposed amendment to Art. VII, Sec. II, Par. I. *Laws, 1929,* 143–144. Defeated Nov. 4, 1930.

[36] Richard Brevard Russell, Jr., son of Chief Justice Russell, was born in Winder, Jackson (now Barrow) County, Georgia, November 2, 1897. He was educated at Gordon Institute and at the University of Georgia (B.L., 1918). He served in the United States Navy in 1918 and returned to Winder to practice law. Elected to the General Assembly in 1920, he became Speaker of the House seven years later. Elected to succeed William J. Harris, he has served in the United States Senate since 1933. *Georgia's Official Register, 1931,* p. 17.

## Amendments and More Amendments

held between Russell and Carswell, the leading candidates. Holder, opposed to any diversion of highway funds, now supported Russell, who won.[37]

In his inaugural address Governor Russell repeated his pledge to carry out a reorganization of the State administration and called upon the General Assembly for action. The Reorganization Act of 1931 which followed abol-

[37] The vote in the first primary was as follows: Russell, 56,177; Carswell, 51,851; Rivers, 47,121; Holder, 44,318; Perry, 6,594; in the runover, Russell, 99,505; Carswell, 47,157.

## A Constitutional History of Georgia

ished fifty-three boards, commissions, and bureaus, and twenty-seven administrative offices. Among the most important changes effected was a consolidation of the power formerly vested in twenty-seven boards of trustees of separate educational institutions in one Board of Regents of the University System of Georgia.[38]

The legislature of 1930 also revised the congressional districts within the State, reducing the number from twelve to ten in conformity with the reduction in Georgia's representation in Congress under the apportionment based on the census of 1930.[39]

Six amendments to the Constitution were passed during the administration of Governor Russell, five of them of general application, relating to highway indebtedness, qualifications for voting, consolidation of schools, contracts by school districts, and sessions of the General Assembly.

The first amendment provided that the State should take over the indebtedness incurred by the counties and by the Coastal Highway District for the construction of highways in conformity with the provisions of the Highway Act of August 18, 1919. This indebtedness was to be paid at a rate of not less than ten per cent *per annum*, beginning in 1936, from the funds of the State Highway Department.[40]

---

[38] Merritt B. Pound, "A Descriptive Account of Reorganization in Georgia" in the *Proceedings of the Southern Political Science Association* (October, 1933). A convenient survey of the administrative departments is given in the *Government Manual, State of Georgia, 1938*, edited by Richard C. Job for the Works Progress Administration.

[39] The number of representatives from Georgia in the lower house of Congress under previous apportionments was as follows: Constitutional apportionment—3; 1790 (1st Census)—2; 1800—4; 1810—6; 1820—7; 1830—9; 1840—8; 1850—8; 1860—7; 1870—9; 1880—10; 1890—11; 1900—11; 1910—12; 1920 (no apportionment).

[40] Amendment to Art. VII, Sec. VIII, Par. I. *Laws, 1931*, 97-101. Ratified Nov. 8, 1932. The date of retirement was extended by an amendment of 1939.

## Amendments and More Amendments

The second amendment dropped as a requirement for voting the payment of all taxes due and substituted therefor the payment of all poll taxes due.[41] The depression beginning in 1929 had caused many of the best citizens to fall in arrears with their tax payments, and this amendment was clearly an outgrowth of this economic situation.

The third amendment authorized the consolidation of two or more school districts, any one or more of which might have a bonded indebtedness, provided such consolidation was approved by a two-thirds vote of the qualified voters of each district affected. The indebtedness of any districts would, upon consolidation, be assumed by the entire new district.[42]

The fourth amendment authorized county boards of education, independent school systems, and local school districts to contract with each other for the education, transportation, and care of children of school age.[43]

The fifth amendment provided for a split session of the General Assembly, and changed the date for the inauguration of the Governor and the beginning of terms of State officials from June to January. The General Assembly would convene biennially on the second Monday in January for a ten day session for organization, election of officers and committees, introduction and first reading of bills and resolutions, and inauguration of the Governor-elect and other Statehouse officers with concurrent terms. The General Assembly should reconvene for its regular biennial session of not more than sixty days on the second Monday after the 4th of July.[44] The object of

---

[41] Amendment to Art. II, Sec. I, Par. III. *Laws, 1931,* 102–103. Ratified Nov. 8, 1932.

[42] Amendment to Art. VIII, Sec. IV, Par. I. *Laws, 1931,* 103–105. Ratified Nov. 8, 1932.

[43] Amendment to Art. VIII, Sec. IV, Par. I. *Laws, 1931,* 105–106. Ratified Nov. 8, 1932.

[44] Amendment to Art. III, Sec. IV, Par. III. *Laws, 1931,* 1053–55. Ratified Nov. 8, 1932.

this amendment was to give members of the General Assembly ample time to study bills introduced in January before reconvening to vote upon them in July. But since the amendment authorized the General Assembly at the ten day special session to fix a date prior to July for reconvening, and every General Assembly did this, the only effects of the amendment were to change the date of meetings from July to January, lengthen the sessions by ten days, and diminish the "lame duck" period between the election and inauguration of State officials.

The sixth amendment struck the exemption made for Richmond County in the amendment adopted in 1928 authorizing abolition of justices of the peace in counties having within their borders a city with a population of 20,000 or more.[45]

## Eugene Talmadge, 1933–1937

UNITED STATES Senator William J. Harris was opposed in the election of 1930 by former Governor John M. Slaton, but Harris carried every county except Evans. His death on April 18, 1932, led Governor Russell to enter the race for the Senate. He was opposed by Charles Crisp, dean of the Georgia delegation in Congress.[46] Many people sup-

---

[45] Amendment to Art. VI, Sec. VII, Par. I. *Laws, 1931*, 1051–53. Ratified Nov. 8, 1932.

[46] Charles Robert Crisp was the son of Charles Frederick Crisp, Speaker of the United States House of Representatives from 1891 to 1895. During that period Charles Robert served as Parliamentarian of the House, and upon the death of his father in 1896 he was elected to fill the remainder of his term in Congress, but was not a candidate for reelection, preferring to resume his law practice in Americus. In the Sixty-Second Congress (1911–1913) he was again elected Parliamentarian of the House, and in 1912 was again elected as a member of Congress from Georgia and served continuously until 1931. *Biographical Dictionary of the American Congress*, 861.

## Amendments and More Amendments

ported Crisp because of his long experience in Congress, but Russell won.

Six candidates, Eugene Talmadge,[47] Abit Nix, Tom Hardwick, John N. Holder, H. B. Edwards, and John I. Kelley, entered the race for Governor; but Talmadge won more than twice as many county unit votes as his five opponents combined.[48] His platform called for a $3 automobile tag, taxing hidden wealth and reducing the *ad valorem* tax, reducing power, telephone, and freight rates, and slashing red tape in government. In 1934 he was reelected in a campaign against Claude Pittman and E. D. Gilliam.[49]

Only three amendments to the Constitution were passed during Talmadge's first two administrations. Two of these were of local application, relating to the debt of Spalding County and to zoning laws in the City of Moultrie.[50] The other amendment related to procedure in appeals to the Supreme Court, providing that a case should not be dismissed because of unavoidable delay in transmittal of the record by the clerk of the trial court.[51] Five

---

[47] Eugene Talmadge was born in Forsyth, Monroe County, Georgia, September 23, 1884. He attended the University of Georgia and was graduated with an LL.B. degree in 1907. He began the practice of law in Atlanta, but within a year moved to Telfair County where he purchased a farm on Sugar Creek. The next fifteen years of his life were divided between farming and country law practice. He was Solicitor of the City Court of McRae from 1918 to 1920, Attorney of Telfair County from 1920 to 1923, and State Commissioner of Agriculture from 1927 to 1933. *Georgia's Official Register, 1933*, p. 7; Allen Lumpkin Henson, *Red Galluses, A Story of Georgia Politics* (Boston, 1945), Ch. I, II. Henson's book, largely a biography, portrayed Talmadge as a defender of Southern tradition against the inroads of the New Deal.

[48] The popular vote was as follows: Talmadge, 116,381; Nix, 78,588; Hardwick, 35,252; Holder, 19,697; Edwards, 12,897; Kelley, 12,115.

[49] The vote was: Talmadge, 178,406; Pittman, 87,049; Gilliam, 5,073.

[50] Amendments to Art. VII, Sec. VII, Par. I. *Laws, 1933*, 29. Ratified Nov. 6, 1934; and to Art. III, Sec. VII, Par. XXV. *Laws, 1935*, 1243. Ratified Nov. 3, 1936.

[51] Amendment to Art. VI, Sec. II, Par. VI. *Laws, 1935*, 1238-40. Ratified Nov. 3, 1936.

amendments, including one changing the term of the Governor to four years, were passed by the General Assembly in 1935 but defeated by the people.

## Eurith D. Rivers, 1937–1941

IN 1936 Governor Talmadge, severe critic of Roosevelt's "New Deal," who termed Senator Russell a "rubber stamp of Washington bureaucrats," ran for the United States Senate, but Russell was reelected. E. D. Rivers,[52] Charles D. Redwine of Fayetteville, and Blanton Fortson of Athens ran for Governor. Rivers, who had long advocated a New Deal for Georgia similar to that which President Roosevelt had given the nation, was elected by a landslide.[53]

In 1938 political interest was centered in the contest for the United States senatorship. Walter F. George, seeking reelection, was openly denounced by President Roosevelt in a speech delivered at Barnesville celebrating the completion of a rural electrification project. George had opposed some of the New Deal program, notably the scheme to pack the Supreme Court. The national administration supported Lawrence S. Camp, a United States District Attorney, as successor to Senator George. Eugene Talmadge also entered the race for Senator, but George was reëlected. In the gubernatorial campaign, Governor

---

[52] Eurith Dickinson Rivers was born in Center Point, Arkansas. He was graduated from Young Harris College with an A.B. degree in 1914, and received an LL.B. degree in 1923 from La Salle Extension University. He taught school in Toombs and Decatur Counties, Georgia, and in 1916 began the practice of law at Cairo. He later moved to Lakeland and was elected mayor of the city. Entering the Georgia House of Representatives in 1925, he became Speaker in 1933. *Georgia's Official Register, 1933*, p. 8.

[53] The vote was: Rivers, 233,503; Redwine, 123,095; Fortson, 32,715.

## Amendments and More Amendments

Rivers, opposed by Hugh Howell, J. J. Mangham, and Robert F. Wood, was elected for a second term.[54]

Eighty-two amendments were passed during Rivers' administration! Sixty-six of these were of local application and sixteen of general interest.

A total of twenty-six amendments were passed in 1937, twelve of general interest and fourteen of local application.[55] The first amendment of general interest provided that when one or more justices of the Supreme Court were disqualified from deciding a case, the qualified justices should designate a judge or judges of the Superior Courts to serve.[56] This authority had formerly been vested in the Governor. In the case of *Daniel vs. Citizens & Southern National Bank*,[57] involving the authority of the Governor to suspend the State Treasurer, four justices of the Supreme Court had disqualified and Governor Talmadge had designated four judges of the Superior Courts to serve in their place. The Court thus constituted had ruled unanimously in favor of the Governor.

The second amendment exempted from all *ad valorem* taxation personal property, including clothing, household and kitchen furniture, domestic animals, tools and

---

[54] The vote was: Rivers, 160,459; Howell, 134,121; Mangham, 19,537; Wood, 2,220.

[55] The fourteen amendments of local application were as follows: Amendments to Art. III, Sec. VII, Paragraphs XXV and XXVI, authorizing zoning laws in Forsyth, Milledgeville, Cordele, Carrollton, Eastman, Fort Valley, McRae, Dalton, and Quitman. Amendments to Art. VII, Sec. VI, Par. I, authorizing a promotional tax for Waycross. Amendment to Art. VII, Sec. VI, Par. II, authorizing special forms of taxation in Chatham, Fulton, DeKalb, and Ware Counties. Amendments to Art. VII, Sec. VII, Par. I, relating to the debt of Albany, Atlanta, Dublin, and Swainsboro and to Richmond County. Amendment to Art. XI, Sec. I, Par. VII, relating to the taxing power of DeKalb County. *Georgia Laws, 1937*, 1114–1140, *passim*. All ratified June 8, 1937.

[56] Amendment to Art. VI, Sec. II, Par. II. *Laws, 1937*, 33–34. Ratified June 8, 1937.

[57] 182 Georgia 384.

## A Constitutional History of Georgia

implements of trade, but not motor vehicles, to the extent of $300.[58]

A third amendment exempted a residence and homestead to the value of $2,000 from all *ad valorem* taxation for State, county and school purposes, except taxation to pay interest on and to retire bonded indebtedness, provided the same was actually occupied by the owner. This did not apply to municipal taxation. The General Assembly was authorized to lower this exemption to $1,250.[59]

The fourth amendment authorized the classification of property for purposes of taxation as tangible property and one or more classes of intangible personal property, including money, and the use of different rates for different classes of property.[60] The Constitution had formerly required that all taxes be uniform on the same class of subjects and *ad valorem*.

The fifth amendment authorized taxation for assistance to aged persons, to needy blind, to dependent children, and for other welfare work.[61] The sixth amendment authorized counties to levy taxes for the same purposes.[62]

The seventh amendment authorized counties to levy taxes to pay county agricultural and home demonstration agents.[63]

The eighth empowered the General Assembly to con-

---

[58] Amendment to Art. VII, Sec. II, Par. II. *Laws, 1937*, 38. Ratified June 8, 1937.

[59] Amendment to Art. VII, Sec. II, Par. VII. *Laws, 1937*, 1122-24. Ratified June 8, 1937.

[60] Amendment to Art. VII, Sec. II, Par. I. *Laws, 1937*, 39-41. Ratified June 8, 1937. This amendment has not resulted in the anticipated increase in revenue. For an evaluation of it, see R. P. Brooks, *Financing Government in Georgia* (Athens, 1946), 18-21.

[61] Amendment to Art. VII, Sec. I, Par. I. *Laws, 1937*, 1126-28. Ratified June 8, 1937.

[62] Amendment to Art. VII, Sec. VI, Par. II. *Laws, 1937*, 1124-26. Ratified June 8, 1937.

[63] Amendment to Art. VII, Sec. VI, Par. II. *Laws, 1937*, 1128-29. Ratified June 8, 1937.

## Amendments and More Amendments

vene itself in extraordinary session. It provided that when three-fifths of the members of both branches of the General Assembly should certify to the Governor that an emergency existed, it was mandatory upon him, within five days of the receipt of such certificates, to convene the General Assembly, and in the event of his failure to do so, the General Assembly could convene itself for a period of thirty days.[64] This amendment was an outgrowth of the refusal of Governor Talmadge to call a special session of the General Assembly when the regular session failed to pass a general appropriation bill.

The ninth amendment of 1937 conferred jurisdiction in misdemeanor cases arising under the Highway Patrol Act of 1937 and other traffic laws upon the Court of Ordinary in all counties not having a City or County Court, provided the defendant waived jury trial. Like jurisdiction was also conferred upon the judges of municipal police courts for offenses arising within their jurisdiction.[65]

The tenth amendment created a fifty-second Senatorial District composed of Fulton County.[66]

The eleventh authorized taxation to pay pensions to widows residing in Georgia who were married to Confederate veterans prior to January 1, 1920.[67] This was the ninth amendment relating to pensions for Confederate veterans and their widows!

The twelfth amendment of State-wide application authorized the General Assembly to grant power for zoning and planning to any city or county having a population

---

[64] Amendment to Art. V, Sec. I, Par. XIII. *Laws, 1937*, 1114–16. Ratified June 8, 1937.
[65] Amendment to Art. VI, Sec. VI, Par. II-A. *Laws, 1937*, 116–118. Ratified June 8, 1937.
[66] Amendment to Art. III, Sec. II, Par. I. *Laws, 1937*, 28–32. Ratified June 8, 1937.
[67] Amendment to Art. VII, Sec. I, Par. I. *Laws, 1937*, 1118–1122. Ratified June 8, 1937.

## A Constitutional History of Georgia

of one thousand or more.[68] There had been seven previous amendments on this subject!

Twenty-one of the 23 amendments passed in 1938 were of local application relating mainly to the debts of particular cities.[69] The two amendments of general application added to the enumerated purposes for which counties could levy taxes the following: first, to conserve natural resources (including protection from forest fires) and, second, to furnish medical aid and hospitalization for indigent sick persons.[70]

Thirty-three amendments were passed in 1939, all but three being of local application.[71] One of the amend-

---

[68] Amendment to Art. III, Sec. VII, Par. XXVI. *Laws, 1937*, 24. Ratified June 8, 1937.

[69] Amendments to Art. VII, Sec. VII, Par. I as follows: Adel bonded debt; Baxley refunding bonds; Beaverdam School District bonds; Blue Ridge bonded debt; Dublin bonded debt; Eastman bonds; Fannin County temporary loan; Gainesville debt; Homerville debt; Jefferson debt; Jeffersonville School District debt; Macon temporary loan; Pineview School District bonds; Savannah refunding bonds; Sparks bonded debt; Vidalia refunding bonds; Willacoochee refunding bonds. Amendments to Art. VIII, Sec. IV, Par. I, as follows: Brantley County school tax; Floyd County high school tax. Amendment to Article XI, Sec. I, Par. I, authorizing a special tax for fire prevention in Cobb County. *Laws, 1937–1938*, 7–60, *passim*. All ratified Nov. 8, 1938.

[70] Amendments to Art. VII, Sec. VI, Par. II. *Laws, 1937–38*, 28–29, 39–41. Ratified Nov. 8, 1938.

[71] Amendment to Art. VI, Sec. XIII, Par. I, authorizing DeKalb County to supplement the salary of its Superior Court Judge. Amendment to Art. VII, Sec. VI, Par. I, authorizing a promotional tax for Fitzgerald. Amendment to Art. VII, Sec. VI, Par. II, relating to the civil service and retirement system of Fulton County. Amendment to Art. XI, Sec. III, Par. II, authorizing assistant clerks in Fulton County. Amendments to Art. VII, Sec. VII, Par. I as follows: Atlanta Revenue Certificates; Augusta temporary loans; Bacon County refunding bonds; Blackshear refunding bonds; Bowdon refunding bonds; Carrollton refunding bonds; East Point and College Park school bonds; Fulton, Floyd and DeKalb Counties, temporary loans; Grady County refunding bonds; Greenville debt; Kite Consolidated School District bonds; Macon debt certificates; Nashville refunding bonds; Ocilla debt; Ocilla refunding bonds; Pearson refunding bonds; Quitman debt certificates; Quitman refunding bonds; Ray City refunding bonds; Reidsville School District bonded debt; Savannah debt; Savannah bonded debt; Sylvania debt; Tift County bonded debt; Willie Consolidated School District refunding bonds. *Laws, 1939*, 8–90. All ratified June 6, 1939.

## Amendments and More Amendments

ments of general interest empowered judges of the Superior Courts, on reasonable notice to the parties, to hear and determine in vacation any issue not requiring a verdict by jury.[72] Another authorized the issuance of highway refunding bonds in the aggregate of $7,950,000 to meet payments of highway refunding certificates maturing in 1939, '40 and '50. The bonds were to bear two per cent interest and be retired in installments of one-third in the years 1946, '47, and '48. The object was to postpone payment of highway indebtedness for six years in order to enable the State to match Federal funds available for road construction in the years 1939, '40, and '41.[73] The third authorized a continuation of the Coastal Highway District, created by an amendment of 1924, and authorized it to borrow $4,500,000, eight-ninths of which was to be paid by the State in equal annual installments extending over a period of twelve years.[74]

## Eugene Talmadge, 1941–1943

IN THE campaign of 1940 Eugene Talmadge, opposed by Columbus Roberts and Abit Nix, was again elected Governor.[75] Sixty-two local and six State-wide amendments were adopted in 1941. The most important of these changed from two to four years the term of the Governor and other State officers required by the Constitution to be elected at the same time, for the same term, and in the same manner as the Governor. The Governor was made ineligible to succeed himself until the expiration of four

---

[72] Amendment to Art. VI, Sec. IV, Par. VIII. *Laws, 1939,* 78–79. Ratified June 6, 1939.

[73] Amendment to Art. VII, Sec. VIII, Par. I. *Laws, 1939,* 47–49. Ratified June 6, 1939.

[74] Amendment to Art. VII, Sec. VII, Par. I. *Laws, 1939,* 23–27. Ratified June 6, 1939.

[75] The vote was: Talmadge, 183,133; Roberts, 127,653; Nix, 44,282.

years.[76] An amendment voted on in this election providing for an annual session of the General Assembly was defeated.

Two of the amendments of 1941 related to taxation. One authorized the General Assembly to levy taxes to advertise the resources and facilities of the State;[77] the other exempted from taxation for a period of twenty years coöperative rural electrification corporations.[78]

The fourth amendment of 1941 authorized counties and municipal corporations to contract for a period of thirty years with each other or with any public agency or corporation for the use of any facilities or services (including hospitalization) that such subdivisions were authorized to undertake.[79]

The fifth amendment extended the amount from $100 to $200 for cases within the jurisdiction of justices of the peace.[80]

The sixth changed the name of the State School Commissioner to State School Superintendent and extended his term from two to four years. The provision that his annual salary should not exceed $2,000 was continued.[81]

---

[76] Amendment to Art. V, Sec. I, Par. II. *Laws, 1941*, 86–87. Ratified June 3, 1941.
[77] Amendment to Art. VII, Sec. I, Par. I. *Laws, 1941*, 16–17. Ratified June 3, 1941.
[78] Amendment to Art. VII, Sec. II, Par. II. *Laws, 1941*, 84–85. Ratified June 3, 1941.
[79] Amendment to Art. VII, Sec. VI, Par. III. *Laws, 1941*, 50–51. Ratified June 3, 1941.
[80] Amendment to Art. VI, Sec. VII, Par. II. *Laws, 1941*, 119–21. Ratified June 3, 1941.
[81] Amendment to Art. VIII, Sec. II, Par. I. *Laws, 1941*, 165–166. Ratified June 3, 1941.

The local amendments of 1941 were as follows: Amendment to Art. VII, Sec. II, Par. I, relating to taxation in Macon. Amendment to Art. VII, Sec. II, Par. II, relating to taxation in Macon. Amendment to Art. VII, Sec. VI, Par. I, relating to the construction of wharfs at Savannah. Amendment to Art. VII, Sec. XVIII, Par. I, Hancock County bonded debt. Amendment to Art. VIII, Sec. IV, Par. I, taxation in Chatham County. Amendment to Art. XI, Sec. IV, Par. I, taxation in DeKalb

*Amendments and More Amendments*

## Ellis Gibbs Arnall, 1943–1947

IN 1942 Governor Talmadge was opposed in his campaign for reelection by Attorney General Ellis Arnall.[82] The relation of the Governor to the University of Georgia was the principal issue involved. In 1941 Mrs. Sylla T. Hamilton, an instructor in the College of Education, made a sworn statement to the Governor that Dr. Walter D. Cocking, who came to the University a few years earlier as Dean of the College of Education, was advocating coeducation of the white and colored races. The question

---

County. Amendment to Art. VII, Sec. VII, Par. I, as follows: Abbeville School District bonds; Abbeville refunding bonds; Adrian Consolidated School District bonds; Baker County bonds; Bibb County debt; Calhoun County refunding bonds; Catoosa County bonds; Chattooga refunding bonds; Claxton refunding bonds; Cobb County refunding bonds; Cochran refunding bonds; Cook County refunding bonds; Cordele refunding bonds; Crawford refunding bonds; Crawford School District debt; Dade County bonded debt; Davisboro School District bonds; Dodge County bonded debt; Doerun refunding bonds; Effingham County refunding bonds; Evans County refunding bonds; Excelsior School District bonds; Gainesville bonded debt; Hart County refunding bonds; Hazelhurst refunding bonds; Irwin County refunding bonds; Jeff Davis refunding bonds; Jefferson County School District refunding bonds; Jefferson County School District No. 10 bonds; Johnson Corner School District bonds; Lexington refunding bonds; Macon debt certificates; Miller County bonds; Miller County refunding bonds; Mitchell County Board of Education temporary loan; Oglethorpe County funding bonds; Paulding County funding bonds; Quitman County debt; Reidsville refunding bonds; Sandy Cross School District refunding bonds; Sparks-Adel School District refunding bonds; Stone Mountain refunding bonds; Sunny Hill School District refunding bonds; Toombs County refunding bonds; Unadilla refunding bonds; Vidalia bonds; Walker County bonds; Washington refunding bonds; Waycross debt; Wilcox County bonds; Wilcox County debt; Wrightsville School District bonds. *Laws, 1941,* 9–195. All ratified June 3, 1941.

[82] Ellis Gibbs Arnall was born at Newnan on March 20, 1907, and educated at Mercer University, the University of the South, and at the Lumpkin Law School of the University of Georgia. Before becoming Governor he had held the following public offices: Member of the Georgia House of Representatives and Speaker Pro Tem, 1933 and 1935; Special Assistant Attorney General, 1935; Assistant Attorney General, 1937–39; Attorney General, 1939–43.

387

of evidence to support Mrs. Hamilton's charge became a political controversy, albeit everyone familiar with the social conditions in Georgia knew that there was no real issue of admitting Negroes to the University in Athens. Nevertheless, Governor Talmadge insisted that the Board of Regents reject the recommendation of Dr. Harmon W. Caldwell, President of the University, that the annual contract of Dean Cocking be renewed. To carry his point, the Governor found it necessary to remove several members of the Board of Regents, and the controversy received national publicity. The Southern Association of Colleges and a number of other educational agencies voted to remove the University of Georgia from their accredited lists because of political interference. Several hundred students of the University staged a parade to the State Capitol, burned the Governor in effigy, and subsequently formed a political association intent upon defeating the Governor in his race for reelection. In a public statement Dr. Steadman Vincent Sanford, Chancellor of the University System of Georgia, avowed that the reelection of Talmadge would result in a disintegration of the University System.[83] The University at Athens was the pride and joy of Georgians. With issues thus drawn, even the hold of Talmadge on the masses was broken. Arnall, campaigning upon a platform to remove the University from the possibility of political control by the creation of a constitutional Board of Regents, won by a large majority.[84]

Fifteen amendments of State-wide application and thirteen local amendments[85] were adopted in 1943. Five

---

[83] *Atlanta Journal*, Aug. 30, 1942.

[84] The popular vote was: Arnall, 174,757; Talmadge, 128,394; the county unit vote, 261 to 149.

[85] The local amendments were as follows: Amendment to Art. VI, Sec. VII, Par. I, Glynn County Justice Court; Amendment to Art. VII, Sec. VI, Par. I, Fulton County promotional work; Amendment to Art. VII, Sec. VI, Par. II, DeKalb County educational tax and Richmond County retirement fund; Amendment to Art. XI, Sec. I, Par. VII, Bibb County

## Amendments and More Amendments

State boards were set up as constitutional offices, as follows:

(1) Board of Regents of the University System (composed of one member from each congressional district and five members from the State at large, appointed by the Governor for terms of seven years).

(2) Public Service Commission (composed of five members elected by the people for terms of six years).

(3) Board of Pardons and Paroles (composed of three members appointed by the Governor for terms of seven years).

(4) Board of Education (composed of one member from each congressional district, appointed by the Governor for terms of seven years).

(5) Game and Fish Commission (composed of one member from each congressional district and one member from one of the following counties: Chatham, Bryan, Liberty, McIntosh, Glynn or Camden, appointed by the Governor for seven year terms).

The powers of the Board of Pardons and Paroles were set forth in the Constitution, and the authority of the Board of Regents and the State Board of Education "frozen" by the constitutional provision that they should exercise such power as then provided by law.[86]

The sixth amendment lowered the age qualification for voting to eighteen.[87] The slogan, "Men old enough to fight are old enough to vote," used in support of the amendment, was well adapted to the war psychology then prevailing.

The seventh amendment effected a compromise be-

---

public service districts; Amendment to Art. XI, Sec. II, Par. I, Spalding County Board of Education. Amendments to Art. VII, Sec. VII, Par. I as follows: Cobb County funding bonds, Fulton County temporary loan, Glenwood bonded debt, Ray City debt, Summerville School District bonds. *Laws, 1943,* 7–69. Ratified Aug. 3, 1943.

[86] Amendments to Art. IV, Sec. II, Par. VIII; Art. V, Sec. I, Par. XII and Sec. IV, Par. I; Art. VIII, Sec. II, Par. II and Sec. VI, Par. II. *Laws, 1943,* 28–31, 37–39, 43–47, 55–57, 66–68. Ratified Aug. 3, 1943.

[87] Amendment to Art. II, Sec. I, Par. II. *Laws, 1943,* 39–40. Ratified Aug. 3, 1943.

tween advocates of annual sessions of the General Assembly and advocates of biennial sessions. It abolished the split session, provided that the General Assembly should meet in regular session biennially on the second Monday in January of odd numbered years, limited the total number of days that the General Assembly could stay in regular session to seventy, and further provided that the General Assembly could adjourn before the expiration of seventy days and fix a later date for reassembling. If the General Assembly should adjourn its first regular session before the expiration of seventy days without fixing a date for reconvening, then it would reconvene on the second Monday in January of the next year.[88]

The eighth amendment fixed the compensation of members of the General Assembly at $600 for each full term and $8 per day for extraordinary sessions.[89]

The ninth provided that in civil service regulations both the State and its political subdivisions should accord preferences to veterans equal to those accorded under Federal Civil Service Laws.[90]

The tenth amendment dealt with consolidation of local school districts. It provided that "where one of such local school districts voting on consolidation shall have outstanding any bonds and another school district voting thereon has no outstanding bonds, a majority only of those voting in such district having such bonds shall be sufficient to carry such election in that particular district, while two-thirds of the qualified voters shall be required as to the district having no such outstanding bonds; and

---

[88] Amendment to Art. III, Sec. IV, Par. III. *Laws, 1943*, 51–52. Ratified Aug. 3, 1943.
[89] Amendment to Art. III, Sec. IX, Par. I. *Laws, 1943*, 30–31. Ratified Aug. 3, 1943.
[90] Amendment to Art. III, Sec. VII, adding Par. XXVI. *Laws, 1943*, 10–11. Ratified Aug. 3, 1943. This ambiguous amendment apparently adopted the veterans' preferences then existing under Federal Civil Service Laws.

upon such consolidation, the consolidated district shall possess and retain any and all taxing powers that may have existed in either of such districts, but the levying of such tax shall apply to all property in any consolidated districts without any additional election therefor." [91]

The eleventh amendment of 1943 dealt with disposition of cases in the Supreme Court and the Court of Appeals. The Constitution of 1877 provided that the Superior Court should dispose of every case at the first or second term after a bill of error was brought, and in case the plaintiff in error was not prepared at the first term to prosecute the case, unless prevented by providential cause, the case should be stricken from the docket and the judgment below be affirmed. An amendment of 1935, as pointed out above, provided that if the transmittal of the record was unavoidably delayed by reason of the illness or death of the trial clerk, or of some member of his family, the case should be heard at the next term, which should be regarded as the first term. The amendment of 1943 extended these provisions to the Court of Appeals as well as the Supreme Court and omitted the enumeration of specific causes that would justify a delay in transmission of the record by the clerk of the trial court. Under the amendment, "No writ of error shall be dismissed because of delay in transmission of the bill of exceptions and the copy of the record, or either of them, resulting from the default of the clerk or other cause, unless it shall appear that the plaintiff in error or his counsel caused such delay." [92]

The twelfth amendment authorized cities and counties to issue revenue-anticipation obligations to provide funds

---

[91] Amendment to Art. VIII, Sec. IV, Par. I. *Laws, 1943*, 16–17. Ratified Aug. 3, 1943.
[92] Amendment to Art. VI, Sec. II, Par. VI. *Laws, 1943*, 23–24. Ratified Aug. 3, 1943.

## A Constitutional History of Georgia

for any revenue-producing facility authorized by the Revenue Certificate Law of 1937, as amended in 1939. The principal and interest on such obligations were to be repaid by revenue from the facilities for which they were issued, and no taxes were to be levied for this purpose.[93]

The thirteenth amendment provided that "There shall be exempt from all *ad valorem* intangible taxes in this State the common voting stock of a corporation not doing business in this State, if at least ninety per cent of such voting stock is owned by a Georgia corporation with its principal place of business located in this State and was acquired or is held for the purpose of enabling the parent company to carry on some part of its established line of business through such subsidiary." The amendment was adopted particularly for the benefit of the Coca Cola Company.[94]

The fourteenth amendment authorized taxation by the General Assembly, counties, and cities for a teacher-retirement system, but no indebtedness against the State was ever to be created for this purpose in excess of the taxes levied each year.[95]

The fifteenth amendment authorized a person who had been a resident of a United States Army post within the State for one year to bring an action for divorce in any county adjacent to the Army post.[96]

---

[93] Amendment to Art. VII, Sec. VII, Par. I. *Laws, 1943*, 47. Ratified Aug. 3, 1943.

[94] Amendment to Art. VII, Sec. II, Par. II. *Laws, 1943*, 60-62. Ratified August 3, 1943.

[95] Amendment to Art. VII, Sec. XVIII. *Laws, 1943*, 64-66. Ratified Aug. 3, 1943.

[96] Amendment to Art. VI, Sec. XVI, Par. I. *Laws, 1943*, 68-69. Ratified Aug. 3, 1943.

CHAPTER XVI

## The Constitution of 1945[1]

BY 1943 the Constitution of 1877 had been amended a total of 301 times. Article VII alone, entitled Finance, Taxation and Public Debt, had been amended 188 times, but not more than fifteen per cent of these amendments were of general interest, the greater number being applicable to a single city or county. Recognizing the need for a new constitution the Institute of Public Affairs of the University of Georgia published in 1932 *A Proposed Constitution for Georgia*[2] drawn up by a committee of prominent citizens. This document recommended a thorough revision of the structure of government, including such radical changes as the substitution of 30 districts for the existing 161 counties as the basis of representation in the General Assembly. The publicity given the document served to stimulate interest in constitutional revision, and most of the press of the State actively supported the movement.

In March, 1943, the General Assembly passed a resolution, sponsored by Governor Ellis Arnall, providing for a commission of twenty-three members to revise the Con-

---

[1] The analysis presented here is adapted from Merritt B. Pound and Albert B. Saye, *A Handbook on the Constitutions of the United States and Georgia* (Athens, 1945), pp. 46–55.

[2] *Bulletin of the University of Georgia*, Vol. XXXII (Jan., 1932), No. 4.

## A Constitutional History of Georgia

stitution. The members of this commission, appointed or serving *ex officio* in conformity to the provisions of the act, were as follows: Ellis Gibbs Arnall, Governor of Georgia; David Johnson Arnold, a member of the State Senate and President of the Georgia Bankers Association; David Scarlett Atkinson, Savannah lawyer and member of the State Senate; Thomas Salter Candler, Judge of the Northeastern Circuit; James Vinson Carmichael, Cobb County lawyer and President of Bell Aircraft Corporation; James W. Culpepper, member of the House of Representatives continuously from 1919 to 1943, from Fayetteville; Adie Norman Durden, City Attorney of Albany and member of the House of Representatives; Frank D. Foley, civic leader and businessman of Columbus; Charles Latimer Gowen, Brunswick lawyer and member of the House of Representatives; Warren Grice, Justice of the Supreme Court; Frank Cleveland Gross, Toccoa lawyer and President of the Senate; Mrs. Leonard Haas, civic leader of Atlanta and Vice President of the Georgia League of Women Voters; Frederick Barrow Hand, Pelham businessman and member of the House of Representatives; Roy Vincent Harris, Augusta lawyer and Speaker of the House of Representatives; Thomas Grady Head, Attorney General; Hamilton Tatum Holt, businessman and civic leader of Macon, past President of Kiwanis International; Hatton Lovejoy, LaGrange lawyer and former member of the General Assembly; Hugh James MacIntyre, Judge of the Court of Appeals; Robert E. Lee Majors, publisher of the *Claxton Enterprise;* James Roy McCracken, Louisville lawyer and member of the House of Representatives; Jefferson Austin Pope, City Attorney of Cairo and member of the Senate; William Rufus Smith, Judge of the Alapaha Judicial Circuit; and B. E. Thrasher, Jr., State Auditor.

## The Constitution of 1945

There were two principal arguments in favor of the use of an appointed commission instead of an elected convention to revise the Constitution of Georgia. In the first place, the existing Constitution required a two-thirds vote of the total membership of both houses of the General Assembly to call a constitutional convention, and previous attempts to call a convention had failed. Since the work of the proposed commission would be submitted directly to the General Assembly and subjected to revision before submission to the people, the resolution creating it met with approval whereas a resolution calling a convention would probably have failed. In the second place, the resolution authorizing the commission expressed the view that a revision of the Constitution could be made "more satisfactorily by a small commission . . . than through a constitutional convention."[3] A criticism advanced against the use of an appointed commission was that this method gave the incumbent administration too great an influence in shaping the fundamental law. Governor Arnall himself served as Chairman of the Commission and appointed eight of the other members; yet it should be noted that none of the *ex officio* members (the Attorney General, State Auditor, *etc.*) were appointed to their office by the Governor.

As chairman, Governor Arnall divided the members of the Commission into seven subcommittees, composed of seven members each, to make preliminary studies of designated articles of the Constitution. He also named the chairmen of these subcommittees. Most of the subcommittees did a considerable amount of work, involving public hearings in some cases, before the first meet-

---

[3] *Georgia Laws, 1943*, p. 1680. See also, "Georgia's Proposed New Constitution," by Albert B. Saye in *The American Political Science Review*, XXXIX (June, 1945), 459–463.

## A Constitutional History of Georgia

ing of the full commission in the Supreme Court Room of the State Capitol on January 6, 1944.[4] Prior to the second meeting of the full commission, April 10th–13th, all subcommittees filed written reports with the Governor, and these served as the basis of discussion as the commission proceeded to a consideration of the Constitution, article by article. A portion of the April meeting was devoted to public hearings. Representatives of the Georgia Bar Association, the American Legion, the Petroleum Institute, the Temperance League and other organized groups, and a few individuals acting in a private capacity, spoke before the Commission. Meetings of the full Commission were open to the public. Upon invitation of Governor Arnall, Hatton W. Sumners, Chairman of the Judiciary Committee of the United States House of Representatives, Frank Bane, Executive Director of the Council of State Governments, and Professors W. Brooke Graves and Walter F. Dodd visited a meeting of the Commission in April to become acquainted with the locale and method of procedure so that they might later furnish expert advice. Most members of the Commission were businessmen who made a personal sacrifice to be present at the State Capitol, and fifteen days was the total time the Commission was in session. At its last meeting, on December 9th, the Commission appointed the Governor, the President of the Senate, and the Speaker of the House as a committee on final revision. As revised by this committee, the Constitution was printed and submitted to the General Assembly in January, 1945.

After extensive study and a number of revisions, the General Assembly approved the proposed new Constitution and submitted it to the people for ratification or rejection. The Commission itself had been equally divided

---

[4] Albert B. Saye, ed., *Records of the Commission to Revise the Constitution of Georgia.* 2 vols. (Atlanta, 1946).

*The Constitution of 1945*

on the question of eliminating the constitutional ban against a successive term for the Governor. Governor Arnall, as Chairman, broke the tie by voting to eliminate the ban, but the General Assembly reversed the Commission's action on this controversial issue. At a special election held on August 7, 1945, the new Constitution was approved by a vote of 60,065 to 34,417;[5] and on August 13th the Governor proclaimed the document to be in effect. The adoption of the Constitution of 1945 gave Georgia the distinction of being the first State in the Union to adopt a constitution proposed by a commission rather than by a constitutional convention.[6]

## Changes Made by the New Constitution

FULLY ninety per cent of the provisions in the Constitution of 1945 were taken from the amended Constitution of 1877. The work of the Commission on revision was confined primarily to a revision of form and organization of the document, albeit some of the changes in substance were of great significance.

The principal changes made by the new Constitution of 1945 are as follows:

*Bill of Rights.* The paragraph prohibiting the revocation of special privileges or immunities was replaced by the sentence: "All exemptions from taxation heretofore granted in corporate charters are declared to be henceforth null and void." This action was directed particularly at the tax exemption of the Georgia Railroad. In *Thompson vs. Atlantic Coast Line Railroad Company,* decided on June 6, 1946, the Georgia Supreme Court held the new constitutional provision void. Nevertheless, the Court sus-

---

[5] *Atlanta Constitution,* Aug. 15, 1945.

[6] A few other States have used a commission to formulate constitutional amendments. A commission drew up a new Constitution for New Jersey in 1941, but the document was rejected by the people.

## A Constitutional History of Georgia

tained the Georgia income tax as applied to the Atlantic Coast Line Railroad Company, lessee of the Georgia Railroad, holding that the Charter of the Georgia Railroad and Banking Company of 1833 limiting taxation on "the stock of said company . . . to a tax not exceeding one-half per cent per annum on the net proceeds of their investments" related only to a property tax and had no bearing on an income tax.

*Elective Franchise.* In an effort to overcome objections raised by the United States Supreme Court in *Smith vs. Allwright*[7] to the exclusion of Negroes from primaries, all references to primaries were eliminated. Several obsolete clauses, including the "grandfather clause," were also eliminated.[8]

*Legislature.* The number of Senators was increased from 52 to 54, thus bringing the total membership of the General Assembly to 259! The prohibition against the appointment of a Senator or Representative to any office having an emolument was modified by the clause, "unless he shall first resign his seat, provided, however, that during the term for which he was elected no Senator or Representative shall be appointed to any civil office which has been created during such term." Special sessions of the General Assembly were limited to seventy days. The *per diem* compensation of members was increased to fifteen dollars, and the limitations on clerical expenses of the General Assembly were abolished. The provision for advertising local legislation in the community affected before its introduction in the General Assembly was strengthened, and a safeguard added against legislation ousting elected local officials before the expiration of their terms.

---
[7] 321 U. S. 649.

[8] Payment of a poll tax as a requirement for voting, a statutory provision never incorporated in the Constitution, was abolished by the General Assembly in March, 1945.

## The Constitution of 1945

*Executive.* The office of Lieutenant Governor was created. Following a trend started in 1943 when five State boards were made constitutional offices, three new boards were incorporated in the Constitution: a Veterans Service Board, a Board of Corrections (for the administration of prisons), and a State Personnel Board. The members of all three new boards were to be appointed by the Governor, with terms staggered to give continuity to their personnel.

*Judiciary.* The number of justices on the Supreme Court was increased from six to seven; the requirement of a concurrent verdict of two juries for granting a divorce was abolished; and the annual salary of judges of the Supreme Court, Court of Appeals, and Superior Courts was raised by $1,000.[9]

*Finance and Miscellaneous.* The paragraph of Article VII of the Constitution of 1877 limiting the debt of a county, city, or other political division of the State to 7% of the assessed value of its taxable property had been amended 135 times. The new Constitution authorized cities and counties to incur debts of 3% of the assessed value of their taxable property in addition to the previous 7% limit, but required that this additional debt be repaid within a period of five years. Equally significant was the provision that an increase in debt could be approved by a majority of the qualified voters of the city or county concerned participating in an election for that purpose, which replaced the requirement of a two-thirds vote in the old Constitution.

The new Constitution put an end to the allocation of taxes by providing that all taxes for State purposes be paid into the general fund of the State Treasury, that appropriations for departments and agencies be made in

---

[9] While the new Constitution included the salaries of most State officers, the General Assembly was authorized to change these salaries.

specific sums of money, and that no appropriation allocate to any object the proceeds of any particular tax or fund or a part or percentage thereof. To avoid the complications that had arisen in past years by adjournment of the legislature before the passage of a general appropriation act, the new Constitution provided that each general appropriation act, with such amendments as were adopted from time to time, should continue in force until repealed or another general appropriation act was adopted.

A new article entitled Home Rule was submitted to the General Assembly by the Commission, extending a broad power of legislation in matters of local concern to counties and cities, but under a complicated system of popular initiative and referendum. The General Assembly struck out most of the provisions of this article, and as it appeared in the new Constitution the home rule article simply stipulated that the General Assembly should provide for uniform systems of county and municipal government, with optional plans of both, and should provide for systems of initiative, referendum, and recall in some of the plans.

Another new article, entitled Merit System, provided for a non-salaried state personnel board of three members "to administer a state merit system under which state personnel shall be selected on a basis of merit, fitness, and efficiency according to law."

## Analysis of the Constitution of 1945

THE following statements, made without regard to technicalities of legal phraseology, and subject to the error inherent in all generalizations, point out the main provisions of the Constitution of 1945:

ARTICLE I—BILL OF RIGHTS. The Bill of Rights of the

## The Constitution of 1945

Constitution of Georgia includes all of the guaranties of personal liberty found in the first eight amendments of the Constitution of the United States and many others, among them a prohibition against imprisonment for debt. This long Bill of Rights is derived primarily from the *Declaration of Fundamental Principles* presented to the Convention of 1861 by Thomas R. R. Cobb.

ARTICLE II—ELECTIVE FRANCHISE. The franchise is extended to any citizen eighteen years of age, who has resided in the State one year and in the county in which he offers to vote six months next preceding the election, provided he is of good character and understands the duties of citizenship *or* can read the Constitution and write any paragraph thereof when read to him.

ARTICLE III—THE GENERAL ASSEMBLY. The legislative power of the State is vested in a General Assembly composed of a Senate and House of Representatives. The Senate consists of fifty-four members, one Senator from each of fifty-four senatorial districts, comprising groups of counties, usually three, as designated by the General Assembly.[10] The House of Representatives consists of 205 members, apportioned among the 159 counties as follows: To the 8 counties with the largest population,[11] 3 representatives each; to the 30 next largest counties, 2 representatives each; [11a] and to the remaining 121 counties,

---

[10] A rule (No. 28 in 1947) of the State Democratic Party requires the use of a rotation system for the nomination of State Senators by which each county in turn nominates the Senator for its district. The primary election is thereby confined to the county whose turn it is to nominate a Senator for the district. This rule cannot be waived without the consent of the Democratic executive committee of each county in the district.

[11] Fulton, DeKalb, Chatham, Bibb, Richmond, Muscogee, Floyd, and Troup.

[11a] Baldwin, Bartow, Bulloch, Burke, Carroll, Clarke, Cobb, Coffee, Colquitt, Coweta, Decatur, Dougherty, Emanuel, Glynn, Gwinnett, Hall, Laurens, Lowndes, Meriwether, Mitchell, Polk, Spalding, Sumter, Thomas, Upson, Walker, Ware, Washington, Whitfield, Worth.

## A Constitutional History of Georgia

1 representative each. The term of members of both the Senate and House of Representatives is two years and the *per diem* compensation, fifteen dollars. Regular sessions of the General Assembly are held biennially and are

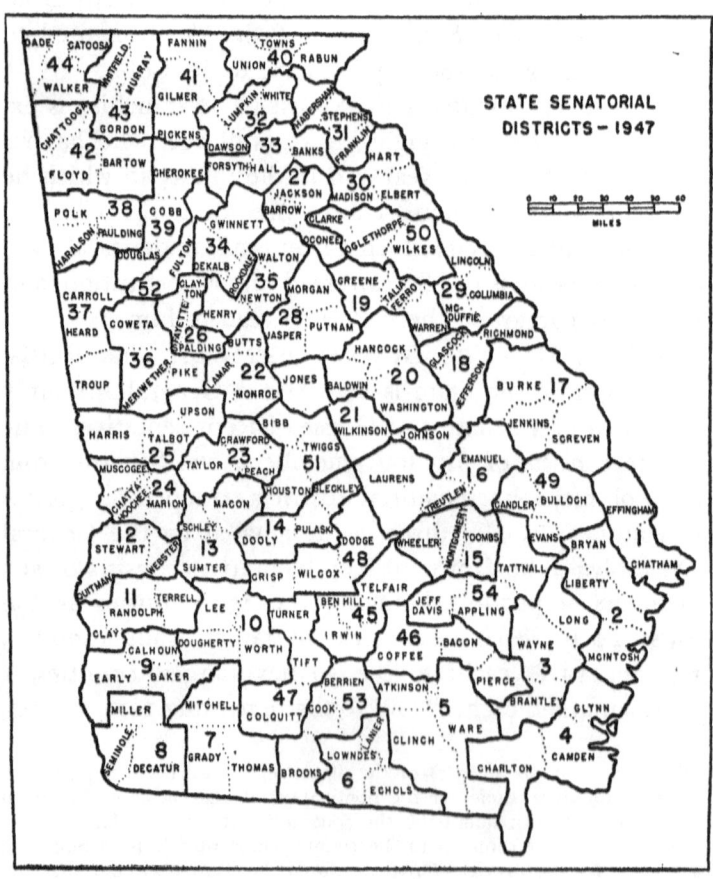

STATE SENATORIAL DISTRICTS – 1947

limited to 70 days, but in case the General Assembly adjourns before 70 days have expired it may set a date for reconvening for the remaining days. The Governor is authorized at any time, and required when petitioned by

*The Constitution of 1945*

three-fifths of the members of both houses, to call a special session of the General Assembly.

ARTICLE IV—PUBLIC UTILITIES AND MISCELLANEOUS PROVISIONS. A Public Service Commission composed of five members elected by the people for six-year terms is established to enforce laws regulating public utilities. The General Assembly is prohibited from regulating utilities owned or operated by a county or municipality, and public utilities are forbidden to give rebates or to do anything to deceive the public as to the real rates charged.

The Federal Constitution prohibits any State from impairing the obligation of contract, and this is construed by the Supreme Court of the United States to apply to contracts to which a State is a party as well as to private contracts. As a safeguard against the perpetuity of contracts against the public interest, the Constitution of Georgia provides that no corporation shall receive a renewal or amendment of its charter or benefit from any law in its favor except upon the condition that its charter be held thereafter subject to the provisions of the Constitution. The significance of this provision becomes clearer when considered in connection with the provision of Article VII that no department of the government shall have authority "to irrevocably give, grant, limit, or restrain" the right of taxation.

Resident life insurance companies are required to deposit $100,000 subject to the order of the Comptroller General of Georgia as a guaranty for the security of policy holders, and non-resident life insurance companies are required to show the Comptroller General that they have a like sum deposited with a responsible officer of the state where they are chartered. The General Assembly is directed to compel fire insurance companies to

## A Constitutional History of Georgia

deposit reasonable securities with the Treasurer of Georgia, to make annual reports to the Comptroller General, and to publish the same at their own expense for the information and protection of the people.

The property of a wife is not liable for the debts of her husband.

ARTICLE V—THE EXECUTIVE. Executive power is vested in a Governor, elected by a majority of the popular vote [12] for a term of four years. He is ineligible to succeed himself until the expiration of four years from the conclusion of his term. He has a veto over acts of the General Assembly, but this may be overridden by a two-thirds vote. The annual salary of the Governor is $12,000. In case of his death or disability, the office passes first to the Lieutenant Governor (the presiding officer of the Senate, elected in the same manner as the Governor) and then to the Speaker of the House of Representatives.

Other executive officers named in the Constitution and elected at the same time and in the same manner as the Governor are the Secretary of State, Attorney General, State School Superintendent, Comptroller General, Treasurer, Commissioner of Agriculture, and Commissioner of Labor. The Constitution also provides for the following executive boards:

(1) Board of Regents of the University System (15 members; terms of 7 years)

(2) State Board of Education (10 members; terms of 7 years)

(3) Public Service Commission (5 members; terms of 6 years)

(4) Board of Pardons and Paroles (3 members; terms of 7 years)

---

[12] The county unit vote, under which each county is given twice the number of unit votes that it has representatives in the General Assembly, is used in the Democratic primary for the nomination of U. S. Senators, the Governor, and the other principal State officials.

## The Constitution of 1945

(5) Board of Corrections (5 members; terms of 5 years)

(6) Game and Fish Commission (11 members; terms of 7 years)

(7) Personnel Board (3 members; terms of 7 years)

(8) Veterans Service Board (7 members; terms of 7 years).

The members of all of these boards, except the Public Service Commission, are appointed by the Governor with confirmation by the Senate, and their terms are staggered in such a way as to give continuity to their personnel. The authority of all of these boards, except three, is subject to the control of the General Assembly. The powers of the Board of Pardons and Paroles are set forth in the Constitution, and the powers of both the Board of Regents and the State Board of Education are "frozen" by the constitutional provision that they "shall have such powers and duties as provided by law and existing at the time of the adoption of this Constitution, together with such further powers and duties as may be hereafter provided by law." The Board of Corrections and the Veterans Service Board are specifically authorized to appoint a director as their executive officer. While the State School Superintendent is elected by popular vote, he is named in the Constitution as the executive officer of the State Board of Education.

ARTICLE VI—THE JUDICIARY. The judiciary of Georgia consists of the following courts:

(1) *Supreme Court.* The Supreme Court is composed of seven justices elected by popular vote for terms of six years. The Supreme Court has no original jurisdiction, but is a court for the correction of errors made by the Superior Courts and City Courts in cases involving: (a) the construction of the Constitution of Georgia or the Constitution or treaties of the United States, (b) title to land, (c) equity, (d) the construction of wills, (e) convic-

tion of a capital felony, (f) *habeas corpus*, (g) extraordinary remedies, and (h) divorce and alimony. The Supreme Court also has authority to bring up by *certiorari* any case from the Court of Appeals.

(2) *Court of Appeals.* The Court of Appeals is composed of six judges,[13] elected by popular vote for terms of six years. This court has appellate jurisdiction over the Superior and City Courts in all cases other than those in which the Supreme Court has jurisdiction. It may certify questions to the Supreme Court whose decisions are binding upon it as precedents. The Court of Appeals was created by an amendment to the Constitution of 1877 in 1906. The number of judges was increased by statute from three to six in 1916, and since that date the Court of Appeals has usually sat in two divisions of three judges each.

(3) *Superior Courts.* The State is divided by statute into thirty-three Superior Court judicial circuits, with one judge in each, except the Atlanta and Macon circuits which have seven and two judges respectively. The Constitution provides that judges of the Superior Courts "shall be elected by the electors of the whole State" for terms of four years, but in the primary they are nominated by the electors of their judicial circuit only. A judge of the Superior Courts must hold court in every county within his circuit at least twice a year. The Superior Courts are the principal State courts of original jurisdiction for both criminal and civil cases, and have exclusive jurisdiction in: (a) cases of divorce, (b) criminal cases where the offender is subjected to loss of life or confinement in the penitentiary, (c) cases respecting titles to land, and (d) equity cases.

There is a Solicitor General for each judiciary circuit, elected in the same manner and for the same term as

---

[13] This number is fixed by statute.

*The Constitution of 1945*

judges of the Superior Courts, to represent the State in cases before the Superior Courts. The county sheriff enforces orders of the Superior Courts.

(4) *Courts of Ordinary.* The Constitution establishes

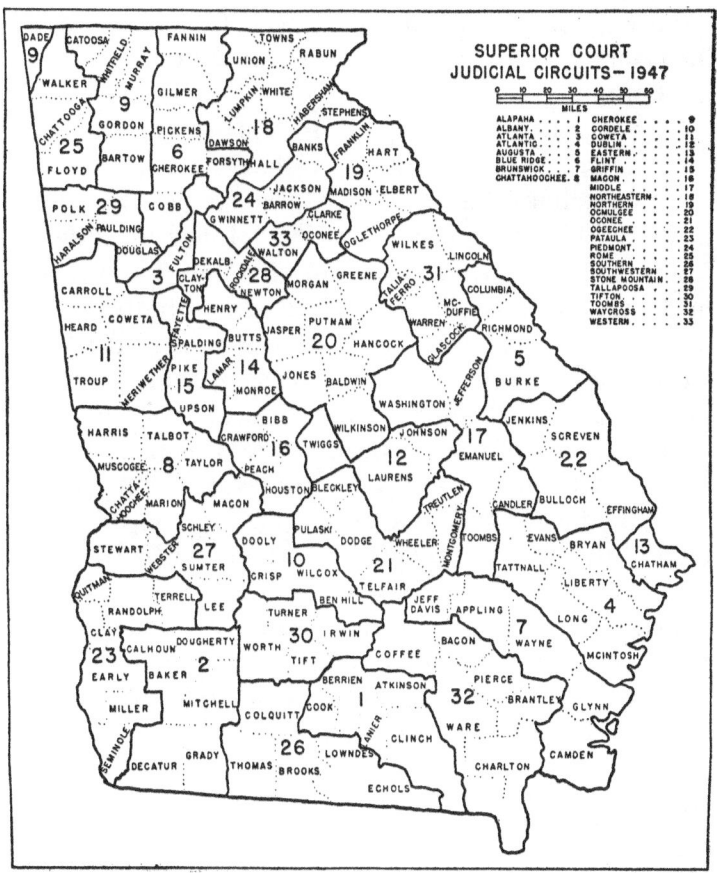

a Court of Ordinary and Probate for each county and provides that the judge of this court, the Ordinary, shall be elected for a term of four years. The jurisdiction of the Court of Ordinary, fixed by statute, covers the probation of wills, administration of estates, appointment of guardians, and issuance of lunacy commissions. The Court of Ordinary has jurisdiction over misdemeanor cases arising under the Highway Patrol Act of 1937 and other traffic laws, and over all cases arising under the Compulsory School Attendance Law in counties not having a City or County Court. Appeals from decisions of the Court of Ordinary are taken to the Superior Court of the County.

In addition to his function as a judge, the Ordinary issues marriage licenses, prints ballots for elections, and exercises administrative power over numerous county matters. The Constitution of 1868 abolished the Inferior Courts that formerly had control of county business and made the Ordinary the principal administrative officer of the county. The Constitution of 1877 vested the Ordinaries with "power in relation to roads, bridges, ferries, public buildings, paupers, county officers, county funds, county taxes, and other county matters as may be conferred on them by law." This provision is carried forward in the Constitution of 1945, but in 149 counties most of these functions have been conferred by law upon boards of county commissioners. Ten counties retain the old type of county government under which the Ordinary is in effect a county manager.[14]

(5) *City and County Courts.* The Constitution mentions City and County Courts, but does not prescribe their organization or jurisdiction. By statute sixty-five counties now have City Courts. The name "City Court" is misleading inasmuch as these are usually courts of county-wide jurisdiction; *e.g.,* the City Court of Macon for Bibb County. These courts are not to be confused with municipal courts. The judges of some of these courts are elected; others are appointed by the Gover-

---

[14] M. Clyde Hughes, *County Government in Georgia* (Athens, 1944), 20.

*The Constitution of 1945*

nor. The term of most of the judges is four years, but this is not uniform. To ascertain the jurisdiction of any particular City Court, it is necessary to consult the act creating it, but in general the City Courts have jurisdiction in misdemeanor cases and in all civil cases except those in which the Superior Court has exclusive jurisdiction. Appeals are made directly from the City Courts to the Superior Courts or to the Court of Appeals. Under authority of an act of 1871, any county (except Walton) not having a City Court may establish a County Court upon the recommendation of the grand jury. "These courts have jurisdiction in all cases of contracts or torts (save where exclusive jurisdiction is vested in the Superior Court) where the principal sum claimed does not exceed $500, and in misdemeanor cases." [15] Appeals are made from the six existing County Courts to the Superior Courts.

(6) *Justices of the Peace*. The smallest political subdivision of the State is the militia district, of which there are today 1,679, used primarily as voting precincts. The Constitution provides for one justice of the peace in each militia district, elected by the people of the district for a term of four years, but authorizes the General Assembly in its discretion to replace justices of the peace by any system of courts deemed advisable in cities having a population above 20,000, or in any county having such a city within its borders. Justices of the peace have jurisdiction in all civil cases arising from contracts or from damage to personal property where the principal sum does not exceed $200. By statute justices of the peace are authorized to aid in conserving peace by issuing warrants for the apprehension of any person charged on oath with crime, and by examining the accused and either committing him to jail to await trial or discharging him.

---

[15] *Code of 1933*. Ed. note, p. 623.

*A Constitutional History of Georgia*

In addition to justices of the peace, the Constitution provides that upon the recommendation of the grand jury of any county the judge of the Superior Court may appoint one commissioned notary public for each militia district, who shall be commissioned by the Governor for a term of four years. These commissioned notaries public are *ex officio* justices of the peace and, except in the method of selection, there is no difference between the office of a commissioned notary public and that of a justice of the peace. These judicial commissioned notaries public are not to be confused with commercial notaries public, or with notaries public of the State at large whose principal authority is to witness signatures and administer oaths.

ARTICLE VII—TAXATION AND PUBLIC DEBT. The purposes for which taxes may be levied by the State are enumerated in the Constitution and the amount of the State tax is limited to five mills on the dollar of taxable property. The bonded debt of the State is never to be increased, and the only debts authorized to be contracted by the State are $500,000 to supply temporary deficits and $3,500,000 to pay public school teachers, which sums must be repaid within the year. Moreover, it is required that the sale of the Western & Atlantic Railroad or any other property of the State be applied to the payment of the bonded debt of the State, and that the General Assembly set up a sinking fund to retire State bonds.

The purposes for which counties may levy taxes are also enumerated, but there is no limit on the amount of county taxes except a 15 mill limit on school taxes. The debt that may be incurred by a county or municipality may not exceed 10% of the assessed value of the taxable property therein, and must be approved by a majority of the qualified voters. Any debt above 7% of the taxable

## The Constitution of 1945

property value is required to be repaid within five years, and other debts must be repaid within thirty years.

ARTICLE VIII—EDUCATION. The State Board of Education, State School Superintendent, and Board of Regents of the University System were described above in the discussion of executive officers. In addition to these officials, Article VIII provides for a board of education and a school superintendent for each county. The county board of education consists of five members selected by the grand jury for terms of five years. The county school superintendent is elected by popular vote for a term of four years. Cities are authorized to maintain existing independent school systems, but no new independent system may be established. "Separate schools shall be provided for the white and colored races."

ARTICLE IX—HOMESTEADS AND EXEMPTIONS. This article provides that the property of the head of a family, and certain others, to the amount of $1,600 shall be exempted from levy and sale by any process whatever. The debtor may waive his right to such exemption. As a result of the economic dislocation resulting from the Civil War, a homestead and exemption clause to protect the debtor against the sale of all his property was included in the Constitution of 1868, and Article IX of the present Constitution is an outgrowth of this provision.

ARTICLE X—THE MILITIA. This article authorizes the General Assembly to provide by law how the militia of the State shall be organized and equipped. The officers and men are not to receive compensation except when in active service.

ARTICLE XI—COUNTIES. Georgia is divided into 159 counties which are administrative divisions of the State, on the one hand, and, on the other, corporate bodies vested by law with certain powers of their own. No new counties can be created, nor county lines changed except by a general law for that purpose. The General Assembly may provide for consolidation of two or more counties, provided two-thirds of the qualified voters of each of the counties affected give their approval in an election held for that purpose. The Constitution requires uniformity in county government, with the following exceptions: In any county the General Assembly may establish Commissioners of Roads and Revenue, abolish the office of Treasurer, and consolidate the office of Tax Receiver and Tax Collector into the office of Tax Commissioner.

The principal governing authority in 149 counties is the Board of County Commissioners who have control of taxation, roads, public buildings, paupers, and other county matters. In ten counties, as noted above, these powers are vested in the Ordinary. The County Commissioners vary in number from one to nine, but most counties have either three or five Commissioners. Most of them are elected, but in a few instances they are appointed by the grand jury.

Officers and agencies usually found in Georgia counties include the ordinary, board of commissioners, sheriff, clerk of the Superior Court, board of education, superintendent of schools, tax collector, tax receiver, treasurer, coroner, justices of the peace, commissioned notaries public, county agricultural agent, county home demonstration agent, county police, welfare board, welfare director, board of tax assessors, registrars, jury commissioners, and constables. Most of these officials are elected by popular vote for a term of four years. The first twelve listed are provided for in the Constitution.[16]

ARTICLE XII—THE LAWS OF GENERAL OPERATION. The laws of general operation in this State are (1) the Constitution of the United States, and the laws and

---
[16] Articles VI, VII, VIII, and XI.

## The Constitution of 1945

treaties of the United States, (2) the Constitution of Georgia, and (3) the statutory laws of Georgia.

ARTICLE XIII—AMENDMENTS TO THE CONSTITUTION. Amendments to the Constitution may be proposed by a two-thirds vote of the members elected to both houses of the General Assembly. They must then be advertised in one or more newspapers in each congressional district for two months prior to the next general election. If an amendment directly affects one or more political subdivisions of the State, it must also be advertised in the area concerned. Amendments are ratified by a majority vote of the people—that is, by a majority of those voting on the proposed amendment, not necessarily a majority of the entire electorate. If the amendment is not one that directly affects the whole State, but only one or more subdivisions thereof, then it must be ratified by a majority vote of those voting thereon both in the State as a whole and in the subdivision or subdivisions affected. When more than one amendment is submitted at the same time, they must be submitted in a way to enable the electors to vote on each amendment separately.

Under the new Constitution, the election at which amendments may be submitted to the people for ratification is the general election "at which election members of the General Assembly are chosen." The Supreme Court had ruled that the term "general election" used in the Constitution of 1877 was not confined to any one election, hence the significance of the altered wording in the Constitution of 1945. In effect it necessitates a delay of two years in amending the Constitution.

The Constitution requires a two-thirds vote of all members of both houses of the General Assembly to call a constitutional convention, and provides that representation in such a convention shall be based on population as near as practicable. Changes in the Constitution proposed by a convention must be submitted to the people and ratified by a two-thirds vote of those voting thereon. There is no provision for revision of the Constitution by an appointed commission; hence the necessity of submitting the work of the Commission on Revision of 1943-44 to the General Assembly and having the General Assembly submit it to the people for ratification as an amendment to the Constitution of 1877, when in effect the revision amounted to a new constitution.[17]

ARTICLE XIV—MERIT SYSTEM. This article provides for a State Personnel Board of three members appointed by the Governor for terms of seven years, to "administer a State Merit System under which state personnel shall be selected on a basis of merit, fitness, and efficiency according to law." No State employee can be a member of this Board. The chances of the effectiveness of this Board are weakened by the provision that it shall be "nonsalaried."

ARTICLE XV—HOME RULE. This article directs the General Assembly to provide uniform systems of county and municipal government, with optional plans, and to provide a method by which a county or municipality may select one of these plans or reject all of them.

Viewing the Constitution of 1945 as a whole, one is impressed more with the large number of provisions that have come down from previous documents than with new provisions, and so it has been with all of Georgia's eight constitutions. Many of the basic governmental in-

---

[17] In *Wheeler vs. Trustees of Fargo School District*, 200 Ga. 323, the Supreme Court held the new constitution to be valid. Referring to the provision of the Bill of Rights of the Constitution of 1877 that "The people of this State have the inherent, sole, and exclusive right of regulating their internal government . . . and of abolishing their constitution whenever it may be necessary to their safety and happiness," the Court rejected the contention that the people were limited to the convention method in adopting a new constitution.

## The Constitution of 1945

stitutions involved are of English and Colonial origin. Association with the other American States under the Articles of Confederation and the Federal Constitution had a salutary effect upon the course of constitutional development in Georgia during the formative period of statehood; and a large percentage of the provisions of all subsequent constitutions can be traced to the Constitution of 1798, the most basic document in Georgia's history. Amendments added from year to year during the nineteenth and twentieth centuries reflected primarily adaptations to local needs as shown by experience, but a mere listing of the dates of her constitutions—1789, 1798, 1861, 1865, 1868, 1877, 1945—reveals the intimate relation of the whole of Georgia's constitutional history to the history of the nation. The ever increasing scope of activity on the part of the National Government and the imperative need of a workable international organization to preserve peace in the new Atomic Age focuses attention on broader fields, but the importance of State and local government must not be overlooked. Writing in 1947, it takes no sage to see that further revisions in Georgia's Constitution of 1945 are needed.

# Bibliography

In *A Short History of Georgia* (Chapel Hill, 1933) E. Merton Coulter offers a well-balanced, eminently readable survey of Georgia history. Amanda Johnson's *Georgia as Colony and State* (Atlanta, 1938) contains more factual material on Georgia history than any other single volume. The chief authorities on the eighteenth century are William B. Stevens (*A History of Georgia*, 2 vol., N. Y. and Philadelphia, 1847–59) and Charles C. Jones (*The History of Georgia*, 2 vol., Boston, 1883). Jones' study is scholarly, detailed, and of superior literary style, but lacks the synthesis of Stevens' work. Hugh M'Call's *History of Georgia* provides valuable information relative to the Revolution and is of particular interest from the early date of its publication (vol. I, 1811; vol. II, 1816). The two most helpful volumes on the nineteenth century are Ulrich B. Phillips, *Georgia and State Rights* (Washington, 1902), and I. W. Avery, *The History of the State of Georgia from 1850 to 1881* (New York, 1881). Among the better known histories of Georgia in several volumes are Lucien Lamar Knight, *A Standard History of Georgia and Georgians* (6 vol., Chicago, 1917), Clark Howell, *History of Georgia* (4 vol., Atlanta, 1926), and Walter R. Cooper, *The Story of Georgia* (4 vol., New York, 1938). Notable among the many excellent biographies of Georgia statesmen are Amos Aschbach Ettinger, *James Edward Oglethorpe: Imperial Idealist* (Oxford, 1936) and C. Vann Woodward, *Tom Watson: Agrarian Rebel* (New York, 1938).

The source *par excellence* for the origin of the Colony of Georgia is the *Diary of John Percival, First Earl of Egmont* (3 vol., London, 1920–23). The State of Georgia has published 26 volumes of *Colonial Records*, 3 volumes of *Revolutionary*

# Bibliography

*Records,* and 5 volumes of *Confederate Records* (ed. by Allen D. Candler, Atlanta, 1904-16). There is sufficient material in the British Public Record Office and in the Archives of the State of Georgia for many more volumes in these series.

Walter McElreath's *Treatise on the Constitution of Georgia* (Atlanta, 1912) is a convenient source for copies of Georgia's first seven constitutions. The original Charter of 1732 has been lost. A photostatic reproduction of the copy in the British Patent Roll is given in Albert B. Saye, ed., *Georgia's Charter of 1732* (Athens, 1942). The original copy of the Constitution of 1777 has also been lost, and there is little information about the convention that framed it other than the fragmentary minutes accompanying copies of the Constitution printed at Savannah by William Lancaster in 1777 (copy in the Library of Congress, Hazard Pamphlet No. 33). Manuscript journals of two of the three conventions held to frame the Constitution of 1789 are available in the State Archives (Rhodes Memorial Building) in Atlanta. The original copy of the Constitutions of 1789, 1798, 1868, 1877, and 1945 are in the office of the Secretary of State in the Capitol. I have been unable to locate the originals of the Constitutions of 1861 and 1865. A manuscript journal of the convention of 1795 is in the State Archives. There appears to be no journal of the convention of 1798. Records of the conventions of 1833 and 1839 are available in printed form under the titles *Journal of the Convention to Reduce and Equalize the Representation of the General Assembly . . . held in Milledgeville . . . in May, 1833* (Milledgeville, 1833) and *Journal of the Convention to Reduce and Equalize the Representation of the General Assembly . . . Assembled in Milledgeville . . . 1839* (Milledgeville, 1839). Journals of the conventions of 1861, 1865, and 1867-68 appear in the *Confederate Records of Georgia*, vol. I, pp. 212-751; vol. V, pp. 133-442; vol. VI, pp. 200-1027. Samuel W. Small's *Stenographic Report of the Proceedings of the Constitutional Convention . . . of 1877* (Atlanta, 1877) gives a fuller record of the framing of the Constitution of 1877 than is available for any of the earlier constitutions. The *Records of the Commission of 1943-44 to Revise the Constitution of Georgia*, 2 vols., ed. by Albert B. Saye (published by the State, 1946) gives a verbatim account of the proceedings of this Commission, but

## A Constitutional History of Georgia

there is no record of the debates in the General Assembly where several amendments were made before the Constitution of 1945 was approved for submission to the people.

The only three formal laws enacted during the Trustee Period are found in *The Colonial Records of Georgia*, I, 31–35. The laws of the Royal Period are found in *Acts Passed by the General Assembly of the Colony of Georgia, 1755 to 1774* (Wormsloe, 1896), and *The Colonial Records of Georgia*, XVIII–XIX. The *Acts and Resolutions of the General Assembly of the State of Georgia* were published following each legislative session, with a few exceptions in the period following the Revolution. Among the many compilations of the laws of the State of Georgia are the following: George and Robert Watkins, *A Compilation of the Laws of Georgia* (Philadelphia, 1800 and 1801. The second edition omitted the Yazoo Act. Neither edition was ever approved by the General Assembly.); Horatio Marbury and Wm. H. Crawford, *Digest of the Laws of Georgia from . . . 1755 to . . . 1800* (Savannah, 1802); Augustin Smith Clayton, *A Compilation of the Laws of the State of Georgia . . . . 1800 to 1810* (Augusta, 1813); Lucius Q. C. Lamar, *A Compilation of the Laws of Georgia, . . . 1800 to . . . 1819* (Augusta, 1821); William Schley, *A Digest of the English Statutes of Force in Georgia* (Philadelphia, 1826); Oliver H. Prince, *A Digest of the Laws of Georgia . . . to 1837* (Athens, 1837); Thomas R. R. Cobb, *A Digest of the Statute Laws of Georgia . . . to 1851*. 2 vols. (Athens, 1851); R. H. Clark, T. R. R. Cobb, and D. Irwin, *The Code of Georgia* (Atlanta, 1863); David Irwin, George N. Lester, and W. B. Hill, *The Code of . . . Georgia* (Macon, 1873); John L. Hopkins, Clifford Anderson, and Joseph R. Lamar, *The Code of . . . Georgia*. 3 vols. (Atlanta, 1896); Orville A. Park, Harry S. Strozier, Bascom S. Deaver, Charles H. Garrett, and Harry B. Skillman, *Park's Annotated Code of . . . Georgia, 1914*. 7 vols. (Atlanta, 1914–16); Thomas Johnson Michie, *The Georgia Code, 1926* (Charlottesville, 1926); Orville A. Park, Harry Strozier, Harry B. Skillman, and Henry H. Cobb, *The Code of Georgia, 1933* (Atlanta, 1935); Orville A. Park, Harry B. Skillman, and Harry S. Strozier, *Code of Georgia Annotated*. 34 vols. (Atlanta, 1936).

The decisions of the Supreme Court of Georgia are avail-

# Bibliography

able in the *Georgia Reports* for the period since 1846. Among the few printed court reports before this date are: Thomas U. P. Charlton, *Reports of Cases in the Superior Courts of the Eastern District of Georgia, 1805–1810* (New York, 1824); Robert M. Charlton, *Report of Decisions Made in the Superior Courts of the Eastern District of Georgia by Judges Berrien, T. U. P. Charlton, Wayne, Davies, Law, Nicoll, and Robert M. Charlton; and in The Middle Circuit, by Thomas U. P. Charlton, 1811–1837* (Savannah, 1838); G. M. Dudley, *Reports of Superior Courts, 1831–1833* (New York, 1837); and *Georgia Decisions 1842–43, Being the Decisions of the Superior Courts* (Published anonymously at Augusta, 1843. Two volumes, but usually bound as one). The two Charltons and Dudley were volunteer reports. *The Georgia Decisions, 1842–43* were published in compliance with statute. In 1845 the office of Recorder was established, and one Kelly was the first to hold the position. The first three volumes of the *Georgia Reports* were published under the name of the reporter, Kelly. All subsequent volumes have been published as *Georgia Reports*. A convenient summary of the early decisions is found in T. R. R. Cobb and W. W. Lumpkin, *A General Digested Index to Georgia Reports Including 1, 2, 3 Kelly, 4 to 10 Georgia Reports, T. U. P. Charlton's Reports, R. M. Charlton's Report, Dudley's Reports and Georgia Decisions, Parts I and II* (Athens, 1852). There have been a dozen subsequent digests of Georgia cases, the most recent and extensive entitled *Georgia Digest*, 23 vols., by the West Publishing Co. (St. Paul, 1942). The names of the judges of the Superior Courts and the Solicitors General in Georgia from 1790 to 1857 are given in an appendix to Stephen F. Miller, *The Bench and Bar of Georgia: Memoirs and Sketches*, vol. II (Philadelphia, 1858), 369–378. The names of the chief justices are given in vol. I, pages 269–270, of Warren Grice, *The Georgia Bench and Bar* (Macon, 1931), a source of much information on the personnel and history of the Georgia judiciary. The *Georgia Bar Journal*, vol. VI–VII (Feb., 1944–Nov., 1945), contains a "History of the Supreme Court of Georgia, The First Hundred Years," written by prominent members of the Bar.

The *Journals* of the House of Representatives from 1821 and of the Senate from 1808, published after each session of

*A Constitutional History of Georgia*

the General Assembly, are available in the Library of the University of Georgia, and most of the earlier legislative journals are in the State Archives. These formal journals do not contain a full record of debates; hence contemporary newspapers constitute a valuable supplement on the legislative record. The newspaper collections found most helpful for this study are in the British Museum, the Library of the University of Georgia, the Library of Congress, the Georgia State Library, and the Carnegie Library of Atlanta. Georgia's first and only colonial newspaper was the *Georgia Gazette,* begun at Savannah on April 17, 1763, by James Johnston.

A convenient reference to the principal secondary sources on Georgia is given in the selected bibliography of E. Merton Coulter's *Georgia, A Short History* (Chapel Hill, 1947), pp. 456–474. The most extensive bibliography on Georgia for both primary and secondary sources is the *Catalogue of the Wymberley Jones De Renne Georgia Library at Wormsloe, Isle of Hope near Savannah, Georgia* (3 vol., privately printed, Wormsloe, 1931). Two other useful bibliographies are Robert Preston Brooks, *A Preliminary Bibliography of Georgia History* (Bulletin of the University of Georgia, Athens, 1910) and Ella May Thornton, *Finding-List of Books and Pamphlets Relating to Georgia and Georgians* (Atlanta, 1928).

The following summary of the sources cited in the footnotes above is given for convenience of reference:

### Primary Sources

*Acts and Resolutions of the General Assembly* (Published contemporaneously. See note above).

"Account of a Voyage to Georgia," *Political State of Great Britain,* XLV (June, 1733), 543–44.

*Biographical Dictionary of the American Congress.* Washington, 1928.

Board of Trade, *Journal of the Commissioners for Trade and Plantations, 1704–82.* 14 vol. London, H. M. Stationery Office, 1920–38.

Bureau of the Census, *A Century of Population Growth from the First Census of the United States to the Twentieth, 1790–1900.* Washington, 1909.

*Bibliography*

Candler, Allen D., ed., *The Colonial Records of the State of Georgia*. 26 vols. Atlanta, 1904–16.
Candler, Allen D., ed., *The Revolutionary Records of the State of Georgia*. 3 vols. Atlanta, 1908.
Candler, Allen D., ed., *The Confederate Records of the State of Georgia*. 5 vols. Atlanta, 1909–11.
*Collections of Georgia Historical Society*. 9 vols. Savannah, 1840–1916.
Coulter, E. Merton, ed., "Minutes of the Georgia Convention Ratifying the Federal Constitution," *Georgia Historical Quarterly*, X (September, 1926), 224–237.
Constitution, Amendments, 1795. *Articles Adopted as Additions and Amendments to the Present Constitution*. Louisville, 1795(?). Copy in the De Renne Collection.
*Documentary History of the Constitution*, vol. II. House Doc. No. 529, 56th Congress, 2nd Session. Washington, 1894.
*Documents Illustrative of the Formation of the Union of the American States*. House Doc. No. 398, 69th Congress, 1st Session.
Elliot, Jonathan, ed., *Debates in the Several State Conventions, on the Adoption of the Federal Constitution*. 5 vols. Philadelphia, 1896.
*Executive Minutes, 1798–1799*. Manuscript in State Archives.
Farrand, Max, *Records of the Federal Convention of 1787*. 3 vols. New Haven, 1911.
*Federalist, The*, Everyman's Library edition, New York, 1934.
*Georgia Facts in Figures*. Athens, Georgia, 1946.
*Georgia's Official Register*, compiled by the State Historian and published biennially by the Dept. of Archives and History, 1923–43.
Grant, W. L., and Munro, James, ed., *Acts of the Privy Council, Colonial Series*. Vols. III–VI. London, 1910–12.
Headlam, Cecil and Newton, Arthur Percival, ed., *Calendar of State Papers, Colonial Series: America and West Indies, 1732*. London, 1930.
*Historical Register, The*, XVI. London, 1732.
Journals of Constitutional Conventions (See note above).
*Journal of the House of Commons, 1732–52*.
Journal of the House of Representatives (Published contemporaneously. See note above).

## A Constitutional History of Georgia

Journal of the Senate (See note above).
*Journal of the State Convention, held in Milledgeville in December, 1850.* Milledgeville, 1850.
Labaree, Leonard Woods, *Royal Instructions to the British Colonial Governors, 1670–1776.* Vol. I. New York, 1935.
Macdonald, William, *Documentary Source Book of American History, 1606–1898.* New York, 1902.
McElreath, Walter, *A Treatise on the Constitution of Georgia.* Atlanta, 1912.
Martyn, Benjamin, *A New and Accurate Account of Georgia and South Carolina.* London, 1732.
*Particular Case of the Georgia Loyalists, The: In addition to the General Case and Claim of the American Loyalists which was lately Published by Order of their Agent.* London (?), 1783. Copy in De Renne Collection.
Pierce, William, *Reliques.* A bound volume of manuscript notes by William Pierce in the Connecticut State Library. Most of these notes were published in the *American Historical Review*, III (July, 1898), 311 ff.
*Political State of Great Britain, The*, XLV (March 22, 1733).
*Poor Richard to the Free Working Men of the Eastern District of Georgia.* Pole Hall, Sept. 20, 1833 (Pamphlet in De Renne Collection).
Poore, Benjamin Perley, *The Federal and State Constitutions, Colonial Charters, and other Organic Laws of the United States.* 2 vols. Washington, 1877.
*Proposed Constitution for Georgia Presented to the Round Table Session of the Institute of Public Affairs, University of Georgia, A*, Bulletin of the University of Georgia, vol. XXXII (January, 1932), No. 4.
Prince, Oliver H., *A Digest of the Laws of the State of Georgia.* Athens, 1837.
Rand, Benjamin, ed., *Berkeley and Percival: The Correspondence of George Berkeley, afterwards Bishop of Cloyne, and Sir John Percival, afterwards Earl of Egmont.* Cambridge, England, 1914.
Roberts, R. A., ed., *Diary of John Percival, First Earl of Egmont* (Hist. MSS. Reports). 3 vols., London, 1920–23.
Saye, Albert B., *Georgia's Charter of 1732.* Athens, 1942.
Saye, Albert B., ed., "The Commission and Instructions of Governor John Reynolds," *Georgia Historical Quarterly*, XXX (June, 1946), 125–162.

# Bibliography

Saye, Albert B., ed., *Records of the Commission of 1943-44 to Revise the Constitution of Georgia*. 2 vols. Atlanta, 1946.
Small, Samuel W., *A Stenographic Report of the Proceedings of the Constitutional Convention Held in Atlanta, Georgia, 1877*. Atlanta, 1877.
Stokes, Anthony, *A View of the Constitution of the British Colonies*. London, 1783.
Thornton, Ella May, *The Constitution of the State of Georgia, 1877, as amended through 1941*. Atlanta, 1942.
Watkins, Robert and George, *Digest of the Laws of the State of Georgia*. Philadelphia, 1801.
*Weekly Miscellany, The* (London). Dec. 1, 1733.
White, George, *Historical Collections of Georgia*. New York, 1855.

### SECONDARY WORKS ON GEORGIA

Almand, Bond, "The Supreme Court of Georgia: An Account of Its Delayed Birth," *Georgia Bar Journal*, VI (November 1, 1943), 105 ff.
*Annual Report of the Georgia Bar Association, 1884-1943*.
Arnett, Alex Mathews, *The Populist Movement in Georgia*. New York, 1922.
Averitt, Jack N., *The Election of 1860 in Georgia*. M.A. thesis. The University of Georgia, 1945.
Avery, I. W., *The History of the State of Georgia from 1850 to 1881*. New York, 1881.
Bonner, James C., et. al., *Studies in Georgia History and Government*. Athens, 1940.
Brooks, Robert Preston, *The Agrarian Revolution in Georgia, 1865-1912*. Madison, Wisconsin, 1914.
Brooks, R. P., *Financing Government in Georgia*. Athens, 1946.
Charlton, T. U. P., *Life of General James Jackson*. Augusta, 1809.
Cooper, Walter G., *The Story of Georgia*. 4 vols. New York, 1938.
Coleman, Kenneth, *The Constitutional Convention of 1877*. M.A. thesis. The University of Georgia, 1940.
Coulter, E. Merton, *College Life in the Old South*. New York, 1928.
Coulter, E. Merton, *A Short History of Georgia*. Chapel Hill, 1933.

Coulter, E. Merton, "The Nullification Movement in Georgia," *Georgia Historical Quarterly*, V (March, 1921), 3–39.
Ettinger, Amos Aschbach, *James Edward Oglethorpe: Imperial Idealist*. Oxford, 1936.
Felton, Mrs. William H., *My Memoirs of Georgia Politics*. Atlanta, 1911.
Fielder, Herbert, *A Sketch of the Life and Times and Speeches of Joseph E. Brown*. Springfield, 1883.
Flippin, Percy Scott, "The Royal Government in Georgia," *Georgia Historical Quarterly*, IX (Sept., 1925), 187–245 and X (Dec., 1926), 261 ff.
Garrett, Jean A., *Amendments and Proposed Amendments to the Constitution of 1798*. M.A. thesis. The University of Georgia, 1944.
Gosnell, Cullen B., *Government and Politics of Georgia*. New York, 1936.
Graybeal, John M., *The Georgia Primary Election System*. M.A. thesis. Emory University, 1932.
Grice, Warren, *The Bench and Bar of Georgia*. Macon, 1931.
Harris, Nathaniel Edwin, *Autobiography*. Macon, 1927.
Henson, Allen Lumpkin, *Red Galluses, A Story of Georgia Politics*. Boston, 1945.
Howell, Clark, *History of Georgia*. 4 vols. Chicago, 1926.
Hughes, M. Clyde, *County Government in Georgia*. Athens, 1944.
Jenkins, Charles Francis, *Button Gwinnett*. New York, 1926.
Job, Richard C., *Government Manual of Georgia*. Atlanta (?), 1938.
Jones, Charles C., *The History of Georgia*. 2 vols. Boston, 1883.
Lamar, Clarinda Pendleton, *The Life of Joseph Rucker Lamar, 1857–1916*. New York, 1926.
Lamar, Joseph R., "The Bench and Bar of Georgia during the Eighteenth Century," *Annual Report of the Georgia Bar Association, 1913*, 90 ff.
Lawrence, Alexander A., *James Moore Wayne, Southern Unionist*. Chapel Hill, 1943.
McLendon, S. G., *History of the Public Domain of Georgia*. Atlanta, 1924.
McCain, James Ross, *Georgia as a Proprietary Province*. Boston, 1917.

# Bibliography

M'Call, Hugh, *History of Georgia*. 2 vols. Savannah, 1811–1816.

Montgomery, Horace, *Party Development in Georgia, 1846–1861*. Ph. D. dissertation. The University of Georgia, 1939.

Nixon, Raymond B., *Henry W. Grady, Spokesman of the New South*. New York, 1943.

Northen, William Jonathan, *Men of Mark in Georgia*. 7 vols. Atlanta, 1907–12.

Park, Orville A., "The Military Record of the Georgia Bar," *Annual Report of the Georgia Bar Association, 1918*, 62 ff.

Pearce, Haywood J., Jr., *Benjamin H. Hill*. Chicago, 1928.

Phillips, Ulrich Bonnell, *Georgia and State Rights*. Washington, 1902.

Phillips, Ulrich Bonnell, *The Life of Robert Toombs*. New York, 1913.

Pound, Merritt B., "A Descriptive Account of Reorganization in Georgia," *Proceedings of the Southern Political Science Association*, October, 1933.

Pound, Merritt B. and Saye, Albert B., *A Handbook on the Constitutions of the United States and Georgia*. Athens, 1945.

Reese, William M., "The Constitution of Georgia," *Annual Report of the Georgia Bar Association, 1885*, 97 ff.

Roberts, L. E., "Sectional Factors in the Movement for Legislative Reapportionment and Reduction in Georgia, 1776–1860," *Studies in Georgia History and Government*, ed. by James C. Bonner and Lucien E. Roberts, 94–122. Athens, 1940.

Saye, Albert B., *New Viewpoints in Georgia History*. Athens, 1943.

Shryock, Richard Harrison, *Georgia and the Union in 1850*. Durham, 1926.

Smith, Charles Henry, *Bill Arp So-Called*. New York, 1866.

Stephens, Alexander H., *More of Georgia and Ohio*. Washington, 1855. (Pamphlet in De Renne Collection.)

Stevens, William Bacon, *A History of Georgia*. 2 vols. New York and Philadelphia, 1847–59.

Strickland, Reba Carolyn, *Religion and the State in Georgia in the Eighteenth Century*. New York, 1939.

Thompson, C. Mildred, *Reconstruction in Georgia*. New York, 1915.

*A Constitutional History of Georgia*

Von Abele, Rudolph, *Alexander H. Stephens.* New York, 1946.
Wade, John Donald, *Augustus Baldwin Longstreet.* New York, 1924.
Ware, Ethel K., *A Constitutional History of Georgia.* New York, 1947.
Woodward, C. Vann, *Tom Watson, Agrarian Rebel.* New York, 1938.

### GENERAL WORKS

Andrews, Charles M., *The Colonial Background of the American Revolution.* New Haven, 1924.
Baker, Ray Stannard, *Woodrow Wilson, Life and Letters.* 8 vols. New York, 1927–39.
Becker, Carl, *The Declaration of Independence.* New York, 1922.
Beer, George L., *British Colonial Policy, 1754–1765.* New York, 1907.
Bolton, H. E. and Ross, M., *The Debatable Land.* Berkeley, California, 1925.
Bryce, James, *The American Commonwealth.* 2 vols. New York, 1888.
Channing, Edward, *A History of the United States.* Vol. II. New York, 1904.
Corwin, E. S., "The Progress of Political Theory between the Declaration of Independence and the Meeting of the Philadelphia Convention," *American Historical Review,* XXX (April, 1925), 527 ff.
Destler, Chester M., *Studies in Social Progress.* Vol. II. Athens, Georgia, 1935.
*Dictionary of National Biography.* 20 vols. Allen Johnson and Dumas Malone, eds. New York, 1929–1936.
Dodd, Walter F., *The Revision and Amendment of State Constitutions.* Baltimore, 1910.
Frothingham, Richard, *The Rise of the Republic of the United States.* Tenth edition, Boston, 1910.
Gee, Joshua, *The Trade and Navigation of Great Britain Considered.* London, 1729.
Green, Fletcher M., *Constitutional Development in the South Atlantic States, 1776–1860.* Chapel Hill, 1930.
Holcombe, Arthur N., *State Government in the United States.* New York, 1916.

*Bibliography*

Jameson, John Alexander, *A Treatise on Constitutional Conventions*. Chicago, 1887.
Jones, Charles Colcock, *The Old South: Addresses Delivered before the Confederate Survivors Association . . . by His Excellency, Governor John B. Gordon and by Col. Charles C. Jones, Jr., L.L.D.* Augusta, Georgia, 1887.
Labaree, Leonard Woods, *Royal Government in America*. New Haven, 1930.
Martin, Asa Earl, *A History of the United States.* vol. I. New York, 1928.
McLaughlin, Andrew Cunningham, *The Confederation and the Constitution*. New York, 1904.
McMaster, J. B., *A History of the People of the United States*. Vol. I. New York, 1884.
McPherson, J. H. T. "The Making of the Constitution," *Studies in Social Progress*, II, 165 ff., ed. by Chester M. Destler. Athens, 1935.
Mobly, Gabriel Bonnot de, *Observations sur le gouvernement et les lois des Etats-Unis d'Amerique*. Amsterdam, 1774.
Morey, William C., "The First State Constitutions," *Annals of the American Academy of Political and Social Science,* IV (September, 1893), 201–232.
Nevins, Allan, *The American States During and After the Revolution*. New York, 1924.
Osgood, Herbert L., *The American Colonies in the Eighteenth Century*. New York, 1924.
Randall, J. G., *The Civil War and Reconstruction*. New York, 1937.
Schlesinger, Arthur Meier, *The Colonial Merchants and the American Revolution*. New York, 1918.
Smith, Samuel (?), *Publick Spirit Illustrated in the Life and Designs of the Reverend Thomas Bray*. London, 1746.
Stephens, Alexander H., *A Constitutional View of the Late War Between the States*. 2 vols. Philadelphia, 1868–70.
Van Tyne, Claude H., "The Influence of the Clergy and of Religion and Sectarian Forces on the American Revolution," *Amer. Hist. Rev.*, XIX (Oct., 1913), 44–64.
Webster, William Clarence, "Comparative Study of State Constitutions of the American Revolution," *Annals of the American Academy of Political and Social Science,* IX (May, 1897), 380–419.

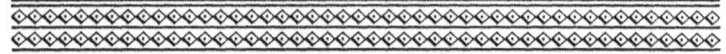

# Governors of Georgia

## Colonial:

JAMES EDWARD OGLETHORPE,
  Resident Trustee................Feb. 12, 1733–July 23, 1743
WILLIAM STEPHENS, President...............Oct. 7, 1741–1750
HENRY PARKER, President..................Sept. 26, 1750–1752
PATRICK GRAHAM, President.........................1752–1754
JOHN REYNOLDS........................Oct. 30, 1754–1757
HENRY ELLIS..........................Feb. 16, 1757–1760
JAMES WRIGHT.......................Oct. 31, 1760–1776 [1]

## Revolutionary:

WILLIAM EWEN,
  President of Council of Safety...............June 22, 1775–1775
GEORGE WALTON, President of Council of Safety.Dec. 11, 1775–1776
WILLIAM EWEN, President of Council of Safety..Feb. 20, 1776–1776
ARCHIBALD BULLOCH, President............April 15, 1776–1777
BUTTON GWINNETT, President..............Feb. 22, 1777–1777
JOHN ADAMS TREUTLEN....................May 8, 1777–1778
JOHN HOUSTOUN.........................Jan. 10, 1778–1779
JOHN WEREAT, Pres. of Supreme Exec. Council...Aug. 6, 1779–1780
GEORGE WALTON, Pres. of faction opposing Wereat Nov. 4, 1779–1780
RICHARD HOWLEY........................Jan. 4, 1780–1780
STEPHEN HEARD, President of Exec. Council...May 24, 1780–1781
NATHAN BROWNSON......................Aug. 16, 1781–1782
JOHN MARTIN...........................Jan. 3, 1782–1783

[1] James Habersham served as President of the Executive Council and Commander in Chief during the absence of Governor Wright on a visit to England, July 13, 1771–Feb. 1773. Wright fled from Georgia on Feb. 11, 1776. After the British captured Savannah, Wright was restored as Royal Governor from July 14, 1779, to June 14, 1782.

## Governors of Georgia

### State:[2]

| | | |
|---|---|---|
| Lyman Hall | Jan. 8, | 1783–1784 |
| John Houstoun | Jan. 9, | 1784–1785 |
| Samuel Elbert | Jan. 7, | 1785–1786 |
| Edward Telfair | Jan. 9, | 1786–1787 |
| George Mathews | Jan. 9, | 1787–1788 |
| George Handly | Jan. 26, | 1788–1789 |
| George Walton | Jan. 7, | 1789–1790 |
| Edward Telfair | Nov. 9, | 1790–1793 |
| George Mathews | Nov. 7, | 1793–1796 |
| Jared Irwin | Jan. 15, | 1796–1798 |
| James Jackson | Jan. 12, | 1798–1801 |
| David Emanuel, *President of Senate* | Mar. 3, | 1801–1801 |
| Josiah Tattnall, Jr. | Nov. 7, | 1801–1802 |
| John Milledge | Nov. 4, | 1802–1806 |
| Jared Irwin | Sept. 23, | 1806–1809 |
| David B. Mitchell | Nov. 10, | 1809–1813 |
| Peter Early | Nov. 5, | 1813–1815 |
| David B. Mitchell | Nov. 10, | 1815–1817 |
| William Rabun | Mar. 4, | 1817–1819 |
| Matthew Talbot, *President of Senate* | Oct. 24, | 1819–1819 |
| John Clark | Nov. 5, | 1819–1823 |
| George M. Troup | Nov. 7, | 1823–1827 |
| John Forsyth | Nov. 7, | 1827–1829 |
| George R. Gilmer | Nov. 4, | 1829–1831 |
| Wilson Lumpkin | Nov. 9, | 1831–1835 |
| William Schley | Nov. 4, | 1835–1837 |
| George R. Gilmer | Nov. 8, | 1837–1839 |
| Charles J. McDonald | Nov. 6, | 1839–1843 |
| George W. Crawford | Nov. 8, | 1843–1847 |
| George W. Towns | Nov. 3, | 1847–1851 |
| Howell Cobb | Nov. 5, | 1851–1853 |
| Herschel V. Johnson | Nov. 9, | 1853–1857 |
| Joseph E. Brown | Nov. 6, | 1857–1865 |
| James Johnson, *Provisional Governor* | June 17, | 1865–1865 |
| Charles J. Jenkins | Dec. 14, | 1865–1868 |
| Brig. Gen. Thomas H. Ruger, *Provisional Gov.* | Jan. 13, | 1868–1868 |
| Rufus E. Bullock | July 4, | 1868–1871 |

[2] The dates given here are taken largely from *Georgia's Official and Statistical Register, 1923*, pp. 166–69.

## A Constitutional History of Georgia

BENJAMIN CONLEY, *President of Senate*.........Oct. 30, 1871–1872
JAMES M. SMITH........................Jan. 12, 1872–1877
ALFRED H. COLQUITT....................Jan. 12, 1877–1882
ALEXANDER H. STEPHENS..........Nov. 4, 1882–1883 (Mar. 4)
JAMES S. BOYNTON, *President of Senate*........Mar. 5, 1883–1883
HENRY D. MCDANIEL..................May 10, 1883–1886
JOHN B. GORDON......................Nov. 4, 1886–1890
WILLIAM J. NORTHEN..................Nov. 8, 1890–1894
WILLIAM Y. ATKINSON.................Oct. 27, 1894–1898
ALLEN D. CANDLER....................Oct. 29, 1898–1902
JOSEPH M. TERRELL...................Oct. 26, 1902–1907
HOKE SMITH..........................June 29, 1907–1909
JOSEPH M. BROWN.....................June 26, 1909–1911
HOKE SMITH..........................July 1, 1911–1911
JOHN M. SLATON, *President of Senate*........Nov. 16, 1911–1912
JOSEPH M. BROWN.....................Jan. 25, 1912–1913
JOHN M. SLATON......................June 28, 1913–1915
NATHANIEL E. HARRIS.................June 26, 1915–1917
HUGH M. DORSEY......................June 30, 1917–1921
THOMAS WILLIAM HARDWICK.............June 25, 1921–1923
CLIFFORD MITCHELL WALKER............June 30, 1923–1927
LAMARTINE GRIFFIN HARDMAN...........June 25, 1927–1931
RICHARD BREVARD RUSSELL, JR.........June 27, 1931–1933
EUGENE TALMADGE.....................Jan. 10, 1933–1937
EURITH DICKINSON RIVERS.............Jan. 12, 1937–1941
EUGENE TALMADGE.....................Jan. 14, 1941–1943
ELLIS GIBBS ARNALL..................Jan. 12, 1943–1947

# Appendix

# The Constitution of Georgia[1]

## PREAMBLE

To perpetuate the principles of free government, insure justice to all, preserve peace, promote the interest and happiness of the citizen, and transmit to posterity the enjoyment of liberty, we, the people of Georgia, relying upon the protection and guidance of Almighty God, do ordain and establish this Constitution.

## ARTICLE I
## BILL OF RIGHTS
### Section I

PARAGRAPH I. *Origin and Foundation of Government.* All government of right, originates with the people, is founded upon their will only, and is instituted solely for the good of the whole. Public officers are the trustees and servants of the people, and at all times, amenable to them.

PARAGRAPH II. *Protection the Duty of Government.* Protection to person and property is the paramount duty of government, and shall be impartial and complete.

PARAGRAPH III. *Life, Liberty, and Property.* No person shall be deprived of life, liberty, or property, except by due process of law.

PARAGRAPH IV. *Right to the Courts.* No person shall be deprived of the right to prosecute or defend his own cause in any of the courts of this State, in person, by attorney, or both.

---

[1] From the manuscript copy in the *Georgia Laws of 1945* preserved in the office of the Secretary of State.

## A Constitutional History of Georgia

PARAGRAPH V. *Benefit of Counsel; Accusation; List of Witnesses; Compulsory Process; Trial by Jury.* Every person charged with an offense against the laws of this State shall have the privilege and benefit of counsel; shall be furnished, on demand, with a copy of the accusation, and a list of the witnesses on whose testimony the charge against him is founded; shall have compulsory process to obtain the testimony of his own witnesses; shall be confronted with the witnesses testifying against him; and shall have a public and speedy trial by an impartial jury.

PARAGRAPH VI. *Crimination of Self Not Compelled.* No person shall be compelled to give testimony tending in any manner to criminate himself.

PARAGRAPH VII. *Banishment and Whipping as Punishment for Crime.* Neither banishment beyond the limits of the State, nor whipping, as a punishment for crime, shall be allowed.

PARAGRAPH VIII. *Jeopardy of Life or Liberty More Than Once Forbidden.* No person shall be put in jeopardy of life or liberty, more than once for the same offense, save on his, or her own motion for a new trial after conviction, or in case of mistrial.

PARAGRAPH IX. *Bail; Fines; Punishment; Arrest, Abuse of Prisoners.* Excessive bail shall not be required, nor excessive fines imposed, nor cruel and unusual punishments inflicted; nor shall any person be abused in being arrested, while under arrest, or in prison.

PARAGRAPH X. *Costs.* No person shall be compelled to pay costs except after conviction on final trial.

PARAGRAPH XI. *Habeas Corpus.* The writ of Habeas Corpus shall not be suspended.

PARAGRAPH XII. *Freedom of Conscience.* All men have the natural and inalienable right to worship God, each according to the dictates of his own conscience, and no human authority should, in any case, control or interfere with such right of conscience.

PARAGRAPH XIII. *Religious Opinions; Liberty of Conscience.* No inhabitant of this State shall be molested in person or property, or prohibited from holding any public office, or trust, on account of his religious opinions; but the right of liberty of conscience shall not be so construed as to

## The Constitution of Georgia

excuse acts of licentiousness, or justify practices inconsistent with the peace and safety of the State.

PARAGRAPH XIV. *Appropriations to Churches, Sects, Etc., Forbidden.* No money shall ever be taken from the public Treasury, directly or indirectly, in aid of any church, sect, or denomination of religionists, or of any sectarian institution.

PARAGRAPH XV. *Liberty of Speech or of the Press Guaranteed.* No law shall ever be passed to curtail, or restrain the liberty of speech, or of the press; any person may speak, write and publish his sentiments, on all subjects, being responsible for the abuse of that liberty.

PARAGRAPH XVI. *Searches, Seizures, and Warrants.* The right of the people to be secure in their persons, house, papers, and effects, against unreasonable searches and seizures, shall not be violated; and no warrant shall issue except upon probable cause, supported by oath, or affirmation, particularly describing the place, or places, to be searched, and the persons or things to be seized.

PARAGRAPH XVII. *Slavery and Involuntary Servitude.* There shall be within the State of Georgia neither slavery nor involuntary servitude, save as a punishment for crime after legal conviction thereof.

PARAGRAPH XVIII. *Status of the Citizen.* The social status of the citizen shall never be the subject of legislation.

PARAGRAPH XIX. *Civil Authority Superior to Military.* The civil authority shall be superior to the military, and no soldier shall, in time of peace, be quartered in any house, without the consent of the owner, nor in time of war, except by the civil magistrate, in such manner as may be provided by law.

PARAGRAPH XX. *Contempts.* The power of the Courts to punish for contempt shall be limited by legislative acts.

PARAGRAPH XXI. *Imprisonment for Debt.* There shall be no imprisonment for debt.

PARAGRAPH XXII. *Arms, Right to Keep and Bear.* The right of the people to keep and bear arms, shall not be infringed, but the General Assembly shall have power to prescribe the manner in which arms may be borne.

PARAGRAPH XXIII. *Legislative, Judicial, and Executive Powers, Separate.* The legislative, judicial and executive powers shall forever remain separate and distinct, and no person discharging the duties of one, shall, at the same time, exercise the functions of either of the others, except as herein provided.

PARAGRAPH XXIV. *Right to Assemble and Petition.* The people have the right to assemble peaceably for their common good and to apply to those vested with the powers of government for redress of grievances by petition or remonstrance.

PARAGRAPH XXV. *Citizens, Protection of.* All citizens of the United States, resident in this State, are hereby declared citizens of this State, and it shall be the duty of the General Assembly to enact such laws as will protect them in the full enjoyment of the rights, privileges and immunities due to such citizenship.

## SECTION II

PARAGRAPH I. *Libel; Jury in Criminal Cases; New Trials.* In all prosecutions or indictments for libel the truth may be given in evidence; and the jury in all criminal cases, shall be the judges of the law and the facts. The power of the judges to grant new trials, in case of conviction, is preserved.

PARAGRAPH II. *Treason.* Treason against the State of Georgia, shall consist in levying war against her; adhering to her enemies; giving them aid and comfort. No person shall be convicted of treason, except on the testimony of two witnesses to the same overt act, or confession in open court.

PARAGRAPH III. *Conviction, Effect of.* No conviction shall work corruption of blood, or forfeiture of estate.

PARAGRAPH IV. *Lotteries.* All lotteries, and the sale of lottery tickets, are hereby prohibited; and this prohibition shall be enforced by penal laws.

PARAGRAPH V. *Lobbying; Penalties.* Lobbying is declared to be a crime, and the General Assembly shall enforce this provision by suitable penalties.

PARAGRAPH VI. *Fraud; Concealment of Property.* The General Assembly shall have the power to provide for the punishment of fraud; and, shall provide by law, for reaching property of the debtor concealed from the creditor.

## SECTION III

PARAGRAPH I. *Private Ways; Just Compensation.* In case of necessity, private ways may be granted upon just compensa-

## The Constitution of Georgia

tion being first paid by the applicant. Private property shall not be taken, or damaged, for public purposes, without just and adequate compensation being first paid.

PARAGRAPH II. *Attainder; Ex Post Facto and Retroactive Laws, Etc.* No Bill of Attainder, ex post facto law, retroactive law, or law impairing the obligation of contracts, or making irrevocable grant of special privileges or immunities, shall be passed.

PARAGRAPH III. *Revocation of Tax Exemptions.* All exemptions from taxation heretofore granted in corporate charters are declared to be henceforth null and void.

### SECTION IV

PARAGRAPH I. *General Laws; Uniform Operation; How Varied.* Laws of a general nature shall have uniform operation throughout the State, and no special law shall be enacted in any case for which provision has been made by an existing general law. No general law affecting private rights, shall be varied in any particular case, by special legislation, except with the free consent, in writing, of all persons to be affected thereby; and no person under legal disability to contract, is capable of such consent.

PARAGRAPH II. *What Acts Void.* Legislative acts in violation of this Constitution, of the Constitution of the United States, are void, and the Judiciary shall so declare them.

### SECTION V

PARAGRAPH I. *State Rights.* The people of this State have the inherent, sole and exclusive right of regulating their internal government, and the police thereof, and of altering and abolishing their Constitution whenever it may be necessary to their safety and happiness.

PARAGRAPH II. *Enumeration of Rights Not Denial of Others.* The enumeration of rights herein contained as a part of this Constitution shall not be construed to deny to the people any inherent rights which they may have hitherto enjoyed.

### SECTION VI

PARAGRAPH I. *Tidewater Titles; Confirmed.* The Act of the General Assembly approved December 16, 1902, which extends the title of ownership of lands abutting on tidal water to low water mark is hereby ratified and confirmed.

## ARTICLE II
## ELECTIVE FRANCHISE
### SECTION I

PARAGRAPH I. *Elections by Ballot; Registration of Voters.* Elections by the people shall be by ballot, and only those persons shall be allowed to vote who have been first registered in accordance with the requirements of law.

PARAGRAPH II. *Who Shall Be An Elector Entitled to Register and Vote.* Every citizen of this State who is a citizen of the United States, eighteen years old or upwards, not laboring under any of the disabilities named in this Article, and possessing the qualifications provided by it, shall be an elector and entitled to register and vote at any election by the people: Provided, that no soldier, sailor or marine in the military or naval services of the United States shall acquire the rights of an elector by reason of being stationed on duty in this State.

PARAGRAPH III. *Who Entitled to Register and Vote.* To entitle a person to register and vote at any election by the people, he shall have resided in the State one year next preceding the election, and in the county in which he offers to vote six months next preceding the election.

PARAGRAPH IV. *Qualifications of Electors.* Every citizen of this State shall be entitled to register as an elector, and to vote in all elections in said State, who is not disqualified under the provisions of Section II of Article II of this Constitution, and who possesses the qualifications prescribed in Paragraphs II and III of this Section or who will possess them at the date of the election occurring next after his registration, and who in addition thereto comes within either of the classes provided for in the two following subdivisions of this paragraph.

1. All persons who are of good character and understand the duties and obligations of citizenship under a republican form of government; or,

2. All persons who can correctly read in the English language any paragraph of the Constitution of the United States or of this State and correctly write the same in the English language when read to them by any one of the registrars, and

## The Constitution of Georgia

all persons who solely because of physical disability are unable to comply with the above requirements but who can understand and give a reasonable interpretation of any paragraph of the Constitution of the United States or of this State that may be read to them by any one of the registrars.

PARAGRAPH V. *Appeal From Decision of Registrars.* Any person to whom the right of registration is denied by the registrars upon the ground that he lacks the qualifications set forth in the two subdivisions of Paragraph IV shall have the right to take an appeal, and any citizen may enter an appeal from the decision of the registrars allowing any person to register under said subdivisions. All appeals must be filed in writing with the registrars within ten days from the date of the decision complained of, and shall be returned by the registrars to the office of the clerk of the superior court to be tried as other appeals.

PARAGRAPH VI. *Judgment of Force Pending Appeal.* Pending an appeal and until the final decision of the case, the judgment of the registrars shall remain in full force.

### SECTION II

PARAGRAPH I. *Registration of Electors; Who Disfranchised.* The General Assembly may provide, from time to time, for the registration of all electors, but the following classes of persons shall not be permitted to register, vote or hold any office, or appointment of honor, or trust in this State, to-wit: 1st. Those who shall have been convicted in any court of competent jurisdiction of treason against the State, of embezzlement of public funds, malfeasance in office, bribery or larceny, or of any crime involving moral turpitude, punishable by the laws of this State with imprisonment in the penitentiary, unless such persons shall have been pardoned. 2nd. Idiots and insane persons.

### SECTION III

PARAGRAPH I. *Privilege of Electors from Arrest.* Electors shall, in all cases, except for treason, felony, larceny, and breach of the peace, be privileged from arrest during their attendance on elections, and in going to and returning from the same.

## Section IV

**Paragraph I.** *Holder of Public Funds.* No person who is the holder of any public money, contrary to law, shall be eligible to any office in this State until the same is accounted for and paid into the Treasury.

## Section V

**Paragraph I.** *Sale of Liquors on Election Days.* The General Assembly shall by law forbid the sale of intoxicating drinks in this State or any political subdivision thereof on all days for the holding of any election in the area in which such election is held and prescribe punishment for any violation of the same.

## Section VI

**Paragraph I.** *Returns Made to Whom.* Returns of election for all civil officers elected by the people, who are to be commissioned by the Governor, and also for members of the General Assembly, shall be made to the Secretary of State, unless otherwise provided by law.

# ARTICLE III
# LEGISLATIVE DEPARTMENT
## Section I

**Paragraph I.** *Power Vested in General Assembly.* The legislative power of the State shall be vested in a General Assembly which shall consist of a Senate and House of Representatives.

## Section II

**Paragraph I.** *Number of Senators and Senatorial Districts.* The Senate shall consist of not more than fifty-four members and there shall be not more than fifty-four Senatorial Districts with one Senator from each District as now constituted, or as hereafter created. The various Senatorial Districts shall be comprised of the counties as now provided, and the General Assembly shall have authority to create, rearrange and change these Districts within the limitations herein stated.

# The Constitution of Georgia

## Section III

PARAGRAPH I. *Number of Representatives.* The House of Representatives shall consist of representatives apportioned among the several counties of the State as follows: To the eight counties having the largest population, three representatives each; to the thirty counties having the next largest population, two representatives each; and to the remaining counties, one representative each.

PARAGRAPH II. *Apportionment Changed, How.* The above apportionment shall be changed by the General Assembly at its first session after each census taken by the United States Government in accordance with the provisions of Paragraph I of Section III of this article.

## Section IV

PARAGRAPH I. *Term of Members.* The members of the General Assembly shall be elected for two years, and shall serve until the time fixed by law for the convening of the next General Assembly.

PARAGRAPH II. *Election, When.* The first election for members of the General Assembly, under this Constitution shall take place on Tuesday after the first Monday in November, 1946, and subsequent elections biennially, on that day, until the day of election is changed by law.

PARAGRAPH III. *Meeting of the General Assembly.* The General Assembly shall meet in regular session on the second Monday in January 1947, and biennially thereafter on the same day until the date shall be changed by law. By concurrent resolution, adopted by a majority of members elected to both Houses, the General Assembly may adjourn any regular session to such later date as it may fix for reconvening in regular session, but shall remain in regular session no longer than seventy (70) days, in the aggregate, during the term for which the members were elected. If it shall adjourn the first regular session before the expiration of seventy (70) days without fixing a date for reconvening, the General Assembly shall reconvene in regular session on the second Monday in January of the next year unless it shall have adjourned sine die. All business pending in the Senate or House at the adjournment of any regular session may be considered at any later regular session of the same General Assembly as if there had been no adjournment. Nothing herein shall be construed to affect the power of the Governor to convoke the General Assembly in extraordinary session, or the duty of the Governor to convene the General Assembly in extraordinary session upon the certificate of three-fifths of the members elected to the Senate and the House of Representatives, as provided in Article V, Section I, Paragraph XII of this Constitution. If an impeachment trial is pending at the end of any regular or extraordinary session, the Senate may continue in session until such trial is completed. The provisions of Paragraph III, Section IV of Article III of the Constitution which this Constitution supersedes which apply to the meetings of the General Assembly shall continue in force until the second Monday in January, 1947.

PARAGRAPH IV. *Quorum.* A majority of each House shall constitute a quorum to transact business; but a smaller number may adjourn from day to day and compel the presence of its absent members, as each House may provide.

PARAGRAPH V. *Oath of Members.* Each Senator and Representative, before taking his seat, shall take the following oath, or affirmation, to-wit: "I will support the Constitution of this State and of the United States, and on all questions and measures which may come before me, I will so conduct myself, as will, in my judgment, be most conducive to the interests and prosperity of this State."

PARAGRAPH VI. *Eligibility; Appointments Forbidden.* No person holding a military commission, or other appointment, or office, having any emolument, or compensation annexed thereto, under this State, or the United States, or either of them except Justices of the Peace and officers of the militia, nor any defaulter for public money, or for any legal taxes required of him shall have a seat in either house; nor shall any Senator, or Representative, after his qualification as such, be elected by the General Assembly, or appointed by the Governor, either with or without the advice and consent of the Senate, to any office or appointment having any emolument annexed thereto, during the time for which he shall have been elected, unless he shall first resign his seat, provided, however, that during the term for which he was elected no Senator or Representative shall be appointed to any civil office which has been created during such term.

## The Constitution of Georgia

PARAGRAPH VII. *Removal From District or County, Effect of.* The seat of a member of either house shall be vacated on his removal from the district or county from which he was elected.

### SECTION V

PARAGRAPH I. *Qualifications of Senators.* The Senators shall be citizens of the United States, who have attained the age of twenty-five years, and who shall have been citizens of this State for four years, and for one year residents of the district from which elected.

PARAGRAPH II. *President.* The presiding officer of the Senate shall be styled the President of the Senate. A President Pro Tempore shall be elected viva voce from the Senators and shall act in case of the death, resignation or disability of the President, or in the event of his succession to the executive power.

PARAGRAPH III. *Impeachments.* The Senate shall have the sole power to try impeachments.

PARAGRAPH IV. *Trial of Impeachments.* When sitting for that purpose, the members shall be on oath, or affirmation, and shall be presided over by the Chief Justice or the Presiding Justice of the Supreme Court. Should the Chief Justice be disqualified, the Senate shall select a Justice of the Supreme Court to preside. No person shall be convicted without the concurrence of two-thirds of the members present.

PARAGRAPH V. *Judgments in Impeachments.* Judgments, in cases of impeachment, shall not extend further than removal from office, and disqualification to hold and enjoy any office of honor, trust, or profit, within this State; but the party convicted shall nevertheless, be liable, and subject, to indictment trial, judgment, and punishment, according to law.

### SECTION VI

PARAGRAPH I. *Qualifications of Representatives.* The Representatives shall be citizens of the United States who have attained the age of twenty-one years, and who shall have been citizens of this State for two years, and for one year residents of the counties from which elected.

PARAGRAPH II. *Speaker.* The presiding officer of the House of Representatives shall be styled the Speaker of the House of

## A Constitutional History of Georgia

Representatives, and shall be elected viva voce from the body.

PARAGRAPH III. *Power to Impeach.* The House of Representatives shall have the sole power to vote impeachment charges against all persons who shall have been or may be in office.

### SECTION VII

PARAGRAPH I. *Election, Returns, Etc.; Disorderly Conduct.* Each House shall be the judge of the election, returns, and qualifications of its members and shall have power to punish them for disorderly behavior, or misconduct, by censure, fine, imprisonment, or expulsion; but no member shall be expelled, except by a vote of two-thirds of the House to which he belongs.

PARAGRAPH II. *Contempts, How Punished.* Each House may punish by imprisonment, not extending beyond the session, any person, not a member, who shall be guilty of a contempt, by any disorderly behavior in its presence, or who shall rescue, or attempt to rescue, any person arrested by order of either House.

PARAGRAPH III. *Privilege of Members.* The members of both Houses shall be free from arrest during their attendance on the General Assembly, and in going thereto, or returning therefrom, except for treason, felony, larceny, or breach of the peace; and no member shall be liable to answer in any other place for anything spoken in debate in either House.

PARAGRAPH IV. *Journals and Acts.* Each House shall keep a journal of its proceedings, and publish it immediately after its adjournment. The General Assembly shall provide for the publication of the laws passed by each session.

PARAGRAPH V. *Where Journals Kept.* The original journal shall be preserved after publication, in the office of the Secretary of State, but there shall be no other record thereof.

PARAGRAPH VI. *Yeas and Nays, When Taken.* The yeas and nays on any question shall, at the desire of one-fifth of the members present, be entered on the Journal.

PARAGRAPH VII. *Bills to Be Read.* Every bill, before it shall pass, shall be read three times, and on three separate days, in each House, unless in cases of actual invasion, or insurrection, but the first and second reading of each local bill,

## The Constitution of Georgia

shall consist of the reading of the title only, unless said bill is ordered to be engrossed.

PARAGRAPH VIII. *One Subject Matter Expressed.* No law shall pass which refers to more than one subject matter, or contains matter different from what is expressed in the title thereof.

PARAGRAPH IX. *General Appropriation Bill.* The General appropriation bill shall embrace nothing except appropriations fixed by previous laws, the ordinary expenses of the Executive, Legislative and Judicial Departments of the Government, payment of the public debt and interest thereon, and for support of the public institutions and educational interests of the State. All other appropriations shall be made by separate bills, each embracing but one subject.

PARAGRAPH X. *Bills For Revenue.* All bills for raising revenue, or appropriating money, shall originate in the House of Representatives, but the Senate may propose, or concur in amendments, as in other bills.

PARAGRAPH XI. *Public Money, How Drawn.* No money shall be drawn from the Treasury except by appropriation made by law.

PARAGRAPH XII. *Bills Appropriating Money.* No bill or resolution appropriating money shall become a law unless, upon its passage, the yeas and nays, in each house, are recorded.

PARAGRAPH XIII. *Acts Signed; Rejected Bills.* All acts shall be signed by the President of the Senate and the Speaker of the House of Representatives, and no bill or resolution, intended to have the effect of a law, which shall have been rejected by either house, shall be again proposed during the same session, under the same or any other title, without the consent of two-thirds of the House by which the same was rejected.

PARAGRAPH XIV. *Majority of Members to Pass Bill.* No bill shall become a law unless it shall receive a majority of the votes of all the members elected to each House of the General Assembly, and it shall, in every instance, so appear on the Journal.

PARAGRAPH XV. *Notice of Intention to Ask Local Legislation Necessary.* No local or special bill shall be passed, unless notice of the intention to apply therefor shall have been published in the newspaper in which the Sheriff's advertisements for the locality affected are published, once a week for three weeks during a period of sixty days immediately preceding its introduction into the General Assembly. No local or special bill shall become law unless there is attached to and made a part of said bill a copy of said notice certified by the publisher, or accompanied by an affidavit of the author, to the effect that said notice has been published as provided by law. No office to which a person has been elected shall be abolished, nor the term of the office shortened or lengthened by local or special bill during the term for which such person was elected unless the same be approved by the people of the jurisdiction affected in a referendum on the question. Where any local law shall add any member or members to any municipal or county governing authority, the members of which are elected by the people, such local law must provide that the member or members so added must be elected by a majority vote of the qualified voters of the political subdivision affected.

PARAGRAPH XVI. *Statutes and Sections of Code, How Amended.* No law, or section of the code, shall be amended or repealed by mere reference to its title, or to the number of the section of the Code, but the amending, or repealing act, shall distinctly describe the law to be amended or repealed, as well as the alteration to be made.

PARAGRAPH XVII. *Corporate Powers, How Granted.* The General Assembly shall have no power to grant corporate powers and privileges to private companies, to make or change election precincts, nor to establish bridges or ferries, nor to change names of legitimate children; but it shall prescribe by law the manner in which such powers shall be exercised by the courts; it may confer this authority to grant corporate powers and privileges to private companies to the judges of the superior courts of this State in vacation. All corporate powers and privileges to banking, trust, insurance, railroad, canal, navigation, express and telegraph companies shall be issued and granted by the Secretary of State in such manner as shall be prescribed by law; and if in any event the Secretary of State should be disqualified to act in any case, then in that event the legislature shall provide by general laws by what person such charter shall be granted.

## The Constitution of Georgia

PARAGRAPH XVIII. *Recognizances.* The General Assembly shall have no power to relieve principals or securities upon forfeited recognizances, from the payment thereof, either before or after judgment thereon, unless the principal in the recognizance shall have been apprehended and placed in the custody of the proper officers.

PARAGRAPH XIX. *Yeas and Nays to Be Entered, When.* Whenever the Constitution requires a vote of two-thirds of either or both houses for the passage of an act or resolution, the yeas and nays on the passage thereof shall be entered on the Journal.

PARAGRAPH XX. *Powers of the General Assembly.* The General Assembly shall have the power to make all laws consistent with this Constitution, and not repugnant to the Constitution of the United States, which they shall deem necessary and proper for the welfare of the State.

PARAGRAPH XXI. *Signature of Governor.* No provision in this Constitution for a two-thirds vote of both houses of the General Assembly shall be construed to waive the necessity for the signature of the Governor as in any other case, except in the case of the two-thirds vote required to override the veto, to submit constitutional amendments, and in case of prolongation of a session of the General Assembly.

PARAGRAPH XXII. *Adjournments.* Neither House shall adjourn for more than three days, or to any other place, without the consent of the other, and in case of disagreement between the two Houses, on a question of adjournment, the Governor may adjourn either, or both of them.

PARAGRAPH XXIII. *Zoning and Planning Laws.* The General Assembly of the State shall have authority to grant the governing authorities of the municipalities and counties authority to pass zoning and planning laws whereby such cities or counties may be zoned or districted for various uses and other or different uses prohibited therein, and regulating the use for which said zones or districts may be set apart, and regulating the plans for development and improvements on real estate therein.

PARAGRAPH XXIV. *Civil Service—Equal Preference to Veterans.* Neither the State of Georgia, nor any political subdivision thereof, shall inaugurate or maintain any civil service scheme of any nature whatever which fails to provide for honorably discharged veterans of any war, and the said State of Georgia, or any political subdivision shall, if a civil service scheme is originated or is already in force, provide equal preferences accorded to such veterans as now exist under Federal Civil Service Laws.

PARAGRAPH XXV. *Street Railways.* The General Assembly shall not authorize the construction of any street passenger railway, within the limits of any incorporate town or city, without the consent of the Corporate Authorities.

SECTION VIII

PARAGRAPH I. *Officers of the Two Houses.* The officers of the two houses, other than the President of the Senate and Speaker of the House, shall be a President Pro Tempore and Secretary of the Senate and Speaker Pro Tempore and Clerk of the House of Representatives, and such assistants as each House may provide for.

SECTION IX

PARAGRAPH I. *Compensation, Expense and Mileage.* The per diem of members of the General Assembly shall be $10.00 per day plus the additional sum of $5.00 per day for maintenance expense; and the mileage shall not exceed 10 cents for each mile traveled by the nearest practical route in going to and returning from the Capitol; but the President Pro Tem of the Senate, when serving as presiding officer thereof, and the Speaker of the House of Representatives, shall each receive $15.00 per day as per diem plus the additional sum of $5.00 per day for maintenance expense.

SECTION X

PARAGRAPH I. *Viva Voce Vote; Place of Meeting.* All elections by the General Assembly shall be viva voce, and the vote shall appear on the Journal of the House of Representatives. When the Senate and House of Representatives unite for the purpose of election, they shall meet in the Representative Hall, and the President of the Senate shall, in such cases, preside and declare the result.

SECTION XI

PARAGRAPH I. *Salaries of Elective Officials; How Changed.* The General Assembly may, at any time, by a majority vote

*The Constitution of Georgia*

of both branches prescribe other and different salaries for all of the elective officers provided for in this Constitution, but no such change shall affect the officers then in commission.

## ARTICLE IV
## PUBLIC UTILITIES, EMINENT DOMAIN, POLICE POWER, INSURANCE COMPANIES, CONTRACTS, ETC.

### Section I

PARAGRAPH I. *Public Utility Tariffs and Charges.* The power and authority of regulating railroad freight and passenger tariffs and of charges of public utilities for their services, of preventing unjust discriminations, and requiring reasonable and just rates of freight and passenger tariffs and of charges of public utilities, are hereby conferred upon the General Assembly, whose duty it shall be to pass laws from time to time, to regulate such tariffs and charges, to prohibit unjust discriminations by the various railroads and public utilities of this State, and to prohibit said railroads and public utilities from charging other than just and reasonable rates and to enforce the same by adequate penalties, provided, nevertheless, that such power and authority shall never be exercised in any way to regulate or fix charges of such public utilities as are or may be owned or operated by any county or municipality of this State; except as provided in this Constitution.

PARAGRAPH II. *Rebates.* No public utility company shall give, or pay, any rebate, or bonus in the nature thereof, directly or indirectly, or do any act to mislead or deceive the public as to the real rates charged or received for freight or passage or services furnished, any such payments shall be illegal and void; and these prohibitions shall be enforced by suitable penalties.

### Section II

PARAGRAPH I. *Right of Eminent Domain.* The exercise of the right of eminent domain shall never be abridged, nor so construed as to prevent the General Assembly from taking property and franchises, and subjecting them to public use.

PARAGRAPH II. *Police Power.* The exercise of the police

power of the State shall never be abridged, nor so construed as to permit the conduct of business in such manner as to infringe the equal rights of others, or the general wellbeing of the State.

## Section III

PARAGRAPH I. *Charters Revived or Amended Subject to Constitution.* The General Assembly shall not remit the forfeiture of the charter of any corporation now existing, nor alter or amend the same, nor pass any other general or special law, for the benefit of said corporation, except upon the condition that such corporation shall thereafter hold its charter subject to the provisions of this Constitution; and every amendment of any charter of any corporation in this State, or any special law for its benefit, accepted thereby, shall operate as a novation of said charter and shall bring the same under the provision of this Constitution.

## Section IV

PARAGRAPH I. *Contracts to Defeat Competition.* All contracts and agreements, which may have the effect, or be intended to have the effect, to defeat or lessen competition, or to encourage monopoly, shall be illegal and void. The General Assembly of this State shall have no power to authorize any such contract or agreement.

PARAGRAPH II. *General Assembly to Enforce Article.* The General Assembly shall enforce the provisions of this Article by appropriate legislation.

PARAGRAPH III. *Public Service Commission as Constitutional Officers.* There shall be a Public Service Commission for the regulation of utilities, vested with the jurisdiction, powers and duties now provided by law or that may hereafter be prescribed by the General Assembly, not inconsistent with other provisions of this Constitution. Such Commission shall consist of five members, who shall be elected by the people. A Chairman shall be selected by the members of the Commission from its membership. The first Commission under this amendment shall consist of the commissioners in office at the time of the adoption of this Constitutional amendment and they shall serve until December 31st after the general election at which the successor of each member is elected.

*The Constitution of Georgia*

Thereafter all succeeding terms of members shall be for six years. The qualifications, compensations, filling of vacancies, manner and time of election, power and duties of members of the Commission, including the chairman shall be such as are now or may hereafter be provided by the General Assembly.

SECTION V

PARAGRAPH I. *Wife's Separate Estate.* All property of the wife at the time of her marriage, and all property given to, inherited or acquired by her, shall remain her separate property, and not be liable for the debts of her husband.

SECTION VI

PARAGRAPH I. *Nonresident Insurance Companies.* All life insurance companies now doing business in this State, or which may desire to establish agencies and do business in the State of Georgia, chartered by other States of the Union, or foreign States, shall show that they have deposited with the Comptroller General of the State in which they are chartered, or of this State, the Insurance Commissioner, or such other officer as may be authorized to receive it, not less than one hundred thousand dollars, in such securities as may be deemed by such officer equivalent to cash, subject to his order, as a guarantee fund for the security of policy-holders.

PARAGRAPH II. *License by Comptroller General.* When such showing is made to the Comptroller General of the State of Georgia by a proper certificate from the State official having charge of the funds so deposited, the Comptroller General of the State of Georgia is authorized to issue to the company making such showing, a license to do business in the State, upon paying the fees required by law.

PARAGRAPH III. *Resident Insurance Companies; Guarantee Fund.* All life insurance companies chartered by the State of Georgia, or which may hereafter be chartered by the State, shall, before doing business, deposit with the Comptroller General of the State of Georgia, or with some strong corporation, which may be approved by said Comptroller General, one hundred thousand dollars, in such securities as may be deemed by him equivalent to cash, to be subject to his order, as a guarantee fund for the security of the policy-holders of

# A Constitutional History of Georgia

the company making such deposit, all interest and dividends from such securities to be paid, when due, to the company so depositing. Any such securities as may be needed or desired by the company may be taken from said department at any time by replacing them with other securities equally acceptable to the Comptroller General, whose certificate for the same shall be furnished to the company.

PARAGRAPH IV. *General Assembly to Enact Laws for People's Protection, Etc.* The General Assembly shall, from time to time enact laws to compel all fire insurance companies, doing business in this State, whether chartered by this State, or otherwise, to deposit reasonable securities with the Treasurer of this State, to secure the people against loss by the operations of said companies.

PARAGRAPH V. *Reports By Insurance Companies.* The General Assembly shall compel all insurance companies in this State, or doing business therein, under proper penalties, to make annual reports to the Comptroller General, and print the same at their own expense, for the information and protection of the people.

## ARTICLE V
## EXECUTIVE DEPARTMENT
### Section I

PARAGRAPH I. *Governor; Term of Office; Salary, Etc.* The executive power shall be vested in a Governor, who shall hold his office during the term of four years, and until his successor shall be chosen and qualified. The Governor serving at the time of the adoption of this constitution and future Governors shall not be eligible to succeed themselves and shall not be eligible to hold the office until after the expiration of four years from the conclusion of his term of office. He shall have a salary of seven thousand five hundred dollars per annum until January 1, 1947. The salary of the Governor for each year thereafter shall be twelve thousand dollars per annum until otherwise provided by a law passed by a majority vote of both branches of the General Assembly, which shall not be increased or diminished during the period for which he shall have been elected; nor shall he receive, within that time, any other emolument from the United States, or either of them, or from any foreign power. The

## The Constitution of Georgia

State officers, required by this Constitution to be elected at the same time, for the same term, and in the same manner as the Governor shall also hold office for four years.

PARAGRAPH II. *Election for Governor.* The first election for Governor, under this Constitution, shall be held on Tuesday after the first Monday in November of 1946, and the Governor-elect shall be installed in office at the next session of the General Assembly. An election shall take place quadrennially thereafter, on said date, until another date be fixed by the General Assembly. Said election shall be held at the places of holding general elections in the several counties of this State, in the manner prescribed for the election of members of the General Assembly, and the electors shall be the same.

PARAGRAPH III. *Returns of Elections.* The returns for every election of Governor shall be sealed up by the managers, separately from other returns, and directed to the President of the Senate and Speaker of the House of Representatives, and transmitted to the Secretary of State, who shall, without opening said returns, cause the same to be laid before the Senate on the day after the two houses shall have been organized, and they shall be transmitted by the Senate to the House of Representatives.

PARAGRAPH IV. *How Returns Published.* The members of each branch of the General Assembly shall convene in the Representative Hall, and the President of the Senate and Speaker of the House of Representatives shall open and publish the returns in the presence and under the direction of the General Assembly; and the person having the majority of the whole number of votes, shall be declared duly elected Governor of this State; but, if no person shall have such majority, then from the two persons having the highest number of votes, who shall be in life, and shall not decline an election at the time appointed for the General Assembly to elect, the General Assembly shall immediately, elect a Governor viva voce; and in all cases of election of a Governor by the General Assembly, a majority of the members present shall be necessary to a choice.

PARAGRAPH V. *Contested Elections.* Contested elections shall be determined by both houses of the General Assembly in such manner as shall be prescribed by law.

PARAGRAPH VI. *Qualifications of Governor.* No person

shall be eligible to the office of Governor, who shall not have been a citizen of the United States fifteen years, and a citizen of the State six years, and who shall not have attained the age of thirty years.

PARAGRAPH VII. *Lieutenant Governor. Succession to Executive Power.* There shall be a Lieutenant Governor, who shall be elected at the same time, for the same term, and in the same manner as the Governor. He shall be President of the Senate, and shall receive the sum of $2,000.00 per annum. In case of the death, resignation, or disability of the Governor, the Lieutenant Governor shall exercise the executive power and receive the compensation of the Governor until the next general election for members of the General Assembly, at which a successor to the Governor shall be elected for the unexpired term; but if such death, resignation, or disability shall occur within thirty days of the next general election, or if the term will expire within ninety days after the next general election, the Lieutenant Governor shall exercise the executive power and receive the compensation of the Governor for the unexpired term. If the Lieutenant Governor shall become a candidate for the unexpired term of the Governor, he shall thereby resign his office as Lieutenant Governor, effective upon the qualification of the Governor elected for the unexpired term, and his successor for the unexpired term shall be elected at such election. In case of the death, resignation, or disability of both the Governor and the Lieutenant Governor, the Speaker of the House of Representatives shall exercise the executive power until the removal of the disability or the election and qualification of a Governor at a special election, which shall be held within sixty days from the date on which the Speaker of the House of Representatives shall assume the executive power. A Lieutenant Governor shall be elected at the general election in 1946 and shall qualify at the same time as the Governor. Until the qualification of a Lieutenant Governor the provisions of Article V, Section I, Paragraph VIII of the Constitution of Georgia of 1877 shall remain of full force and effect.

PARAGRAPH VIII. *Unexpired Terms, Filling of.* The General Assembly shall have power to provide by law, for filling unexpired terms by special elections, except as provided in this Constitution.

## The Constitution of Georgia

PARAGRAPH IX. *Oath of Office.* The Governor shall, before he enters on the duties of his office, take the following oath or affirmation: "I do solemnly swear (or affirm, as the case may be) that I will faithfully execute the office of Governor of the State of Georgia, and will, to the best of my ability, preserve, protect, and defend the Constitution thereof, and the Constitution of the United States of America."

PARAGRAPH X. *Commander-in-Chief.* The Governor shall be commander-in-chief of the army and navy of this State, and of the militia thereof.

PARAGRAPH XI. *Reprieves and Pardons; State Board of Pardons and Paroles.* The Governor shall have power to suspend the execution of a sentence of death, after conviction, for offenses against the State, until the State Board of Pardons and Paroles, hereinafter provided, shall have an opportunity of hearing the application of the convicted person for any relief within the power of such Board, or for any other purpose which may be deemed necessary by the Governor. Upon conviction for treason the Governor may only suspend the execution of the sentence and report the case to the General Assembly at the next meeting thereof, when the General Assembly shall either pardon, commute the sentence, direct its execution or grant a further reprieve. The Governor shall, at each session of the General Assembly, communicate to that body each case of suspension of sentence, stating the name of the convict, the offense for which he was convicted, the sentence and its date, the date of the reprieve or suspension, and the reasons for granting the same. He shall take care that the laws are faithfully executed, and shall be a conservator of the peace throughout the State. There shall be a State Board of Pardons and Paroles composed of three members, who shall be appointed by the Governor and confirmed by the Senate. Appointments made at times when the Senate is not in session shall be effective ad interim. The first members shall be appointed for terms of three, five, and seven years, respectively, to be designated by the Governor, and all subsequent appointments shall be for a period of seven years, except in case of an unexpired term. The Governor shall not be a member of the State Board of Pardons and Paroles. The members of the State Board of Pardons and Paroles shall each receive an annual salary of $5,000.00, payable monthly. The State

## A Constitutional History of Georgia

Board of Pardons and Paroles shall have power to grant reprieves, pardons and paroles, to commute penalties, remove disabilities imposed by law, and may remit any part of a sentence for any offense against the State, after conviction except in cases of treason or impeachment, and except in cases in which the Governor refuses to suspend a sentence of death. Provided that such board shall act on all applications within 90 days from the filing of same, and in all cases a majority shall decide the action of the Board. Except if any member for any cause is unable to serve in any case involving capital punishment, the Governor shall act as the third member of said Board and the action so taken in such instance shall be by unanimous vote. The State Board of Pardons and Paroles shall at each session of the General Assembly communicate to that body in full detail each case of pardon, parole, commutation, removal of disabilities or remission of sentences granted, stating the name of the convict, the offense for which he was convicted, the sentence and its date, the date of the pardon, parole, commutation, removal of disabilities or remission of sentence and the reasons for granting the same, and the State Board of Pardons and Paroles may make rules and regulations as may be authorized by law. The first Board of Pardons and Paroles under this provision may be those in office under an act of the General Assembly creating such a Board existing at the time of the adoption of this amendment, which, if so existing shall be in lieu of such a Board to be created by the General Assembly subsequent to the adoption of this amendment, and which Board shall have all the rights, privileges, powers, and duties the same as if it was so subsequently created, and the terms of members of such Board shall date from the time specified in the existing Act of the General Assembly. The General Assembly may enact laws in aid of, but not inconsistent with, this amendment.

PARAGRAPH XII. *Writs of Election; Called Sessions of the General Assembly.* The Governor shall issue writs of election to fill all vacancies that may happen in the Senate and the House of Representatives, and shall give the General Assembly, from time to time, information of the State of the Commonwealth, and recommend to their consideration such measures as he may deem necessary or expedient. The Governor

## The Constitution of Georgia

shall have power to convoke the General Assembly on extraordinary occasions, but no law shall be enacted at called sessions of the General Assembly, except such as shall relate to the object stated in his proclamation convening them; providing that such called sessions of the General Assembly shall not exceed 70 days in length, unless at the expiration of said period there shall be pending an impeachment trial of some officer of the State Government in which event the General Assembly will be authorized to remain in session until such trial shall have been completed.

Provided, however, that when three-fifths of the members elected to the House of Representatives and three-fifths of the members elected to the Senate shall have certified to the Governor of the State of Georgia that in their opinion an emergency exists in the affairs of the State of Georgia, it shall thereupon be the duty of said Governor and mandatory upon him, within five days from the receipt of such certificate or certificates, to convene said General Assembly in extraordinary session for all purposes; and in the event said Governor shall, within said time, Sundays excluded, fail or refuse to convene said General Assembly as aforesaid, then and in that event said General Assembly may convene itself in extraordinary session, as if convened in regular session, for all purposes, provided that such extraordinary, self convened session shall be limited to a period of 30 days, unless at the expiration of said period, there shall be pending an impeachment trial of some officer of the State Government, in which event the General Assembly shall be authorized to remain in session until such trial shall have been completed.

The members of the General Assembly shall receive the same per diem and mileage during such extraordinary session as is now or may be hereafter provided.

PARAGRAPH XIII. *Filling Vacancies.* When any office shall become vacant, by death, resignation, or otherwise, the Governor shall have power to fill such vacancy, unless otherwise provided by law; and persons so appointed shall continue in office until a successor is commissioned, agreeably to the mode pointed out by this Constitution, or by law in pursuance thereof.

PARAGRAPH XIV. *Appointments Rejected.* A person once rejected by the Senate, shall not be reappointed by the Governor to the same office during the same session, or the recess thereafter.

PARAGRAPH XV. *Governor's Veto.* The Governor shall have the revision of all bills passed by the General Assembly before the same shall become laws, but two-thirds of each house may pass a law notwithstanding his dissent; and if any bill should not be returned by the Governor within five days (Sunday excepted) after it has been presented to him, the same shall be a law; unless the General Assembly, by their adjournment, shall prevent its return. He may approve any appropriation, and disapprove any other appropriation, in the same bill, and the latter shall not be effectual, unless passed by two-thirds of each House.

PARAGRAPH XVI. *Governor to Approve Resolutions, Etc.* Every vote, resolution, or order, to which the concurrence of both houses may be necessary, except on a question of election or adjournment, shall be presented to the Governor, and before it shall take effect be approved by him, or, being disapproved, shall be repassed by two-thirds of each house, provided, however, that nothing contained in this Article shall be construed to confer on the Governor the right to veto or enter his disapproval of any proposal made by the General Assembly to amend this Constitution.

PARAGRAPH XVII. *Information From Officers and Employees; Suspension of Officers.* The Governor may require information in writing from Constitutional officers, department heads, and all State employees, on any subject relating to the duties of their respective offices or employment. The General Assembly shall have authority to provide by law for the suspension of any Constitutional officer or departmental head from the discharge of the duties of his office, and also for the appointment of a suitable person to discharge the duties of the same.

SECTION II

Other Executive Officers

PARAGRAPH I. *Executive Officers, How Elected.* The Secretary of State, Attorney General, State School Superintendent, Comptroller General, Treasurer, Commissioner of Agriculture, and Commissioner of Labor shall be elected by the persons qualified to vote for members of the General Assembly

## The Constitution of Georgia

at the same time, and in the same manner as the Governor. The provisions of the Constitution as to the transmission of the returns of the election, counting the votes, declaring the results, deciding when there is no election, and when there is a contested election, applicable to the election of Governor, shall apply to the election of the above named executive officers; they shall be commissioned by the Governor and hold their offices for the same time as the Governor.

PARAGRAPH II. *Duties, Authority, and Salaries of Other Executive Officers.* The General Assembly shall have power to prescribe the duties, authority, and salaries of the executive officers, and to provide help and expenses necessary for the operation of the department of each.

PARAGRAPH III. *Profit From Use of Public Money.* No State official shall be allowed, directly or indirectly, to receive any fee, interest, or reward from any person, bank, or corporation, for the deposit, or use, in any manner, of the public funds, and the General Assembly shall enforce this provision by suitable penalties.

PARAGRAPH IV. *Qualifications.* No person shall be eligible to the office of the Secretary of State, Attorney General, State School Superintendent, Comptroller General, Treasurer, Commissioner of Agriculture, and Commissioner of Labor, unless he shall have been a citizen of the United States for ten years, and shall have resided in this State for six years next preceding his election, and shall be twenty-five years of age when elected. All of said officers shall give bond and security, under regulation to be prescribed by law, for the faithful discharge of their duties.

PARAGRAPH V. *Fees and Perquisites Denied.* No State official named in Paragraph I of this Section shall be allowed any fee, perquisite or compensation other than their salaries as prescribed by law, except their necessary expenses when absent from the seat of government on business for the State.

### SECTION III

PARAGRAPH I. *Great Seal; What Constitutes; Custody; When Affixed to Instruments.* The great seal of the State shall be deposited in the office of the Secretary of State and shall not be affixed to any instrument of writing except by order of the Governor or General Assembly, and that now in use shall be the great seal of the State until otherwise provided by law.

## Section IV

PARAGRAPH I. *Game and Fish Commission.* There is hereby created a State Game and Fish Commission. Said Commission shall consist of one member from each Congressional District in this State, and one additional member from one of the following named counties, to-wit: Chatham, Bryan, Liberty, McIntosh, Glynn, or Camden. The first members of the Commission shall consist of those in office at the time this Constitution is adopted, with terms provided by law. Thereafter, all succeeding appointments shall be made by the Governor and confirmed by the Senate for a term of seven years from the expiration of the previous term. All members of the Commission shall hold office until their successors are appointed and qualified. Vacancies in office shall be filled by appointment of the Governor and submitted to the Senate for confirmation at the next session of the General Assembly after the making of the appointment.

The Commission shall have such powers, authority, duties, and shall receive such compensation and expenses as may be delegated or provided for by the General Assembly.

## Section V
## State Board of Corrections

PARAGRAPH I. *State Board of Corrections; How Composed, Director.* There shall be a State Board of Corrections composed of five members in charge of the State Penal System. The Board shall have such jurisdiction, powers, duties and control of the State Penal System and the inmates thereof as shall be provided by law. The Board shall elect a Director of Corrections who shall be the executive officer of the Board. The Board of Corrections shall be appointed by the Governor with the consent of the Senate. The first appointment shall be for terms of one, two, three, four and five years and their successors shall be appointed for terms of five years each. The compensation of the Director and members of the Board shall be fixed by law.

# The Constitution of Georgia

## Section VI
### State Department of Veterans Service

PARAGRAPH I. *Veterans Service Board; How Composed; Director.* There shall be a State Department of Veteran Service and Veterans Service Board composed of seven members, who shall have such control, duties, powers and jurisdictions of the State Department of Veterans Service as shall be provided by law. Said Board shall appoint a director who shall be the executive officer of the Department. Members of the Board shall be appointed by the Governor with the advice and consent of the Senate and all members of the Board and the Director shall be veterans of some war in which the United States has engaged.

The first appointments shall be for terms of one, two, three, four, five, six and seven years. Thereafter all terms and appointments, except in case of vacancy, shall be for seven years. Vacancies shall be filled by appointment of the Governor.

# ARTICLE VI
## *JUDICIARY*
### Section I

PARAGRAPH I. *Courts Enumerated.* The judicial powers of this State shall be vested in a Supreme Court, a Court of Appeals, Superior Courts, Courts of Ordinary, Justices of the Peace, Notaries Public who are ex-officio Justices of the Peace, and such other Courts as have been or may be established by law.

### Section II

PARAGRAPH I. *Supreme Court Justices; Quorum.* The Supreme Court shall consist of seven associate justices, who shall from time to time as they may deem proper, elect one of their member as Chief Justice, and one as Presiding Justice; the office of Chief Justice as it has heretofore existed under this Constitution being hereby converted into the office of an associate justice, with the same right of incumbency and the same succession as to terms, as applied to the former office. The Chief Justice so elected by the other Justices shall be the chief presiding and administrative officer of the court, and the Presiding Justice, elected in like manner, shall perform all the duties devolving upon the Chief Justice, when he is absent or disqualified. A majority of the court shall constitute a quorum.

PARAGRAPH II. *Court to Designate Judges to Preside, When; Means for Supreme Court to Prevent Delay in Congested Dockets.* When one or more of the Justices of the Supreme Court are disqualified from deciding any case by interest or otherwise, the qualified Justices shall designate a judge or judges of the Superior Court to preside in said case, provided, that if all the justices are disqualified, they or a majority of them shall, despite their disqualification, select seven judges of the superior court to preside in the cause, but they shall make such selections by lot and in open court from not less than twelve names of such superior court judges.

PARAGRAPH III. *Terms of Office.* The Justices aforesaid shall hold their offices for six years, and until their successors are qualified. They shall be elected by the people at the same time and in the same manner as members of the General Assembly; provided, that the successors to the two incumbents whose terms will expire on December 31, 1946, shall be elected for the succeeding terms at the time of electing members of the General Assembly during that year; successors to the two incumbents whose terms will expire on December 31, 1948, shall be elected in like manner during that year; successors to the two incumbents whose terms will expire on December 31, 1950, shall be elected in like manner during that year and provided further that an additional or seventh Justice shall be immediately appointed by the Governor, his tenure under such appointment to expire on December 31, 1946, and his successor for the ensuing regular term of six years to be elected at the time and in the manner aforesaid at such general election to be held during that year; and all terms (except unexpired terms) shall be for six years. In case of any vacancy which causes an unexpired term, the same shall be filled by executive appointment, and the person appointed by the Governor shall hold his office until the next regular election, and until his successor for the balance of the unexpired term shall have been elected

## The Constitution of Georgia

and qualified. The return of such elections shall be made to the Secretary of State, who shall certify the result to the Governor, and commission shall issue accordingly.

PARAGRAPH IV. *Jurisdiction of Supreme Court.* The Supreme Court shall have no original jurisdiction but shall be a court alone for the trial and correction of errors of law from the superior courts and the city courts of Atlanta and Savannah, as existed on August 16, 1916, and such other like courts as have been or may hereafter be established in other cities, in all cases that involve the construction of the Constitution of the State of Georgia or of the United States, or of treaties between the United States and foreign governments; in all cases in which the constitutionality of any law of the State of Georgia or of the United States is drawn in question; and, until otherwise provided by law, in all cases respecting title to land; in all equity cases; in all cases which involve the validity of, or the construction of wills; in all cases of conviction of a capital felony; in all habeas corpus cases; in all cases involving extraordinary remedies; in all divorce and alimony cases, and in all cases certified to it by the Court of Appeals for its determination. It shall also be competent for the Supreme Court to require by certiorari or otherwise any case to be certified to the Supreme Court from the Court of Appeals for review and determination with the same power and authority as if the case had been carried by writ of error to the Supreme Court. Any case carried to the Supreme Court or to the Court of Appeals, which belongs to the class of which the other court has jurisdiction, shall, until otherwise provided by law, be transferred to the other court under such rules as the Supreme Court may prescribe, and the case so transferred shall be heard and determined by the court which has jurisdiction thereof. The General Assembly may provide for carrying cases or certain classes of cases to the Supreme Court and the Court of Appeals from the trial courts otherwise than by writ of error, and may prescribe conditions as to the right of a party litigant to have his case reviewed by the Supreme Court or Court of Appeals. The Supreme Court shall also have jurisdiction of and shall decide cases transferred to it by the Court of Appeals because of an equal division between the judges of that Court when sitting as a body for the determination of cases.

PARAGRAPH V. *Cases, How Disposed Of.* The Supreme Court and the Court of Appeals shall dispose of every case at the term for which it is entered on the court's docket for hearing, as provided by Paragraph VIII of this Article and Section, or at the next term. If the plaintiff in error shall not be prepared to prosecute the case at the term for which it is so entered for hearing, unless prevented by providential cause, it shall be stricken from the docket and the judgment below shall stand affirmed. No writ of error shall be dismissed because of delay in transmission of the bill of exceptions and the copy of the record, or either of them, resulting from the default of the clerk or other cause, unless it shall appear that the plaintiff in error or his counsel caused such delay. Nothing herein shall be construed to excuse the clerk for any omission of duty or to relieve him of any liability resulting therefrom.

PARAGRAPH VI. *Judgments May Be Withheld.* In any case the Court may in its discretion withhold its judgment until the next term after the same is argued.

PARAGRAPH VII. *The Supreme Court; How Cases To Be Heard and Determined.* The Supreme Court shall have power to hear and determine cases when sitting in a body, under such regulations as may be prescribed by it.

PARAGRAPH VIII. *Court of Appeals.* The Court of Appeals shall consist of the Judges provided therefor by law at the time of the ratification of this amendment, and of such additional Judges as the General Assembly shall from time to time prescribe. All terms of the Judges of the Court of Appeals after the expiration of the terms of the Judges provided for by law at the time of the ratification of this amendment, except unexpired terms, shall continue six years, and until their successors are qualified. The times and manner of electing Judges, and the mode of filling a vacancy which causes an unexpired term, shall be the same as are or may be provided for by the laws relating to the election and appointment of Justices of the Supreme Court. The Court of Appeals shall have jurisdiction for the trial and correction of errors of law from the superior courts and from the City Courts of Atlanta and Savannah, as they existed on August 19, 1916, and such other like courts as have been or may hereafter be established in other cities, in all cases in which

## The Constitution of Georgia

such jurisdiction has not been conferred by this Constitution upon the Supreme Court, and in such other cases as may hereafter be prescribed by law; except that where a case is pending in the Court of Appeals and the Court of Appeals desires instruction from the Supreme Court, it may certify the same to the Supreme Court, and thereupon a transcript of the record shall be transmitted to the Supreme Court, which, after having afforded to the parties an opportunity to be heard thereon, shall instruct the Court of Appeals on the question so certified, and the Court of Appeals shall be bound by the instruction so given. But if by reason of equal division of opinion among the Justices of the Supreme Court no such instruction is given, the Court of Appeals may decide the question. The manner of certifying questions to the Supreme Court by the Court of Appeals, and the subsequent proceedings in regard to the same in the Supreme Court, shall be as the Supreme Court shall by its rules prescribe, until otherwise provided by law. No affirmance of the judgment of the court below in cases pending in the Court of Appeals shall result from delay in disposing of questions or cases certified from the Court of Appeals to the Supreme Court, or as to which such certificate has been required by the Supreme Court as hereinbefore provided. All writs of error in the Supreme Court or the Court of Appeals, when received by its clerk during a term of the Court and before the docket of the term is by order of the Court closed, shall be entered thereon, and when received at any other time, shall be entered on the docket of the next term; and they shall stand for hearing at the term for which they are so entered, under such rules as the Court may prescribe, until otherwise provided by law. The Court of Appeals shall appoint a clerk and a sheriff of the court. The reporter of the Supreme Court shall be reporter of the Court of Appeals until otherwise provided by law. The laws relating to the Supreme Court as to qualifications and salaries of Judges, the designation of other Judges to preside when members of the Court are disqualified, the powers, duties, salaries, fees and terms of officers, the mode of carrying cases to the Court, the powers, practice, procedure, times of sitting, and costs of the Court, the publication of reports of cases decided therein, and in all other respects, except as otherwise provided in this Constitution or by the laws as to the Court of Appeals at the time of the ratification of this amendment, and until otherwise provided by law, shall apply to the Court of Appeals so far as they can be made to apply. The decisions of the Supreme Court shall bind the Court of Appeals as precedents. The Court of Appeals shall have power to hear and determine cases when sitting in a body, except as may be otherwise provided by the General Assembly.

In the event of an equal division of judges on any case when the Court is sitting as a body, the case shall be immediately transferred to the Supreme Court.

SECTION III

Superior Courts

PARAGRAPH I. *Terms, Etc., of Superior Court Judges.* There shall be a judge of the Superior Courts for each judicial circuit, whose term of office shall be for four years, and until his successor is qualified. He may act in other circuits when authorized by law. The legislature shall have authority to add one or more additional judges of the superior court for any judicial circuit in this State, and shall have authority to regulate the manner in which the judges of such circuits shall dispose of the business thereof, and shall fix the time at which the term or terms of office of such additional judge or judges shall begin, and the manner of his appointment or election, and shall have authority from time to time to add to the number of such judges in any judicial circuit; or to reduce the number of judges in any judicial circuit; provided that at all times there shall be at least one judge in every judicial circuit of this State.

PARAGRAPH II. *Elections, When to Be Held.* The successors to the present and subsequent incumbents shall be elected by the electors of the whole State entitled to vote for members of the General Assembly, at the general election held for such members, next preceding the expiration of their respective terms.

PARAGRAPH III. *Terms Begin, When.* The terms of the judges to be elected under the Constitution, except to fill vacancies, shall begin on the first day of January after their elections. Every vacancy occasioned by death, resignation, or

## The Constitution of Georgia

other causes shall be filled by appointments of the Governor until the first day of January after the general election held next after the expiration of thirty days from the time such vacancy occurs, at which election a successor for the unexpired term shall be elected.

### Section IV

Paragraph I. *Exclusive Jurisdiction.* The Superior Courts shall have exclusive jurisdiction in cases of divorce; in criminal cases where the offender is subjected to loss of life, or confinement in the penitentiary, in cases respecting titles to land, and equity cases.

Paragraph II. *Equity May Be Merged in Common Law Courts.* The General Assembly may confer upon the Courts of common law all the powers heretofore exercised by Courts of equity in this State.

Paragraph III. *General Jurisdiction.* Said Courts shall have jurisdiction in all civil cases, except as hereinafter provided.

Paragraph IV. *Appellate Jurisdiction.* They shall have appellate jurisdiction in all such cases as may be provided by law.

Paragraph V. *Certiorari, Mandamus, Etc.* They shall have power to correct errors in inferior judicatories by writ of certiorari, which shall only issue on the sanction of the Judge, and said Courts, and the judges thereof shall have power to issue writs of mandamus, prohibition, scire facias, and all other writs that may be necessary for carrying their powers fully into effect, and shall have such other powers as are, or may be conferred on them by law.

Paragraph VI. *New Trials.* The Superior and City Courts may grant new trials on legal grounds.

Paragraph VII. *Judgment of the Court.* The Court shall render judgment without the verdict of a jury in all civil cases, except actions ex delicto, where no issuable defense is filed except as otherwise provided in this Constitution, and subject to the right of trial by a jury on written demand of either party.

Paragraph VIII. *Sessions.* The Superior courts shall sit in each county not less than twice in each year, at such times as have been, or may be appointed by law. The judges of said courts may, on reasonable notice to the parties, at any time, in vacation, at chambers, hear and determine, by interlocutory or final judgment, any matter or issue, where a jury verdict is not required, or may be waived.

PARAGRAPH IX. *Presiding Judge Disqualified.* The General Assembly may provide by law for the appointment of some proper person to preside in cases where the presiding judge is from any cause disqualified.

### SECTION V

PARAGRAPH I. *Judges of Superior and City Courts May Alternate, When.* In any county within which there is, or hereafter may be, a city Court the Judge of said Court, and of the Superior Court may preside in the Courts of each other in cases where the judge of either Court is disqualified to preside.

### SECTION VI

PARAGRAPH I. *Appeals From Ordinary.* The powers of a Court of Ordinary and of Probate shall be vested in an Ordinary for each county, from whose decision there may be an appeal, or by consent of parties, without a decision to the Superior Court under regulations prescribed by law.

PARAGRAPH II. *Powers.* The courts of ordinary shall have such powers in relation to roads, bridges, ferries, public buildings, paupers, county officers, county funds, county taxes and other county matters as may be conferred on them by law.

The court of ordinary shall have jurisdiction to issue warrants, try cases, and impose sentences thereon in all misdemeanor cases arising under the Act known as the Georgia State Highway Patrol Act of 1937, and other traffic laws, and in all cases arising under the Compulsory School Attendance law in all counties of this State in which there is no city or county court, provided the defendant waives a jury trial. Like jurisdiction is also conferred upon the judges of the police courts of incorporated cities and municipal court judges for offense arising under the act known as the Georgia State Highway Patrol Act of 1937, and other traffic laws of the State within their respective jurisdiction.

PARAGRAPH III. *Term of Office.* The Ordinary shall hold

## The Constitution of Georgia

his office for the term of four years and until his successor is elected and qualified.

### Section VII
### Justices of the Peace

PARAGRAPH I. *Number and Term of Office.* There shall be in each militia district one justice of the peace, whose official term, except when elected to fill an unexpired term, shall be for four years: Provided, however, that the General Assembly may, in its discretion, abolish justice courts and the office of justice of the peace and of notary public ex-officio justice of the peace in any city of this State having a population of over twenty thousand, and establish in lieu thereof such court or courts or system of courts as the General Assembly may, in its discretion, deem necessary, conferring upon such new court or courts or system of courts, when so established, the jurisdiction as to subject matter now exercised by justice courts and by justices of the peace and notaries public ex-officio justices of the peace, together with such additional jurisdiction, either as to amount or subject-matter, as may be provided by law, whereof some other court has not exclusive jurisdiction under this Constitution; together with such provision as to rules and procedure in such courts, and as to new trials and the correction of errors in and by said courts, and with such further provision for the correction of errors by the Superior Court, or Court of Appeals, or the Supreme Court, as the General Assembly may, from time to time, in its discretion, provide or authorize. Any court so established shall not be subject to the rules of uniformity laid down in Paragraph I of Section IX of Article VI of the Constitution of Georgia: Provided, however, that the General Assembly may, in its discretion, abolish justice courts and the office of justice of the peace and notary public ex-officio justice of the peace in any county in this State having within its borders a city having a population of over twenty thousand, and as well in the County of Glynn, and establish in lieu thereof such court or courts or system of courts as the General Assembly may, in its discretion, deem necessary; or conferring upon existing courts, by extension of their jurisdiction as to subject matter now exercised by justice courts and by justices of the peace and notaries public ex-officio justices of the peace; together with such additional jurisdiction, either as to amount or to subject-matter, as may be provided by law, whereof some other court has not exclusive jurisdiction under this Constitution; together also with such provisions as to rules and procedure in such courts and as to new trials and the correction of errors in and by said courts, and with such further provision for the correction of errors by the Superior Court or the Court of Appeals or the Supreme Court as the General Assembly may, from time to time, in its discretion, provide or authorize. The civil court of Fulton County shall have jurisdiction in Fulton County and outside the city limits of Atlanta either concurrently with, or supplemental to, or in lieu of justice courts, as may be now or hereafter provided by law. Any court so established shall not be subject to the rules of uniformity laid down in Paragraph I of Section IX of Article VI of the Constitution of Georgia.

PARAGRAPH II. *Jurisdiction.* Justices of the peace shall have jurisdiction in all civil cases arising ex contractu and in cases of injury or damage to and conversion of personal property, when the principal sum does not exceed two hundred dollars, and shall sit monthly at fixed times and places but in all cases there may be an appeal to a jury in said court, or an appeal to the Superior Court under such regulation as may be prescribed by law.

PARAGRAPH III. *Elections and Commissions.* Justices of the peace shall be elected by the legal voters in their respective districts, and shall be commissioned by the Governor. They shall be removable on conviction for malpractice in office.

## SECTION VIII
## Notaries Public

PARAGRAPH I. *Appointment; Number; Term; Removal.* Commissioned notaries public, not to exceed one for each militia district, may be appointed by the judges of the Superior Courts in their respective circuits, upon recommendation of the grand juries of the several counties. They shall be commissioned by the Governor for the term of four years and shall be ex-officio justices of the peace, and shall be removable on conviction for malpractice in office.

# The Constitution of Georgia

## Section IX
## Uniformity of Courts

PARAGRAPH I. *Uniformity Provided For.* Except as otherwise provided in this Constitution, the jurisdiction, powers, proceedings and practice of all courts or officers invested with judicial powers (except City Courts) of the same grade or class, so far as regulated by law, and the force and effect of the process, judgment and decree, by such courts, severally, shall be uniform. This uniformity must be established by the General Assembly, and in case of City Courts, may be established by the General Assembly.

## Section X
## Attorney General

PARAGRAPH I. *Election; Term of Office.* There shall be an Attorney General of this State, who shall be elected by the people at the same time, for the same term and in the same manner as the Governor.

PARAGRAPH II. *Duties.* It shall be the duty of the Attorney General to act as the legal adviser of the Executive Department, to represent the State in the Supreme Court in all Capital felonies; and in all Civil and Criminal Cases in any Court when required by the Governor and to perform such other services as shall be required of him by law.

## Section XI
## Solicitors General

PARAGRAPH I. *Number; Term of Office; Vacancies.* There shall be a solicitor general for each judicial circuit, whose official term (except to fill a vacancy) shall be four years. The successors of present and subsequent incumbents shall be elected by the electors of the whole State, qualified to vote for members of the General Assembly, at the general election held next preceding the expiration of their respective terms. Every vacancy occasioned by death, resignation, or other cause shall be filled by appointment of the Governor, until the first day of January after the general election held next after the expiration of 30 days from the time such vacancy occurs, at which election a successor for the unexpired term shall be elected.

# A Constitutional History of Georgia

PARAGRAPH II. *Duties.* It shall be the duty of the Solicitor General to represent the State in all cases in the Superior Courts of his Circuit and in all cases taken up from the superior courts of his Circuit to the Supreme Court, and Court of Appeals and to perform such other services as shall be required of him by law.

## SECTION XII
### Salaries of Justices, Judges and Solicitors General

PARAGRAPH I. *Salaries of Justices, Judges and Solicitors General.* The Justices of the Supreme Court each shall have out of the treasury of the State salaries of $8,000 per annum; the Judges of the Court of Appeals each shall have out of the treasury of the State salaries of $8,000 per annum, the Judges of the Superior Courts each shall have out of the treasury of the State salaries of $6,000 per annum and the Solicitors General shall each have out of the treasury of the State a salary of $250.00 per annum with the right of the General Assembly to authorize any county to supplement the salary of a judge of the Superior Court and Solicitor General of the Judicial Circuit in which such county lies, out of county funds, provided, however, where such salary is, at the time of the adoption of this Constitution, being supplemented out of county funds under existing laws, such laws shall remain in force until altered by the General Assembly. Provided further, that the Board of County Commissioners of Richmond County, or the Ordinary, or such other board or person as may from time to time have charge of the fiscal affairs of said county, shall without further legislative action continue to supplement from said County's treasury, the salary of the judge of Superior Court of the circuit of which the said County of Richmond is a part, by the sum of Two Thousand ($2,000) Dollars per annum, which shall be in addition to the amount received by said judge out of the State treasury; and such payments are declared to be a part of the court expenses of said county, and such payment shall be made to the judge now in office during his present or subsequent terms, as well as to his successors, with the authority in the General Assembly to increase such salary from the County treasury as above provided.

## The Constitution of Georgia

PARAGRAPH II. *Powers to Abolish or Reinstate Fees of Solicitor General.* The General Assembly shall have power, at any time, by a majority vote of each branch, to abolish the fees at present accruing to the office of solicitor general in any particular judicial circuit, and in lieu thereof to prescribe a salary for such office, without regard to the uniformity of such salaries in the various circuits; and shall have the further power to determine what disposition shall be made of the fines, forfeitures and fees accruing to the office of solicitor general in any such judicial circuit where the fees are abolished; and likewise shall have the further power, if it so, desires, to abolish such salary and reestablish such fees; but in either event, when so changed, the change shall not become effective until the end of the term to which the solicitor general was elected.

### SECTION XIII
### Qualifications of Justices, Judges, Etc.

PARAGRAPH I. *Age; Citizenship; Practice of Law.* No person shall be Justice of the Supreme Court, Court of Appeals, Judge of Superior Courts, or Attorney General, unless, at the time of his election, he shall have attained the age of thirty years, and shall have been a citizen of the State three years, and have practiced law for seven years; and no person shall be hereafter elected Solicitor General, unless at the time of his election he shall have attained twenty-five years of age, shall have been a citizen of the State for three years, and shall have practiced law for three years next preceding his election.

### SECTION XIV
### Venue

PARAGRAPH I. *Divorce Cases.* Divorce cases shall be brought in the county where the defendant resides, if a resident of this State; if the defendant be not a resident of this State, then in the county in which the plaintiff resides, provided, that any person who has been a resident of any United States Army Post or military reservation within the state of Georgia for one year next preceding the filing of the petition may bring an action for divorce in any county adjacent to said United States Army Post or military reservation.

PARAGRAPH II. *Land Titles.* Cases respecting titles to land shall be tried in the county where the land lies, except where a single tract is divided by a county line, in which case the Superior Court of either county shall have jurisdiction.

PARAGRAPH III. *Equity Cases.* Equity cases shall be tried in the county where a defendant resides against whom substantial relief is prayed.

PARAGRAPH IV. *Suits Against Joint Obligors, Co-partners, Etc.* Suits against joint obligors, joint promissors, co-partners, or joint trespassers, residing in different counties, may be tried in either county.

PARAGRAPH V. *Suits Against Maker, Endorser, Etc.* Suits against the maker and endorser of promissory notes, or drawer, acceptor and endorser of foreign or inland bills of exchange, or like instruments, residing in different counties, shall be brought in the county where the maker or acceptor resides.

PARAGRAPH VI. *All Other Cases.* All other civil cases shall be tried in the county where the defendant resides, and all criminal cases shall be tried in the county where the crime was committed, except cases in the Superior Courts where the Judge is satisfied that an impartial jury cannot be obtained in such county.

## SECTION XV
## Change of Venue

PARAGRAPH I. *Power to Change Venue.* The power to change the venue in civil and criminal cases shall be vested in the Superior Courts to be exercised in such manner as has been, or shall be, provided by law.

## SECTION XVI
## Jury Trial

PARAGRAPH I. *Right of Trial By Jury.* The right of trial by jury, except where it is otherwise provided in this Constitution, shall remain inviolate, but the General Assembly may prescribe any number, not less than five, to constitute a trial, or traverse jury, except in the superior court.

PARAGRAPH II. *Selection of Jurors.* The General Assembly shall provide by law for the selection of the most experi-

## The Constitution of Georgia

enced, intelligent and upright men to serve as grand jurors, and intelligent and upright men to serve as traverse jurors. Nevertheless, the grand jurors shall be competent to serve as traverse jurors. The General Assembly shall have the power to require jury service of women also, under such regulations as the General Assembly may prescribe.

PARAGRAPH III. *Compensation of Jurors.* It shall be the duty of the General Assembly by general laws to prescribe the manner of fixing compensation of jurors in all counties in this State.

### SECTION XVII
### County Commissioners

PARAGRAPH I. *Power to Create County Commissioners.* The General Assembly shall have power to provide for the creation of county commissioners in such counties as may require them, and to define their duties.

### SECTION XVIII
### What Courts May Be Abolished

PARAGRAPH I. *Power to Abolish Courts.* All courts not specially mentioned by name in the first section of this Article may be abolished in any county at the discretion of the General Assembly.

PARAGRAPH II. *Supreme Court Cost. Pauper Oath.* The cost in the Supreme Court and Court of Appeals shall not exceed $15.00 until otherwise provided by law. Plaintiffs in error shall not be required to pay costs in said courts when the usual pauper oath is filed in the court below.

### ARTICLE VII
### FINANCE, TAXATION AND PUBLIC DEBT
### SECTION I
### Power of Taxation

PARAGRAPH I. *Taxation, a Sovereign Right.* The right of taxation is a sovereign right—inalienable, indestructible—is the life of the State, and rightfully belongs to the people in all republican governments, and neither the General Assembly, nor any, nor all other departments of the Government established by this Constitution, shall ever have the authority to irrevocably give, grant, limit, or restrain this right; and all laws, grants, contracts, and all other acts, whatsoever, by said government, or any department thereof, to affect any of these purposes, shall be, and are hereby, declared to be null and void, for every purpose whatsoever; and said right of taxation shall always be under the complete control of, and revocable by, the State, notwithstanding any gift, grant or contract, whatsoever, by the General Assembly.

The power to tax corporations and corporate property, shall not be surrendered or suspended by any contract, or grant to which the State shall be a party.

PARAGRAPH II. *Taxing Power Limited.*

1. The General Assembly shall not by vote, resolution or order, grant any donation or gratuity in favor of any person, corporation or association.

2. The General Assembly shall not grant or authorize, extra compensation to any public officer, agent or contractor after the service has been rendered or the contract entered into.

3. The levy of taxes on property for any one year by the General Assembly for all purposes, except to provide for repelling invasions, suppressing insurrections, or defending the State in time of war, shall not exceed five (5) mills on each dollar of the value of the property taxable in the State.

4. No poll tax shall be levied to exceed one dollar annually upon each poll.

PARAGRAPH III. *Uniformity; Classification of Property.* All taxes shall be levied and collected under general laws and for public purposes only. All taxation shall be uniform upon the same class of subjects within the territorial limits of the authority levying the tax. Classes of the subjects for taxation of property shall consist of tangible property and one or more classes of intangible personal property including money. The General Assembly shall have the power to classify property including money for taxation, and to adopt different rates and different methods for different classes of such property.

PARAGRAPH IV. *Exemptions From Taxation.* The General Assembly may, by law, exempt from taxation all public property; places of religious worship or burial; all institutions of purely public charity; all intangible personal property

## The Constitution of Georgia

owned by, or irrevocably held in trust for the exclusive benefit of, religious, educational and charitable institutions, no part of the net profit from the operation of which can inure to the benefit of any private person; all buildings erected for and used as a college, incorporated academy or other seminary of learning, and also all funds of property held or used as endowment by such colleges, incorporated academies or seminaries of learning, provided the same is not invested in real estate; and provided, further, that said exemptions shall only apply to such colleges, incorporated academies or other seminaries of learning as are open to the general public; provided further, that all endowments to institutions established for white people, shall be limited to white people, and all endowments to institutions established for colored people, shall be limited to colored people; the real and personal estate of any public library, and that of any other literary association, used by or connected with such library; all books and philosophical apparatus and all paintings and statuary of any company or association, kept in a public hall and not held as merchandise or for purposes of sale or gain; provided the property so exempted be not used for the purpose of private or corporate profit and income, distributable to shareholders in corporations owning such property or to other owners of such property, and any income from such property is used exclusively for religious, educational and charitable purposes, or for either one or more of such purposes and for the purpose of maintaining and operating such institution; this exemption shall not apply to real estate or buildings other than those used for the operation of such institution and which is rented, leased or otherwise used for the primary purpose of securing an income thereon; and also provided that such donations of property shall not be predicated upon an agreement, contract or otherwise that the donor or donors shall receive or retain any part of the net or gross income of the property. The General Assembly shall further have power to exempt from taxation farm products, including baled cotton grown in this State and remaining in the hands of the producer, but not longer than for the year next after their production.

All personal clothing, household and kitchen furniture, personal property used and included within the home, domestic animals and tools, and implements of trade of manual laborers, but not including motor vehicles, are exempted from all State, County, Municipal and School District ad valorem taxes, in an amount not to exceed $300.00 in actual value.

The Homestead of each resident of Georgia actually occupied by the owner as a residence and homestead, and only so long as actually occupied by the owner primarily as such, but not to exceed $2,000.00 of its value, is hereby exempted from all ad valorem taxation for State, county and school purposes, except taxes levied by municipalities for school purposes and except to pay interest on and retire bonded indebtedness, provided, however, should the owner of a dwelling house on a farm, who is already entitled to homestead exemption, participate in the program of rural housing and obtain a new house under contract with the local housing authority, he shall be entitled to receive the same homestead exemption as allowed before making such contract. The General Assembly may from time to time lower said exception to not less than $1250.00. The value of all property in excess of the foregoing exemptions shall remain subject to taxation. Said exemptions shall be returned and claimed in such manner as prescribed by the General Assembly. The exemption herein provided for shall not apply to taxes levied by municipalities.

All cooperative, non-profit, membership corporations organized under the laws of this State for the purpose of engaging in rural electrification, as defined in sub-section 1 of Section 3 of the Act approved March 30, 1937, providing for their incorporation, and all of the real and personal property owned or held by such corporations for such purpose, are hereby exempted from all taxation, state, county, municipal, school district and political or territorial subdivisions of the State having the authority to levy taxes. The exemption herein provided for shall expire December 31, 1961.

There shall be exempt from all ad valorem intangible taxes in this State, the common voting stock of a subsidiary corporation not doing business in this State, if at least ninety per cent of such common voting stock is owned by a Georgia Corporation with its principal place of business located in

## The Constitution of Georgia

this State and was acquired or is held for the purpose of enabling the parent company to carry on some part of its established line of business through such subsidiary.

All laws exempting property from taxation, other than the property herein enumerated, shall be void.

PARAGRAPH V. *Exemptions of Certain Industries Continued.* Existing exemptions under the amendment to the Constitution providing for the exemption of certain industries from taxation appearing in Acts of the General Assembly of 1923, extra session, page 67, ratified November 4, 1924, shall continue of force until the expiration of the term for which granted.

SECTION II

Purposes and Method of Taxation

PARAGRAPH I. *Taxation, How and For What Purposes Exercised.* The powers of taxation over the whole State shall be exercised by the General Assembly for the following purposes only:

1. For the support of the State Government and the public institutions.

2. For educational purposes.

3. To pay the principal and the interest on the public debt, and to provide a sinking fund therefor.

4. To suppress insurrection, to repel invasion, and defend the State in time of war.

5. To make provision for the payment of pensions to ex-Confederate soldiers and to the widows of Confederate soldiers who were married to such soldiers prior to January 1, 1920, and who are unmarried.

6. To construct and maintain State buildings and a system of State highways, airports, and docks.

7. To make provision for the payment of old-age assistance to aged persons in need, and for the payment of assistance to the needy blind, and to dependent children and other welfare benefits; provided that no person shall be entitled to the assistance herein authorized, who does not qualify for such provisions in every respect, in accordance with enactments of the General Assembly, which may be in force and effect, prescribing the qualifications for beneficiaries hereunder: Provided no indebtedness against the State shall

## A Constitutional History of Georgia

ever be created for the purpose herein stated, in excess of the taxes lawfully levied each fiscal year under Acts of the General Assembly authorized hereunder for such purposes.

8. To advertise and promote the agricultural, industrial, historic, recreational and natural resources of the State of Georgia.

9. For public health purposes.

PARAGRAPH II. *Teacher Retirement System—Taxation For.* The powers of taxation may be exercised by the State through the General Assembly and by counties and municipalities, for the purpose of paying pensions and other benefits and costs under a teacher retirement system or systems; provided no indebtedness against the State shall ever be created for the purpose herein stated in excess of the taxes lawfully levied each fiscal year under Acts of the General Assembly authorized hereunder.

PARAGRAPH III. *Revenue to Be Paid Into General Fund.* All money collected from taxes, fees and assessments for State purposes, as authorized by revenue measures enacted by the General Assembly, shall be paid into the General Fund of the State Treasury and shall be appropriated therefrom, as required by this Constitution, for the purposes set out in this Section and for these purposes only.

PARAGRAPH IV. *Tax Returns of Public Utilities.* The General Assembly may provide for a different method and time of returns, assessments, payment and collection of ad valorem taxes, of public utilities, but not at a greater basis of value or at a higher rate of taxation than other properties.

### SECTION III
### State Debt

PARAGRAPH I. *Purposes For Which Contracted.* No debt shall be contracted by, or on behalf of, the State, except to supply such temporary deficit as may exist in the treasury in any year for necessary delay in collecting the taxes of that year, to repel invasion, suppress insurrection and defend the State in time of war, or to pay the existing public debt; but the debt created to supply deficiencies in revenue shall not exceed, in the aggregate, five hundred thousand dollars, and any loan made for this purpose shall be repaid out of the taxes levied for the year in which the loan is made. How-

## The Constitution of Georgia

ever, said debt may be increased in the sum of three million, five hundred thousand dollars for the payment of the public school teachers of the State only. The principal amount borrowed for payment of teachers shall be repaid each year out of the common school appropriation, and the interest paid thereon shall be paid each year out of the general funds of the State.

PARAGRAPH II. *Bonded Debt Increased, When.* The bonded debt of the State shall never be increased, except to repel invasion, suppress insurrection or defend the State in time of war.

PARAGRAPH III. *Form of Laws to Borrow Money.* All laws authorizing the borrowing of money by or on behalf of the State shall specify the purpose for which the money is to be used and the money so obtained shall be used for the purpose specified and for no other.

PARAGRAPH IV. *State Aid Forbidden.* The credit of the State shall not be pledged or loaned to any individual company, corporation or association and the State shall not become a joint owner or stockholder in or with, any individual, company, association or corporation.

PARAGRAPH V. *Assumption of Debts Forbidden.* The State shall not assume the debt, nor any part thereof, of any county, municipal corporation or political subdivision of the State, unless such debt be contracted to enable the State to repel invasion, suppress insurrection or defend itself in time of war: Provided, however, that the amendment to the Constitution proposed by the General Assembly and set forth in the published Acts of the General Assembly of the year 1931 at page 97, which amendment was ratified on November 8, 1932, and which amendment provided for the assumption by the State, of indebtedness of the several counties of the State, as well as that of the Coastal Highway District, and the assessments made against the counties of said district for the construction and paving of the public roads or highways, including bridges, of the State, under certain conditions and for the issuance of certificates of indebtedness for such indebtedness so assumed, is continued of full force and effect until such indebtedness assumed by the State is paid and such certificates of indebtedness retired.

PARAGRAPH VI. *Profit on Public Money.* The receiving,

## A Constitutional History of Georgia

directly or indirectly, by any officer of State or county, or member or officer of the General Assembly of any interest, profits or perquisites, arising from the use or loan of public funds in his hands or moneys to be raised through his agency for State or county purposes, shall be deemed a felony, and punishable as may be prescribed by law, a part of which punishment shall be a disqualification from holding office.

PARAGRAPH VII. *Certain Bonds Not to Be Paid.* The General Assembly shall have no authority to appropriate money either directly or indirectly, to pay the whole, or any part, of the principal or interest of the bonds, or other obligations which have been pronounced illegal, null and void by the General Assembly and the Constitutional amendments ratified by a vote of the people on the first day of May, 1877; nor shall the General Assembly have authority to pay any of the obligations created by the State under laws passed during the late War Between the States, nor any of the bonds, notes or obligations made and entered into during the existence of said war, the time for the payment of which was fixed after the ratification of a treaty of peace between the United States and the Confederate States; nor shall the General Assembly pass any law, or the Governor or any other State official, enter into any contract or agreement whereby the State shall be made a party to any suit in any court of this State, or of the United States instituted to test the validity of any such bonds, or obligations.

PARAGRAPH VIII. *Sale of State's Property to Pay Bonded Debt.* The proceeds of the sale of the Western and Atlantic Railroad, and any other property owned by the State, whenever the General Assembly may authorize the sale of the whole or any part thereof, shall be applied to the payment of the bonded debt of the State, and shall not be used for any other purpose whatsoever, so long as the State has any existing bonded debt; provided that the proceeds of the sale of the Western and Atlantic Railroad shall be applied to the payment of the bonds for which said railroad has been mortgaged, in preference to all other bonds.

PARAGRAPH IX. *State Sinking Fund.* The General Assembly shall raise by taxation each year, in addition to the sum required to pay the public expenses, such amounts as

## The Constitution of Georgia

are necessary to pay the interest on the public debt and the principal of the public debt maturing in such year and to provide a sinking fund to pay off and retire the bonds of the State which have not been matured. The amount of such annual levy shall be determined after consideration of the amount then held in the sinking fund. The taxes levied for such purposes and the said sinking fund, shall be applied to no other purpose whatever. The funds in the said sinking fund may be invested in the bonds of the State, and also in bonds and securities issued by the Federal Government and subsidiaries of the Federal Government, fully guaranteed by that government. If the said bonds are not available for purchase, the funds in the sinking fund may be loaned by the Treasurer of the State, with the approval of the Governor, upon terms to be fixed by such officials and when amply secured by bonds of the State or Federal Government.

### Section IV
### Taxation by Counties

PARAGRAPH I. *Taxing Power of Counties.* The General Assembly shall not have power to delegate to any county the right to levy a tax for any purpose, except:

1. To pay the expenses of administration of the county government.
2. To pay the principal and interest of any debt of the county and to provide a sinking fund therefor.
3. For educational purposes upon property located outside of independent school systems, as provided in Article 8 of this Constitution.
4. To build and repair the public buildings and bridges.
5. To pay the expenses of courts, the maintenance and support of prisoners and to pay sheriffs and coroners and for litigation.
6. To build and maintain a system of county roads.
7. For public health purposes in said county, and for the collection and preservation of records of vital statistics.
8. To pay county police.
9. To support paupers.
10. To pay county agricultural and home demonstration agents.
11. To provide for payment of old age assistance to aged

persons in need, and for the payment of assistance to needy blind, and to dependent children and other welfare benefits, provided that no person shall be entitled to the assistance herein authorized who does not qualify for such assistance in every respect, in accordance with enactments of the General Assembly which may be in force and effect prescribing the qualifications for beneficiaries hereunder; provided no indebtedness or liability against the county shall ever be created for the purpose herein stated, in excess of the taxes lawfully levied each fiscal year under acts of the General Assembly authorized hereunder for such purposes.

12. To provide for fire protection of forest lands and for the further conservation of natural resources.

13. To provide medical or other care and hospitalization, for the indigent sick people of the county.

14. To acquire, improve and maintain airports, public parks, and public libraries.

15. To provide for workmen's compensation and retirement or pension funds for officers and employees.

16. To provide reasonable reserves for public improvements as may be fixed by law.

PARAGRAPH II. *Districting of Counties.* The General Assembly may district the territory of any county, outside the limits of incorporated municipalities, for the purpose of providing systems of waterworks, sewerage, sanitation, and fire protection; and authorize such counties to levy a tax only upon the taxable property in such district for the purpose of constructing and maintaining such improvements.

## SECTION V

PARAGRAPH I. *Taxing Power and Contributions of Counties, Cities and Political Division Restricted.* The General Assembly shall not authorize any county, municipal corporation or political division of this State, through taxation, contribution or otherwise, to become a stockholder in any company, corporation or association, or to appropriate money for, or to loan its credit to any corporation, company, association, institution or individual except for purely charitable purposes. This restriction shall not operate to prevent the support of schools by municipal corporations within their respective limits.

# The Constitution of Georgia

## Section VI

Paragraph I. *Contracts For Use of Public Facilities.* (a) The State, state institutions, any city, town, municipality or county of this State may contract for any period not exceeding fifty years, with each other or with any public agency, public corporation or authority now or hereafter created for the use by such subdivisions or the residents thereof of any facilities or services of the State, state institutions, any city, town, municipality, county, public agency, public corporation or authority, provided such contracts shall deal with such activities and transactions as such subdivisions are by law authorized to undertake.

(b) Any city, town, municipality or county of this State is empowered, in connection with any contracts authorized, by the preceding paragraph, to convey to any public agency, public corporation or authority now or hereafter created, existing facilities operated by such city, town, municipality or county for the benefit of residents of such subdivisions, provided the land, buildings and equipment so conveyed shall not be mortgaged or pledged to secure obligations of any such public agency, public corporation or authority and provided such facilities are to be maintained and operated by such public agency, public corporation or authority for the same purposes for which such facilities were operated by such city, town, municipality or county. Nothing in this section shall restrict the pledging of revenues of such facilities by any public agency, public corporation or authority.

(c) Any city, town, municipality or county of this State, or any combination of the same, may contract with any public agency, public corporation or authority for the care, maintenance and hospitalization of its indigent sick, and may as a part of such contract obligate itself to pay for the cost of acquisition, construction, modernization or repairs of necessary buildings and facilities by such public agency, public corporation or authority, and provide for the payment of such services and the cost to such public agency, public corporations or authority of acquisition, construction, modernization or repair of buildings and facilities from revenues realized by such city, town, municipality or county from any taxes authorized by the Constitution of this State or revenues derived from any other sources.

## Section VII
## Limitation on County and Municipal Debts

PARAGRAPH I. *Debts of Counties and Cities.* The debt hereafter incurred by any county, municipal corporation or political division of this State except as in this Constitution provided for, shall never exceed seven per centum of the assessed value of all the taxable property therein, and no such county, municipality or division shall incur any new debt except for a temporary loan or loans, to supply casual deficiencies of revenue, not to exceed one-fifth of one per centum of the assessed value of the taxable property therein, without the assent of a majority of the qualified voters of the county, municipality or other political subdivision voting in an election for that purpose to be held as prescribed by law; and provided further that all laws, charter provisions and ordinances heretofore passed or enacted providing special registration of the voters of counties, municipal corporations and other political divisions of this State to pass upon the issuance of bonds by such counties, municipal corporations and other political divisions are hereby declared to be null and void; and the General Assembly shall hereafter have no power to pass or enact any law providing for such special registration, but the validity of any and all bond issues by such counties, municipal corporations or other political divisions made prior to January 1, 1945, shall not be affected hereby; provided, that any county or municipality of this State may accept and use funds granted by the Federal Government, or any agency thereof, to aid in financing the cost of architectural, engineering, economic investigations, studies, surveys, designs, plans, working drawings, specifications, procedures, and other action preliminary to the construction of public works, and where the funds so used for the purposes specified are to be repaid within a period of ten years.

PARAGRAPH II. *Levy of Taxes to Pay Bonds.* Any county, municipal corporation or political division of this State which shall incur any bonded indebtedness under the provisions of this Constitution, shall at or before the time of so doing, provide for the assessment and collection of an annual tax sufficient in amount to pay the principal and interest of

## The Constitution of Georgia

said debt, within thirty years from the date of the incurring of said indebtedness.

PARAGRAPH III. *Additional Debt Authorized, When.* In addition to the debt authorized in Paragraph I of this section, to be created by any county, municipal corporation or political subdivision of this State, a debt may be incurred by any county, municipal corporation or political subdivision of this State, in excess of seven per centum of the assessed value of all the taxable property therein, upon the following conditions: Such additional debt, whether incurred at one or more times, shall not exceed in the aggregate, three per centum of the assessed value of all the taxable property in such county, municipality, or political subdivision; such additional debt shall be payable in equal installments within the five years next succeeding the issuance of the evidences of such debt; there shall be levied by the governing authorities of such county, municipality or political subdivision prior to the issuance of such additional debt, a tax upon all of the taxable property within such county, municipality or political subdivision collectable annually, sufficient to pay in full the principal and interest of such additional debt when as due; such tax shall be in addition to and separate from all other taxes levied by such taxing authorities, and the collections from such tax shall be kept separate and shall be held, used and applied solely for the payment of the principal and interest of such additional indebtedness; authority to create such additional indebtedness shall first have been authorized by the General Assembly; the creation of such additional indebtedness shall have been first authorized by a vote of the registered voters of such county, municipality or political subdivision at an election held for such purpose, pursuant to and in accordance with the provisions of this Constitution and of the then existing laws for the creation of a debt by counties, municipal corporations, and political subdivisions of this State, all of which provisions, including those for calling, advertising, holding and determining the result of, such election and the votes necessary to authorize the creation of an indebtedness, are hereby made applicable to an election held for the purpose of authorizing such additional indebtedness.

PARAGRAPH IV. *Temporary Loans Authorized; Conditions.*

## A Constitutional History of Georgia

In addition to the obligations hereinbefore allowed, each county, municipality and political subdivision of the State authorized to levy taxes, is given the authority to make temporary loans between January 1st and December 31st in each year to pay expenses for such year, upon the following conditions: The aggregate amount of all such loans of such county, municipality or political subdivision outstanding at any one time, shall not exceed seventy-five per centum of the total gross income of such county, municipality or political subdivision, from taxes collected by such county, municipality or political subdivision in the last preceding year. Each such loan shall be payable on or before December 31st of the calendar year in which such loan is made. No loan may be made in any year under the provisions of this paragraph when there is a loan then unpaid which was made in a prior year under the provisions of this paragraph. Each such loan shall be first authorized by resolution fixing the terms of such loan, adopted by a majority vote of the governing body of such county, city or political subdivision, at a meeting legally held, and such resolution shall appear upon the minutes of such meeting. No such county, municipality or subdivision shall incur in any one calendar year, an aggregate of such temporary loans and other contracts or obligations for current expenses, in excess of the total anticipated revenue of such county, municipality or subdivision for such calendar year, or issue in one calendar year notes, warrants or other evidences of such indebtedness in a total amount in excess of such anticipated revenue for such year.

PARAGRAPH V. *Revenue Anticipation Obligations.* Revenue anticipation obligations may be issued by any county, municipal corporation or political subdivision of this State, to provide funds for the purchase or construction, in whole or in part, of any revenue-producing facility which such county, municipal corporation or political subdivision is authorized by the Act of the General Assembly approved March 31, 1937, known as "The Revenue Certificate Laws of 1937," as amended by the Act approved March 14, 1939, to construct and operate, or to provide funds to extend, repair or improve any such existing facility, and to buy, construct, extend, operate and maintain gas or electric generating and distribution systems, together with all necessary appurte-

*The Constitution of Georgia*

nances thereof. Such revenue anticipation obligations shall be payable, as to principal and interest, only from revenue produced by revenue-producing facilities of the issuing political subdivision, and shall not be deemed debts of, or to create debts against, the issuing political subdivisions within the meaning of this paragraph or any other of this Constitution. This authority shall apply only to revenue anticipation obligations issued to provide funds for the purchase, construction, extension, repair or improvement of such facilities and undertakings as are specifically authorized and enumerated by said Act of 1937, as amended by said Act of 1939; and to buy, construct, extend, operate and maintain gas or electric generating and distribution systems, together with all necessary appurtenances thereof; provided further any revenue certificates issued to buy, construct, extend, operate and maintain gas or electric generating and distribution systems shall, before being undertaken, be authorized by a majority of those voting at an election held for the purpose in the county, municipal corporation or political subdivision affected, and provided further that a majority of the registered voters of such county, municipal corporation or political subdivision affected shall vote in said election, the election for such to be held in the same manner as is used in issuing bonds of such county, municipal corporation or political subdivision and the said elections shall be called and provided for by officers in charge of the fiscal affairs of said county, municipal corporation or political subdivision affected; and no such issuing political subdivision of the State shall exercise the power of taxation for the purpose of paying the principal or interest of any such revenue anticipation obligations or any part thereof.

Provided that after a favorable election has been held as set forth above, if municipalities, counties or other political subdivisions shall purchase, construct, or operate such electric or gas utility plants from the proceeds of said revenue certificates, and extend their services beyond the limits of the county in which the municipality or political subdivision is located, then its services rendered and property located outside said county shall be subject to taxation and regulation as are privately owned and operated utilities.

PARAGRAPH VI. *Refunding Bonds.* The General Assembly

is hereby authorized to create a commission and to vest such commission with the power to secure all necessary information and to approve or disapprove the issuance of bonds for the purpose of refunding any bonded indebtedness of any county, municipality or political subdivision of this State issued prior to the adoption of this Constitution, including the authority to approve or disapprove the amount and terms of such refunding bonds, together with such other powers as to the General Assembly may seem proper, but not in conflict with the provisions of the Constitution. Such refunding bonds shall be authorized only where such county, municipality or political subdivision has not the funds available to meet the payment of outstanding bonded indebtedness through failure to levy and collect the required taxes, or through failure to maintain the required sinking fund for such bonds. The General Assembly may approve the issuance of the said refunding bonds under the conditions stated. Such refunding bonds shall not, together with all other outstanding bonded indebtedness, exceed the limits fixed by this Constitution for the maximum amount of bonded indebtedness which may be issued by such county, municipality or political subdivision and shall be otherwise governed by all of the terms and provisions of this Constitution. No bonds shall be issued under this paragraph to refund any bonds issued after the adoption of this Constitution.

PARAGRAPH VII. *Refunding Bonds to Reduce Bonded Indebtedness.* The General Assembly is further authorized to give to the said Commission the power and authority to approve or disapprove the issuance of bonds to refund any outstanding bonded indebtedness of any county, municipality or political subdivision now or hereafter issued, for the purpose of reducing the amount payable, principal or interest, on such bonded indebtedness, and upon the condition that, the issuance of such refunding bonds will reduce the amounts payable upon such outstanding bonds, principal or interest. Such refunding bonds shall replace such outstanding bonded indebtedness. The said Commission shall have the authority to approve or disapprove the terms of any such proposed refunding bonds. The General Assembly may authorize the issuance of such refunding bonds issued for the said purpose, when approved by the said Commission and authorized by

## The Constitution of Georgia

the governing authority of such county, municipality or subdivision, without an election by the qualified voters as otherwise required, but in all other respects such refunding bonds shall comply with the provisions of this Constitution.

### Section VIII

PARAGRAPH I. *Sinking Funds For Bonds.* All amounts collected from any source for the purpose of paying the principal and interest of any bonded indebtedness of any county, municipality or subdivision and to provide for the retirement of such bonded indebtedness, above the amount needed to pay the principal and interest on such bonded indebtedness due in the year of such collection, shall be placed in a sinking fund to be held and used to pay off the principal and interest of such bonded indebtedness thereafter maturing.

The funds in such sinking fund shall be kept separate and apart from all other moneys of such county, municipality or subdivision, and shall be used for no purpose other than that above stated. The moneys in such sinking fund may be invested and reinvested by the governing authorities of such county, municipality or subdivision or by such other authority as has been created to hold and manage such sinking fund, in the bonds of such county, municipality or subdivision, and in bonds or obligations of the State of Georgia, of the counties and cities thereof and of the government of the United States, of subsidiary corporations of the Federal Government fully guaranteed by such government, and no other. Any person or persons violating the above provisions shall be guilty of malpractice in office and shall also be guilty of misdemeanor, and shall be punished, when convicted, as prescribed by law for the punishment of misdemeanors, until the General Assembly shall make other provisions for the violation of the terms of this paragraph.

### Section IX
### Appropriation Control

PARAGRAPH I. *Preparation and Submission of General Appropriation Bill.* The Governor shall submit to the General Assembly within fifteen days after its organization, a budget

## A Constitutional History of Georgia

message accompanied by a draft of a General Appropriation Bill, which shall provide for the appropriation of the funds necessary to operate all the various departments and agencies, and to meet the current expenses of the State for the ensuing fiscal year.

PARAGRAPH II. *Continuation of General Appropriation Act.* Each General Appropriation Act, with such amendments as are adopted from time to time, shall continue in force and effect for each fiscal year thereafter until repealed or another General Appropriation Act is adopted; provided, however, that each section of the General Appropriation Act in force and effect on the date of the adoption of this Constitution, of general application and pertaining to the administration, limitation and restriction on the payment of appropriations and each section providing for appropriation of Federal Grants and other continuing appropriations and adjustments on appropriations shall remain in force and effect until specifically and separately repealed by the General Assembly.

PARAGRAPH III. *Other or Supplementary Appropriations.* In addition to the appropriations made by the General Appropriation Act and amendments thereto, the General Assembly may make additional appropriations by Acts, which shall be known as supplementary appropriation Acts, provided no such supplementary appropriation shall be available unless there is an unappropriated surplus in the State Treasury or the revenue necessary to pay such appropriation shall have been provided by a tax laid for such purpose and collected into the General Fund of the State Treasury. Neither House shall pass a Supplementary Appropriation Bill until the General Appropriation Act shall have been finally adopted by both Houses and approved by the Governor.

PARAGRAPH IV. *Appropriations to Be For Specific Sums.* The appropriation for each department, officer, bureau, board, commission, agency or institution for which an appropriation is made, shall be for a specific sum of money, and no appropriation shall allocate to any object, the proceeds of any particular tax or fund or a part or percentage thereof.

PARAGRAPH V. *Appropriations Void, When.* Any appropriation made in conflict with either of the foregoing provisions shall be void.

# The Constitution of Georgia

### SECTION X

PARAGRAPH I. *Existing Amendments Continued of Force.* Amendments to the Constitution of the State of Georgia of 1877 in effect at the date of the ratification by the voters of the State, of this Constitution, shall continue of full force and effect after the ratification of this Constitution, where such amendments are of merely local, and not, general application, including the amendments pertaining to the Coastal Highway District of this State. There is also continued under this provision in force and effect, amendments to the Constitution of 1877 applicable to counties and cities having a population in excess of a number stated in such amendments, amendments applicable to counties having a city wholly or partly therein with a population in excess of, or not less than a number stated in such amendment, and amendments applicable to cities lying in two counties, where such amendments are in force and effect at the time of the ratification of this Constitution. Provided the amendment of Paragraph I of Section II of Article XI of the Constitution of 1877 proposed by Georgia Laws, 1943, page 53, and ratified August 3, 1943, authorizing election by the people of the County Board of Education of Spalding County; prescribing rules of eligibility of members of the Board; providing for election by the Board of the County Superintendent of Schools shall not be continued of force.

## ARTICLE VIII
## *EDUCATION*
### SECTION I

PARAGRAPH I. *System of Common Schools; Free Tuition, Separation of Races.* The provision of an adequate education for the citizens shall be a primary obligation of the State of Georgia, the expense of which shall be provided for by taxation. Separate schools shall be provided for the white and colored races.

### SECTION II

PARAGRAPH I. *State Board of Education; Method of Appointment.* There shall be a State Board of Education, composed of one member from each Congressional District in the State, who shall be appointed by the Governor, by and with the advice and consent of the Senate. The Governor shall not be a member of the State Board of Education. The first State Board of Education under this Constitution shall consist of those in office at the time this Constitution is adopted, with the terms provided by law. Thereafter, all succeeding appointments shall be for seven year terms from the expiration of the previous term. Vacancies upon said Board caused by expiration of term of office shall be similarly filled by appointment and confirmation. In case of a vacancy on said Board by death, resignation, or from any other cause other than the expiration of such member's term of office, the Board shall by secret ballot elect his successor, who shall hold office until the end of the next session of the General Assembly, or if the General Assembly be then in session to the end of that session. During such session of the General Assembly the Governor shall appoint the successor member of the Board for the unexpired term and shall submit his name to the Senate for confirmation. All members of the Board shall hold office until their successors are appointed and qualified. The members of the State Board of Education shall be citizens of this State who shall have resided in Georgia continuously for at least five years preceding their appointment. No person employed in a professional capacity by a private or public education institution, or by the State Department of Education, shall be eligible for appointment or to serve on said Board. No person who is or has been connected with or employed by a school book publishing concern shall be eligible to membership on the Board, and if any person shall be so connected or employed after becoming a member of the Board, his place shall immediately become vacant. The said State Board of Education shall have such powers and duties as provided by law and existing at the time of the adoption of this Constitution, together with such further powers and duties as may be hereafter provided by law.

## Section III

Paragraph I. *State School Superintendent; Election, Term, Etc.* There shall be a State School Superintendent, who shall

## The Constitution of Georgia

be the executive officer of the State Board of Education, elected at the same time and in the same manner and for the same term as that of the Governor. The State School Superintendent shall have such qualifications and shall be paid such compensation as may be fixed by law. No member of said Board shall be eligible for election as State School Superintendent during the time for which he shall have been appointed.

SECTION IV

PARAGRAPH I. *University System of Georgia; Board of Regents.* There shall be a Board of Regents of the University System of Georgia, and the government, control, and management of the University System of Georgia and all of its institutions in said system shall be vested in said Board of Regents of the University System of Georgia. Said Board of Regents of the University System of Georgia shall consist of one member from each Congressional District in the State, and five additional members from the State-at-large, appointed by the Governor and confirmed by the Senate. The Governor shall not be a member of the said Board. The first Board of Regents under this Constitution shall consist of those in office at the time this Constitution is adopted, with the terms provided by law. Thereafter all succeeding appointments shall be for seven year terms from the expiration of the previous term. Vacancies upon said Board caused by expiration of term of office shall be similarly filled by appointment and confirmation. In case of a vacancy on said Board by death, resignation of a member, or from any other cause other than the expiration of such member's term of office, the Board shall by secret ballot elect his successor, who shall hold office until the end of the next session of the General Assembly, or if the General Assembly be then in session to the end of that session. During such session of the General Assembly the Governor shall appoint the successor member of the Board for the unexpired term and shall submit his name to the Senate for confirmation. All members of the Board of Regents shall hold office until their successors are appointed. The said Board of Regents of the University System of Georgia shall have the powers and duties as provided by law existing at the time of the adoption of this Constitution, together with such further powers and duties as may be hereafter provided by law.

## Section V

PARAGRAPH I. *County System; Board of Education; Election, Term, Etc.* Authority is granted to Counties to establish and maintain public schools within their limits. Each County, exclusive of any independent school system now in existence in a County, shall compose one school district and shall be confined to the control and management of a County Board of Education. The Grand Jury of each County shall select from the citizens of their respective Counties five freeholders, who shall constitute the County Board of Education. Said members shall be elected for the term of five years except that the first election of Board members under this Constitution shall be for such terms that will provide for the expiration of the term of one member of the County Board of Education each year. In case of a vacancy on said Board by death, resignation of a member, or from any other cause other than the expiration of such member's term of office, the Board shall by secret ballot elect his successor, who shall hold office until the next Grand Jury convenes at which time said Grand Jury shall appoint the successor member of the Board for the unexpired term. The members of the County Board of Education of such County shall be selected from that portion of the County not embraced within the territory of an independent school district.

The General Assembly shall have authority to make provision for local trustees of each school in a county system and confer authority upon them to make recommendations as to budgets and employment of teachers and other authorized employees.

## Section VI

PARAGRAPH I. *County School Superintendent; Election, Term, Etc.* There shall be a County School Superintendent, who shall be the executive officer of the County Board of Education. He shall be elected by the people and his term of office shall be for four years and run concurrently with other county officers. The qualifications and the salary of the County School Superintendent shall be fixed by law.

# The Constitution of Georgia

### Section VII

PARAGRAPH I. *Independent Systems Continued; New Systems Prohibited.* Authority is hereby granted to municipal corporations to maintain existing independent school systems, and support the same as authorized by special or general law, and such existing systems may add thereto colleges. No independent school system shall hereafter be established.

### Section VIII

PARAGRAPH I. *Meetings of Boards of Education.* All official meetings of County Boards of Education shall be open to the public.

### Section IX

PARAGRAPH I. *Contracts For Care of Pupils.* County Boards of Education and independent school systems may contract with each other for the education, transportation, and care of pupils.

### Section X

PARAGRAPH I. *Certain Systems Protected.* Public schools systems established prior to the adoption of the Constitution of 1877 shall not be affected by this Constitution.

### Section XI

PARAGRAPH I. *Grants, Bequests and Donations Permitted.* The State Board of Education and the Regents of the University System of Georgia may accept bequests, donations and grants of land, or other property, for the use of their respective systems of education.

PARAGRAPH II. *Grants, Bequests and Donations to County Boards of Education and Independent School Systems.* County Boards of Education and independent school systems may accept bequests, donations and grants of land, or other property, for the use of their respective systems of education.

### Section XII

PARAGRAPH I. *Taxation by Counties For Education.* The fiscal authority of the several Counties shall levy a tax for the support and maintenance of education not less than five mills nor greater than fifteen mills (as recommended by the County Board of Education) upon the dollar of all taxable property in the County located outside independent school systems. The independent school system of Chatham County and the City of Savannah, being co-extensive with said County, the levy of said tax shall be on all property in said County as recommended by the governing body of said system.

## ARTICLE IX
## HOMESTEADS AND EXEMPTIONS
### Section I

PARAGRAPH I. *Amount of Homestead and Exemptions.* There is hereby exempt from levy and sale, by virtue of any process whatever under the laws of this State, the property of every head of a family, or guardian, or trustee of a family of minor children, or every aged or infirm person, or person having the care and support of dependent females of any age, who is not the head of a family, realty or personalty, or both, to the value in the aggregate of sixteen hundred dollars; and the General Assembly shall have authority to provide the manner of exempting said property, the sale, alienation and encumbrance thereof, and to provide for the waiver of said exemption by the debtor.

PARAGRAPH II. *Homestead and Exemption Laws Continued.* The laws now of force with respect to homestead and exemptions shall remain in full force until changed by law.

## ARTICLE X
## MILITIA
### Section I

PARAGRAPH I. *Organization of Militia.* A well regulated militia being essential to the peace and security of the State, the General Assembly shall have authority to provide by law how the militia of this State shall be organized, officered, trained, armed and equipped; and of whom it shall consist.

PARAGRAPH II. *Volunteers.* The General Assembly shall have power to authorize the formation of volunteer companies, and to provide for their organization into battalions, regiments, brigades, divisions, and corps, with such restric-

## The Constitution of Georgia

tions as may be prescribed by law, and shall have authority to arm and equip the same.

PARAGRAPH III. *Pay of Militia and Volunteers.* The officers and men of the militia and volunteer forces shall not be entitled to receive any pay, rations, or emoluments, when not in active service by authority of the State.

## ARTICLE XI
## COUNTIES AND MUNICIPAL CORPORATIONS
### SECTION I

PARAGRAPH I. *Counties a Corporate Body; Boundaries.* Each county shall be a body corporate with such powers and limitations as may be prescribed by law. All suits by or against a county shall be in the name thereof; and the metes and bounds of the several counties shall remain as now prescribed by law, unless changed as hereinafter provided.

PARAGRAPH II. *Number Limited.* There shall not be more than one hundred and fifty-nine counties in this State.

PARAGRAPH III. *New Counties Permitted, When.* No new county shall be created except by the consolidation or merger of existing counties.

PARAGRAPH IV. *Consolidation of Counties; Method.* The General Assembly shall have power, with the concurrence of two-thirds of the qualified voters of each of the counties to be affected who participate in elections held for that purpose, to provide for the consolidation of two or more counties into one, or the merger of one or more counties into another, or the division of a county, and the merger of portions thereof into other counties.

PARAGRAPH V. *Dissolution of Counties; Method.* Any County may be dissolved and merged with a contiguous county or counties by two-thirds of the qualified voters of each of the counties affected who participate in elections held for that purpose.

PARAGRAPH VI. *County Governments Uniform; Exceptions.* Whatever tribunal, or officers, may be created by the General Assembly for the transaction of county matters, shall be uniform throughout the State, and of the same name, jurisdiction, and remedies, except that the General Assembly may provide for Commissioners of Roads and Revenues in any

# A Constitutional History of Georgia

county, may abolish the office of County Treasurer in any county, may fix the compensation of County Treasurers, and may consolidate the offices of Tax Receiver and Tax Collector in the office of Tax Commissioner, and may fix his compensation, without respect to uniformity.

PARAGRAPH VII. *Consolidation of Governments; Submission to Voters.* The General Assembly may provide by general law optional systems of consolidated county and municipal government, providing for the organization and the powers and duties of its officers. Such optional systems shall become effective when submitted to the qualified voters of such county and approved by a majority of those voting.

PARAGRAPH VIII. *County Lines.* County lines shall not be changed, unless under the operation of a general law for that purpose.

PARAGRAPH IX. *County Sites Changed; Method.* No County site shall be changed or removed, except by a two-thirds vote of the qualified voters of the county, voting at an election held for that purpose and by a majority vote of the General Assembly.

### SECTION II

PARAGRAPH I. *County Officers; Election; Term; Removal; Eligibility.* The county officers shall be elected by the qualified voters of their respective counties or districts, and shall hold their office for four years. They shall be removed upon conviction for malpractice in office; and no person shall be eligible for any of the offices referred to in this paragraph unless he shall have been a resident of the county for two years and is a qualified voter.

PARAGRAPH II. *Compensation of County Officers.* County officers may be on a fee basis, salary basis, or fee basis supplemented by salary, in such manner as may be directed by law.

## ARTICLE XII
### THE LAWS OF GENERAL OPERATION IN FORCE IN THIS STATE
#### SECTION I

PARAGRAPH I. *Supreme Law.* The laws of general operation in this State are, first: As the Supreme Law: The Constitution of the United States, the laws of the United States in pur-

## The Constitution of Georgia

suance thereof and all treaties made under the authority of the United States.

PARAGRAPH II. *Second in Authority.* Second. As next in authority thereto: This Constitution.

PARAGRAPH III. *Third in Authority.* Third. In subordination to the foregoing: All laws now of force in this State, not inconsistent with this Constitution shall remain of force until the same are modified or repealed by the General Assembly.

PARAGRAPH IV. *Local and Private Acts.* Local and private acts passed for the benefit of counties, cities, towns, corporations and private persons, not inconsistent with the Supreme Law, nor with this Constitution and which have not expired nor been repealed, shall have the force of Statute Law, subject to judicial decision as to their validity when passed, and to any limitations imposed by their own terms.

PARAGRAPH V. *Proceedings of Courts Confirmed.* All judgments, decrees, orders, and other proceedings, of the several courts of this State, heretofore made within the limits of their several jurisdictions, are hereby ratified and reaffirmed, subject only to reversal by motion for a new trial, appeal, bill of review or other proceedings, in conformity with the law of force when they were made.

PARAGRAPH VI. *Existing Officers.* The officers of the Government now existing shall continue in the exercise of their several functions until their successors are duly elected or appointed and qualified. But nothing herein is to apply to any officer, whose office may be abolished by this Constitution.

## ARTICLE XIII
## *AMENDMENTS TO THE CONSTITUTION*
### SECTION I

PARAGRAPH I. *Proposed by General Assembly; Submission to People.* Any amendment or amendments to this Constitution may be proposed in the Senate or House of Representatives and if the same shall be agreed to by two-thirds of the members elected to each of the two houses, such proposed amendment or amendments shall be entered on their journals, with the yeas and nays taken thereon. The General Assembly shall cause such amendment or amendments to be published in one or more newspapers in each Congressional

District, for two months previous to the time of holding the next general election at which election members of the General Assembly are chosen; and if such proposed amendment directly affects only one or more political subdivisions of the State, then it shall also be advertised in the area to be directly affected thereby; and shall also provide for a submission of such proposed amendment or amendments to the people at said next general election, and if the people shall ratify such amendment or amendments, by a majority of the electors qualified to vote for members of the General Assembly voting thereon, such amendment or amendments shall become a part of this Constitution; provided that if the proposed amendment is not one that directly affects the whole State, but only one or more subdivisions thereof, said amendment shall not become a part of this Constitution unless it receive both a majority of the electors qualified to vote voting thereon in the State as a whole, and also a majority of the electors qualified to vote voting thereon in the particular subdivision or subdivisions affected. When more than one amendment is submitted at the same time they shall be so submitted as to enable the electors to vote on each amendment separately.

PARAGRAPH II. *Convention, How Called.* No convention of the people shall be called by the General Assembly to revise, amend or change this Constitution, unless by the concurrence of two-thirds of all members of each house of the General Assembly. The representation in said convention shall be based on population as near as practicable. This Constitution shall not be revised, amended, or changed by the Convention until the proposed revision, amendment, or change has been submitted and ratified by the people in the manner provided for submission and ratification of amendments proposed by the General Assembly.

PARAGRAPH III. *Veto Not Permitted.* The Governor shall not have the right to veto any proposal by the General Assembly to amend the Constitution.

## ARTICLE XIV
## MERIT SYSTEM
### SECTION I

PARAGRAPH I. *State Personnel Board.* A non-salaried State Personnel Board comprised of three citizens of this State, of

*The Constitution of Georgia*

known interest in the improvement of public administration, shall administer a State Merit System under which state personnel shall be selected on a basis of merit, fitness, and efficiency according to law. The members of the State Personnel Board shall be appointed by the Governor with the advice of the Senate. The first members shall be appointed for terms of three, five and seven years, respectively, the terms to be designated by the Governor. All subsequent appointments shall be for a period of seven years, except unexpired terms. No State official or employee shall be a member of the State Personnel Board.

PARAGRAPH II. *Retirement System. Appropriation.* The General Assembly is authorized to establish an actuarially sound retirement system for employees under a merit system. Adequate appropriations shall be provided for the operation of a merit system and the State Personnel Board.

## ARTICLE XV
## *HOME RULE*
### SECTION I

PARAGRAPH I. *Uniform Systems of County and Municipal Government.* The General Assembly shall provide for uniform systems of county and municipal government, and provide for optional plans of both, and shall provide for systems of initiative, referendum and recall in some of the plans for both county and municipal governments. The General Assembly shall provide a method by which a county or municipality may select one of the optional uniform systems or plans or reject any or all proposed systems or plans.

# INDEX

Abbeville School District, bonds of, 387 note
Abercorn, early settlement, 22
Abolitionists, 237
Ackerman, Amos T., 265
Adel, debt of, 384 note
Administrative reorganization, 375
Adrian Consolidated School District, bonds of, 387 note
Agricultural agents, taxation for, 305
Agricultural and mechanic schools, 335
Agricultural College, 335
Albany Conference, 119
Albany, debt of, 381 note
Alexander, Hooper, candidate for Governor, 349
Alleviating laws, unconstitutional, 190
Alliance, Farmers', 324
Allocation of taxes, forbidden, 399
Altamaha River, boundary, 148
Amending process, under Constitution of
  1777, 113
  1789, 145
  1798, 162–63
  1861, 246
  1868, 271
  1877, 289–90
  1945, 413
American Legion, denounced by Tom Watson, 366
American System, Clay's, 207
"Anarchists," 248
*Ann*, frigate transports original settlers, 19

Appointments, by General Assembly, criticized, 166
Appomattox, 250
Appropriation Bill, General, 284–85, 400
Arbor Day, 327
Arnall, Ellis Gibbs, *biographical sketch of, 387 note;* elected Governor, 388; sponsors constitutional revision, 393; favors Governor succeeding himself, 397
Arnold, David Johnson, 394
Arp, Bill, 258
Arsenal, Federal, at Augusta, 241
Articles of Confederation, 121–25, 219
Atkins, James, 277
Atkinson County, created, 360; boundaries redefined, 362
Atkinson, David Scarlett, 394
Atkinson, William Y., elected Governor, 329
Atlanta, burned, 248; capital, 270, 283; debt of, 381 note; revenue certificates of, 384 note
*Atlanta Constitution,* quoted, 282, 346
*Atlanta Journal,* founded, 326; supports Hoke Smith, 337; requests new trial for Leo Frank, 352
Attorney General, under Royal government, 64; under Constitution of 1877, 287, 404
Augusta, early settlement, 22; capital, 115; debt of, 346, 384 note
*Augusta Chronicle,* 151, 202, 209

# Index

Augusta Chronicle and Sentinel, 262
Austrian Succession, War of, 40
Avery, I. W., quoted, 233

Bacon, Augustus O., Speaker, 317, 319; Senator, 353; how defeated, 357
Bacon County, created, 350; debt of, 355; bonds of, 384 note
Bailiffs, early judges at Savannah, 21, 24
Baker County, bonds, 387 note
Baldwin, Abraham, delegate to Federal Convention, 126, *127 note;* signs Constitution, 131; land commissioner, 153
Baltimore Convention of 1860, 216
Bane, Frank, 396
Banks, inspection of, 327, 340
Baptists, 66
Barnett, N. C., Secretary of State, 267
Barrow County, 350
Bartow, Francis S., member of Secession Convention, 231, 232; delegate to Montgomery convention, 241
Baxley, debt of, 384 note
Beaverdam School District, bonds of, 384 note
Bedford, Gunning, Jr., quoted, 129
Belcher, William, member of Convention of 1776-77, 99
Bell, John, candidate for President, 216, 217, 233
Ben Hill County, created, 336; given representation, 341
Benning, Henry L., member of Secession Convention, 281
Berrien, John McPherson, Attorney General, 199; sponsors political convention, 203
Bibb County, debt of, 387 note; public service districts in, 389 note
Bill of rights, in Constitution of
   1777, 101
   1789, 145
   1798, 158
   1861, 244

1865, 256
1868, 267
1877, 283-84, 290
1945, 397-98, 400-01
Bishop of London, authority over colony, 55
Blackshear, bonds of, 384 note
Bleckley County, 349
Bleckley, Justice Logan, 332 note
Blind, taxation for, 305
Blodgett, Foster, candidate for Senate, 272; elected to Senate, 275
Blue Ridge, debt of, 384 note
Board of Regents, see Regents, Board of
Board of Trade, devises plan of government for Colony, 49
Bonds, repudiated, 277-78; limited under Constitution of 1877, 287; for highways, 306
Books, free texts, proposed, 374
Booth, John Wilkes, 251
Bosomworth, Thomas, 44-45
Boundary, under Charter of 1732, 14; extended, 59, 70; summary statement on, 148; sale of western land, 152-53, 205
Bourbon Democracy, defined, 210
Bowdon, bonds of, 384 note
Boynton, James S., Acting Governor, 317
Bradley, Aaron Alpeoria, 264
Brantley County, created, 364; school tax, 384 note
Bray, Rev. Thomas, D.D., philanthropist, 6
Breckenridge, John C., candidate for President, 216, 233
Brigadier generals, election of, 165
British colonial policy, 47, 48-51
Brown, B. Gratz, 277
Brown, Joseph E., opposes Compromise of 1850, 212; *biographical sketch of,* 226-27; advocates secession, 227, 229-30; invited to Secession Convention, 231; seizes Fort Pulaski, 240; War Governor, 248-49; resigns office of Governor, 252; advises submission, 262; candidate for Sen-

# Index

ate, 272; industrialist, 311–12; philanthropist, 312; appointed to Senate, 315; elected to Senate, 316
Brown, Joseph M., *biographical sketch of, 344 note;* elected Governor, 344–46, 349
Brown, Walter R., candidate for Governor, 366
Brunswick, debt of, 369
Bryan, William J., 330
Bryce, James, 90
Buchanan, James, receives Georgia's electoral vote, 214
Bulloch, Archibald, 82, 84, 86, 88, 94, 97, 113
Bullock, Rufus B., influence in Convention of 1867, 264; elected Governor, 271; *biographical sketch of, 274–75;* Provisional Governor, 275; resigns, 276; tried, 277
Burns, John T., Comptroller General, 267

Cabinet government, 242
Caldwell, Harmon W., President of University, 388
Calhoun County, bonds, 387 note
Calhoun, John C., influence on Georgia politics, 210
Camden County, origin of name, 104
Camp, Lawrence S., candidate for Senate, 380
Campbell County, consolidated, 291
Campbell, Tunis G., 264
Candler, Allen D., member of General Assembly, 279; *biographical sketch of, 334;* historian, 347
Candler County, 350
Candler, Thomas Salter, 394
Cape Bluff, early settlement, 22
Capital, 115, 147, *169,* 270
Capitol, 275
Carmichael, James Vinson, member of Constitutional Commission, 394; candidate for Governor, 359 note

Carpetbaggers, 264, 265
Carrollton, debt of, 384 note
Carswell, George H., candidate for Governor, 371, 374
Carteret, George, Carolina proprietor, 14
Castell, Robert, architect, imprisoned, 5
Catholics, besmeared by Tom Watson, 366. See Papists
Catoosa County, bonds, 387 note
Causton, Thomas, storekeeper, 24
Census, 69 note, 197 note
Chappell, A. H., 256
Charleston, Convention of 1860 in, 215
Charter of 1732, steps in issuance of, 9–10; provisions of, 12–18; surrendered, 45
Chatham County, origin of name, 104; debt of, 372; taxation in, 381 note, 386 note
Chattahoochee River, 148, 153
Chattooga, bonds, 387 note
Checks and balances, a restraint upon the President, 228
Child labor, restricted, 340
Children, dependent, taxation for, 305
*Chisholm vs. Georgia,* 200
Church of England, rites of to be followed, 36, 55; established, 66
Circuit riding, by Chief Justice, 112; by Supreme Court justices, 187
City Courts, 408
Citizens, defined, 240
Civil Rights Bill, 260
Civil service, veterans' preference, 294, 390, 400
Clark, John, seeks to remove Secretary of State, 192; party leader, 201, 205
Clark Party, 200–05
Clark, Richard H., prepares *Code,* 247
Clarke, Elijah, 201
Claxton, bonds of, 387 note
Clayton, Judge A. S., 203
Clerical expenses, limited, 285–86; of Governor, raised, 295; limi-

## Index

tations on Treasurer, Secretary of State, and Comptroller General abolished, 296

Coastal Highway District, 368, 376, 385

Cobb County, fire prevention in, 384 note; bonds of, 387 note

Cobb, Howell, Speaker of House, 199; Secretary of Treasury, 199; political leader, 210; supports Compromise of 1850, 211; Governor, 212; endorsed as Presidential candidate, 215; favors secession, 230; invited to Secession Convention, 231; delegate to Montgomery convention; "monarchist," 248

Cobb, Thomas R. R., author of provision in Constitution of 1861, vii; favors secession, 228; member of Secession Convention, 231, 232; delegate to Montgomery Convention, 241; part in writing Constitution of 1861, 243, 244; publishes *Code*, 246; author of Bill of Rights, 401

Coca Cola Company, 392

Cochran, bonds of, 387 note

Cocking, Walter D., educator, 387

Code of 1863, 246-47

College Park, bonds of, 384 note

Colonial agents, 62

Colquitt, Alfred H., member of Secession Convention, 231; mentioned, 280, 282; *biographical sketch of, 313;* Governor, 313-16

Columbus, debt of, 372

Commissioners, County Board of, 412

Common Council of Trustees, 16-17

Compromise of 1850, 210-11

Comptroller General, popular election of, 285; report of, 288; salary of, 372

Confederate Government, nature of, 219-20, 241-42

Confederate Veterans, care for, 302, 318, 319, 331, 334, 341, 362, 363, 383

Congressional districts, number of, 375 note

Conley, Benjamin F., mentioned, 265; Acting Governor, 276

Conscription, 248

Conservation, taxation for, 305, 384

Consolidation of city and county, 369

Constables, officers of early court, 21; under Royal government, 64

Constitution of
1776, 93
1777, 99-114
1789, 142-45
1798, 158-63
1861, 242-47
1865, 256-58
1868, 267-71
1877, 283-90
1945, 400-415, 433-503

Constitution of Confederacy, 241-42

Constitution of the United States, signers of, 131; ratified, 132; used as model in Georgia, 142

Constitutional Commission of 1943-44, 394-96

Constitutional Convention of
1776-77, 97-98
1788-89, 136-42
1795, 145-47
1798, 155-57
1833, 170-72
1839, 173-74
1861, 229-34, 242-46
1865, 252-56
1867-68, 264-67
1877, 279-83

Constitutional conventions, power of, 137-38

Constitutional Union Party, 210-12

Continental Congress, delegates to, 86; recognized as supreme, 95-96

Contracts, by cities and counties, 306-07; impairment of, 397, 403

Convict lease system, abolished, 341

Cook County, created, 360; bonds of, 387 note

508

*Index*

Cooper, John R., candidate for Senate, 353
Cooperatives, rural electric, exempt from taxation, 304
Cordele, bonds of, 387 note
Cornelia, debt of, 373 note
Cornerstone Speech, 238–40
Corporate powers, how granted, 165, 294, 327, 349
Corporation Courts, 182–83
Corporations, subsidiary, 304
Corrections, Board of, 399, 405
Cotton, declining price of, 232; money crop, 323; baled, exempt from taxation, 349
Council of Governor, 56–57, 94, 102, 108
Council of Safety, formed, 87, 88
Counties, colony divided into two, 36; southern county abolished, 48; authorized under Royal government, 59; eleven in 1788, 133; rapid increase in number, 169; ninety-two in 1838, 173; under Constitution of 1868, 270; under Constitution of 1877, 289; number increased, 291; amendments relating to, 309; number increased, 336; term of officers, 351; general comments on, 411–12
County Agents, 382
County Courts, 408–09
County police, 305, 341
County unit rule, 345, 357–59, 404 note
Court of Appeals, 298–99, 336, 354, 406
Courthouse rings, attacked, 315
Courts of Conscience, 65, 112, 180–81
Crane, James M., quoted, 199
Crawford, bonds of, 387 note
Crawford, George W., President of Secession Convention, 230
Crawford, Martin J., delegate to Montgomery Convention, 241
Crawford School District, debt of, 387 note

Crawford, William H., denounces Yazoo fraud, 151; Secretary of Treasury, 199; early life, 201; candidate for President, 202–03
Creighton, Alexander, 80
Crimes, severe penalties in Colonial period, 25
Crisp, Charles F., Speaker of House, 328
Crisp, Charles Robert, *biographical sketch of*, 378 note
Crisp County, debt of, 369
Critical Period, 125
Culpepper, James W., 394

Dade County, debt of, 387 note
D'Allone, Abel Tassin, 7
Darien, early settlement, 22
Davis, Jefferson, President of Confederacy, 248; visits Georgia, 319
Davisboro School District, bonds of, 387 note
Debtors, imprisoned, released, 6; not sent to Georgia, 8–9; relief of, 265–66
Debts, under Constitution of 1877, 287, 305–07, 348, 362, 370, 385, 399, 410
Declaration of Independence, quoted, 74–75; news of received in Georgia, 96
DeKalb County, taxation by, 381 note; temporary loan, 384 note; taxation in, 386 note; educational tax, 388 note
Delegated powers, 219
Democratic Party, 206–218; regains control in 1870, 276; opposition to, 314; uses two-thirds rule in convention of 1880, 316; supremacy of, 333; position of Executive Committee, 339; State regulation of, 356–59
District Courts, under Constitution of 1868, 269; abolished, 286
Divorce, 164, 302, 392
Dixie Highway, 368
Dodd, Walter F., 113, 394
Dodge County, debt of, 387 note

509

# Index

Dominion of New England, 119
Dorsey, Hugh M., prosecutes Leo Frank, 352; elected Governor, 355; *biographical sketch of*, 355 *note*; defeated, 366
Douglas, Stephen A., advocate of popular sovereignty, 214; candidate for President, 216, 217, 233
Dublin, debt of, 381 note, 384 note
Duels, 115, 201
Duke of Newcastle, 10
Durden, Adie Norman, 394

Eastman, debt of, 384 note
East Point, bonds of, 384 note
Ebenezer, early settlement, 22
Education, provisions of Constitution for, in 1798, 160; under Constitution of 1868, 270; special taxes allocated to, 270; under Constitution of 1877, 288; tax exemptions, 303; amendments relating to, 307–08; local taxes for, 307–08; high schools, 307; consolidation, 308; taxation for, 326, 362; consolidation of districts, 377; State Board of, 389, 404; consolidation of local districts, 390–91; teacher-retirement, 392; general provisions for, 411
Edwards, H. B., candidate for Governor, 379
Effingham County, origin of name, 104
Egmont, First Earl of, identified, 7; quoted, 8, 9; aids in securing Charter, 10; first President of the Georgia Corporation, 18; quoted, 30; his *Diary*, 32
Elberton, debt of, 373 note
Election procedure, under Royal government, 59–60
Electoral vote, in *ante bellum* period, 200
Electorate,
  for choosing first assembly, 43
  under Royal government, 59
  for Provincial congresses, 92
  for Convention of 1776–77, 96
  under Constitution of
    1777, 106
    1789, 143
    1798, 162
    1868, 267–68
    1877, 284, 290, 377, 389
    1945, 398, 401
Electrification, rural, 304, 386
Eleventh Amendment, 221
Ellis, Henry, colonial Governor, quoted, 64; arrives in Savannah, 66
Empire State, 197–98
Enumerated powers, 219
Estill, John H., candidate for Governor, 337
Evans County, given representation, 360; bonds, 387 note
Everett, Edward, candidate for Vice-President, 216
Ewen, William, President of Council of Safety, 87
Excelsior School District, bonds of, 387 note
Executive: under
  Charter of 1732, 19–20, 33–40
  Royal government, 51–56
  Rules of 1776, 93
  Constitution of
    1777, 107–10
    1789, 143–44
    1798, 160–61, 175–77
    1861, 245–46
    1865, 256–57
    1868, 267–68
    1877, 285–86, 295–97, 385
    1945, 399, 404–05
Exemptions, see Homestead and Taxation

Fannin County, debt of, 384 note
Farm products, tax exempt, 303
Farmers' Alliance, 324
Farrow, H. P., elected to Senate, 275; not seated, 276
Federal Convention, 126–31
Federal dualism, 219
Federal government, nature of, 219–223

*Index*

Federal ratio, 159, 171
Felder, Thomas B., candidate for Senate, 353
Felton, Rebecca Latimer, 367
Felton, William H., *biographical sketch of, 215*
Fertilizer, inspection of, 327
Few, William, member of Constitutional Convention of 1776–77, 99; delegate to Congress, 121; delegate to Federal Convention, 126, *127 note;* signs Constitution, 131; in Georgia convention ratifying United States Constitution, 133; delegate to Constitutional Convention of 1788, 137
Fifteenth Amendment, ratified, 274; circumvented, 342–43
Fishing, on Sunday, 340
Fitzgerald, tax in, 384 note
*Fletcher vs. Peck,* 153
Flint River, 148
Floyd County, tax, 384 note; temporary loan, 384 **note**
Foley, Frank D., 394
Forests, fire protection, 305
Forsyth, John, Minister to Spain, 199; Secretary of State, 199; opposes nullification, 204
Fort King George, 4
Fort Pulaski, 240
Foster, Ira A., 248
Fourteenth Amendment, rejected, 260; ratified, 272; reratified, 275
Frank, Leo M., 351–52
Franklin, Benjamin, colonial agent, 62; plan of union by, 119
Frederica, military post, 22; government of, 36, 38
Freedmen's Bureau, 259, 265
Freight rates, 285
Fulton County, consolidated with Milton and Campbell, 291; a separate Senatorial district, 291; taxation in, 370; debt of, 372; water and fire system, 373 note; taxation by, 381; a Senatorial District, 383; civil service in, 384 note; assistant clerks in, 384

note; loan by, 384 note; promotional work, 388 note

Gainesville, debt of, 384 note, 387 note
Game and Fish Commission, 297, 389, 405
Gartrell, Lucius J., member of Convention of 1877, 280, 281
Gee, Joshua, writer, 4
General appropriation act, 400
General Assembly,
  compensation of members, 361, 390, 398
  number of members, 364
  sessions of, 368, 377, 383, 386, 390
  eligibility of members to executive offices, 398
  composition of, 401–02
  See Legislature
George, Walter F., elected to Senate, 367; *biographical sketch, 367 note;* reëlected to Senate, 371, 380
*Georgia and State Rights,* 125
*Georgia Gazette,* colonial newspaper, 74, 79, 84, 85, 87, 114
Georgia Platform, 211
Georgia Society, 8
*Georgia vs. Stanton,* 262
Gibbons, William, president of Constitutional convention, 141
Gillian, E. D., candidate for Governor, 379
Glen, John, leader in Revolution, 84
Glover, Arthur, executed, 345
Glynn County, origin of name, 104; authorized to abolish Justices of the Peace, 301; taxation in, 374; justice courts, 388 note
Goldsmith, W. L., Comptroller General, 314
Gordon, John B., candidate for Governor, 271; elected to Senate, 277; supports Constitution of 1877, 283; *biographical sketch of, 312;* resigns from Senate, 315; elected Governor,

511

## Index

319; elected to Senate, 326; supported by Grady, 357
Governors, list of, 428–30; see Executive
Gowen, Charles Latimer, 394
Grady County, bonds of, 384 note
Grady, Henry W., New South Speech, 310–11; political influence, 319, 357; death of, 320
Graham, Patrick, Agent to Indians, 48
Grandfather clause, 341–43, 398
Grange, 323
Great Britain, expected to aid South, 227–28
Great Ogeechee, district of, 24
Greeley, Horace, vote for, 277
Greenville, debt of, 384 note
Grice, Warren, 394
Gross, Frank Cleveland, 394
Guerry, T. L., member of Secession Convention, 231; member of Convention of 1877, 280
*Guinn vs. United States*, 343
Gunn, James, land speculator, 149, 150
Gwinnett, Button, signer of Declaration of Independence, 94; member of Constitutional Convention of 1776–77, 99; President of Council of Safety, 113; in duel, 115

Haas, Mrs. Leonard, 359 note, 394
*Habeas corpus*, suspension of, 248
Habersham & Harris, commercial firm, 43
Habersham, James, Sr., Secretary in colony, 48; Acting Governor, 82
Habersham, James, Jr., leader in Revolution, 79, 84
Hall, Joseph Hill, candidate for Governor, 349
Hall, Lyman, leader in Revolution, 87, 88; signer of Declaration of Independence, 94
Hamilton, Alexander, quoted, 220
Hamilton, Sylla T., 387
Hamlin, Hannibal, Vice-President, 233

Hammond, Abner, Secretary of State, 192
Hamstead, early settlement, 22
Hancock County, debt of, 386 note
Hand, Frederick Barrow, 394
Handly, George, president of Convention of 1788, 137
Hanna, Mark, 330
Hansel, A. N., 281
Hardman, L. G., candidate for Governor, 353, 356; Governor, 371–74; *biographical sketch, 371 note;* reëlected Governor, 371
Hardwick, Thomas W., elected to Senate, 353; elected Governor, 366; *biographical sketch, 366 note;* candidate for Senate, 370; candidate for Governor, 379
Harris, Francis, first speaker of colonial assembly, 43; an Assistant to President, 49
Harris, Nathaniel E., Governor, 352–55; *biographical sketch, 353 note*
Harris, Roy Vincent, 394
Harris, S. W., 281
Harris, William J., elected to Senate, 356; reëlected, 370, 378
Hart County, bonds, 387 note
Hartford Convention, 221–22
Hazelhurst, bonds of, 387 note
Head, Thomas Grady, 394
Head-right land system, 148
Health, taxation for, 384
Heard's Fort, capital, 115
Hegel, philosophy of, 74
Highgate, early settlement, 22
High schools, 363
Highway Patrol Act, 301, 383
Highways, county debts for assumed by State, 306; taxation for, 370; bonds for, 385
Hill, Benjamin H., leader of Know-Nothing Party, 213; member of Secession Convention, 231, 232; delegate to Montgomery Convention, 241; "monarchist," 248; articles by, 262; Senator, 311

512

## Index

Hill, Joshua, elected Senator, 272; refused seat, 273; seated, 276; supports Constitution of 1877, 283
Hines, James K., elected Governor, 329
Hobby, W. J., owner of the *Augusta Chronicle*, 202
Holder, John N., candidate for Governor, 366, 371, 374, 379
Holsey, Hopkins, supports Compromise of 1850, 212
Holt, Hamilton Tatum, 394
Home demonstration agents, taxation for, 305, 382
Home rule, 400, 414
Homerville, debt of, 384 note
Homestead, exemption from sale, 266, 270, 289, 441; exemption from taxation, 303, 382
Hospitals, 305, 384, 386
House of Representatives, see Legislature
Houstoun, John, leader in Revolution, 84, 86, 88; Governor, 115
Houstoun, William, delegate to Federal Convention, 126, 127 note
Howell, Clark, Speaker, 326; candidate for Governor, 337, 338
Howell, Evan P., editor, 325, 326
Howell, Hugh, candidate for Governor, 381
Howley, Richard, delegate to Congress, 121
Hulbert, Colonel Edward, 263
Hutchins, G. A., candidate for Senate, 353
Hutchinson's Island, 22

Immigrants, 196
Income tax, proposed, 374
Incorporation, see corporate powers
Independent Democrats, 314–17
Indians, trade with restricted, 28; fear of, 120–21; removal of, 204–05
Industrialization, 310
Inferior Courts, 180

Initiative, popular, for constitutional amendment, 100, 113
Institute of Public Affairs, 393
Insurance companies, 327, 403
Interest rate, limited, 340
Irwin County, bonds of, 387 note
Irwin, David, 247, 271
Irwin, Jared, President of Convention of 1798, 155
*Irwin's Code*, 270

Jackson, Andrew, following in Georgia, 206–07; quoted, 222
Jackson, James, denounces Yazoo Fraud, 151; land commissioner, 153; member of Convention of 1798, 155; *biography of, 156–57*; "Prince of Duelists," 114, 201
Jeff Davis County, bonds of, 387
Jefferson County School District, bonds of, 387 note
Jefferson County School District No. 10, bonds of, 387 note
Jefferson, debt of, 384 note
Jefferson, Thomas, quoted, vii, 75, 76; cited, 239
Jeffersonville School District, debt of, 384 note
Jenkins, Charles J., supports Compromise of 1850, 210; in Convention of 1865, 254; Governor, 258, 259; opposes Congressional Reconstruction, 262, 266, 267, 277; President of Convention of 1877, 280, 281–82
Jenkins' Ear, War of, 39
Johnson, Abda, 281
Johnson, Andrew, characterized, 251; relations with Georgia, 252; appeals to country, 261
Johnson Corner School District, bonds of, 387 note
Johnson, Herschel V., opposes Compromise of 1850, 212; candidate for Vice-President, 216; member of Secession Convention, 231, 232; President of Convention of 1865, 254; elected to Senate, 258

## Index

Johnson, James, Provisional Governor, 252, 257, 258
Johnston, James, publisher, 79, 114
Johnston, Joseph E., surrender of, 250
Jones, Charles Colcock, historian, quoted, 320
Jones, John, Treasurer, 266
Jones, Noble, assistant to President, 48
Jones, Noble Wymberly, Revolutionary leader, 82, 84, 86, 88; President of Convention of 1795, 146
Judicial review, background of, 60; early history of, 188–95
Judiciary: under
  Charter of 1732, 20–26
  Royal Government, 63–65
  Rules of 1776, 93
  Constitution of
    1777, 111–13
    1789, 145
    1798, 161–62, 177–95
    1861, 246
    1865, 257–58
    1877, 286–87, 297–302, 321–32, 334, 336–37, 354, 379, 385, 391
    1945, 399, 405–10
Justice of the peace, early officers called conservators of the peace, 22; under Royal government, 64; under Constitution of 1877, 287, 301, 349, 372, 386, 409. See Courts of Conscience and Judiciary

Kelley, John I., candidate for Governor, 379
Kenan, Augustus H., delegate to Montgomery Convention, 241
Kimball, Hannibal I., financial adviser of Governor, 275
Kimball House, 275
King George's War, 40
King Legacy, 7
Kite Consolidated School District, bonds of, 384 note
Know-Nothing Party, 213

Knox, William, colonial agent, 62
Ku Klux Klan, 273

Labor Day, 327
LaGrange, debt of, 372
Lakeland, debt of, 373 note
Lamar, Albert R., Secretary of Secession Convention, 230
Lamar County, 364
Lamar, J. B., supports Compromise of 1850, 212
Lamar, Joseph R., quoted, 25, 247 note; Justice of Supreme Court, 346
Land policy, under Trustees, 29–30; under Royal government, 55; early State, 148
Lane, Joseph, candidate for Vice-President, 216, 217
Langworthy, Secretary of Convention of 1776–77, 99
Lanier County, 364
Laws enacted by Trustees, 18, 26–31
Laws of general operation, 258
Lawton, Alexander R., member of Convention of 1877, 281
League of Nations, 365
Lease, Mrs. Elizabeth, quoted, 321
Lee, Robert E., surrender of, 250
Legislature: under
  Trustees, 26, 41–45
  Royal government, 57–63
  Rules of 1776, 93
  Constitution of
    1777, 102–06
    1789, 142–43
    1798, 159–60
    Amendment of 1842–43, 174
  Constitution of
    1861, 245
    1865, 256
    1868, 268
    1877, 284–85, 290–95, 327, 351
    1945, 398, 401–03
Lexington, bonds of, 387 note
Liberty County, origin of name, 104
Liberty Hall, home of Alexander H. Stephens, 224
Liberty Hall, scene of Revolutionary meeting, 80

514

# Index

Libraries, tax exempt, 303
Lien laws, 322–23
Lieutenant Governor, 399
Lincoln, Abraham, quoted, 76, 94; elected President, 217; plan of reconstruction, 250; assassinated, 251
Liquor, prohibited in Colony, 27; law violated openly, 29; prohibited in 1907, 340
Livingston, T. F., candidate for Governor, 325
Local legislation, enacted by General Assembly, 166; restricted, 285; restriction removed, 293, 318; restricted, 398
Locke, John, influence on American Revolution, 75
Long County, 364
Louisville, capital, 147
Lovejoy, Hatton, 394
Lowndes County, college in authorized, 370
Loyalists, numerous in Georgia, 78
Lumpkin, Joseph Henry, justice of Supreme Court, 187
Lumpkin, Wilson, supporter of Clark party, 202; opposes nullification, 204; Democratic leader, 211; favors secession, 230

Mably, Abbé de, quoted, 105
MacIntyre, Hugh James, 394
Macon, taxation in, 304, 386 note; debt certificates, 384 note, 387 note
Madison, James, in Virginia legislature, 126; on the nature of the Union, 220
Major generals, election of, 165
Majors, Robert E. Lee, 394
Manufactures, few in colony, 72; receive special protection, 236
Maps:
  Congressional Districts, 375
  Senatorial Districts, 402
  Judicial Circuits, 407
Married Women's Act, 270
Marshall, John, decision by, 154; rules in favor of Indians, 205

Martyn, Benjamin, Secretary of the Trustees, 48; agent of Board of Trade, 48; complaint against, 62
Mathews, George, relation to Yazoo land fraud, 150
Maugham, J. J., candidate for Governor, 381
McCay, N. K., 265
McCracken, James Roy, 394
McDaniel, Henry D., Governor, 317–18
McElreath, Walter, quoted, 163
McIntosh County, taxation by, 374
McKinley, William, 330–31
McPherson, John Hanson Thomas, quoted, 117
Meade, General George C., 266, 271, 272
Medical care, taxation for, 305
Mercer, Jesse, member of Convention of 1798, 155
Merchant-planter, 322
Merit system, 400, 414
Mexican War, 210, 234
Midway Puritans, 119–20
Militia, 270, 289, 411
Milledge, John, land commissioner, 153
Milledgeville, capital, 169; captured, 248
Milledgeville *Federal Union*, 230
Miller County, bonds of, 387 note
Miller, H. V. M., elected to Senate, 272; refused seat, 273; seated, 275
Milton County, consolidated, 291
Ministers, itinerant, 66
Mitchell County Board of Education, loan by, 387 note
Mobley, James M., 281
Model royal colony, 49 note
Money bills, originate in Commons House, 62
Montgomery, convention in, 241
Montgomery, Sir Robert, 3
Morrill Act, 276
Moultrie, debt of, 379
Municipal courts, 301
Mynott, Pryor L., 281

515

# Index

Narcotic drugs, 340
Nashville, bonds of, 384 note
Natural resources, conservation of, 305
Negroes, brought into colony, 29 note; marriage with whites forbidden, 258; suffrage, 261; jury service, 263; suffrage, 263; in Convention of 1867, 264; suffrage, 271; expelled from House, 272; eligible to hold office, 273; Ku Klux Klan restrains, 273; reseated in General Assembly, 275; separate schools for, 288, 303; university for, 308; irresponsible, 321; education of, 327; political influence, 333; race riot, 339; suffrage, 341–43, 359 note; coeducation, 387; suffrage, 398. See Slavery and Census
Neill, Cecil W., 358
Neill Primary Act, 356–59
New England Confederation, 119
New Jersey Plan of Union, 128
Newspapers, in *ante bellum* period, 209
Nisbet, Eugenius A., justice of Supreme Court, 188; leader of Know-Nothing Party, 214; member of Secession Convention, 231, 232, 233; delegate to Montgomery Convention, 241
Nisbet, R. B., 281
Nix, Abit, candidate for Governor, 379, 385
Non-importation agreement, 81
Northen, William J., elected Governor, 325–26; reëlected, 329; historian, 347
Norwood, Thomas M., Senator, 311; candidate for Governor, 316

Ocilla, debt of, 384 note; refunding bonds, 384 note
Ogeechee, early settlement, 22
Oglethorpe County, bonds, 387 note
Oglethorpe, James Edward, early life, 5; interest in imprisoned debtors, 5; secures charter for Georgia, 6–11; accompanies first settlers, 18; never Governor of Georgia, 19–20; absorbed in military affairs, 39–40
Old age pensions, 305
*Old South, The*, 320
Olmsted, Frederick Law, quoted, 199
Ordinary, Court of, 182, 269, 286, 301, 383, 407
Orr, Gustavus J., School Commissioner, 314
Osgood, Herbert L., quoted, 15, 27

Paintings, tax exempt, 303
Papists, discriminated against, 16, 66, 366
Pardons and Paroles, State Board of, 296, 389, 404
Parishes, colony divided into eight, 58; four new ones, 59
Parker, Henry, bailiff, 24; President of colony, 48
Parrot, J. R., 264
Patronage, abused in colonial period, 54
Patrons of Husbandry, 323
Paulding County, bonds, 387 note
Peach County, created, 291
Pearson, bonds of, 384 note
Peek, W. L., candidate for Governor, 329
Pendleton, Nathaniel, delegate to Federal Convention, 126
Pension agent, United States, 240
Pensions, see Confederate Veterans and Old age
People's Party, 328–31
*People's Party Paper*, 329
Percival, Viscount, see Egmont
Perry, James A., candidate for Governor, 374
Personnel Board, State, 399, 405
Phagan, Mary, murdered, 351
Phillips, Ulrich Bonnell, quoted, 223, 230–31
Piedmont region, rapid growth of, 143, 146, 169
Pierce, Franklin, receives Georgia's electoral vote, 213

516

*Index*

Pierce, William, quoted, 118; delegate to Federal Convention, 126, 127 note; brings United States Constitution to Georgia, 132
Pineview School District, bonds of, 384 note
Pittman, Claude, candidate for Governor, 379
Poll tax, 270, 377, 398 note
Pope, General John, 262, 263, 266, 271
Pope, Jefferson Austin, 394
Popular election, increased use of, 165
Population, number of charity settlers, 8; see Census
Populist Party, 320–31
Powell, James, member of Convention of 1798, 157
Presbyterians, 66
President, in colonial government, 36; under Rules of 1776, 93
Primary elections, regulated, 327, 340, 344, 356–59
Privy Council, right of appeal to, 65
Probate, registers of, 112
Prohibition, 27, 248, 340
Property qualification, for membership in General Assembly, dropped, 167–68
*Proposed Constitution, A,* 393
Provincial Congress,
 First, 85–86
 Second, 88
 Composition of, 91–92
 Powers of, 93–99
Provost Marshall, colonial official, 59; duties described, 64
Public Service Commission, established, 295; constitutional board, 389, 403. See Railroad Commission
Purry, Jean Pierre, Swiss colonizer, 3–4
Purysburg, 4

Quitman County, debt certificates, 384 note; refunding bonds, 384 note; debt of, 387 note

Quit rent, 30, 44

Railroad Commission, 295, 326, 340
Randolph of Roanoke, John, opposes Yazoo settlement, 153
Ray City, bonds, 384 note
Reconstruction, Congressional, 261 ff.
Recorder, of first court, 21
Redwine, Charles D., candidate for Governor, 380
Reese, Augustus, member of Secession Convention, 231, 232; judge, 271
Referendum, use of, 163, 172
Regents, Board of, 308, 375, 389, 404
Reidsville, bonds of, 387 note
Reidsville School District, debt of, 384 note
Religion, tax exemption, 303
Religion, freedom of, under Charter of 1732, 16. See Bill of Rights
Renfroe, J. W., Treasurer, 314
Reorganization Act of 1931, 375
Republican Party, 237
Republican Party (Jeffersonian), 200–01
Rescinding Act of 1796, 152
Revenue anticipation obligations, 306, 391–92
Revenue Certificate Law, 306, 392
Reynolds, John, Governor, 49; his commission and instructions, 51; arrives in Savannah, 66
Richmond Convention of 1860, 216
Richmond County, origin of name, 104; debt of, 372, 381 note; retirement fund, 388 note
Rivers, Eurith Dickinson, candidate for Governor, 371, 374; *biographical sketch of, 380 note;* reëlected Governor, 381
Roberts, Columbus, candidate for Governor, 385
Robinson, Pickering, member of local government in 1754, 49
Rockwell, Captain Charles F., 267
*Royal Georgia Gazette,* 114
Ruger, Brigadier General Thomas H., 267

# Index

Rules and Regulations of 1776, 92
Rural Free Delivery, 328
Russell, Richard B., Sr., candidate for Governor, 337, 338; candidate for Senate, 371
Russell, Richard B., Jr., *biographical sketch, 374 note;* elected to Senate, 378–79

Sandy Cross School District, bonds of, 387 note
Sanford, Steadman Vincent, Chancellor of University System, 388
Sanitation, 305, 341
Savannah, captured during Revolution, 115; debt of, 384 note; wharfs at, 386 note
Savannah *Georgia Journal,* 202, 223
*Savannah News,* 209
Scalawags, 264
Scheibley, P. M., 264
School Commissioner, State, office created, 270; under Constitution of 1877, 288, 308; elected, 331; name changed, 386
School districts, consolidation of, 377
School Superintendent, State, 308, 386. See School Commissioner, State
Schools, see Education
Scotch Highlanders, settle at Darien, 22
Seal, Great, preserved by Governor Jenkins, 267, 277
Secession, arguments for and against, 222, 227–240, *passim;* Ordinance of, rescinded, 254
Secretary of State, popular election of, 285–86; power to grant corporate powers, 294, 327; salary of, 372
Sectionalism, 171–72
Seminole County, 364
Senate, see Legislature
Separation of powers, in Constitution of 1777, 102; principle violated, 167, 398
Sewall, Arthur, 330
Seward, James L., 281

Seward, William H., 258
Sherman, William T., 248, 249
Shryock, Richard Harrison, historian, 211
Sibley, Samuel, 359 note
Silk, production of encouraged, 26, 42
Simmons, James M., secretary of Convention of 1788, 137
Simmons, Thomas J., member of Convention of 1877, 287
Sinking fund, 288
Skidaway, early settlement, 22
Slaton, John M., acting Governor, 348; Governor, 349–52; candidate for Senate, 358, 378
Slavery, prohibited in colony, 26; discussed at Federal Convention, 130; importation from foreign states forbidden, 158–59; affects representation in General Assembly, 159, 171; value in 1860, 223; protected under Constitution, 235–37; justified by Stephens, 238–40; abolished, 254–55
Smith, Charles Henry, 258 note
Smith, Hoke, elected Governor, 337–39; *biographical sketch, 339 note;* defeated by Joseph M. Brown, 344–46; elected Governor, 347; elected to Senate, 347; reëlected, 353; defeated, 360
Smith, James M., elected Governor, 276; candidate for Governor, 337–38
Smith, Kirby, 250
*Smith vs. Allwright,* 359 note, 398
*Smith vs. Atlanta,* 373
Smith, William Rufus, 394
Society for the Propagation of the Gospel in Foreign Parts, 66
Solicitor General, under Constitution of 1877, 287; popular election of, 301, 331; methods of selection, 334 note; salary of, 355
*Soul of the People, The,* 209
Soule, Andrew M., educator, 335

# Index

South Atlantic Coastal Highway, 368
Spalding County, debt of, 379
Spalding County Board of Education, 389 note
Spanish-American War, 331
Sparks, debt of, 384 note
Sparks-Adel School District, bonds, 387 note
Special sessions of General Assembly, 296, 403
Specie payment suspended, 226
Speer, Emory, elected to Congress, 315
Split session of General Assembly, 292
St. Johns Parish, inhabitants of represented in Second Continental Congress, 87
St. Mary's River, boundary, 148
Stamp Tax, opposed, 79–81
*Stare decisis*, 192
State Normal School, 327
States' rights, defended by Georgia, 220 ff.
State Rights Party, 206–18
Stephens, Alexander H., proposal for reducing membership in General Assembly, 174; presents glowing picture of Georgia's prosperity, 197; member of United States House of Representatives, 199; a Whig, 207; supports Compromise of 1850, 211; joins Democratic Party, 213; *biographical sketch of*, 224–25; opposes secession, 228; member of Secession Convention, 231, 232; Cornerstone Speech, 238–40; delegate to Montgomery Convention, 241; differs with Davis, 248; imprisoned, 252; released, 253; elected to Senate, 259; opposes fusion with Liberal Republicans, 277; elected to House of Representatives, 277; Governor, 317; death of, 317
Stephens County, Debt of, 373 note
Stephens, Thomas, wayward son of William Stephens, 28
Stephens, William, colonial secretary, 34–41, 48
Stevens, Thaddeus, 260
Stokes, Anthony, Chief Justice, quoted, 54; importance of, 64; quoted, 71; returns during Revolution, 114
Stone Mountain, bonds of, 387 note
Street improvement bonds, 363
Sumner, Charles, 260, 273
Sumners, Hatton W., 396
Sunday, fishing on, 340
Sunny Hill School District, bonds of, 387 note
Superior Courts, created, 111–12; amendments relating to, 300; decisions in vacation, 385, 406. See Judiciary
Supreme Court, movement for, 183–88; procedure in, 332 note, 379, jurisdiction defined, 354; disposition of cases in, 391; membership increased, 399. See Judiciary
Swainsboro, debt of, 381 note
Sylvania, debt of, 384 note

Taft, William Howard, visits Georgia, 346
Talmadge, Eugene, platform in 1946, 359 note; Commissioner of Agriculture, 371; *biographical sketch of, 379 note;* candidate for Senate, 380; elected Governor, 385; campaign of 1942, 387–88
Tariff, controversy over, 203–04
Tax Collector, 369, 412
Tax Commissioner, 412
Tax Receiver, 369, 412
Taxation, special, for schools, 270; alienation of right prohibited, 285; under Constitution of 1877, 287, 302–07; classification for, 303; exemptions from, 303–04; 5 mill limit, 326; for schools, 326; date of returns, 348; farm products exempted, 349; prop-

519

## Index

erty of colleges exempted, 360; for schools, 362; new industries exempted, 368; personal property exemption, 381–82; home, exemption, 382; classification for, 382; for welfare work, 382; for advertising, 386; rural electrification, exempted, 386; on corporations, 392; general provisions for, 410

Taylor, Richard, 250
Teen age vote, 389
Terrell, James M., Governor, 335
Terry, General Alfred H., 274
Terry's Purge, 275
Texts, free, 374
Thirteenth Amendment, ratified, 258
Thomas, Major General G. H., 251
Thomas, W. W., 254
*Thompson vs. Atlantic Coast Line Railroad Company*, 397
Thompson, W. T., 281
Thorpe, early settlement, 22
Thrasher, B. E., Jr., 394
Thunderbolt, early settlement, 22
Tift County, debt of, 384 note
Title of Act, 160, 194
Tondee's Tavern, 84
Toombs County, bonds of, 387 note
Toombs' Oak, 225
Toombs, Robert, dates of his service in Congress, 199; member of Whig Party, 208; supports Compromise of 1850, 211; joins Democratic Party, 213; biographical sketch of, 225–26; favors secession, 230; member of Secession Convention, 231 232, 234; delegate to Montgomery Convention, 241; opposes Congressional reconstruction, 262–63; prosecutes Bullock, 277; in Convention of 1877, 281–82
Trammell, L. N., candidate for Congress, 314
Treasurer, county, 350, 412
Treasurer, State, popular election of, 285; quarterly report required, 288; salary increased, 295, 361, 372
Treutlen County, created, 360
Treutlen, John Adams, first Governor of State, 113
Troup, George M., on removal of Indians, 204–05; Whig leader, 211
Troup Party, 200–05
Trustees, powers of under Charter of 1732, 15–17; names of most active, 32; method of work, 32–33
Truth, the power of, 229
Tuberculosis sanitarium, 340
Turner, H. M., 264
Tybee, early settlement, 22
Tythingmen, officers of early court, 21

Unadilla, bonds of, 387 note
Unicameral legislature, 103
Union Party, 206–218
Unitary government, nature of, 219–20
University of Georgia, scene of party caucuses, 202; closed, 263; issue in campaign of 1942, 387–88; Institute of Public Affairs, 393. See Regents, Board of

Valdosta, college in authorized, 370
Van Tyne, Claude H., quoted, 74
Venue, 183
Vernon, James, active Trustee, 35
Vestrymen, duties of, 66
Veterans, see Confederate Veterans and Civil Service
Veterans Service Board, 399, 405
Veterinary examiners, 340
Vidalia, debt of, 384 note; bonds of, 387 note
Virginia and Kentucky Resolutions, 221
Virginia Plan of Union, 128; supported by Georgia, 129
Vital statistics, 305, 370
Voting, compulsory, 106

Waddell, J. B., Secretary of Convention of 1865, 254

# Index

Wade-Davis Bill, 251
Walker, Clifford, candidate for Governor, 366; elected Governor, 367; *biographical sketch of, 367–68 note;* reëlected Governor, 370
Walker County, bonds of, 387 note
Walker, Dawson, candidate for Governor, 277
Walton, George, leader in Revolution, 84; signs Declaration of Independence, 95; lays claim to office of Governor, 115; delegate to Congress, 121; named as delegate to Federal Convention, 126; delegate to Georgia Convention of 1788, 137
War debt, 255–56
War of 1812, 221
Ware County, debt of, 372; taxation by, 381 note
Warner, Hiram, justice of Supreme Court, 187–88; member of Secession Convention, 231; Chief Justice, 259
Washington, bonds of, 387 note
Washington County, debt of, 373 note
Watkins, Robert, compiles *Digest,* 157
Watson, Joseph, held prisoner, 26
Watson, Tom, quoted, 321; elected to Congress, 326; *biographical sketch, 328 note;* Vice-Presidential candidate, 330; supports Hoke Smith, 337–38; opposes Smith, 345; influence, 352; supports N. E. Harris, 354; elected to Senate, 366; death of, 367
*Watson's Jeffersonian,* 352, 356
Waycross, promotion tax, 381 note; debt of, 387 note
Wayne, James M., President of Convention of 1833, 170; of 1839, 173; Justice of Supreme Court, 199

Wells, George, member of Convention of 1776–77, 99; fights duel, 114
Wereat, John, claimed title to Governor, 115; president of Convention ratifying Federal Constitution, 133
West, William S., Senator, 353
Westbrook, early settlement, 22
West Point, bonds for, 363
Wheaton, Captain Charles, 267
Wheeler County, 349
Whig Party, see State Rights Party
White, Hugh L., receives electoral vote of Georgia, 207
Whitely, R. H., elected to Senate, 275; not seated, 276
Wife, property of, 270
Wilcox County, bonds and debt, 387 note
Willacoochee, debt of, 384 note
Williams, C. J., member of Secession Convention, 231
Willie Consolidated School District, bonds of, 384 note
Wilmot Proviso, 213
Wilson, Woodrow, quoted, 317–18
Wine, production of encouraged, 26
Wood, J. O., candidate for Governor, 371
*Worcester vs. Georgia,* 222
Wright, Augustus R., 241, 287
Wright, Sir James, appointed Governor, 68; successful, 68–69; delays Revolutionary action, 79, 85; flees Colony, 89; quoted, 95; returns, 114
Wright, Seaborn, 329
Wrightsville School District, bonds of, 387 note
Writ of error, dismissal of, 299

Yazoo land fraud, 147–54

Zoning, 294, 373, 383
Zubly, Rev. John Joachim, 89

www.ingramcontent.com/pod-product-compliance
Lightning Source LLC
Chambersburg PA
CBHW021845300426
44115CB00005B/21